# SOCIAL CONTEXTS OF EARLY EDUCATION, AND RECONCEPTUALIZING PLAY (II)

# ADVANCES IN EARLY EDUCATION AND DAY CARE

Series Editor: Stuart Reifel

Recent Volumes:

ADVANCES IN EARLY EDUCATION AND DAY CARE
VOLUME 13

# SOCIAL CONTEXTS OF EARLY EDUCATION, AND RECONCEPTUALIZING PLAY (II)

EDITED BY

## STUART REIFEL
*University of Texas at Austin, TX, USA*

## MAC H. BROWN
*University of South Carolina, SC, USA*

2004

ELSEVIER
JAI

Amsterdam – Boston – Heidelberg – London – New York – Oxford
Paris – San Diego – San Francisco – Singapore – Sydney – Tokyo

| ELSEVIER B.V. | ELSEVIER Inc. | **ELSEVIER Ltd** | ELSEVIER Ltd |
| --- | --- | --- | --- |
| Radarweg 29 | 525 B Street, Suite 1900 | **The Boulevard, Langford** | 84 Theobalds Road |
| P.O. Box 211 | San Diego | **Lane, Kidlington** | London |
| 1000 AE Amsterdam | CA 92101-4495 | **Oxford OX5 1GB** | WC1X 8RR |
| The Netherlands | USA | **UK** | UK |

First edition 2004

British Library Cataloguing in Publication Data
A catalogue record is available from the British Library.

ISBN: 0-7623-1146-0
ISSN: 0270-4021 (Series)

♾ The paper used in this publication meets the requirements of ANSI/NISO Z39.48-1992 (Permanence of Paper). Printed in The Netherlands.

## Working together to grow libraries in developing countries

www.elsevier.com | www.bookaid.org | www.sabre.org

**ELSEVIER**    **BOOK AID** International    Sabre Foundation

# CONTENTS

# LIST OF CONTRIBUTORS

| | |
|---|---|
| *Debra J. Ackerman* | Graduate School of Education, Rutgers, the State University of New Jersey, New Brunswick, NJ, USA |
| *Mac H. Brown* | Department of Instruction and Teacher Education, University of South Carolina, SC, USC/Gateway Child Development and Research Center, Columbia, SC, USA |
| *Sheralyn Campbell* | Centre for Equity and Innovation in Early Childhood, University of Melbourne, Australia |
| *Judith A. Chafel* | Department of Curriculum and Instruction, Indiana University, Bloomington, IN, USA |
| *Jody Eberly* | Department of Elementary and Early Childhood Education, The College of New Jersey, NJ, USA |
| *Belinda Bustos Flores* | College of Education and Human Development, The University of Texas at San Antonio, San Antonio, TX, USA |
| *Nancy K. Freeman* | Department of Instruction and Teacher Education, University of South Carolina, USC/Gateway Child Development and Research Center, Columbia, SC, USA |
| *Susan L. Golbeck* | Department of Educational Psychology, Graduate School of Education, Rutgers, the State University of New Jersey, New Brunswick, NJ, USA |
| *Priscilla Hoke* | Department of Curriculum & Instruction, University of Texas, Austin, TX, USA |
| *Glenda MacNaughton* | Centre for Equity and Innovation in Early Childhood (CEIEC), Department of Learning and Educational Developments, The University of Melbourne, Victoria, Australia |

| | |
|---|---|
| *Paula McMurray-Schwarz* | College of Health and Human Services, Ohio University Eastern Campus, St. Clairsville, OH, USA |
| *Heidi L. Malloy* | Department of Psychology, Metropolitan State University, St. Paul, MN, USA |
| *Carin Neitzel* | Department of Teaching and Learning, Vanderbilt University, Nashville, TN, USA |
| *Jane Page* | Centre for Equity and Innovation in Early Childhood, University of Melbourne, Australia |
| *Dianne Pape* | Department of Curriculum & Instruction, University of Texas, Austin, TX, USA |
| *Stuart Reifel* | Department of Curriculum & Instruction, University of Texas, Austin, TX, USA |
| *Mari Riojas-Cortez* | College of Education and Human Development, The University of Texas at San Antonio, San Antonio, TX, USA |
| *Sharne Rolfe* | Centre for Equity and Innovation in Early Childhood, University of Melbourne, Australia |
| *Karen VanderVen* | Psychology in Education, School of Education, University of Pittsburgh, Pittsburgh, PA, USA |
| *Deborah Wisneski* | Department of Curriculum & Instruction, University of Texas, Austin, TX, USA |
| *Irma Cantú Woods* | Child Development/Early Childhood, Del Mar College, Corpus Christi, TX, USA |

# INTRODUCTION TO VOLUME 13: SOCIAL CONTEXTS OF EARLY EDUCATION, AND RECONCEPTUALIZING PLAY (II)

Volume 13 of the *Advances in Early Education and Day Care* series marks twenty years that the series has attempted to provide a forum for current scholarship that might further our thinking about early childhood education and care. This, my ninth volume as series editor, is intended to serve the continuing intent of the series to provide multi-disciplinary and interdisciplinary perspectives on a field that by its nature requires diverse perspectives. Early childhood practices have drawn on ideas from child development, curriculum studies, social work, nursing, sociology, anthropology, and other fields that inform us about children, their care, and the settings in which we implement our programs. *Advances* has always attempted to respect the necessary diversity of perspectives that can inform the field, and to support work that may not fit in a tidy disciplinary nook.

This volume allows us to revisit a number of themes that have appeared in earlier *Advances* publications. In 1995, we explored some of the Social Contexts of Early Development and Education (Reifel, 1995), and in 2001 we began what was intended as an on-going look at Reconceptualizing Play (Reifel & Brown, 2001). Volume 13 returns to those themes, with new investigations of those topics. As with the 2001 volume, Mac Brown has served as co-editor of the section on Reconceptualizing Play (II).

Volume 13's look at Social Contexts begins with Judith A. Chafel and Carin Neitzel's empirical exploration of "Young Children's Ideas about Poverty: Gender, Race, Socioeconomic Status, and Setting Differences." In their effort to understand the roots of thinking in childhood about poverty, these authors looked at children's responses to poverty in literature and found unique response patterns based on gender, race, SES, and urban/rural differences. Children's views of the topic are not monolithic, and suggest the importance of not assuming homogeneity in what children bring to their thinking about important features of our societal context.

Boys and girl's thinking in the interactional social context of playful problem solving is described in "Blocks, Building and Mathematics: Influences of Task Format and Gender of Play Partners Among Preschoolers," by Jody L. Eberly and Susan L. Golbeck. This look at the influence of conditions of peer interaction (divergent or convergent thinking) shows a significant, differential influence on how boys and girls play/construct. The construction tasks involved in the study are explicitly linked by Eberly and Golbeck to mathematics skills.

Those two chapters reflect relatively traditional developmental approaches to the field, and contrast methodologically with an analysis conducted by Glenda MacNaughton and her colleagues. In "Beyond Quality, Advancing Social Justice and Equity: Interdisciplinary Explorations of Working for Equity and Social Justice in Early Childhood Education," Sheralyn Campbell, Glenda MacNaughton, Jane Page, and Sharne Rolfe take a uniquely early childhood view of "socially just equity practice." Their post-modern view of practices and inquiry provides a multi-layered perspective on the complexities of practice, as it presents a systematic, fascinating interpretation of classroom life. Views such as this are opening new vistas in the field (Grieshaber & Cannella, 2001).

New social contexts for early education and care often require that we aim our inquiry at social conditions that have not existed in the past. Debra J. Ackerman does that in her analysis of teacher preparation that was mandated by a legislature: "Between a Rock and a Hard Place: Teachers' Experiences in Meeting the *Abbott* Mandate." A new requirement, that teachers in New Jersey's community-based preschools have a bachelor's degree or lose their jobs, creates frustration for teachers in the system. Efforts to support teacher education in this program appear to be at odds with the circumstances of the concerned teachers. Ackerman tells us a great deal about early childhood teachers, how they think about their work, and policy that does not seem really to speak to practice.

A different view of policy, professional standards, and discontinuities in practice is provided by Irma Cantu Woods' ethnography on "Lessons From Home: A Look at Culture and Development." The particular focus of this chapter is on culturally sensitive use of terms of endearment in a predominantly Mexican-American community and its Head Start program. By living in the community and teaching in the Head Start center, Woods is able to document how families and teachers in the community make use of *nombres de carino*, and how adults make use of relational names to provide comfort and identity for children and other adults. Woods relates these customs to professional guidelines, Head Start standards, and dominant culture research that create dissonance for teachers in this culture's program. Implications for sensitivity to cultural differences are drawn, based on a rich appreciation of developmental and cultural scholarship.

These studies of some of the social contexts of early education point to how many of the needs of the field are unique, depending on where and when we do our work, and whom we work with. The policies we create, social issues and trends, political decisions, community practices, classroom interactions, all provide important influences that we need to understand. I believe that each of these chapters contributes to that understanding on one or more levels.

Part II of this volume, Reconceptualizing Play (II), continues a discussion begun in Volume 11 of this series (Reifel & Brown, 2001). Actually, the discussion was begun two years earlier, at an American Educational Research Association roundtable presentation on early childhood play. Mac Brown took a leading role in the roundtable, and has continued to develop the topic through two publication cycles of *Advances*. The five chapters here reflect our collaboration on that project. As with the 2001 volume, our concern has been new conceptions of an abiding set of practices in early childhood programs, those things we call *play*. Our interest has been in exploring new conceptions, especially those that move beyond developmentally appropriate practice (DAP) (Bredekamp & Copple, 1997).

Karen VanderVen introduces this section for us with "Beyond Fun and Games Towards a Meaningful Theory of Play: Can a Hermeneutic Perspective Contribute?" Building on her own long-standing inquiry into the meaning of play, VanderVen goes deeply into hermeneutic philosophy and methodology to re-frame our thinking about play. After orienting the reader to the basic ideas of hermeneutics, she leads us to the significance of perspective and methodology (approach to inquiry and interpretation). These ideas are applied to classroom play, only after existing hermeneutic treatment of play is presented. The importance of carefully situated narrative is affirmed.

Our own work on "From Context to Texts: DAP, Hermeneutics, and Reading Classroom Play" (Stuart Reifel, Priscilla Hoke, Dianne Pape, and Debora Wisneski) complements VanderVen, by delineating the narrative assumptions in DAP's treatment of play. How are teachers and researchers to understand the meanings of play? What hermeneutic tools might help us make connections between practice, research and theory? With classroom activities as meaningful as play, what narratives are necessary and sufficient for relating to play? This chapter explores those ideas and presents a case of play that illustrates some of the challenges in "reading" and studying play narratives in contexts. Hermeneutic understandings may help us elaborate our own practice-based rhetoric of play (Reifel, 1999; Sutton-Smith, 1997, 1999).

Nancy K. Freeman and Mac H. Brown reinterpret a problematic play activity in "Reconceptualizing Rough and Tumble Play: Ban the Banning." The story of rough and tumble activity is re-framed, pointing to the benefits of the activity as well as the pretend nature of the violent-seeming play. Basing their perspective on extensive research, they provide tools for interpreting rough and tumble from other forms of activity, and for supporting children's development through play. The issue of problematic, violent seeming play is also addressed by Heidi L. Malloy and Paula McMurray-Schwarz in "War Play, Aggression, and Peer Culture: A Review of the Research Examining the Relationship between War Play and Aggression." A thorough review of research on aggression and war play reveals biases and ambiguities in methodologies and interpretations. These authors provide teachers and researchers with ways of seeing such play as part of peer culture, where it has its own meanings that should be studied.

All of the chapters in this part of the volume, point to the multiple perspectives that teachers, researchers, parents, and children bring to our understanding of play. Mari Riojas-Cortez and Belinda Bustos Flores add a cultural dimension to this reconceptualization, by assessing the views of bilingual teachers and parents ("*Los Padres y Los Maestros*: Perspectives of Play among Bilingual Stakeholders in Public Schools"). This chapter details how Mexican-American teachers and parents vary in their views of how play functions in the education and development of children. While adults from a common cultural background may share beliefs about children's play, those beliefs seem to transform in the professional setting. And the value of play may require special attention as these adults communicate with one another about children and school. The value and meanings of play activities in one culture do not translate directly into another setting (Frost, Wortham & Reifel, 2001), and we need research to sort out the relationship of beliefs to practice to outcomes.

As Part I of this volume does, Part II raises questions of social contexts, as well as intellectual frameworks for making sense of activity in contexts. Culture, policy, belief, and values prove to be worthy lenses for enhancing our developmental views of childhood play and practice. Our hope is that others will build on some of these reconceptualizations, to assist teachers and families to improve the lives of children in their programs. I am especially grateful to Mac Brown for the leadership he provided over the course of this project, and for the thoughtful reviewing he provided for manuscripts submitted for review.

Any reviewed volume involves the conscientous work not just of editors, but also of many outside reviewers who deserve our eternal graditude for their contributions. The following individuals provided helpful critiques of submissions, and I want to express my thanks to them: Sandra Briley, University of Texas at Austin; Cary Buzzelli, Indiana University; Lisa Cary, University of Texas at Austin; Susan Empson, University of Texas at Austin; Olga Janett, Georgia State University; Alice Meckley, Millersville University; Patricia Ramsey, Mount Holyoke College; Chandler Stolp, University of Texas at Austin; John Sutterby, University of Texas at Brownsville; Rachel Theilheimer, Borough of Manhattan College; Candra Thornton, Auburn University; and June Yeatman, Austin Community College.

Stuart Reifel
*Series Editor*

# REFERENCES

Bredekamp, S., & Copple, C. (1997). *Developmentally appropriate practice in early childhood programs serving children from birth throughage 8.* Washington, DC: National Association for the Education of Young Children.

Frost, J. L., Wortham, S., & Reifel, S. (2001). *Play and child development.* Upper Saddle River, NJ: Merrill/Prentice-Hall.

Grieshaber, S., & Cannella, G. (2001). *Embracing identities in early childhood education: Diversity and possibilities.* New York: Teachers College Press.

Reifel, S. (1995). Social contexts of early development and education. In: *Advances in Early Education and Day Care* (Vol. 7). Greenwich, CT: JAI Press.

Reifel, S. (1999). Play research and the early childhood profession. In: S. Reifel (Ed.), *Foundations, Adult Dynamics, Teacher Education and Play: Advances in Early Education and Day Care* (Vol. 10, pp. 201–212). Stamford, CT: JAI Press.

Reifel, S., & Brown, M. H. (2001). Early education and care, and reconceptualizing play. In: *Advances in Early Education and Day Care* (Vol. 11). Oxford: JAI Press/Elsevier.

Sutton-Smith, B. (1997). *The ambiguity of play.* Cambridge, MA: Harvard University Press.

Sutton-Smith, B. (1999). The rhetorics of adult and child play theories. In: S. Reifel (Ed.), *Advances in Early Education and Day Care* (Vol. 10, pp. 149–161). Greenwich, CT: JAI Press.

# PART I:
# SOCIAL CONTEXTS
# OF EARLY EDUCATION

# YOUNG CHILDREN'S IDEAS ABOUT POVERTY: GENDER, RACE, SOCIOECONOMIC STATUS, AND SETTING DIFFERENCES

Judith A. Chafel and Carin Neitzel

## ABSTRACT

*What are children's responses to storybook characters portrayed as socioeconomically disadvantaged? Do these responses vary by gender, race, socioeconomic status, and setting? Sixty-two 8-year-old-children individually listened and responded to a story about a soup kitchen using two different communication systems: drawings and words. Categories generated from the data were analyzed using chi-square analyses, yielding statistically significant findings for each of the variables of interest. Results offer a unique, detailed picture of the conceptual schemas of 8-year-old children about poverty.*

For more than a half a century, a small body of literature has been accumulating on what children think about social and economic inequality in American society. These studies have focused on children of diverse ages, ranging from preschool to adolescence, to examine class-related attitudes, awareness of status differences, explanations and justifications given for these differences, and notions of social mobility and change (Estvan, 1952; Flanagan et al., 1997; Flanagan & Tucker,

Social Contexts of Early Education, and Reconceptualizing Play (II)
Advances in Early Education and Day Care, Volume 13, 3–37
ISSN: 0270-4021/doi:10.1016/S0270-4021(04)13001-2

1999; Furby, 1979; Harrah & Friedman, 1990; Leahy, 1981, 1983a; Ramsey, 1991; Simmons & Rosenberg, 1971; Stendler, 1949; Tudor, 1971; Weinstein, 1958) (Chafel, 1997a). The findings emanating from these studies have yielded some intriguing insights, but numerous areas of inquiry await investigation.

The present effort was undertaken with two aims: (1) to develop another approach to studying children's conceptions of poverty; and (2) using this method, to engage in further inquiry about their ideas. About two decades ago, Leahy (1983b) suggested that a variety of methods were needed to examine children's class concepts. The present study was undertaken with the assumption that another methodology might elicit dimensions of understanding untapped by prior research (Bombi, 1995/1998). An exploratory effort, it extended past work by requiring participants to represent their knowledge using two different communication systems: drawings and words. Participants selected for study were 8 years of age.

Existing research has studied children's ideas about social and economic inequality using largely an interview methodology. Procedures have consisted of verbal questions presented alone or in conjunction with drawings, photographs, or pictures (see, for example, Estvan, 1952; Furby, 1979; Leahy, 1981, 1983a; Ramsey, 1991; Simmons & Rosenberg, 1971; Stendler, 1949; Tudor, 1971) (Chafel, 1995). Typically, children have been asked questions (with or without stimuli) (e.g. "Describe poor people. What are they like?"), and a verbal response has been required (Leahy, 1981, p. 525). When children have been presented with stimuli, they have been asked to respond verbally to questions posed about the stimuli and/or to sort, group, match, or point out the stimuli (e.g. Mookherjee & Hogan, 1981; Ramsey, 1991; Stendler, 1949; Tudor, 1971). Work by Mookherjee and Hogan, and Tudor stands out because the data appear to have been secured requiring little, if any, verbalization from children.

Researchers have enhanced our knowledge of children's developing conceptions of social and economic inequality using the measures just described. Studies conducted by Ramsey (1991) and Leahy (1981, 1983a) are particularly relevant to the present work because of the broad outlines they provide of children's thinking, from preschool to adolescence.

## CHILDREN'S UNDERSTANDINGS
## OF CLASS CONCEPTS

Interested in the understandings of very young children, Ramsey (1991) showed white preschoolers (3, 4, and 5 years of age) from low- and middle-SES families photographs. The children's descriptions of the photographs (given in response to the prompt, "Tell me about the person in this picture") indicated that they rarely spoke spontaneously about class differences (p. 76). They grouped the photographs as "rich" or "poor" upon request, after explaining what the two concepts meant. Although they sorted correctly significantly more often than chance expectation, displaying an ability to perceive gross distinctions between status groups, they correctly identified more poor than rich people. Asked about the two classes being alike or different, more children replied that they were different. A question about the cause of poverty ("why some people had more money than others") failed to elicit an answer from most children (p. 78). Ramsey emphasized that her findings demonstrated that even very young children are aware of social class differences, although they display limited concepts that are based on concrete cues.

Leahy (1981, 1983a) examined the conceptions of children representing a broader spectrum of ages (5 through 18 years), races (black, white) and status groups (lower, working, middle, and upper-upper middle) with a Piagetian clinical interview. He asked his participants for descriptions and comparisons of rich and poor, and questioned them about the causes and justification of economic inequality, and social mobility and change. To illustrate, he asked, "Why are some people poor, while others are rich?" "Should some people be poor, while others are rich?" (Leahy, 1983a, p. 113).

He found a trend toward increasing decentration in the descriptions and comparisons of rich and poor that the children gave, when divided by age (6–11 years, 11–14 years, 14–17 years). The youngest children spoke in *peripheral* terms about external, observable qualities; the middle group in *psychological* terms about inferred, internal states; and the oldest in *sociocentric* terms about relationships within society. The contents of the children's thoughts at these levels, respectively, emphasized: (1) behaviors, possessions, appearances; (2) thoughts, traits; and, (3) class consciousness, life chances. He similarly observed a developmental progression in the children's explanations and justifications of economic inequality, and concepts of social mobility and change. Older children explained and justified status in terms of equity (e.g. effort, ability) more frequently than younger children. Their justifications of wealth and poverty, and ideas about social change were also more likely to exhibit fatalism.

The youngest children in Leahy's sample (6–11 years of age), unable to use causal reasoning, explained and justified class distinctions with definitional criteria, as exemplified by this statement (about the cause of poverty) made by a 6-year-old:

> The poor people don't have no jobs. They couldn't pay for no jobs because they don't have no money to get a job (Leahy, 1983b, p. 81).

They largely saw social mobility and change as being brought about by donations of money, a view that also reflects the peripheral aspects of poverty. Not yet possessing a multiple-classificatory structure, children of this age spoke more about differences between rich and poor than similarities. As the same 6-year-old told the interviewer,"They ain't the same" (Leahy, 1983b, p. 81). Leahy's findings confirm that even young children have something to say about economic inequality, and that qualitative shifts become evident in children's thinking as they mature.

## CORRELATES OF CHILDREN'S IDEAS

Past research has examined whether certain demographic variables are associated with children's ideas about social and economic inequality. Findings with respect to gender and socioeconomic status are mixed and inconclusive (Chafel, 1995), although some studies do suggest a greater awareness of class-related concepts by girls than boys. To illustrate briefly, Ramsey (1991) expected girls to be more aware of social class cues than boys as a result of being socialized to take better note of how people look and feel. Whereas the boys in her sample identified correctly only poor people more often than chance expectation girls were able to do so for rich and poor. Furthermore, she found girls more accurate than boys when responding to tasks about *rich* people. Bombi (1995/1998) observed that girls were better able than boys to distinguish the personal conditions (appearance, well-being, value) associated with economic inequality.

Leahy (1983a) predicted class (and race) effects in children's ideas about inequality by looking to social conflict and social functional theory. Social conflict theory suggests that different perspectives on inequality stem from "competing interests" tied to race and class, and social functional theory that all children internalize "a shared ideology" about its legitimacy (Leahy, 1983a, p. 113). Although he noted a few differences between the socioeconomic status (and racial) groups in his study, he decided that the data overall brought to light more agreement than disagreement among the children (Leahy, 1983a, b; 1990). In other words, the findings supported social functionalist theory.

With a few notable exceptions (e.g. Flanagan & Tucker, 1999; Leahy, 1981, 1983a; Simmons & Rosenberg, 1971), race has largely escaped the attention of researchers. Although Leahy commented on the infrequent reference to race by his black and white participants when explaining wealth and poverty, Cook et al. (1996) more than a decade later observed low-income, inner-city African-American boys showing in their aspirations and expectations a class- and race-based system of occupational differentiation.

Setting has likewise been unexplored as a factor, although it is reasonable to assume that environmental context does have an influence. Furnham and Stacey

(1991, p. 8), for example, have written that "a cut-off rural environment compared to an urban inner-city environment exposes young people to a quite different set of people, institutions and experiences which help shape their ideas." Findings reported by Flanagan et al. (1997) are suggestive. They sampled 7th–12th grade youth residing in different locations (wealthy suburbs, the urban ring, the inner city) and found that their attributions about poverty varied.

Inasmuch as gender, socioeconomic status, race, and setting each involve a unique set of socialization experiences, it is puzzling as to why past research has failed to substantiate a stronger connection between these variables and children's perspectives about poverty. The present study deliberately sampled participants to obtain contrasting groups of these variables and expected differences to emerge in the findings, but made no specific predictions given the study's exploratory methodology.

## RESEARCH QUESTIONS

The present effort reports findings obtained with 8-year-old children. This age group was targeted for two reasons. First, children of this age, while still falling within the early childhood years, are able to articulate their ideas better than younger children. Secondly, they experience a shift from preoperational to concrete operational thinking about this time, which means that children of this age should also display more developmentally advanced conceptions. Studies by Danziger (1958) and Short (1991) also highlighted findings with 8-year-olds. Working with Australian children of mainly working-class families, Danziger (1958) found that only the 8-year-olds, the older group in his sample, showed a rudimentary understanding of capital accumulation, when responding to questions about wealth and poverty. Short (1991, p. 92) sought to ascertain if this age "might mark a watershed" with respect to the thinking of British children representing different social classes. Consistent with person perception theory, he found that by the age of 8 children believed that being wealthy was "not an unmixed blessing" (p. 96). He interpreted the finding as supporting Livesley and Bromley's (1973) intermediate stage of person perception. At this stage, children are able to take into account more than one aspect of a person's behavior. In summing up his findings, Short (1991, p. 104) concluded that the youngest children in his sample (6-year-olds) "seemed far less 'in touch' with socio-economic reality" than the older children (8- and 10-year-olds). Thus, while the age of 8 still encompasses the early years of growth, it also provides an opportunity to assess the child's maturing conceptual schemas. Inasmuch as the present study offers a picture of the conceptual schemas of a particular age group, it may be considered developmental, although it does not report age-related comparisons nor focus on the processes involved in constructing social meaning.

Two sets of reasons argue for the importance of studying young children's conceptions of poverty (Chafel, 1995). First, the findings of such inquiry would extend existing research and theory on a socially significant aspect of child development that has been largely overlooked. Secondly, they would illuminate further the contents of children's thoughts. Knowing the thoughts of *young* children is particularly important because of the opportunity it provides to intervene, if necessary, at a time when concept and attitude formation is not yet complete. If children display limited concepts or have any misconceptions, they can be addressed through educational interventions (Chafel, 1997a, b; Short, 1991). With more enlightened conceptions, children may eventually work as adults to bring about greater social justice.

The study addressed two questions: What are children's responses to storybook characters portrayed as economically disadvantaged? Do these responses vary according to the child's gender, race, setting, or socioeconomic status? Participants in this study were given open-ended tasks similar to their daily-life activities in their natural environment (Donaldson, 1978; Nelson, 1978, 1979, 1986) (Chafel, 1995). They listened to a story, drew a picture about the story, and responded verbally to questions. These "school-like" tasks required them to express their knowledge using two different communication systems: drawings and words.

Whereas in past research, stimuli such as drawings, photographs, or pictures have sometimes been used to elicit children's ideas about social and economic inequality, the present study employed a story in conjunction with a drawing task. The procedure was undertaken with the assumption that exposure to economically disadvantaged storybook characters would stimulate a *variety* of responses in the children (Cox & Many, 1992; Piaget & Inhelder, 1969; Rosenblatt, 1978, 1985). Rosenblatt's (1995) transactional theory of reader-response supports the expectation:

> In the past, reading has too often been thought of as an interaction, the printed page impressing its meaning on the reader's mind or the reader extracting the meaning embedded in the text. Actually, reading is a constructive, selective process over time in a particular context.... Meaning emerges as the reader carries on a give-and-take with the signs on the page .... the two-way, reciprocal relation explains why meaning is not "in" the text or "in" the reader. Both reader and text are essential to the transactional process of making meaning (p. 26).

In other words, textual meaning results from a process of *active* construction, and the construction is influenced by developmental ability, emotions, values, past experiences, and so forth (Cox & Many, 1992). As Cox and Many (1992, p. 39) put it, "In the end they [children; brackets added] evoke yet another entity, the virtual literary work, or "poem," with each version of that poem as unique as the individuals themselves."

The present study asked participants to respond to literature via drawing to explore an alternative methodology for studying children's ideas about poverty. Past research has largely drawn on children's spoken words to assess their understandings (Chafel, 1995). For example, Leahy's (1983a) study captured children's knowledge about inequality exclusively via language (through a clinical interview), and while Ramsey (1991) required the participants in her study to group photographs, she nonetheless expected a verbal response to other task demands. The children in these studies may have possessed undisclosed concepts that might have come to light if other methodologies had been employed (Furnham & Stacey, 1991). Children may respond differently via drawing than language because the challenge of communicating one's knowledge poses a fundamentally different task.

Art has been described as "a process by which thoughts, feelings, behaviors, and relationships can be translated into concrete images"(Burgess & Hartman, 1993, p. 161). When children draw, content, skill, and experience combine to yield a visual representation (L. Lackey, personal communication, September 27, 2002). The task of drawing presents the child with a "cognitive challenge"(Smith and the Drawing Study Group, 1998, p. 15). The challenge entails identifying content (from observation, imagination, memory, and other sources) on which to focus, and finding a way to transpose that content onto paper using graphic materials (Smith and the Drawing Study Group, 1998). Past experience influences the meaning assigned to the content of a drawing as well as the selection, invention, and execution of drawing strategies (Smith and the Drawing Study Group, 1998). Other factors that influence children's ability to draw include culture, art education, development, and individual differences (Smith and the Drawing Study Group, 1998).

Typically, by eight years, the age targeted by this study, young children's drawings have advanced beyond the unidentifiable scribbles of the preschool child. Now, more visually realistic representations depict "a more varied range of marks, lines, and shapes," as a result of a better attention to detail and more developed fine motor skills (Smith and the Drawing Study Group, 1998, p. 68; Thomas & Silk, 1990). While the drawings of younger children may lack part-whole coordination (Thomas & Silk, 1990), "a subtle interplay of parts and whole" may be found in the creations of eight-year-olds (Smith and the Drawing Study Group, 1998, p. 67). Children of this age are also more concerned with problems of proportion, viewpoint, and depth (Thomas & Silk, 1990).

Past research confirms that children's drawings can be analyzed to yield valid inferences (see, for example, Clark, 1993; Coles, 1964; Farver et al., 2000;

Harris, 1963; Hummel et al., 1995; Lewis & Osofsky, 1997). Studies utilizing drawing as a methodological tool have focused on a wide variety of topics, such as child abuse (Hibbard & Hartman, 1990) and exposure to civil war (Garbarino et al., 1991), but only a few have attempted to assess poverty-related issues like children's perceptions of wealth and poverty (e.g. Bombi, 1995/1998), neighborhood violence (Lewis & Osofsky, 1997), or the worlds that low-income city children envision in their play (Middlebrooks, 1998). In their inquiries about various topics, researchers have sometimes employed drawings together with other approaches (e.g. interviews, story narratives, fantasy play) (Farver et al., 2000).

Only a few studies to date (see, for example, Bombi, 1995/1998, 1996, 2002) have utilized drawings to assess children's ideas about wealth and poverty. A method such as drawing may elicit new dimensions of understanding untapped by prior research (Bombi, 1995/1998). Whereas Bombi (1995/1998, p. 6) asked children "to draw a rich person and a poor person," the present study posed a more open-ended task to evoke children's ideas about poverty.

# METHODOLOGY AND DATA ANALYSIS

## *Participants*

Sixty-two 8-year-old children served as participants for the study. They were recruited from 15 classrooms situated in 9 schools (6 urban and 3 rural) serving families of diverse socioeconomic status backgrounds. Every child in these classrooms was given an opportunity to take part in the study when the teacher sent home with each child a letter requesting parental consent. Parental consent was obtained for 95 children. A survey designed to yield information about a child's socioeconomic status and race was subsequently sent home with each child for whom parental consent had been given. Completed surveys were returned by 69 children (73%). Several children were eliminated from the study: one because of missing interview data, another because the interviewer inadvertently provided an interpretation of the story, and the remainder because they turned 9 years old before they could be interviewed. The resulting sample of 62 children consisted of 31 boys and 31 girls; 27 children of higher socioeconomic status and 35 children of lower socioeconomic status; 41 white, 17 black, and 4 biracial children; and 42 urban children and 20 rural children. Tables 1, 2, and 3 show the gender, racial, and socioeconomic status distribution of the sample.

Information provided by the survey made it possible to ascertain the socioeconomic status and race of each child. Socioeconomic status was determined using demographic characteristics commonly employed by the U.S. Bureau of

***Table 1.*** Gender Distribution of Participants in the Study.

| | Gender | |
| --- | --- | --- |
| | Boys | Girls |
| Race | | |
| White | 20 | 21 |
| Black/Biracial | 11 | 10 |
| Setting | | |
| Rural | 10 | 10 |
| Urban | 21 | 21 |
| SES | | |
| Low | 17 | 18 |
| High | 14 | 13 |

***Table 2.*** Racial Distribution of Participants in the Study

| | Race | |
| --- | --- | --- |
| | White | Black/Biracial |
| Setting | | |
| Rural | 20 | 0 |
| Urban | 21 | 21 |
| SES | | |
| Low | 20 | 15 |
| High | 21 | 6 |

the Census: (1) father's education level; (2) mother's education level; (3) father's occupation; (4) mother's occupation; and (5) family income. Occupational data were recoded with the Duncan Socioeconomic Index of Occupations (Duncan, 1961), a numerical index that rates the level or social position of an occupation. The five pieces of data were then summed to create an estimate of socioeconomic status

***Table 3.*** Socioeconomic Status of Participants in the Study.

| | SES | |
| --- | --- | --- |
| | Low | High |
| Setting | | |
| Rural | 9 | 11 |
| Urban | 26 | 16 |

for each family. Using a mean split, each child was assigned to one of two groups (lower or higher) based on these estimates. Average income for the sample fell between $36,000 and $39,000 per year (ranging from less than $9,999–$80,000, with a standard deviation of $12,000). On average, the parents of the children possessed some college education. The children were classified by race on the basis of parental response to a question about race, resulting in two groups: white and other (black and biracial).

## Stimuli

Two forms of stimuli were employed in the study to elicit children's ideas about poverty: (1) a commercially produced picture book; and (2) participants' drawings made in response to the story. These stimuli constitute a natural part of children's everyday lives inasmuch as they involve tasks frequently done by children in schools (namely, listening to a story and drawing a picture about the story). The book employed in the study has been analyzed by one of the authors in previous research: namely, *Uncle Willie and the Soup Kitchen* by DyAnne DiSalvo-Ryan (New York: Morrow Junior Books, 1991) (see Chafel et al., 1997). The book was selected because it focuses on a central theme related to poverty, the concept of a soup kitchen, and does so in a manner that is engaging and developmentally appropriate for children of this age.

Briefly, the story tells of a boy who accompanies his "Uncle Willie" to a soup kitchen. While walking to and from school, the boy has seen a Can Man pushing his cart along a sidewalk, and a woman sleeping on a park bench. Curious about the soup kitchen, where Uncle Willie works, he asks, "Why do you work there, anyway?" Uncle Willie replies, "Sometimes people need help."His mother responds to the child's curiosity by suggesting a visit. On their way to the soup kitchen, the boy and Uncle Willie stop at a neighborhood meat market to pick up donated food. They proceed to the soup kitchen, where they meet a group of workers, and assist with meal preparation. When the meal they have prepared is ready, they serve it to a large crowd of hungry people who have been waiting outside. The boy and Uncle Willie assist with clean up, and then walk home.

A sympathetic account of giving, the story portrays its characters in matter-of-fact terms, although it conveys to the reader at a couple of points in the text that the boy feels both fear and sadness when encountering the poor people depicted in the story. Other than the illustrations (which were not shown to the children), there are no clues provided in the story about the race/ethnicity of the major story characters, although they are apparently middle-class as conveyed by the child's lack of familiarity with poor people. No information is given as to why the crowd of people are going to the soup kitchen other than the fact that they are hungry, nor why people are poor.

## *Procedures*

The study's procedures were implemented in two phases. During the *pre-data collection phase of the study*, a white, female graduate student visited each classroom setting on several different occasions. On each occasion, she read a story to the entire class, asked the children as a group open-ended questions about the story, distributed drawing materials, and invited the children to individually draw a picture about the story just read and to talk about their drawings. This was done to acclimate the children to the study's procedures. None of the books and questions used during this phase was about poverty. For the *data collection phase*, each subject was taken by the graduate student to a resource room/area in the school or to a hallway, and individually asked to listen to the story, *Uncle Willie and the Soup Kitchen*. The graduate student read from a script that consisted only of text. In other words, no illustrations were shown to the children.

Following the story, each subject was given two sets of tasks. They were asked: (1) to respond verbally to a series of questions about the nature, causes, justification, and alleviation of poverty; and (2) to draw a picture about the story, and then to respond verbally to two questions and their prompts (see below). The order of presentation of these tasks was counterbalanced across the sample to control for the possible influence of task sequence on the children's responses. Only findings elicited with the second set of tasks are reported here.

Participants were asked to respond to the story by drawing a picture. On the task, participants were told, "Now, I'd like you to think about the story I just read to you, and to draw a picture about the story. In your picture, I'd like you to show me what this story about being poor means to you. There are no right or wrong pictures." Participants were given twelve minutes to complete the task, and as they worked, the same prompt ("I am interested to see what being poor means to you") was employed at 3–6- and 9-minute intervals to ensure that the drawing focused on the theme of poverty. If a child stopped drawing before the end of the twelve minutes, the graduate student administered a different prompt. (Examples: "Is there anything else you can draw about what being poor means to you?", or "Now what else can you show me about what it means to be poor?"). Each child was given the same amount of time to complete the drawing, and the same materials to work with: namely, three crayons (red, yellow, and blue), and a large piece of drawing paper (18 inches by 12 inches). When the drawing had been completed, each child was asked to respond verbally to the questions, "Tell me about your drawing." "Tell me some more about your drawing." "Is there anything else you want to tell me about your drawing?" Then each child was asked, "What does being poor mean?" (Karniol, 1985, p. 794). "Tell me some more." "Is there anything else you want to tell me?" Throughout the interview, the graduate student was instructed to respond to the children's replies in a neutral, yet friendly fashion. The responses to the questions just noted as well as any spontaneous comments made by the children while drawing were audiotaped, and then transcribed.

## Analyses

Participants' responses to the task demands of the study were scrutinized consistent with the constant comparative method, until discrete categories emerged from three sources of data: (1) their drawings; (2) their spontaneous comments made while drawing; and (3) their verbal responses to each of the two interview questions ("Tell me about your drawing," and "What does being poor mean?") and their prompts (Glaser & Strauss, 1967). The category generation process was completed in several phases. First, the principal investigator of the study and a nationally known art educator (Gilbert Clark) together studied each child's drawing, and composed a brief, verbal description and interpretation of each one. They then identified categories grounded in the data. Once these categories were identified, they rated the data. The principal investigator of the study then trained a doctoral student in art education in the use of the categories, and asked her to apply them to a random selection of drawings. When it became apparent that inter-rater agreement could not be obtained for the two sets of ratings, the principal investigator asked the same student to examine transcripts of the verbal data. Using the "old" categories derived from the drawings as a guide, the student studied the transcripts to ascertain how the nonverbal schema might appear verbally. Continuous readings of the verbal data resulted in a set of groupings that consisted of "old" categories, refinements of some "old" categories, and some "new" categories. The principal investigator, the second author of this chapter, the graduate student, and a second doctoral student in art education (who was being trained to code the data) (see below), then discussed the category system. These discussions brought about a further refinement of some category definitions, and the elimination of one category.

Forty categories resulted from the process just described. These categories were used to rate the data. After the data were rated, the more precise schema were grouped into a set of 12 superordinate categories to conduct the statistical analyses. Table 4 contains a working definition of each category along with examples of its manifestations. Many of the examples shown in the table were taken directly from the data; others were added for training purposes.

***Table 4.*** Categories.

---

*Awareness of the Poor*

1. *Acknowledgment of the poor*

A cognizance of the poor, which may take the form of verbal or non-verbal interaction, or other act of recognition between figures. One of the figures may be the child (that is, the subject). A poor person may be aware of another poor person. Examples: (a) looking towards a figure in poverty; (b) tossing a can into the can man's cart; (c) "I (the subject) saw the poor lady and said hello"; and (d) "he was going to throw it to him and he said 'here.' " Overall awareness demonstrated by the child's response to the interview questions should not be scored as evidence of this category.

2. *Spatial proximity between poor and non-poor*

Physical closeness, direct interaction, or contact between figures. Examples: (a) putting money into cup of a person begging; (b) "they talk together instead of staying away"; (c) "she gave him a little money and sat down together"; and (d) talking to a figure in patched clothing lying on a park bench. Score only if proximity seems to be important.

3. *Personal acquaintance with poor people*

Child knows someone who is poor or has direct contact with people in poverty. Examples: (a) "I have a poor person in my family"; (b) "I worked in a soup kitchen three times"; and (c) "we gave a poor person a ride one day."

4. *Personal experience of being poor*

Child places self in image or story, or reveals that he or she is or has been poor. Examples: (a) " I don't like it when I'm poor"; and (b) "This is me and I'm barefoot and hungry."

*Lack of Awareness of the Poor*

1. *Lack of personal knowledge*

Child expresses ignorance about poverty. Examples: (a) "I don't know what being poor means"; (b) "I have never known anybody who was homeless"; and (c) "Nobody in my family has ever been poor."

2. *Contradicts self*

Child demonstrates, but then disclaims personal knowledge of poverty. Examples: (a) "Being poor means not having any food . . . but I don't know anything about being poor"; and (b) "I worked in a soup kitchen once, but I don't know any poor people."

*Causes of Poverty*

1. *Poverty is due to lack of good-paying job*

People are poor because they don't have a job or don't make enough money at their job. Examples: (a) "poor people have to find a way to make a living so they can get money"; and (b) "that man is poor because his job doesn't pay him enough to buy food."

2. *Intergenerational transmission of poverty*

People are poor because their parents are/were poor. Examples: (a) "her parents are poor so she didn't have a place to live"; and (b) "my dad is poor, my mom is poor, and I'm poor, too."

*The Negative Look of Poverty*

1. *Lack of acknowledgment of the poor*

Lack of cognizance of the poor, verbal or non verbal interaction, or other act of recognition. Examples: (a) one person is shown walking by a person begging without seeming to notice; (b) "some people don't think about a hungry person even when they right in their face"; and (c) "some people don't pay attention to them."

**Table 4.**   (*Continued*)

2. *Solitariness or isolation of figures in poverty*
Used when: (1) only one figure is present and the figure appears to be alone, or (2) a person in poverty seems to be alone, even though other figures are present, or (3) when two or more figures are present and appear to be alone because a barrier exists between them. (The barrier may be physical, social, emotional or other.) A lack of friends or support network may be indicated. Examples: (a) a mother and a frowning child walking at a distance past a woman sleeping alone on a park bench; (b) a figure walking alone towards a soup kitchen with a crowd of people waiting for a bus nearby; (c) "nobody cares about them"; (d) "you have to travel around and leave your friends"; (e) a sole figure sleeping on a park bench beside a neighboring tree; (f) two figures "alone," each in his or her respective dwelling; (g) "she was outside looking in the window at all the people"; (h) "she lives between two little cracks"; (i) "She is never invited to any parties because she is poor." Score only if aloneness appears to be important.

3. *Spatial distance between poor and non-poor*
Physical separation or lack of interaction between figures. Examples: (a) a figure looks on from a distance at a woman sleeping on a park bench; (b) "we saw some people begging and crossed over to the other side of the street to get away from them"; (c) "my mama told me to stay as far away from them as possible." Score only if a distance relationship seems to be important.

4. *Depiction of an economically depressed setting*
Two or more characteristics usually associated with a rundown area, or a single direct verbal reference to the setting. Examples: (a) garbage can *and* street litter; (b) "no plants grow in that empty lot"; (c) "the slums where the poor people live"; and (d) a large pile of refuse *and* a vacant lot with automobile parts strewn about.

5. *Negative affect displayed by figures in poverty*
A figure who is frowning, bent down, weeping, frustrated, angry, and so on. Examples: (a) person with tears rolling down cheeks; (b) figure hunched over in despair; and (c) "he's really angry about something." Negative affect is always scored regardless of whether there is differentiation of affect in the same drawing.

6. *Disability of the poor*
Physical impairment of a poor person. Examples: (a) a figure with crutches or a seeing-eye-dog; (b) "she broke her leg and had to stay in bed."

7. *Vulnerability to medical problems*
People in poverty are susceptible to disease or death, need medical assistance or aren't able to get medical attention. Examples: (a) "they are starving to death"; and (b) "when you get sick you can't get a doctor to come help you."

*Environmental Context of Poverty*
1. *Depiction of poor people in an apparently rural setting*
Two or more characteristics usually associated with a rural setting, or a single direct verbal reference to a rural setting. Examples: (a) a tree ripe with fruit *and* flowers blooming; (b) cows grazing in a pasture and a silo nearby; (c) "walking in the woods"; and (d) "poor people don't have big farms."

2. *Depiction of poor people in an apparently urban setting*
Two or more characteristics usually associated with an urban setting, or a single characteristic *only* associated with cities, or a single direct verbal reference to an urban setting, or typical "city life." Examples: (a) "in that part of the city there's lots of soup kitchens"; (b) a big apartment building, sidewalks, and traffic sign; (c) visually busy conglomeration of images suggestive of urban scene; and (d) a row house.

## Table 4. (Continued)

*Helplessness of the Poor*

1. *Lack of agency (Dependency)*
People in poverty are powerless to change their circumstances, or can only wait for someone else to do something for them. Examples: (a) "they can't do anything about their raggedy clothes"; and (b) "those poor people just wait and wait for someone to feed them."

2. *Seeking assistance on the part of the poor*
People in poverty verbally asking for help. Examples: (a) figure says, "Take me to your house, please"; (b) a crying child with patched clothing says to a passerby, "Help me!"; (c) "he's asking her for money"; and (d) "he says, I need food, please."

3. *Needing protection from the elements*
A threatening relationship between a figure in poverty and the natural environment. Examples: (a) small figure sleeping alone on a park bench with storm clouds overhead; (b) a scantily clothed figure in patched attire huddled beside a building with snowflakes falling from the sky; (c) "it was raining and they didn't have warm clothes to wear"; and (d) "You have to live on the streets and you're always cold."

4. *Vulnerability in general (Victimization)*
People in poverty are susceptible to attack, to crime or to violence or otherwise susceptible to harm. They cannot depend on police protection. Examples: (a) "they get kicked by other people"; (b) "he had no way to call the police" or "that car ran over him" or " he was treated mean"; and (c) "they got kicked out of their house."

*A Sense of Obligation or Empathy Towards the Poor*

1. *Willingness to help the poor*
A manifestation of giving. When the scene is a soup kitchen, but no human figures are present, do not categorize as willingness to serve the poor. Examples: (a) feeding the hungry; (b) giving cans to the Can Man; and (c) "I'd help them if I could."

2. *Expansive generosity toward the poor*
A superlative expression of giving. Examples: (a) huge steaming pots of food in a soup kitchen busy with activity; (b) a homeless shelter with many workers, a table laden with food and clothing, and several beds; (c) "that bowl was so full of food, and then they came back for more and ate and ate and ate"; and (d) "I would give them food and clothing and a house and maybe even my car if I had one." The category may supercede "willingness to help the poor."

3. *Value statement about the poor*
Expresses a sense of obligation toward people in poverty. Examples: (a) "you really should be kind to people who are poor"; and (b) "it's good if you try to help them and it's bad if you try to hurt them."

4. *Empathy*
Child expresses sympathy, or personal affinity with people in poverty. Examples: (a) "If I'm ever poor, I'll be sad"; (b) "I think it's a shame that people don't have enough food"; and (c) "What does poor mean to you?" "Sad."

*The Poor as a Group Set Apart*

1. *Class conflict depicted*
Antagonism or hostility between poor and non-poor. Examples: (a) remarks suggestive of hostility or discord between figures; (b) "rich people treat poor people really bad"; (c) "they hate people who throw garbage on them and stuff" and (d) "some people are mean to the poor people."

*Table 4.* (*Continued*)

2. *Class differences are clearly depicted*

A clear juxtaposition of contrasting socioeconomic status between two or more figures, or a verbal acknowledgment of differences between socioeconomic groups. Differences may include actions, behaviors, possessions, or other characteristics that clearly set people apart. The emphasis here is on *difference* rather than *disapproval* (criticism of poverty) or *antagonism* (class conflict.) Examples: (a) figure in patched clothing points to a person in fancy clothing and says, "You're rich and I'm poor!" (b) a mother and a frowning child looking towards and walking at a distance past a woman sleeping alone on a park bench; (c) "I wish that poor people could be like us and have a home"; and (d) "they said goodbye to the Can Man and went inside the restaurant to eat."

3. *Criticism of poverty*

Disapproval of poverty. Examples: (a) figure says that poverty is bad; (b) "sometimes they make fun of poor people because they think they are nothing"; and (c) "they are a bad influence."

4. *Unwillingness to help the poor*

People are not willing to help people in poverty. Examples: (a) "my mama helped them once but didn't ever do it again"; (b) "nobody likes them so they won't give them any money."

5. *Poverty is associated with criminal behavior*

People in poverty commit crimes. Examples: (a) "they sell drugs to get the money they need to live"; and (b) "they gotta steal money just to get something to eat."

6. *Poverty is associated with negative behaviors (bad habits, bad decisions)*

People in poverty make bad choices regarding drunkenness, poor financial management, and so forth. Examples: (a) "they leave the kids at home alone while they go drinking with their friends"; and (b) "poor means spending all your money on stuff you don't need like beer and then not having money left for rent."

*The Positive Look of Poverty*

1. *Depiction of poor people in a pleasant, carefree setting*

Two or more characteristics depicting a happy, positive environment, or a single direct verbal reference to a happy setting. Examples: (a) a person dozing soundly on a park bench *and* birds flying in the air; (b) "the soup kitchen was so fun"; and (c) a smiling Can Man rolling his cart along a busy street *and* children happily playing with balloons nearby.

2. *Poor people are not isolated or alone (Support Network)*

People in poverty help each other out, or keep each other company, or someone they know will take care of them. Support may be provided by a family member, neighbor, stranger, and so forth, but do not score instances of institutional support (e.g. the soup kitchen). Examples: (a) "if one poor person has food, he can share it with the others"; (b) "their friends will give them a place to stay when they are poor"; and (c) "I saw some homeless people sitting on a bench together playing cards."

3. *People in poverty have a sense of agency (Self Reliance)*

Poor people can "help themselves," or are willing to try to improve their own situations, or have to rely on their own efforts. Examples: (a) "they can collect cans to cash in to get money for food"; (b) "they know they can go hunt for food"; and (c) "they try to get inside that place and build a fire out of old wood because it is cold outside."

4. *Positive affect displayed by figures in poverty*

A clear differentiation of affect between figures, or positive affect that goes beyond the formulaic, or direct verbal indication of gladness or joy. Examples: (a) one figure is shown frowning and another is shown smiling; (b) figure is shown with open toothy smile and big pink cheeks; and (c) "the people in this part are really happy."

## *Table 4.* (*Continued*)

5. *Depiction of the natural environment implies support of the poor*
A protective relationship between a figure in poverty and the natural environment. Examples: (a) an umbrella-shaped tree shelters a person sleeping on a park bench; (b) a scantily clad figure seeks shelter from the rain inside a cave; and (c) "all they have to eat would be apples off of a tree."

*Poor People Are Shown Undifferentiated and Formulaically*
People in poverty are perceived to be virtually the same. Examples: (a) a crowd of people (all shown alike) lined up to enter a soup kitchen; (b) several people (all shown alike) sitting at a table inside a soup kitchen; and (c) "all poor people wear raggedy clothes and smell bad." Restrict use of category to large groups of people.

*Poverty is Complex*
1. *Associates poverty with other social issues*
Description draws connection between poverty and war, or poverty and slavery, or poverty and corporate layoffs, and so forth.
2. *Poverty is multidimensional*
Recognizes the many-faceted nature of poverty with respect to its causes, permanence, or other aspects. Examples: (a) "sometimes it's their fault and sometimes it's not"; (b) "they didn't always used to be poor but now they are"; and (c) "poor people can be old, but they can also be young."

*Defining Poverty (Being Without/Concrete Manifestations)*
Behavior or appearance typically characteristic of a person in poverty, or neediness of someone in poverty (e.g. hunger, homelessness, begging, hitchhiking), or lacking what others have (e.g. good fortune, schooling). Examples: (a) someone is shown waiting at soup kitchen for food; (b) figure speaks about needing shoes or a place to stay; (c) "you don't have money to buy clothes"; (d) "you lost your bed"; (e) "their parents couldn't afford to send them to school"; (f) patched or ripped clothing; (g) eating from garbage can; (h) the Can Man pushing his cart; (i) "they are dirty and they have no teeth"; and (j) "he lives inside a box."

---

Two raters with experience as elementary-school art teachers (one of the previously mentioned doctoral students in art education and an in-service teacher with a master's degree in art education) were trained to use the category coding system over approximately a three-week period. Both coders were unaware of the study's guiding questions and participants' sociodemographic characteristics. They independently read a transcription of each child's verbal comments while drawing and responses to the two interview questions and prompts, and examined the drawing. In the case of the first question, the raters were instructed to rate only verbal comments that corresponded with images found in the drawing. Initially, an attempt was made to analyze the children's drawings apart from the verbal data, as alluded to earlier, but adequate reliability could not be obtained on these analyses. Analyzing the visual representations in conjunction with the verbal data made it possible to code the children's drawings reliably. All data for the two interview questions were analyzed for the presence of a category rather than the number of times it appeared.

***Table 5.*** Frequencies (Percentages) and Interrater Agreement for the Poverty Coding Categories ($N = 62$).

| Categories | Number of Children Responding (Percentage) | | Intercoder Agreement | |
|---|---|---|---|---|
| | Drawings | Verbal | Percent Agreement | Cohen's Kappa |
| 1. Awareness of the poor | 15 (24) | 2 (3) | | |
| Acknowledgment of the poor | 13 (20) | 1 (2) | 94 | 0.93 |
| Spatial proximity between poor and non-poor | 8 (13) | 0 (0) | 92 | 0.91 |
| Personal acquaintance with poor people | 1 (2) | 0 (0) | 100 | 1.00 |
| Personal experience of being poor | 1 (2) | 1 (2) | 100 | 1.00 |
| 2. Lack of awareness of the poor | 2 (3) | 5 (8) | | |
| Lack of personal knowledge | 2 (3) | 5 (8) | 96 | 0.95 |
| Contradicts self | 2 (3) | 2 (3) | 100 | 1.00 |
| 3. Causes of poverty | 0 (0) | 10 (16) | | |
| Poverty is due to lack of a good-paying job | 0 (0) | 8 (13) | 94 | 0.93 |
| Intergenerational transmission of poverty | 0 (0) | 3 (5) | 96 | 0.94 |
| 4. The negative look of poverty | 21 (34) | 11 (18) | | |
| Solitariness/isolation of figures in poverty | 14 (23) | 10 (16) | 92 | 0.91 |
| Spatial distance between poor/non-poor | 2 (3) | 2 (3) | 100 | 1.00 |
| Lack of acknowledgment of the poor | 1 (2) | 2 (3) | 94 | 0.89 |
| Negative affect of people in poverty | 7 (11) | 0 (0) | 100 | 1.00 |
| Depiction of economically depressed setting | 3 (5) | 0 (0) | 98 | 0.96 |
| Disability of the poor | 2 (3) | 1 (2) | 100 | 1.00 |
| Vulnerability to medical problems | 3 (5) | 10 (16) | 100 | 1.00 |
| 5. Environmental context of poverty | 5 (8) | 0 (0) | | |
| Depiction of rural setting | 1 (2) | 0 (0) | – | – |
| Depiction of urban setting | 4 (7) | 0 (0) | 97 | 0.95 |
| 6. Helplessness of the poor | 12 (19) | 15 (24) | | |
| Lack of agency (dependency) | 2 (3) | 4 (6.5) | 94 | 0.92 |
| Seeking assistance on the part of the poor | 6 (10) | 3 (5) | 98 | 0.97 |
| Need protection from the elements | 6 (10) | 3 (5) | 73 | 0.61 |
| Vulnerability (victimization) | 1 (1.5) | 5 (8) | 78 | 0.69 |
| 7. Obligation toward the poor | 34 (55) | 7 (10) | | |
| Willingness to help the poor | 29 (47) | 4 (6.5) | 90 | 0.89 |
| Expansive generosity towards the poor | 6 (10) | 0 (0) | 50 | 0.36 |
| Value statement about the poor | 3 (5) | 2 (3) | 96 | 0.95 |
| Empathy | 3 (5) | 3 (5) | 98 | 0.96 |

**Table 5.** *(Continued)*

| Categories | Number of Children Responding (Percentage) | | Intercoder Agreement | |
|---|---|---|---|---|
| | Drawings | Verbal | Percent Agreement | Cohen's Kappa |
| 8. The poor as a group set apart | 20 (32) | 22 (35) | | |
| Class differences | 14 (23) | 15 (24) | 79 | 0.77 |
| Class conflict | 2 (3) | 4 (6.5) | 94 | 0.89 |
| Criticism of poverty | 4 (6.5) | 5 (8) | 92 | 0.90 |
| Unwillingness to help the poor | 2 (3) | 1 (1.5) | 96 | 0.95 |
| Poverty is associated with criminal behavior | 1 (2) | 2 (3) | 75 | 0.50 |
| Poverty is associated with negative behavior | 2 (3) | 1 (2) | 93 | 0.79 |
| 9. The positive look of poverty | 23 (37) | 8 (13) | | |
| People in poverty have a sense of agency | 9 (15) | 8 (13) | 90 | 0.88 |
| Poor people are not isolated or alone | 6 (10) | 0 (0) | 94 | 0.92 |
| People in poverty display positive affect | 9 (16) | 0 (0) | 96 | 0.94 |
| Pleasant, carefree environmental setting | 10 (16) | 0 (0) | 96 | 0.95 |
| Depiction of the environment implies support of the poor | 2 (3) | 1 (1.5) | 100 | 1.00 |
| 10. Defining poverty (being without/concrete manifestations) | 59 (95) | 58 (94) | 90 | 0.75 |
| 11. Poor people are shown undifferentiated and formulaically | 1 (2) | 0 (0) | – | – |
| 12. Poverty is complex | 3 (5) | 6 (10) | | |
| Associates poverty with other social issues | 0 (0) | 0 (0) | – | – |
| Poverty is multidimensional | 3 (5) | 6 (10) | 85 | 0.60 |

*Note:* For ease of reference, children's verbal comments corresponding with images found in the drawing are referred to as the "drawing task," and those made in reply to the question about what poverty meant are referred to as the "verbal task."

One coder read and rated the data for all 62 children. To assess inter-coder agreement for each of the coding categories, a second coder independently coded 24 (39%) of the 62 transcripts. Percent agreement was calculated using an estimate of accuracy proposed by Berry and Mielke (1988), and corrected for chance agreement using a variation of Cohen's Kappa appropriate for dichotomous variables (Bartko & Carpenter, 1976). Estimates of accuracy for the 40 categories ranged from 50 to 100%; Kappas from 0.36 to 1.00 (see Table 5).

# RESULTS

Figure 1 shows a drawing made by one of the study's participants. The protocol developed for the drawing and the child's description of the drawing, given in response to the question, "Tell me about your drawing," are presented below. The protocol was written by the Principal Investigator of the Study and a nationally known art educator (Gilbert Clark).

## Protocol of a Child's Drawing

### Description of Drawing
There are two clouds and a sun drawn in the sky. There is printed text with the words, "I think everyone should have homes. I think being poor is wrong," appearing in the inner space of the page and filling the open area above two figures. There is a baseline, with the same two stick figures and a park bench with another stick figure drawn on it.

### Interpretation of Drawing
This image is interpretable by itself, although words on the page add greatly to the interpretation. The drawing appears to depict elements of the story as read.

*Fig. 1.*

Words drawn by the artist, clearly indicating the artist's feelings, are integrated into the image. The drawing is relatively unsophisticated. A mother and child are stick figures on a baseline, facing toward the viewer. A woman (also a stick figure) on a park bench on the same baseline is shown as a solitary image at a distance from the other two figures.

### Child's Description of Drawing

Interviewer: "Tell me about your drawing."
      Child: "Well, uhm, this is when they were walking through the park and they saw the lady sleeping on the bench."

Every child in the study offered a response to each of the two interview questions. Of the 62 children interviewed, 58% commented a lot while drawing and in response to the question, "Tell me about your drawing"; 19% said something; and 23% said little or nothing. In their drawings, verbal comments while drawing, and response to the above question, the children typically depicted elements of the story as read (82%), although several children appeared to go beyond the story (42%), or did not appear to deal with the theme of poverty (7%). Urban children were more likely than rural children to go beyond the story as read ($\chi^2 = 5.83, p = 0.02$). The children's comments while drawing and in response to the question focused on most parts of the drawing (97%). Some children commented on content not shown in their drawing (15%). Simple percentage agreement between the two coders on the ratings of these items ranged from 83 to 96%, and agreement corrected for chance (Cohen's Kappa) from 81 to 96%. The frequency data presented in Table 5 show that some categories figured more prominently in the children's responses than others, and that the number of children whose responses reflected a given category varied with the task demand. There were no differences in the children's responses based on order of administration of the verbal and nonverbal tasks. Tables 5 and 6 show two columns entitled "Drawings" and "Verbal." The first column refers to the children's verbal comments that corresponded with images found in the drawing, and the second column to their verbal comments about what poverty meant.

A central expectation of the study was that when asked questions about poverty, children would respond differentially based on gender, race, socioeconomic status, and setting. In order to examine this expectation, a series of two-way contingency table analyses were conducted (see Table 6). The relations of each of the four grouping variables to the superordinate coding categories for each of the two interview questions ("Tell me about your drawing." "What does being poor mean?") were examined separately. The results of each of these analyses are reported below.

*Table 6.*  Two-Way Contingency Analyses Examining Differences in Proportions of Children's Responses to Questions About Poverty by Gender, Race, Setting, and Socioeconomic Status

| Categories[a] | Gender ($\chi^2$) | | Race ($\chi^2$) | | SES ($\chi^2$) | | Setting ($\chi^2$) | |
|---|---|---|---|---|---|---|---|---|
| | Drawing | Verbal | Drawing | Verbal | Drawing | Verbal | Drawing | Verbal |
| 1. Awareness of poverty | 0.09 | 2.07 | 0.46 | 4.04** | 0.77 | 1.60 | 0.01 | 0.98 |
| 2. Lack of awareness of poverty | 2.07 | 1.96 | 1.06 | 2.79* | 5.36** | 2.94* | 0.98 | 0.15 |
| 3. Causes of poverty | – | 0.00 | – | 0.08 | – | 0.06 | – | 2.70* |
| 4. The negative look of poverty | 3.53* | 0.11 | 0.25 | 5.29** | 0.01 | 1.44 | 0.20 | 1.21 |
| 5. Environmental context of poverty | 1.96 | – | 0.47 | – | 7.05** | – | 0.37 | – |
| 6. Helplessness of the poor | 3.75** | 0.79 | 0.40 | 0.33 | 0.63 | 0.84 | 0.36 | 1.36 |
| 7. Obligation toward people in poverty | 2.35 | 0.16 | 1.84 | 0.28 | 2.70* | 0.72 | 0.32 | 0.05 |
| 8. The poor as a group set apart | 0.30 | 1.13 | 0.50 | 2.04 | 0.03 | 0.58 | 0.07 | 0.26 |
| 9. The positive look of poverty | 0.62 | 0.57 | 2.40 | 0.32 | 6.98** | 1.34 | 0.79 | 3.84** |

[a] Analyses were not conducted on three categories, Defining Poverty (being without/concrete manifestations), Poor People are Shown Undifferentiated and Formulaically, and Poverty is Complex, because of a lack of variance in the data.

* $p < 0.10$.
** $p < 0.05$.

## Gender

In response to the first question, "Tell me about your drawing?", there were statistically significant differences between the proportions of girls and boys whose responses communicated the helplessness of the poor, Pearson $\chi^2$ (1, $N = 62$) = 3.75, $p = 0.05$, Cramer's $V = 0.25$; and the negative look of poverty, Pearson $\chi^2$ (1, $N = 62$) = 3.53, $p = 0.06$, Cramer's $V = 0.24$. The proportions of girls and boys who responded with the helplessness of the poor were 0.29 and 0.10, respectively. The probability of children communicating this response was about 2.9 times more likely when the child was a girl than a boy. The proportions of girls and boys who responded with the negative look of poverty were 0.45 and 0.23, respectively. Girls were 1.96 times more likely to communicate this response than were boys. In response to the second question, "What does being poor mean?", there were no statistically significant differences in the children's comments based on gender.

## Race

In response to the first question, "Tell me about your drawing?", there were no statistically significant differences in children's responses based on race. In response to the second question, "What does being poor mean?", there were statistically significant differences in the proportions of children from different racial groups whose verbal comments communicated an awareness of the poor, Pearson $\chi^2$ (1, $N = 62$) = 4.04, $p = 0.05$, Cramer's $V = 0.26$, a lack of awareness of the poor, Pearson $\chi^2$ (1, $N = 62$) = 2.79, $p = 0.09$, Cramer's $V = 0.21$, and the negative look of poverty, Pearson $\chi^2$ (1, $N = 62$) = 5.29, $p = 0.02$, Cramer's $V = 0.30$. The proportions of children who displayed an awareness of the poor were 0.10 for children who were black or biracial and 0.00 for children who were white. Black or biracial children were infinitely more likely than white children to communicate an awareness of the poor. The proportions of children who displayed a lack of awareness of the poor were 0.12 for children who were white and 0.00 for children who were black or biracial. White children were infinitely more likely than black or biracial children to communicate a lack of awareness of the poor. The proportions of black or biracial children and white children responding with the negative look of poverty were 0.33 and 0.09, respectively. The probability of a child communicating the negative look of poverty was about 3.7 times more likely when the child was black or biracial as opposed to being white.

## Socioeconomic Status

In response to the first question, "Tell me about your drawing?", there were statistically significant differences between the proportions of children from lower and higher socioeconomic groups who communicated a lack of awareness of the poor, Pearson $\chi^2$ (1, $N = 62$) $= 5.36$, $p = 0.03$, Cramer's $V = 0.24$. The proportions of children from the lower and higher socioeconomic groups whose data conveyed a lack of awareness of the poor were 0.01 and 0.11, respectively. The probability of a child communicating a lack of awareness of the poor was about 11 times more likely when the child's socioeconomic status was higher as opposed to lower.

There were statistically significant differences between the proportions of children from lower and higher socioeconomic groups whose responses communicated the positive look of poverty, Pearson $\chi^2$ (1, $N = 62$) $= 6.98$, $p = 0.01$, Cramer's $V = 0.34$. The proportions of children from lower and higher socioeconomic groups whose responses conveyed the positive look of poverty were 0.23 and 0.56, respectively. The probability of a child responding with this category of poverty was about 2.44 times more likely when the child was from a higher socioeconomic background as opposed to a lower background.

There were statistically significant differences between the proportions of children from lower and higher socioeconomic groups whose responses communicated the environmental context of poverty, Pearson $\chi^2$ (1, $N = 62$) $= 7.05$, $p = 0.01$, Cramer's $V = 0.34$. The proportions of children from lower and higher socioeconomic groups who responded with the environmental context of poverty were 0.00 and 0.19, respectively. Higher socioeconomic status children were infinitely more likely than lower socioeconomic status children to communicate this category of poverty.

There were statistically significant differences between the proportions of children from lower and higher socioeconomic groups whose responses communicated an obligation or empathy towards the poor, Pearson $\chi^2$ (1, $N = 62$) $= 2.70$, $p = 0.10$, Cramer's $V = 0.21$. The proportions of children from lower and higher socioeconomic groups whose responses conveyed a sense of obligation or empathy towards the poor were 0.46 and 0.67, respectively. The probability of a child responding with this category of poverty was about 1.5 times more likely for children from higher socioeconomic backgrounds than for those children from lower socioeconomic backgrounds. In response to the second question, "What does being poor mean?", there were no statistically significant differences in the children's responses based on socioeconomic status.

In response to the second question, "What does being poor mean?", there were statistically significant differences between the proportions of children from lower and higher socioeconomic groups who communicated a lack of awareness of the poor, Pearson $\chi^2$ (1, $N = 62$) $= 2.94$, $p = 0.09$, Cramer's $V = 0.21$. The proportions of children from the lower and higher socioeconomic groups whose data conveyed a lack of awareness of the poor were 0.03 and 0.15, respectively.

The probability of a child communicating a lack of awareness of the poor was about 5 times more likely when the child's socioeconomic status was higher as opposed to lower.

*Setting*
In response to the first question, "Tell me about your drawing?", there were no statistically significant differences in children's responses by setting. In response to the second question, "What does being poor mean?", there were statistically significant differences in the proportions of children from rural vs. urban settings whose responses reflected the positive look of poverty, Pearson $\chi^2$ (1, $N = 62$) = 3.84, $p = 0.05$, Cramer's $V = 0.25$ and the causes of poverty, Pearson $\chi^2$ (1, $N = 62$) = 2.70, $p = 0.10$, Cramer's $V = 0.21$. The proportions of children from rural and urban settings who expressed the positive look of poverty were 0.25 and 0.07, respectively. The probability of a child exhibiting this category was about 3.8 times more likely when the child was from a rural setting as opposed to an urban setting. The proportions of children from rural and urban settings who made reference to the causes of poverty were 0.05 and 0.21, respectively. The probability of a child communicating this category of poverty was about 4.2 times more likely when the child was from an urban setting as opposed to a rural setting.

## DISCUSSION

This study addressed two questions: What are children's responses to storybook characters portrayed as economically disadvantaged? Do these responses vary according to the child's gender, race, socioeconomic status, or setting? Use of multiple methods that drew on two different communication systems (drawings, words) made it possible for the children to respond in ways that may have gone unnoticed if only a single method had been employed. This is evident from the fact that the number of children whose responses reflected a given category varied with the task demand.

When analyzing children class-related understandings, studies may apply pre-existing categories to the data, identify themes emerging from the data, or employ a combination of both. A limitation of the first approach is that categories developed *a priori* may not really fit children's understandings because with deductively derived categories, data are viewed from the perspective of adult-conceptualized schema. Schema of this sort may be concerned with the question of "how children come to know" and oriented toward the *future*, whereas emergent categories, grounded in the *present*, more accurately reflect "how children know"(see, for example,

Webley & Lea, 1993). The inductively derived category system used in this study was based on children's present ways of knowing.

Results obtained by this study offer a unique, detailed picture of the conceptual schemas of 8-year-old children about poverty. *First*, the children's knowledge was rich and varied. Forty subordinate and 12 superordinate categories emerged from the data. Every child in the sample had something to say, with more than half commenting a lot while drawing, and when asked to talk about their representation. *Secondly*, the children's responses reflected not only the content of the story, but also their own ideas about poverty. The vast majority of participants depicted elements of the story as read, although nearly half went beyond the story. While the larger proportion suggests a limited knowledge of poverty (staying close to the text), it may also indicate that the children were attending to the task given ("Now, I'd like you to think about the story I just read to you, and to draw a picture about the story"). When considered in this way, these findings may simply mean that some children may have possessed personal views about poverty that were untapped by the study. Interestingly, urban children were more likely than rural children to go beyond the story. *Thirdly*, the children displayed notions of poverty that were realistic and unrealistic. One category emerging from the data (the negative look of poverty) speaks to commonly agreed upon and well-documented aspects of privation (e.g. social isolation, negative affect, disability, vulnerability), but another (the positive look of poverty) portrays some misconceptions (e.g. positive affect, a carefree setting, a support network). Rural children and those of higher socioeconomic status were more likely to convey misconceptions. *Fourthly*, some dimensions of poverty figured more prominently in the children's thinking than others: defining poverty, its negative aspects, its positive aspects, a sense of obligation or empathy towards the poor, and the poor as a group set apart. Leahy (1981, 1983b) similarly found that children of this age tended to emphasize the external, observable (that is, definitional) manifestations of wealth and poverty. The frequency of a sense of obligation or empathy towards the poor in the present study might be attributed to a story text that emphasized a theme of social giving. Yet, the finding is consistent with other research. Ramsey (1991) noted a norm of sharing among the preschool children she studied, and Leahy (1983b) a concern about equalizing wealth (from childhood to early adolescence). The reason for the prominence of the other three categories is unclear. And, finally, the children's understandings conveyed some awareness of the psychological, nonobservable aspects of poverty, a finding also reported by Leahy (1981) for children of this age.

For ease of reference, the discussion that follows on the correlates of children's ideas about poverty refers to the children's verbal comments that corresponded with images found in the drawing as the "drawing task," and those made in reply to the question about what poverty meant as the "verbal task."

## Gender

On the drawing task, girls displayed a greater awareness than boys of the helplessness of the poor as well as the negative look of poverty, although the latter finding was only marginally significant. The categories encompass sad, distressing dimensions of economic disadvantage (e.g. isolation, vulnerability, and more). These results corroborate those of other researchers (Bombi, 1995/1998; Leahy, 1981; Ramsey, 1991) that suggest girls may be more aware than boys of social and economic inequality.

That girls are more attuned than boys to the aspects of poverty just noted seems to fit with traditional conceptions of the feminine gender as being more empathic to the downtrodden in our society. (See, for example, Eisenberg, 1985; Zahn-Waxler et al., 1992). Working with Italian children and also using a drawing task, Bombi (1995/1998) obtained a similar result. When asked "to draw a rich person and a poor person," a larger number of girls than boys portrayed the poor as being "weak" (e.g. mutilated, old, injured, sick) (Bombi, 1995/1998, p. 6). On the other hand, Farver et al. (2000) observed girls from mostly working-class backgrounds in this country depicting more positive elements (e.g. smiling adults/ children) in drawings of their neighborhoods than boys, although no differences emerged for violent content. Differences for violence did emerge in a study by Lewis and Osofsky (1997) who found a significantly higher percentage of low-income girls than boys depicting "smiling" figures in drawings of aggressors, victims, and bystanders. The particular content on which a child is asked to focus a drawing (e.g. poor people generally, one's own neighborhood) may influence the result obtained.

## Race

Like Leahy (1983a) and Simmons and Rosenberg (1971), the present study documented differences in the thinking of children of different races about social and economic inequality. On the verbal task, "What does being poor mean?", black or biracial children were more likely than white to communicate an awareness of the poor as well as the negative look of poverty, and white children were more likely than black or biracial to demonstrate a lack of awareness, although the latter finding was only marginally significant. Of the 21 black or biracial children, 15 were of lower socioeconomic status whereas the white children were almost equally distributed between the two status groups. In other words, race and socioeconomic status were confounded in the study.

By and large a less privileged group, the black or biracial children in the present study were likely speaking about poverty as a phenomenon that they knew something about. All of the black or biracial participants resided in an urban setting. As residents of an urban setting, they may have observed or experienced directly the harsh realities of economic hardship: for example, the loneliness or vulnerability of the poor. Weinger (1998) similarly observed that the low-income Caucasian and African-American children in her study demonstrated an awareness of the burdens of poverty, a finding she interpreted as reflecting realities present in the children's daily lives. In the present study, specific references to race did not appear in the children's comments or drawings. These findings may have been different had the children been presented with a greater choice of colors in the crayons they used: namely, black or brown.

## Socioeconomic Status

On the drawing task, children of higher socioeconomic status were more likely than those of lower socioeconomic status to demonstrate a lack of awareness of the poor and to depict the positive look of poverty. Higher socioeconomic status children were also more likely than lower socioeconomic status children on the verbal task to display a lack of awareness, although the finding was only marginally significant. Some past studies have found upper-status children more socially aware than other groups (Simmons & Rosenberg, 1971), and others have not (Ramsey, 1991). Discrepancies found in the literature on this variable may result, at least in part, from the administration of different tasks (Chafel, 1995).

The findings of the present study with respect to socioeconomic status are intuitively very reasonable. For more privileged children, economic privation apparently represents a human condition that's foreign to their own personal experiences and outlook. Portraying poverty in terms of its positive dimensions (a carefree setting, smiling face, a support network) suggests that children of higher socioeconomic status do not fully appreciate what it means to be poor. The darker side of economic privation (unpleasant living conditions, despair, loneliness) is something they seemingly know little about. In a qualitative study that drew on a small convenience sample of 5–14-year-old children of middle- and low-income status, Weinger (2000) emphasized the underlying similarity in the responses of both groups when questioned about opportunities for career success. Though none of her findings were tested for statistical significance, there is some evidence in the data that low-income children were more aware of the harsher realities of poverty (e.g. discrimination, lack of opportunity) than the middle-income children, not a surprising finding.

On the drawing task, the more privileged children in this study were also more likely than the less privileged group to demonstrate an awareness of the environmental context of poverty. At first glance, this result may seem contradictory inasmuch as the more privileged children, as just noted, also displayed a lack of awareness of the poor. The two sets of findings may be reconciled, if one considers that each category tapped different dimensions of a child's understanding. Why those of more privileged status were more likely to associate poverty with a rural or an urban setting is not entirely clear.

Despite the lack of awareness, higher socioeconomic status children were also more likely than lower to communicate a sense of obligation or empathy toward the poor on the drawing task, although the finding was only marginally significant. On the one hand, the result is reasonable, if one considers that one must be better off (have something to give) in order to help the poor. On the other, notions of obligation/empathy presuppose an ability to "step outside oneself" as a motivation for assisting the needy, which conflicts with a lack of appreciation for the realities of poverty communicated by this group of children. Or perhaps, the finding may simply reflect the fact that this group has been influenced by social messages transmitted by influential others (parents, teachers) about the worthiness of helping the less fortunate in our society.

## Setting

On the question, "What does being poor mean?", rural children were more likely than urban to speak about the positive look of poverty, a finding that may be viewed as a misconception, as pointed out earlier, but that may also reflect an accurate perception by the children of their environment. Though more has been written about urban than rural poverty, researchers have suggested that they differ in important respects. For example, poor children in rural settings are more likely to belong to two-parent families having a lower incidence of welfare, and the poor are more likely to be dispersed than concentrated geographically (Bianchi, 1993). With their emphasis on the positive look of poverty, the rural children in this study may simply have been revealing aspects of economic disadvantage as they knew it. Their responses fell primarily in two subordinate categories: the agency (self-reliance) of the poor and depiction of the environment as providing support for the needy, both of which are consistent with what might reasonably be assumed about poverty in rural settings.

The urban children in the study were more likely than those residing in rural settings to answer the question, "What does being poor mean?", with responses that reflected the causes of poverty, although the finding was only marginally significant. Of the study's 42 urban participants, 26 were from the less privileged group. Like race, the setting variable was thus confounded with socioeconomic status. The urban children may have been communicating an understanding of poverty derived from personal experience with family unemployment, making do on income from a low-paying job, or the intergenerational transmission of poverty.

A number of caveats are in order. First, any interpretations of the data should be viewed with caution given the modest size of the sample. Although statistically significant findings are indicative of large effect sizes with a small sample, they are also fragile. In other words, it is possible for statistical significance to be lost or gained with a change in one child's response. Secondly, chi-square analyses were performed on the data using two-way tables. This means that participants responses to the drawing and verbal tasks were analyzed separately for gender, race, socioeconomic status, and setting. In all likelihood, these variables are highly interrelated, and the conclusions suggested by at least some of the chi-square analyses may be attributed to more than one variable. Thirdly, IQ and drawing ability were not assessed in the study and may have influenced the children's responses. In the case of IQ, the statistically significant findings just reported do no lend credence to this possibility. Two reasons argue against drawing as a potential influence: (1) the quality of the children's representations was not considered when coding the data; and (2) it is unlikely that drawing ability was systematically related to any of the variables of interest. However, future studies should incorporate measures that assess IQ and drawing ability into their research design to test whether they have an influence.

Early in the study, problems were encountered with audiotaping the children's responses, which made it necessary to repeat all of the procedures of the study with 14 participants. Distribution of these children across the variables of interest were as follows: gender (8 girls and 6 boys); race (14 white children); socioeconomic status (4 lower and 10 higher); and setting (14 rural). The children were interviewed a second time no sooner than at least two months following the initial interview. When participants were asked, "Have you ever seen or listened to this story before?", 11 children responding affirmatively had been interviewed previously. Arguably, the re-interviewed children may have had an advantage over those not interviewed a second time, yet the findings reported earlier do not support this conclusion.

This study has offered a glimpse into how four sources of influence (gender, race, setting, and socioeconomic status) operate differently on children's conceptions of poverty, and allowed us to speculate *why*. Future research should move beyond focusing on structural correlates of poverty to examining processes associated with these correlates, using a larger sample, and should recognize that variables do not operate in isolation but rather interact to affect child development. What is it about socioeconomic status, for example, that affects children's conceptions of poverty? And how might processes underlying socioeconomic status (e.g. ethnic identity, family structure, IQ, language ability) function *concurrently* and *differently* for children of various genders, races, and settings? Children are complex, multifaceted beings susceptible to numerous socializing influences. Research designs more sophisticated than simple, univariate analyses are needed to investigate the co-operation of variables: how multiple factors work together, the relative contribution of each, and the degree to which one variable may moderate or mediate the affect of another. Mapping out conceptually and testing systematically the relations among the multitude of influences behind children's thinking about poverty should bring us closer to developing predictive and explanatory theoretical frameworks.

Future research should also seek to refine the use of drawing as a methodology for examining children's ideas about poverty. The data of this and other research (e.g. Bombi, 1995/1998) lend support to the conclusion that children's drawings represent a viable research tool. The present study was unable to secure adequate intercoder agreement when the children's drawings were analyzed apart from the verbal data. The more focused drawing task that Bombi (1995/1998, p. 6) gave her subjects ("to draw a rich person and a poor person") may explain, at least in part, why the researcher succeeded in securing adequate intercoder agreement with a solely nonverbal task. Nonetheless, the combined methodology (drawings and words) employed by the present study did yield fruitful results.

Some have questioned the wisdom of attempting to understand children's artistic endeavors in isolation from other communication modes (e.g. language). Kindler and Darras (1997, p. 23) contend that

> Many drawings are incomplete and reveal little about intentions or abilities of those who produced them if they are detached from a context which includes words, sounds, and gestures.... We argue that pictorial activity not only can be supported by or supportive of other forms of communication and expression, but that in fact it can be regarded as an integral part of a pluri-media process (Kindler & Darras, 1994).

Future work should provide children with opportunities to disclose their understandings of poverty through "a pluri-media process." The present study invited children to talk about their drawings after they were completed. Although spontaneous verbalizations were recorded while drawing, the children rarely spoke. Situations might be created in future studies to encourage more spontaneous verbalizations by children as they draw: for example, by asking them to work alongside other children, in pairs, or in small groups (see, for example, Dyson, 1988). Analyzing how a drawing progresses and the language that accompanies it may yield insight into the processes involved in children's thinking as well as the content.

The findings of this study have implications for educational intervention. They point to themes around which to construct units of study and children to target (e.g. boys, those of higher socioeconomic status). To illustrate briefly, thematic units might be developed on the environmental context of poverty (urban, rural), the causes of poverty (internal, external), or sense of obligation to the poor. Employing literature, field trips, class discussions, and role plays, teachers can help children to construct realistic notions about the poor, to dispel any misconceptions that they may possess, and to extend their perspectives (see, for example, Chafel, 1997a). The prominence of a sense of obligation or empathy in the data suggests that the early childhood years may be an especially fruitful time to cultivate a spirit of altruism towards the less fortunate in our society.

# ACKNOWLEDGMENTS

(1) We acknowledge the contribution of several colleagues in the development of this work: Mary Harnishfeger (data collection), MiWon Choe (rating of the data), and Gladys Newsome (intercoder agreement). The study also benefitted from extensive assistance provided by Gilbert Clark (analysis of the children's drawings) and Melanie Davenport (category generation). Other colleagues (Lee Ehman, Susan Klein, Lara Lackey, Dan Mueller, Myrtle Scott) read and critiqued portions of the paper at various stages of its development. We are also grateful to the children, teachers, parents, and administrative personnel who made it possible for us to obtain data in the schools, and to three anonymous reviewers for their helpful comments on an earlier version of the paper.

(2) The research reported in this article was made possible by grants from the Spencer Foundation and the Proffitt Endowment at Indiana University, Bloomington to Judith Chafel. The data presented, the statements made, and the views expressed are ours alone.

(3) An earlier version of this paper was presented at the Annual Meeting of the American Educational Research Association, New Orleans, LA, April 2, 2002.

(4) We would like to express our appreciation to the study's raters (Mi Won Choe and Gladys Newsome) for suggesting that only the children's verbal comments corresponding to the drawing images be rated, and to Lara Lackey for pointing out the importance of considering other communication modes that children employ while drawing.

(5) The category, poverty is multidimensional, was suggested by Leahy's (1981) discussion of multiple-classificatory structure; defining poverty (being without/concrete manifestations) is similar to Leahy's (1981) peripheral (external) aspects of poverty.

# REFERENCES

Bartko, J. J., & Carpenter, W. T. (1976). On the methods and theory of reliability. *Journal of Nervous and Mental Disease, 163*, 307–328.

Berry, K., & Mielke, P. (1988). A generalization of Cohen's Kappa agreement measure to interval measurement and multiple raters. *Educational and Psychological Measurement, 48*, 921–933.

Bianchi, S. (1993). Children of poverty: Why are they poor? In: J. Chafel (Ed.), *Child Poverty and Public Policy* (pp. 91–125). Washington, DC: Urban Institute Press.

Bombi, A. (1996). Social factors of economic socialization. In: P. Lunt & A. Furnham (Eds), *Economic Socialization: The Economic Beliefs and Behaviours of Young People* (pp. 183–201). Brookfield, VT: Edward Elgar Publishing Company.

Bombi, A. (1998). Pictorial representations of wealth and poverty by children six to eleven years of age (P. Villa, Trans.). *Eta Evolutiva, 50*, 3–18. (Original work published 1995.)

Bombi, A. (2002). The representations of wealth and poverty: Individual and social factors. In: M. Hutchings, M. Fulop & A. Van den dries (Eds), *Young People's Understanding of Economic Issues in Europe* (pp. 105–188). Sterling: Trentham Books.

Burgess, A., & Hartman, C. (1993). Children's drawings. *Child Abuse & Neglect, 17*, 161–168.

Chafel, J. (1995). Children's conceptions of poverty. In: S. Reifel (Ed.), *Advances in Early Education and Day Care* (Vol. 7, pp. 27–57). Greenwich, CT: JAI Press.

Chafel, J. (1997a). Children's views of poverty: A review of research and implications for teaching. *The Educational Forum, 61*, 360–371.

Chafel, J. (1997b). Societal images of poverty: Child and adult beliefs. *Youth and Society, 28*, 432–463.

Chafel, J., Fitzgibbons, S., Cutter, L., & Burke-Weiner, K. (1997). Poverty in books for young children: A content analysis. *Early Child Development and Care, 139*, 13–27.

Clark, G. (1993). Judging children's drawings as measures of art abilities. *Studies in Art Education, 34*, 72–81.

Coles, R. (1964). *Children of crisis*. Boston: Little, Brown and Company.

Cook, T., Church, M., Ajanaku, S., Shadish, W., Kim, J., & Cohen, R. (1996). The development of occupational aspirations and expectations among inner-city boys. *Child Development, 67*, 3368–3385.

Cox, C., & Many, J. (1992). Stance towards a literary work: Applying the transactional theory to children's responses. *Reading Psychology: An International Quarterly, 13*, 37–72.

Danziger, K. (1958). Children's earliest conceptions of economic relationships. *Journal of Social Psychology, 57*, 231–240.

Donaldson, M. (1978). *Children's minds*. New York: W. W. Norton.

Duncan, O. D. (1961). A socioeconomic index for all occupations. In: A. J. Reiss (Ed.), *Occupations and Social Status* (pp. 109–138). New York: Free Press.

Dyson, A. (1988). Appreciate the drawing and dictating of young children. *Young Children, 43*, 25–32.

Eisenberg, N. (Ed.) (1985). *Altruistic emotion, cognition, and behavior*. Hillsdale, NJ: Erlbaum.

Estvan, F. (1952). The relationship of social status, intelligence, and sex of ten- and eleven-year-old children to an awareness of poverty. *Genetic Psychology Monograph, 46*, 3–60.

Farver, J., Ghosh, C., & Garcia, C. (2000). Children's perceptions of their neighborhoods. *Journal of Applied Developmental Psychology, 21*, 139–163.

Flanagan, C., Ingram, P., Gallay, E., & Gallay, E. (1997). Why are people poor? Social conditions and adolescents' interpretations of the social contract. In: R. D. Taylor & M. C. Wang (Eds), *Social and Emotional Adjustment and Family Relations in Ethnic Minority Families* (pp. 53–62). Mahwah, NJ: Erlbaum.

Flanagan, C., & Tucker, C. (1999). Adolescents' explanations for political issues: Concordance with their views of self and society. *Developmental Psychology, 35*, 1198–1209.

Furby, L. (1979). Inequalities in personal possessions: Explanations for and judgements about unequal distribution. *Human Development, 22*, 180–202.

Furnham, A., & Stacey, B. (1991). *Young people's understanding of society.* New York: Routledge.

Garbarino, J., Kostelny, K., & Dubrow, N. (1991). *No place to be a child: Growing up in a war zone.* New York: Lexington Books.

Glaser, B., & Strauss, A. (1967). *The discovery of grounded theory.* Chicago: Aldine.

Harrah, J., & Friedman, M. (1990). Economic socialization in children in a midwestern American community. *Journal of Economic Psychology, 11*, 495–513.

Harris, D. (1963). *Children's drawings as measures of intellectual maturity.* New York: Harcourt, Brace and World.

Hibbard, R., & Hartman, G. (1990). Emotional indicators in human figure drawings of sexually victimized and nonabused children. *Journal of Clinical Psychology, 46*, 211–219.

Hummel, C., Rey, J., & Lalive d'Epinay, C. (1995). Children's drawings of grandparents: A quantitative analysis of images. In: M. Featherstone & A. Wernick (Eds), *Images of aging: Cultural representations of later life* (pp. 149–170). London: Routledge.

Karniol, R. (1985). Children's causal scripts and derogation of the poor: An attributional analysis. *Journal of Personality and Social Psychology, 48*, 791–798.

Kindler, A., & Darras, B. (1994). Artistic development in context: Emergence and development of pictorial imagery in the early childhood years. *Visual Arts Research, 20*, 1–13.

Kindler, A., & Darras, B. (1997). Map of artistic development. In: A. Kindler (Ed.), *Child Development in Art* (pp. 17–44). Reston, VA: National Art Education Association.

Leahy, R. (1981). The development of the conception of economic inequality: I. Descriptions and comparisons of rich and poor people. *Child Development, 52*, 523–532.

Leahy, R. (1983a). Development of the conception of economic inequality: II. Explanations, justifications, and concepts of social mobility and change. *Developmental Psychology, 19*, 111–125.

Leahy, R. (1983b). The development of the conception of social class. In: R. Leahy (Ed.), *The Child's Construction of Social Inequality* (pp. 79–107). New York: Academic Press.

Leahy, R. (1990). The development of concepts of economic and social inequality. *New Directions for Child Development, 46*, 107–120.

Lewis, M., & Osofsky, J. (1997). Violent cities, violent streets: Children draw their neighborhoods. In: J. Osofsky (Ed.), *Children in a Violent Society* (pp. 277–299). London: Guilford Press.

Livesley, W., & Bromley, D. (1973). *Person perception in childhood and adolescence.* London: Wiley.

Middlebrooks, S. (1998). *Getting to know city kids: Understanding their thinking, imagining, and socializing.* New York: Teachers College Press.

Mookherjee, H., & Hogan, H. (1981). Class consciousness among young rural children. *The Journal of Social Psychology, 114*, 91–98.

Nelson, K. (1978). How children represent knowledge of their world in and out of language, a preliminary report. In: R. Siegler (Ed.), *Children's Thinking: What Develops?* (pp. 255–273). Hillsdale, NJ: Lawrence Erlbaum.

Nelson, K. (1979). At morning, it's lunchtime: A scriptal view of children's dialogues. *Discourse Processes, 2*, 73–94.

Nelson, K. (1986). Event knowledge and cognitive development. In: K. Nelson (Ed.), *Event Knowledge: Structure and Function in Development* (pp. 231–247). Hillsdale, NJ: Lawrence Erlbaum.

Piaget, J., & Inhelder, B. (1969). *The psychology of the child.* New York: Basic Books.

Ramsey, P. (1991). Young children's awareness and understanding of social class differences. *The Journal of Genetic Psychology, 152,* 71–82.

Rosenblatt, L. (1978). *The reader, the text, the poem: The transactional theory of the literary work.* Carbondale, IL: Southern Illinois University Press.

Rosenblatt, L. (1985). The transactional theory of the literary work. In: C. R. Cooper (Ed.), *Researching Response to Literature and the Teaching of Literature* (pp. 33–53). Norwood, NJ: Ablex.

Rosenblatt, L. (1995). *Literature as exploration.* New York: Modern Language Association of America.

Short, G. (1991). Perceptions of inequality: Primary school children's discourse on social class. *Educational Studies, 17,* 89–106.

Simmons, R., & Rosenberg, M. (1971). Functions of children's perceptions of the stratification system. *American Sociological Review, 36,* 235–249.

Smith, N., & The Drawing Study Group (1998). *Observation drawing with children: A framework for teachers.* New York: Teachers College Press.

Stendler, C. (1949). *Children of brasstown.* Urbana: University of Illinois Press.

Thomas, G., & Silk, A. (1990). *An Introduction to the psychology of children's drawings.* New York: New York University Press.

Tudor, J. (1971). The development of class awareness in children. *Social Forces, 49,* 470–476.

Webley, P., & Lea, S. (1993). Towards a more realistic psychology of economic socialization. *Journal of Economic Psychology, 14,* 461–472.

Weinger, S. (1998). Poor children "know their place": Perceptions of poverty, class, and public messages. *Journal of Sociology and Social Welfare, 25,* 100–118.

Weinger, S. (2000). Opportunities for career success: Views of poor and middle-class children. *Children and Youth Services Review, 22,* 13–35.

Weinstein, E. (1958). Children's conceptions of occupational stratification. *Sociology and Social Research, 42,* 278–284.

Zahn-Waxler, C., Radke-Yarrow, M., Wagner, E., & Chapman, M. (1992). Development of concern for others. *Developmental Psychology, 28,* 126–136.

# BLOCKS, BUILDING AND MATHEMATICS: INFLUENCES OF TASK FORMAT AND GENDER OF PLAY PARTNERS AMONG PRESCHOOLERS☆

Jody L. Eberly and Susan L. Golbeck

## ABSTRACT

*The influences of gender and task format on children's collaborative activity with blocks were examined. Forty eight (24 same-gender dyads of preschoolers half of whom were girls) played with blocks under either a divergent or a convergent format. Children attended a community based child care center in an urban area and were predominantly Latino and African-American. Level of social interaction was measured by the amount of time the pair of children spent in interaction. The complexity of the block product was measured by: (1) the number of blocks included in the building (quantitative complexity); and (2) quality of structural organization as determined by the spatial and geometric architectural features (spatial and geometric complexity). Results showed effects for both gender and task format. Dyads in the convergent condition interacted more often. Analyses of the block structures showed that boys used more blocks in the convergent format while girls used more blocks in the divergent format. Girl pairs built more architecturally complex structures than boy pairs. These results show an*

---

☆The research described here was completed as a portion of a doctoral dissertation by the first author under the supervision of the second author at Rutgers University.

**Social Contexts of Early Education, and Reconceptualizing Play (II)**
**Advances in Early Education and Day Care, Volume 13, 39–54**
**© 2004 Published by Elsevier Ltd.**
**ISSN: 0270-4021/doi:10.1016/S0270-4021(04)13002-4**

*important task format by gender interaction. Implications for early learning in math are discussed.*

Activities with manipulative materials such as blocks have an enduring place in early childhood education. A wide array of early childhood curricula, developed over a long period of time, incorporate blocks in some form (e.g. Froebel, as cited in Hohman et al., 1979; Montesorri, 1967; Weber, 1984). Although blocks are neither inherently mathematical nor representational, they readily support the expression of spatial, geometric and mathematical understanding. Blocks provide a resource and a means for demonstrating knowledge of numerical relationships, geometry, algebra and other core mathematical concepts (Clements, 2004; Leeb-Lundberg, 1996; NAEYC, 2002; NCTM, 2000; Sarama & Clements, 2004).

Early mathematical knowledge (expressed with blocks and other objects in the world) is constructed by an individual knower reflecting upon interactions with *physical objects* in some kind of social context. This occurs at home and in school, and with adults as well as peers (Ginsburg, Pappas & Seo, 2001). Recent work in cognitive development has underscored the importance of the social context for children's learning (e.g. Howes & Ritchie, 2002; National Research Council, 2001; Rogoff et al., 2001). Children's social relationships provide an ongoing context for the acquisition of important knowledge and skills. Within classrooms, this context is evident among preschoolers engaged in cooperative play and problem solving. Children can be seen supporting each other, sharing responsibility, adapting plans and goals to incorporate one another and enjoying each other's accomplishments and pleasures. How can early childhood educators best structure such situations to support learning? The research described here examines the role of gender and task structure in children's social interaction with blocks.

Young children's social interaction with blocks frequently includes play. Yet, in recent years, early childhood educators have struggled with the complex relationships between free play and guided learning. Teachers are urged to encourage and to support play, to set the stage for play, to be available, to extend concepts and to challenge thinking. Yet, through all of this they are told not to interfere. Teachers are also urged to observe children's play and to make use of their insights to guide instruction. Processes of mutual engagement and collaboration serve an important function in young children's social, emotional and cognitive development. These processes have often been studied in the context of play through a structured observation in which children are left in an observation room with interesting toys. Such work reveals that child characteristics, such as social acceptance and popularity (Black & Hazen, 1990; Hazen & Black, 1989), cultural background (Farver & Shin, 1997), gender (Black, 1989; Leaper, 1991;

Leaper et al., 1999; Sheldon, 1992, 1993), and types of play materials influence communication strategies and patterns of social interaction during play (Goncu, 1993).

More recently, researchers have explored child initiated play activity in classroom environments. Leseman et al. (2001) note that play environments are important contexts for cognitive development among preschoolers although they also emphasize the importance of teacher involvement, particularly in classrooms with a high representation of children living in poverty, or children with low initial cognitive skill and behavioral problems. Farran and Son-Yarbrough (2001) also described changes in children's play and verbal behaviors across the school year in a Title I preschool. They found an interaction between gender and time in verbalizations. Girls talked more to teachers as the year progressed while boys talked less. Both these studies underscore the importance of considering individual level variables for understanding cognitive change in young children. Yet, despite the work on play described here, the nature of ongoing collaboration in the context of children's play with manipulative materials is poorly understood.

Studies of peer problem solving provide a different perspective on peer collaboration with manipulative materials. Unlike the work on play, studies of preschoolers' problem solving has been focused on a product or end result of the problem solving process as well as the communication strategies, characterizing the social interaction. Azmitia (1988) studied both the processes and outcomes of collaboration in preschoolers building with Lego blocks; Perlmutter and colleagues (Perlmutter et al., 1989) studied preschoolers working with peers on computers; Golbeck (1995) considered children's activity with age mates on a spatial reconstruction task. In all of these studies, children were randomly assigned to work alone or with a peer and performance within the two conditions was compared. Talk and related situation information such as gesture, were coded, as children worked or played. Findings to date offer a mixed picture on the benefits of working with a peer during problem solving. Although children's performance can improve by working with another, the probability of improvement is qualified by such issues as conflict expression (Tudge, 1992), shared responsibility within the group (Azmitia & Hesser, 1993), expertise of the partner (Azmitia, 1988; Perlmutter et al., 1989; Tudge, 1992); as well as the age of the children (Azmitia & Hesser, 1993; Perlmutter et al., 1989).

The studies of collaborative problem solving described above have primarily made use of convergent problems possessing a single solution. Examples include requesting children to replicate block structures, to play computer games, to solve problems of physical equivalence, and to reconstruct spatial arrangements with miniature objects. However, as we have already noted, children also collaborate in play, an inherently divergent activity. How does such task structure influence the processes of collaboration? Divergent activities, such as open-ended play, may afford the individual greater flexibility and greater opportunity to coordinate or match activity with a partner.

Implicit in this discussion is the assumption that social interaction influences cognition. Some constructivist perspectives on cognitive change emphasize the importance of negotiation and the active engagement of both individuals for learning (e.g. De Lisi & Golbeck, 1999; DeVries, 1997). Others emphasize the notion that linkages between social interaction and cognition depend upon language and communication (Tudge, 1992; Vygotsky, 1978). A variety of schemes reflecting this range of views have been devised for analyzing young children's discourse in small group situations as well as their talk and gesture during play (e.g. DeVries et al., 1991; Leaper, 1991).

In the study reported here, the effect of task format on children's collaborative activity with blocks was directly examined. Children worked in pairs and were asked to build with wooden unit blocks. In the convergent format, children were asked to work together to replicate a model. In the divergent format, children were asked to work together to build something new, a task structure much like free play. In both conditions, children worked with a peer of the same gender. There was no additional adult intervention. Drawing upon past work (Wanska et al., 1989), children involved in the divergent activity were expected to show a higher rate of social interactive behavior than children in the convergent task since it called for some discussion of what to build.

Past work has revealed a variety of interesting gender differences in spatial tasks among young children. While work with older children suggests that boys outperform girls on at least some spatial problems (Linn & Hyde, 1989), findings from a few studies with preschoolers actually show that girls outperform boys (e.g. Coates, 1972; Goodson, 1982; Liben et al., 1982). Contributing to the confusion is a cultural bias towards viewing block building as a "male" oriented activity (Dunn & Morgan, 1987; Epstein, 1995; Saracho, 1994). Blocks are considered by some to be a "boys" activity. Such social labeling might influence young children's interactions with materials in a variety of ways. Boys and girls may receive differential access to blocks and they may be differentially reinforced for playing with blocks. If boys spend more time playing and working with blocks, will they be more skilled than girls?

Children's block constructions were evaluated with respect to two measures relevant to complexity of thinking and mathematical understanding in geometry and measurement. First we determined the quantitative complexity of the structures by tallying the total number of blocks included in the structure. Second, we measured the architectural complexity of the construction as reflected by elements of spatial orientation and symmetry. Such features have been associated with the sophistication of children's geometric and mathematical thinking (Andrews & Trafton, 2002; Leeb-Lundberg, 1996). More specifically, children's block structures were rated for their inclusion of horizontally and vertically aligned blocks, enclosures, and arches placed in aligned or complementary orientations. The creation of these forms draws upon implicit knowledge of number, geometry and measurement (see Leeb-Lundberg, 1996; Sophian, 1999).

Past work provides conflicting rationales for the effects of both gender and task format. Therefore, we considered the following questions and tentatively posed the following hypothesis:

(1) Does task format affect the time engaged in interactive behavior during joint activity with blocks? Since open-ended activities provide the child with more flexible options for task engagement, we expected that children participating in the divergent condition would show a higher rate of interactive behavior than children in the convergent condition.

(2) Do task format and gender influence the quality of the geometric and mathematical properties of the block structure? More specifically: Do children use more blocks and build more architecturally complex structures in the divergent condition than in the convergent condition? Are there differences between boys and girls in the mathematical complexity of the constructions?

# METHOD

## *Participants*

The participants were recruited from a community childcare center in an urban area within Central New Jersey. The sample consisted of 48 children (24 female) ranging in age from 42 to 67 months ($M = 56.9$, S.D. $= 6.8$). The children came from lower to lower-middle socioeconomic homes. The ethnicities of the participants were the following: 79.2% Latino, 16.7% African American, 2.1% Caucasian, and 2.1% Asian American.

## *Apparatus and Setting*

Children attended a school accredited by the NAEYC that followed a developmentally appropriate curriculum. The school provides full day childcare on a sliding scale basis for children ages two years through kindergarten. The

*Fig. 1.* Block Model.

study was completed towards the end of the school year and most children had been attending since September.

Data collection was carried out in the school but outside the classroom in a room used for meetings and events. Children were familiar with the room. A 6 × 9 ft. rug was placed along one wall of the room where blocks were set up and the observations conducted. Two video cameras on tripods were set up. A back up audio recorder was used. A 35 mm camera was used to photograph completed block constructions.

Blocks were standard unit blocks (unit $= 1\frac{3}{8}'' \times 2\frac{3}{4}'' \times 5\frac{1}{2}''$) made of hard rock maple and were from a standard school supply catalogue. One hundred eighteen blocks were available. These included 32 standard unit blocks, 24 half units, 10 double units, 4 quadruple units, 4 unit triangles, 8 small triangles, 6 pillars, 2 unit ramps, 2 roof boards, 2 quarter circles, 16 half unit sticks, 2 half arches, 2 unit arches and half circles. In the Convergent Condition (see below) a model block arrangement (see Fig. 1) was constructed of 34 blocks (14 standard units, 2 quadruple units, 3 double units, 2 quarter circles, 2 half circles, 1 half circle arch and 2 half unit sticks).

*Design and Procedure*

Children were randomly assigned to dyads with the following constraints: same gender, same classroom, and social compatibility. Each dyad was randomly assigned to either the convergent condition or to the divergent condition, with the stipulation that each condition included 6 pairs of boys and 6 pairs of girls. The sessions were conducted outside the children's classroom in a nearby room used for meetings and special events. Children were familiar with the space. An area in a corner of the room was set up as a block area. Sessions were video and audio taped.

*Convergent Format*
Participants assigned to the convergent format were asked to duplicate a complex construction built of wooden unit blocks. The referent construction was built from 34 blocks varying in shape and size, and incorporated features of an advanced block construction described by Guanella (1934). Following a procedure used by Azmitia (1988) that employed Lego blocks, the children were shown two identical Playmobile toy figurines. The children were told the figures were twins and that the "house" (referring to the model) belonged to one of the twins. The researcher said, "Would you work together using these wooden blocks to build another house for the other twin that looks exactly like this house? While you are building I am going to videotape you because I am trying to learn about how children use blocks together. I have some paperwork to do and will work at that table while you are building together. When you are finished, please let me know." Task sessions lasted 20 minutes or until the children indicated completion.

*Divergent Format*
Pairs of children assigned to the divergent format worked in the same space with the same blocks. The model was present when children entered the room. The researcher said, "This a block structure two children built together. I would like you two to work together and build something. Decide together what to build with the blocks and then work together and help each other. I am going to move the other children's block construction out of the way so that you have more room to build together . . ." The model was then moved out of sight. Sessions lasted 20 minutes or until the children indicated completion.

*Measures*

*Time Engaged in an Interactive State*
To measure the time engaged in interactive behavior, videotapes were segmented into 15-second intervals. Using the procedure described by McLoyd et al. (1984), the number of 15-second intervals each pair of children engaged in interactive behavior was coded. McLoyd et al. (1984) were focused on whether or not the child was interacting with his or her partner. Children who were involved in a shared exchange, who responded to behavior requests, directions and questions of

each other, who made their behaviors contingent on the behavior of the other and appeared to have a common goal were coded as being in an interactive state. This state may or may not have involved verbal exchanges. Children who were clearly engaged in independent activity, including parallel and onlooker behavior were coded as being in a solitary state. To adjust for variations in length of total time of the session, the total absolute number of intervals was converted to a proportion of the total number of possible intervals. A second rater scored 20% of the videotapes. Raters agreed 98.1% of the time.

*Quantitative Complexity of Block Structures*
The number of blocks in the completed structure was calculated. A total of 118 blocks were available for possible inclusion.

1: Piling, non-aligned

Level 4: Enclosure

Level 2: Clustered or sorted

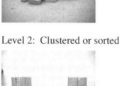

Level 5: Single Arches

Level 3: Flat Spread (Horizontal)

Level 6: Arches Stacked Vertically

Level 3: Flat Spread (Vertical)

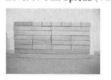

Level 7: Arches Stacked Vertically and Oriented in Different Directions

*Fig. 2.*   Architectural Complexity.

*Architectural Complexity of Block Structures*

Drawing upon pilot work and previous studies of children's block building (Goodson, 1982; Guanella, 1934; Hirsch, 1996) a measure of spatial geometric organization was developed. A 7 point rating system was devised with a low score representing the least complex feature and the high score representing the most complex feature. The scoring system was as follows: (1) Piling or non-aligned arrangement of blocks; (2) clustering or sorting of blocks based on size and or shape but no detectable building; (3) flat spread of blocks on floor such that blocks were lined up in one or two dimensions; (4) some type of enclosure of the blocks, but with all blocks on the floor; (5) a structure including at least one single arch (an arch included one block supported by two other blocks and spanning an empty space); (6) arches of blocks stacked on top of each other vertically; and (7) arches stacked vertically and oriented in different directions (see Fig. 2). Each block construction received a single score based on the highest-level feature present. A second rater scored 20% of the block constructions. The percentage of inter-rater agreement was 95%. Discrepancies were discussed and resolved by the senior coder.

# RESULTS

In the first portion of this section we examine the effects of task structure and gender on the collaborative activity within the dyads. In the second portion we examine the effects of task structure and gender on the block constructions. The alpha is set at 0.05. Significant multivariate effects were followed up with appropriate post hoc tests.

### *Effects of Task Structure and Gender on the Time Engaged in Interactive Behavior*

Each child received a score for the proportion of the total number of 15-second intervals in which he was engaged in a socially interactive state. A proportion score was created by dividing the total number of intervals the child was engaged socially by the total number of intervals coded. To test the effects of task structure and gender, a $2 \times 2$ univariate analysis of variance was performed with gender and condition (convergent or divergent) as between-group factors.

Results of the analysis of variance showed a main effect for condition, $F(1, 44) = 6.4$, $p < 0.001$. Contrary to expectations, children in the convergent condition ($M = 68.7$, S.D. $= 28.2$), spent a larger proportion of time in an interactive state than children in the divergent condition ($M = 48.4$, S.D. $= 37.9$). There was also a main effect for gender, $F(1, 44) = 21.3$, $p < 0.001$. Boys ($M = 77.1$, S.D. $= 23.5$) spent a larger proportion of time in an interactive state than girls ($M = 39.9$, S.D. $= 34.2$). The condition by gender interaction was not significant.

*The Effects of Task Structure and Gender on the Quantitative Complexity*

To examine the effects of gender and task structure on the quantitative complexity of the block structure, the total number of blocks used in the block constructions were tallied and, a $2 \times 2$ univariate analysis of variance (ANOVA) was performed with gender of dyad and format (convergent vs. divergent) as between-group factors. The Least-Significant Differences (LSD) method was used for post hoc tests.

There was an interesting interaction, $F(1, 42) = 6.9$, $p < 0.05$ between task format and gender. Post hoc tests revealed that girls used more blocks in the divergent condition ($M = 79.7$, S.D. $= 32.3$) than in the convergent condition ($M = 47.3$, S.D. $= 33.7$). In contrast, boys used more blocks in the convergent condition ($M = 66.3$, S.D. $= 46.8$) than the divergent condition ($M = 37.4$, S.D. $= 42.9$). There were no main effects.

*The Effects of Task Format and Gender on Spatial and Geometric Complexity*

The architectural quality of children's block structure was evaluated with the measure of spatial and geometric complexity. Each block construction was assigned a score based on the highest-level feature present in the block constructions. The scores ranged from 0 to 7 ($M = 3.59$, S.D. $= 1.97$).

Scores on spatial and geometric complexity (architectural) were analyzed in a $2 \times 2$ univariate analysis of variance with gender and task condition as between group factors. A main effect for gender was found, $F(1, 42) = 8.3$, $p < 0.006$. Girls produced more complex block constructions with respect to spatial and geometric complexity ($M = 4.3$, S.D. $= 1.5$) than did boys ($M = 2.8$, S.D. $= 2.1$). There was no effect for task format and the interaction was not significant.

# DISCUSSION

Our questions focused on preschool children's activities with unit blocks, a common manipulative material in early childhood education. We were especially interested in the effects of task structure on children's collaborative activity. We also had a secondary interest in the differences between pairs of boys and pairs of girls in their interactions in block activity. Finally, we were interested in the effects of task structure and gender on the geometric and mathematical features of structures children created in block activity.

We examined task structure by comparing two formats for block activity, a convergent format in which children were asked to replicate a model structure and a divergent format in which children were encouraged to build something new. We tentatively predicted that the divergent format, which was open-ended and flexible, would lead to increased social interaction and higher levels of collaboration. We found that task structure does indeed influence social interaction and collaboration. However, rather than increased interaction during the divergent format, we found more social interaction occurred in the convergent format. Overall, the young children in this study spent a larger proportion of time in a socially interactive state when asked to copy a model jointly rather than when they were asked to build something new together. We also found that overall, boys were more interactive than girls.

What do these differential rates of social interaction across task format and gender mean? The full answer to this question awaits the results of the discourse analysis, currently in progress (Eberly & Golbeck, 2001a, b). However, analysis of children's talk partially mirrors simple interaction. Overall, more individual speech acts and more exchanges were coded in the convergent condition than in the divergent condition. This is consistent with the effect for task on rate of social interaction. However, *what* was said also differed across task format.

Task format did not influence interaction in the way we expected, although as we noted, we had very little past work upon which to base our hypothesis. We had expected increased collaboration in the divergent activity in part because it was more flexible and would permit children to adapt the activity to their own interests. However, the convergent activity used here, while more focused and less open than the divergent task, still provided a high level of flexibility for children. Indeed, a few pairs of children in the convergent condition appeared to ignore the task directions and instead built their own structures. A convergent task format in which children are offered less flexibility and less opportunity for modifying the activity to suit their own interests would be one follow up to this study. However, our constructivist lens leads us to prefer an approach which closely tracks both the input of the child as well as changes in the learning environment (task format) in any future work. Children, either individually or in a social context, always transform environmental input. The challenge for teachers and researchers is to remain attentive to these processes and creatively measure both the learner and the learning context. We believe our forthcoming discourse analysis will help us better understand these data. In the meantime, these findings offer useful insights for teachers.

Complementing the effect for task format, we also found an effect for gender. We had predicted that boys would be more socially engaged than girls and this expectation was confirmed. Boys spent a larger proportion of their time engaged in social interaction than girls. This was evident across both the convergent and divergent format. Our preliminary analysis of the children's talk, currently in progress, also confirms our expectation that suggests that boys use more controlling and collaborative speech while girls use more withdrawing statements (Eberly & Golbeck, 2001a, b).

A second focus of this study was the block constructions created by boys and girls under the contrasting task formats. Certainly the two measures we devised do not fully capture the complexity of the block structures children created (see Leeb-Lundberg, 1996; Reifel & Greenfield, 1982), but these were a start. While early childhood educators extol the virtues of block building for many dimensions of the early childhood curriculum, surprisingly little empirical work is available on children's activity with blocks and their learning in any content area (see Golbeck, 2001a). We were particularly interested in the architectural features, specifically the spatial and geometric properties of the structures, content with an obvious connection to mathematics (Ginsburg & Golbeck, in press; Golbeck, 1995, 2001b; Sophian, 1999) We expected to see fairly sophisticated block structures from these four and five year old children. We also wondered if boys and girls would create structures of similar size and complexity. Since past work yields somewhat conflicting findings on gender differences in the spatial skills of young children, we made no specific predictions.

Block structures were coded in two ways; first for quantitative complexity, or the total number of blocks included in the structure, and second for the spatial and geometric complexity of the arrangement. The analysis of quantitative complexity (the total number of blocks) used revealed a gender by format interaction. Boys used more blocks in the convergent format than the divergent format. Girls exhibited the opposite pattern, using more blocks in the divergent format. This cross over pattern was not expected. One explanation is that girls in the divergent condition worked relatively independently, each building her own structure and interacting relatively little with her partner. Girls in the convergent condition spent more time talking and less time building. Boys, on the other hand, actually worked together more effectively with the blocks, talking and building simultaneously. This would be consistent with the data on rate of social interaction and discourse. There is some reason to believe that boys engaged in more unrelated dramatic play and it may be that more of this occurred in the divergent condition. While the boys may have been engaged and active, their activity may not always have included the blocks organized into a structure. Additional analysis of the transcripts and videotapes would clarify this.

This explanation is consistent with the analysis of block structure complexity scores. This analysis shows no effect for task format. However, it does show an effect for gender. Girls produced more complex structures than boys. Their structures were more likely to include high level features such as stacked and crossed arches. This finding may appear surprising since much of the literature in spatial cognition has emphasized the superiority of males over females (Linn & Hyde, 1989). As noted earlier however, some previous work, has shown preschool-aged girls outperforming males on spatial problems. (e.g. Goodson, 1982; Liben et al., 1982). We suspect that the slight edge demonstrated by girls may have had more to do with their approach to the task than spatial understanding *per se*. Importantly, girls did not appear less competent than the boys.

How can early childhood practitioners use these findings to enhance young children's mathematical knowledge in the preschool classroom? These data suggest that teachers should provide both convergent and divergent types of experiences with blocks in the early childhood classroom. These findings suggest that convergent activities are especially important for supporting preschoolers' joint engagement in activity. All too often teachers view children's experiences in the block area as a time for "free play" much like the divergent activity used here. Children are left on their own to organize and structure their experience. These findings suggest that children become engaged and work together when given a task such as the convergent task used here. These findings should encourage teachers to think "outside the box" about the presentation of traditional early childhood materials, taking care to recognize the complex interplay between task format and the dynamics of small group interaction in preschool.

Striking about these findings is the complex combination of relationships surrounding gender, task structure, social interaction and block constructions. Distinct gender differences are evident in children's social interactions as well in the products they created. Boy pairs were more interactive than girl pairs. However, the girls generated more spatially complex structures. The scores reported here are group means and both boys and girls showed considerable variation in their building. Future work needs to look more closely at the relationship between ongoing social interaction and children's spatial geometric products in small group settings. Such work is important for understanding the use of manipulatives in mathematics instruction in which children are expected to symbolize quantitative and geometric relationships with physical materials.

Teachers of young children might learn a great deal by watching children closely on tasks such as these. By combining clear goals for mathematical understanding, insights about the strengths and weakness of activities presented in varying task formats and the special needs of individual learners, teachers can be empowered. Such knowledge is detailed, concrete and integrated (Hiebert et al., 2002). Only with an understanding gained through close observation of children will teachers be able to meet the diverse needs of children and provide them with an adequate foundation for future learning.

# REFERENCES

Andrews, A., & Trafton, P. (2002). *Little kids – powerful problem solvers*. Portsmouth, NH: Heinemann.
Azmitia, M. (1988). Peer interaction and problem solving: When are two heads better than one? *Child Development, 59*, 87–96.
Azmitia, M., & Hesser, J. (1993). Why siblings are important agents of cognitive development: A comparison of siblings and peers. *Child Development, 64*, 430–444.
Black, B. (1989). Interactive pretense: Social and symbolic skills in preschool play groups. *Merrill-Palmer Quarterly, 35*(4), 379–397.
Black, B., & Hazen, N. L. (1990). Social status and patterns of communication in acquainted and unacquainted preschool children. *Developmental Psychology, 26*(3), 379–387.
Coates, S. (1972). *Preschool embedded figures test*. Palo Alto, CA: Consulting Psychologists Press.
Clements, D. H. (2004). Geometric and spatial thinking in early childhood education. In: D. Clements & J. Sarama (Eds), *Engaging Young Children in Mathematics: Standards for Early Childhood Mathematics Education* (pp. 267–298). Mahwah, NJ: Lawrence Erlbaum.
De Lisi, R., & Golbeck, S. (1999). Implications of Piagetian theory for peer learning. In: A. M. O'Donnell (Ed.), *Cognitive Perspectives on Peer Learning* (pp. 3–37). Mahwah, NJ: Lawrence Erlbaum.
DeVries, R. (1997). Piaget's social theory. *Educational Researcher, 26*(3), 4–17.
DeVries, R., Reese-Learned, H., & Morgan, P. (1991). Sociomoral development in direct-instruction, eclectic, and constructivist kindergartens: A study of children's enacted interpsersonal understanding. *Early Childhood Research Quarterly, 6*, 474–517.
Dunn, S., & Morgan, V. (1987). Nursery and infant school play patterns: Sex-related differences. *British Educational Research Journal, 13*(3), 271–281.
Eberly, J. L., & Golbeck, S. L. (2001a). Teachers' perceptions of children's block play: How accurate are they? *Journal of Early Childhood Teacher Education, 22*(2), 63–68.
Eberly, J. L., & Golbeck, S. L. (2001b, June). Children's block constructions. Paper presented at the Annual Meetings of the Jean Piaget Society, Montreal, Canada.
Epstein, D. (1995). Girls don't do bricks: Gender and sexuality in the primary classroom. In: J. I. Blatchford (Eds), *Educating the Whole Child: Cross-curricular Skills, Themes and Dimensions* (pp. 56–69). Bristol, PA: Open University Press.
Farran, D., & Son-Yarbrough, W. (2001). Title I funded preschools as a developmental context for children's play and verbal behaviors. *Early Childhood Research Quarterly, 16*(2), 245–262.
Farver, J. M., & Shin, Y. L. (1997). Social pretend play in Korean- and Anglo-American preschoolers. *Child Development, 65*(3), 544–556.
Ginsburg, H., & Golbeck, S. (2004). Thoughts on the future of research on mathematics and science learning in education. *Early Childhood Research Quarterly, 19*(1).
Ginsburg, H., Pappas & Seo (2001). Everyday mathematical knowledge: Asking children what is developmentally appropriate. In: S. L. Golbeck (Ed.), *Psychological Perspectives on Early*

*Childhood Education: Reframing Dilemmas in Research and Practice* (pp. 181–219). Mahwah, NJ: Lawrence Erlbaum.

Golbeck, S. (1995). The social context and children's spatial representations: Recreating the world with blocks, drawings, and models. In: S. Reifel (Ed.), *Advances in Early Education and Care* (7th ed., pp. 213–250). Greenwich, CT: JAI Press.

Golbeck, S. L. (2001a). Instructional models for early childhood: In search of a child-regulated/teacher-guided pedagogy. In: S. L. Golbeck (Ed.), *Psychological Perspectives on Early Childhood Education: Reframing Dilemmas in Research and Practice* (pp. 3–34). Mahwah, NJ: Lawrence Erlbaum.

Golbeck, S. L. (2001b, April). A spatial structural approach to young children's block building. Paper presented at the Biennial Meetings of the Society for Research in Child Development, Minneapolis, MN.

Goncu, A. (1993). Development of intersubjectivity in the dyadic play of preschoolers. *Early Childhood Research Quarterly, 8,* 99–116.

Goodson, B. (1982). The development of hierarchic organization: The reproduction, planning, and perception of multiarch block constructions. In: G. Forman (Ed.), *Action and Thought: From Sensorimotor Schemes to Symbolic Operations.* New York: Academic Press.

Guanella, F. M. (1934). Block building activities of young children. *Archives of Psychology, 174,* 1–91.

Hazen, N. L., & Black, B. (1989). Preschool peer communication skills: The role of social status and interaction context. *Child Development, 60,* 867–876.

Hiebert, J., Gallimore, R., & Stigler, J. (2002). A knowledge base for the teaching profession: What would it look like and how can we get one? *Educational Researcher, 31*(5), 3–15.

Hirsch, E. S. (Ed.) (1996). *The block book* (pp. 35–60). Washington, DC: National Association for the Education of Young Children.

Hohman, M., Banet, B., & Weikart, D. (1979). *Young children in action: A manual for preschool educators.* Ypsilanti, MI: High/Scope Press.

Howes, C., & Ritchie, S. (2002). *A matter of trust: Connecting teachers and learners in the early childhood classroom.* New York: Teachers College Press.

Leaper, C. (1991). Influence and involvement in children's discourse: Age, gender, and partner effects. *Child Development, 62,* 797–811.

Leaper, C., Tenenbaum, H. R., & Shaffer, T. G. (1999). Communication patterns of African American girls and boys from low-income, urban backgrounds. *Child Development, 70*(6), 1489–1503.

Leeb-Lundberg, K. (1996). The block builder mathematician. In: E. S. Hirsch (Ed.), *The Block Book* (pp. 35–60). Washington, DC: National Association for the Education of Young Children.

Leseman, P. M., Rollenberg, L., & Rispens, J. (2001). Playing and working in kindergarten: Cognitive co-construction in two educational situations. *Early Childhood Research Quarterly, 16*(3), 363–384.

Liben, L. S., Moore, M., & Golbeck, S. (1982). Preschoolers' knowledge of their classroom environment: Evidence from small scale and life-size spatial tasks. *Child Development, 53,* 1275–1284.

Linn, M. C., & Hyde, J. S. (1989). Gender, mathematics, and science. *Educational Researcher, 18,* 17–27.

McLoyd, V. C., Thomas, E. A., & Warren, D. (1984). The short-term dynamics of social organization in preschool triads. *Child Development, 55,* 1051–1070.

Montesorri, M. (1967). *The absorbent mind.* New York: Holt, Rinehart & Winston.

NAEYC & NCTM (2002). Early childhood mathematics: Promoting good beginnings. Available at http://www.naeyc.org/resources/position_statements/psmath.pdf.

National Research Council (2001). Eager to learn: Educating our preschoolers. Committee on Early Childhood Pedagogy. In: B. T. Bowman, M. S. Donovan & M. S. Burns (Eds), *Commission on Behavioral and Social Sciences and Education*. Washington, DC: National Academy Press.

NCTM (National Council of Teachers of Mathematics) (2000). *Principles and standards for school mathematics*. Reston, VA: NCTM. Online: http://my.nctm.org/eresources/school_level.

Perlmutter, M., Behrend, S. D., Kuo, F., & Muller, A. (1989). Social influences on children's problem solving. *Developmental Psychology, 25*(5), 744–754.

Reifel, S., & Greenfield, P. (1982). Structural development in a symbolic medium: The representational use of block constructions. In: G. Forman (Ed.), *Action and Thought: From Sensorimotor Schemes to Symbolic Operations* (pp. 203–233). New York: Academic Press.

Rogoff, B. Turkanis, C., & Barlett, L. (2001). *Learning together: Children and adults in a school community*. New York: Oxford University Press.

Saracho, O. N. (1994). The relationship of preschool children's cognitive style to their play preferences. *Early Child Development and Care, 97*, 21–33.

Sarama, J., & Clements, D. (2004). Building Blocks for early mathematics. *Early childhood Research Quarterly*.

Sheldon, A. (1992). Conflict talk: Sociolinguistic challenges to self-assertion and how young girls meet them. *Merrill-Palmer Quarterly, 38*(1), 95–117.

Sheldon, A. (1993). Pickle fights: Gendered talk in preschool disputes. In: D. Tannen (Ed.), *Gender and Conversational Interaction* (pp. 89–103). New York: Oxford University Press.

Sophian, C. (1999). Children's ways of knowing: Lessons from cognitive development research. In: J. Copley (Ed.), *Mathematics in the Early Years* (pp. 11–20). Washington, DC: National Association for the Education of Young Children.

Tudge, J. (1992). Processes and consequences of peer collaboration: A Vygotskian analysis. *Child Development, 63*, 1364–1379.

Vygotsky, L. (1978) *Mind in society: The development of higher psychological processes*. Cambridge, MA: Harvard University Press.

Wanska, S. K., Pohlman, J. C., & Bedrosian, J. L. (1989). Topic maintenance in preschoolers' conversation in three play situations. *Early Childhood Research Quarterly, 4*, 393–402.

Weber, E. (1984). *Ideas influencing early childhood education: A theoretical analysis*. New York: Teachers College Press.

# BEYOND QUALITY, ADVANCING SOCIAL JUSTICE AND EQUITY: INTERDISCIPLINARY EXPLORATIONS OF WORKING FOR EQUITY AND SOCIAL JUSTICE IN EARLY CHILDHOOD EDUCATION

Sheralyn Campbell, Glenda MacNaughton, Jane Page and Sharne Rolfe

## ABSTRACT

*In this chapter, we used a research-based case study titled "The Desirable Prince Meeting" to explore how interdisciplinary theoretical perspectives on the child can be used to prompt critical reflection on socially just equity praxis in early childhood education. We argue that using multiple theoretical perspectives to analyze teaching and learning can generate and drive critical reflection on equity praxis more effectively than using a single perspective that presents a single truth about teaching and learning moments.*

Social Contexts of Early Education, and Reconceptualizing Play (II)
Advances in Early Education and Day Care, Volume 13, 55–91
Copyright © 2004 by Elsevier Ltd.
ISSN: 0270-4021/doi:10.1016/S0270-4021(04)13003-6

# INTRODUCING THE ISSUES

In this chapter, we use interdisciplinary theoretical perspectives on the child to prompt critical reflection on socially just equity praxis in early childhood education. We argue that using multiple theoretical perspectives to analyse teaching and learning can generate and drive critical reflection on equity praxis more effectively than using a single perspective that presents a single truth about teaching and learning moments.

To build our argument we use a research-based teaching and learning scenario from an early childhood classroom titled, *"The Desirable Prince Meeting"* to offer three contrasting readings of how social justice and equity touches young children's lives. Those perspectives are socio-developmental theory, critical futures studies and feminist poststructuralist theory. The contrasting readings of the *"The Desirable Prince Meeting"* built using these three perspectives invites and provokes critical reflection on the place of social justice in early childhood curriculum praxis on two levels. Firstly, they operate to show how a single perspective can limit the range of issues that a teacher might consider when analyzing classroom encounters. Specifically, they do this by:

- highlighting the idea that there is no single perspective that offers guidance on all aspects of equity praxis in early childhood classrooms;
- showing how multiple perspectives can be used to honor the complexity of classroom life;
- illustrating how in using single perspectives much can remain under-explored;
- highlighting the contradictory understandings of the child and classroom practices that are made possible when contrasting readings are placed alongside each other.

Secondly, the contrasting readings illustrate three distinct ways in which equity and social justice can be understood and thus enacted in early childhood pedagogies. In doing so they invite specific reflection on how the use of multiple perspectives might highlight different arenas in and through which an early childhood teacher can build socially just equity praxis.

Our starting point is the research-based teaching and learning scenario *The Desirable Prince Meeting*.

# THE *"DESIRABLE PRINCE MEETING"*: A TEACHING AND LEARNING SCENARIO

The story of the *"Desirable Prince Meeting"* is taken from a doctoral action research project led by Sheralyn Campbell (Campbell, 2002) in which she worked with three teachers – Anne, Meg and Leyla – in the three to five year old room of an inner urban Australian children's center in 1998. The story exposes some of their struggles as they tried to think, speak and act with equity intent to create a socially just classroom as teachers in Australian early childhood education.

We ask you to read Sheralyn's construction of their shared and different voices with respect for the courage of a group of early childhood teachers who explored the dangers and possibilities of resistance to the status quo. The story begins and ends as an acknowledgment of Sheralyn's debt to these critical friends who have changed how she sees and understands the world of early childhood, and who continue to challenge her gaze on their work and the work of early childhood education more broadly.

Anne and Meg had called a classroom meeting to talk about how Gayle *(was) being treated by other children and the way she (was) treating children.* Gayle (4, Australian born) was a new part-time member of the group and recently, Barry (Australian born, 5) had uncharacteristically lost both his patience and temper, when she had repeatedly asked him to be the Prince in her Princess games.

While Barry's strong rejection of Gayle concerned Anne and Meg, they were equally concerned by Gayle's reaction to a suggestion that she choose Mick (5, South Pacific Island born) to be her Prince instead of Barry. Gayle had refused, rolling her eyes in disbelief and disgust. Anne and Meg believed that a meeting with all the children about these issues would provide a forum for Barry, Gayle and others to talk about and solve the problems of exclusions for these two children.

### The "Desirable Prince Meeting"

Anne began the meeting by asking Gayle how she understood Barry's refusal to be her Prince:
Anne: *Gayle is there a reason why you want Barry to be the Prince in your (Princess) game?*
Gayle: *Because I always like playing Princess games . . .*
Anne: *. . . Do you understand why Barry doesn't want to play it?*
Gayle: *No.*

Barry: *. . . I just keep saying NO because she keeps asking me and No means (you're) bothering me.*
Meg: *Can you just tell her . . . 'You're not interested in playing that game?' Next time she asks you over and over again can you just say 'Gayle I'm not interested. Maybe you should ask someone else'. And if, Gayle, your Prince needs to be a boy, there are other boys in the room you can ask.*

Gayle: *I just like Barry . . .*
Anne: *That's fine to like Barry. We all like different people. We are all closer to different people than other people but what Barry is saying is that you're actually annoying him by always asking him to play that game.*

Gayle: *I'm but just asking because I'm always left alone . . .*

Meg: *But Gayle I remember . . . one day when Barry said he didn't want to play, Mick said he would play and you said 'No'.*
Gayle: *Its always a bit too hard for me to play with him . . . because I always want to play with Barry.*

Anne: *Gayle? . . . Can you tell me why you don't ask Mick to play your (Princess) games?*
Gayle: *Because he – I like Barry.*
Anne: *Yeah and that's ok but why is it that you choose not to play with Mick?*
Gayle: *Because I don't, I don't (like) people that are black I – only white people.*

Other children expanded on Mick's difference:
Kaarin: *His hair is curly*
Fiona: *And cos I don't (like curly) either . . . I like only straight . . .*
Gayle: *Because sometimes I um I smell his skin and it smells horrible.*

In what follows we present our three readings of this scenario with a focus on how each of our chosen theoretical perspectives might answer the following questions:

- *What knowledge of the young child can be used to understand the equity issues within this scenario?* Specifically, what do we know from within a chosen perspective about the ways in which young children construct their understandings of their social, educational and cultural worlds and how this impacts on their educational participation and development including what they understand, how they understand it and what these understandings mean for what and how they learn in the early years?
- *What knowledge of the social contexts of the young child can be used to understand the equity issues within this scenario?* Specifically, what do we know from within a chosen perspective about the ways in which young children's social, educational and cultural worlds limits or expands their capacity to experience equitable and just participation and outcomes from services for young children including its impact on how and what young children's learn through their education?
- *What knowledge of the early childhood professional can be used to understand the equity issues within this scenario?* Specifically, what do we know from within a chosen perspective about the ways in which early childhood professionals can most successfully produce equitable experiences and outcomes for young children in their services and the factors that constrain or sustain such work?

As you engage with each of the three readings of *The Desirable Prince Meeting* we invite you to reflect on those questions and how they are answered in each of the readings.

## READING 1: A SOCIO-DEVELOPMENTAL PERSPECTIVE ON THE YOUNG CHILD, SOCIAL CONTEXTS, THE EARLY CHILDHOOD PROFESSIONAL AND A SOCIALLY JUST CURRICULUM

The scenario presented raises several complex issues from a socio-developmental perspective. In the main, these have to do with how the described events (the "experiences") may impact on the individuals participating in them. Here the focus will be on the children rather than the adults, and on how these experiences may effect their psychological wellbeing and their construction of the social world based on them. There are many ways in which these topics might be considered within a social-development framework. The approach chosen for this analysis is based on a resilience perspective (e.g. Clarke & Clarke, 1976, 2000, 2003). This perspective considers how experiences impact on the child, not from a deficit model of development (pinpointing risk factors and showing their negative effects) but based on an identification of sources of strength, i.e. so-called protective factors and their precursors (Werner, 1985).

The developmental-resilience framework had its origins in several longitudinal studies of how various life stresses during the prenatal, infancy and childhood periods are related to psychological and social outcomes in adolescence and adulthood (e.g. Garmezy, 1993; Werner & Smith, 1992). Werner and Smith's research was conducted on the Hawaiian island of Kuaui over a period of more than 40 years, beginning in the mid–1950s. The original sample included almost 700 children and the study was notable, *inter alia*, for the high retention rate of participant families over such an extended time. Although the initial aim of the study was to examine long-term consequences of prenatal and perinatal stress and to document how adverse early experiences impact on cognitive, emotional and physical development, the data inspired the researchers to reconceptualize this approach. That is, although the aim of the study was to understand the negative effects of risk factors, over time the resilience of some children was striking. About 33% of high-risk children in the sample (having been exposed to parental mental illness, parental alcohol abuse, family breakdown and poverty) nonetheless developed into adults who "loved well, worked well and played well" (Werner, 1989, p. 4). What nurtured this ability to withstand stress, "to adapt effectively in the face of adversity" (Berk, 2000, p. 10), became the new focus of research efforts.

Since the initial research studies, there have been many attempts to refine the definition of resilience, to appreciate its complexity and to understand better the experiences that promote it. In general, the conclusions of Werner and her colleagues have been supported. Whilst it would appear that there is a fundamental tendency towards resilience built into the human system, how strongly it is expressed varies widely from individual and is impacted critically by experience (Clarke & Clarke, 2003). The "three most potent influences" (419) identified by Clarke and Clarke (2003) are the inner resources of the individual – sociability, problem solving and self esteem; external support, beginning with the opportunity to form a close, positive relationship with at least one caring adult – although not necessarily the parent – who knows the child well and is committed to that child's wellbeing' and the duration of that support.

Central to all factors is their role in facilitating the child's exposure to positive, nurturing relationship experiences. An easy, outgoing temperament elicits positive responses from others and thus promotes positive interactions (Seifer et al., 1996). At least one secure attachment within the family, or amongst the child's early caregivers, is pivotal to the development of trust, security and later autonomy and initiative. Outside family supports encourage and reinforce feelings of competence, particularly in the later childhood years (Werner & Smith, 1992).

That attachment relationships have a central role in the development of resilience comes as no surprise to those who have followed recent research and writings on the development of the self. The self-concept – who I am – is not present at birth. It develops in the social context of human interactions and relationships: how others respond to us and relate to us during the early years, especially those persons with whom we have significant, sustained relationships. We are the product of our social and cultural milieu. Over development, the sense of self consolidates so that one's self concept does not always remain as fluid as it is in the earliest years but the early years may be particularly potent (see Schore, 1994; Sroufe, 1995).

The importance of interactions and relationships early in life is that they appear to set up expectancy about the self, especially the self in relationship with others. Attachment theorists have referred to these expectancies as a person's 'inner working model'. For example, Bowlby's (1969/1997) concept of an internal working model is in essence a working model of the self, a set of expectations about the social world and the individual within it. In his writing on this topic, Sroufe (1995) integrates attachment theory with the work of psychoanalysts such as Erikson (1963). He conceives of what Erikson has called "basic trust" (the so-called psychosocial task or crisis of the first year of life) as the core element of the self. He describes it as "the individual's fundamental sense of others as caring, the self as worthy, and the world as safe" (p. 221). This fundamental sense of security or trust results from a history of caregiving relationships characterized by sensitivity, consistency and responsiveness.

During the first to the third years, once the child has become mobile, a second layer of the self emerges via attempts at autonomy or independent striving to obtain a goal (Erikson's psychosocial stage of autonomy vs. shame and doubt). The child whose strivings are accepted and valued develops a view of the self as accepted and valued (Sroufe, 1995). A true sense of what Sroufe terms "instrumentality" or autonomous functioning in the absence of adult involvement emerges in the preschool period, when peer friendships, relatively free from adult direction, develop and the child is able to assume some, albeit rudimentary, self-responsibility. Feelings of competence and self-esteem are the end product of caregiving experiences that nurture each of these phases. Unresponsive, inconsistent and/or insensitive care lead to predictable outcomes in terms of the development of the self (Sroufe, 1995).

Importantly for the current discussion, these expectancies which constitute the inner working model of the self can become self-fulfilling, a lens that captures our perception of events to confirm our expectations. Writing from an attachment perspective, Goldberg describes the process in the following way:

> ...the manner in which new information is added to or integrated in the model is shaped by its existing nature. Hence the effects of early experiences are carried forward in these models, even as they undergo change. Furthermore, Bowlby believed that some aspects of these internal working models, particularly those that are not accessible to consciousness, would be particularly resistant to change. Each individual's working model of a particular relationship includes concepts of the self and the other, as well as expectations of this relationship. With development and experience, a general working model of relationships evolves which reflects an aggregation of experiences in different relationships. Presumably some relationships are more influential than others in shaping this model (Goldberg, 2000, p. 9).

Within attachment theory, it is the primary caregiving relationships that are most influential. That early childhood educators are important attachment figures, and hence have potential to influence the developing sense of self in highly significant ways, has profound implications for practice (see Howes, 1999; Rutter & O'Conner, 1999).

### Reading the Scenario from a Socio-Developmental Perspective

From this analytical perspective, how might we understand the scenario of "*The Desirable Prince Meeting*" and its potential impact on the children? Clearly the socio-developmental perspective outlined demands that we situate each child at a developmental stage in regard to the emergence of the internal working model, and how "flexible" it might be at that stage. It also requires that we consider each child as an active participant in a number of different "relationship" contexts, each impacting to a greater or lesser extent on their emerging sense of self. Finally, we need to consider how the experiences may carry forward by adding to the current view of self, and self in relation to others. In Piagetian terms (e.g. Piaget, 1952), we might consider the process as one of adaptation of the working model, of assimilation and accommodation. That is, during the process of assimilation, the child (or adult) interprets new events in their environment according to existing understandings. However, if those existing understandings do not fit with experience, they may be modified to fit, so-called accommodation. The balance between these dual processes changes. At some times, when in Piagetian terms there is equilibrium, the child tends to assimilate new information more than modify existing understandings. At other times, when cognitive development is proceeding more quickly, modification of existing understandings (accommodation) occurs more.

From a socio-developmental perspective there are three understandings that the early childhood professional can draw on to explore the social justice and equity meanings within the *"Desirable Prince Meeting."* They are:

- Understanding 1 – the need to situate the child developmentally.
- Understanding 2 – understanding the child as an active participant.
- Understanding 3 – the 'carry forward' possibilities.

Each will now be discussed in turn.

*Understanding 1 – The Need to Situate the Child Developmentally*

In the *"Desirable Prince Meeting"* scenario, the children are each identified as being in the early childhood stage, Gayle aged 4 years, Mick aged 5 years, and Barry. The setting of the scenario is an Australian children's center, in a room for 3–5 year olds. The internal working model, whilst still flexible at this early stage, will already have been moulded by the myriad of experiences each child has had in the preceding years. As such, the interpretation of the events outlined would be assimilated into those earlier experiences, and the extent of accommodation would reflect various factors. These would include:

- how representative of dynamics in the room the scenario is;
- how many of the children in the room share similar views to the main protagonists (Gayle et al.);
- how adults in the room and the wider early childhood community respond to and redefine the children's views;
- how the community within which the children live values diversity;
- the nature of the inner working model (secure or insecure) each child brings based on cumulative experience.

Gayle brings to the meeting (and to her ongoing interactions with Barry, Mick and the other children) an accrued sense of her own selfhood and values and attitudes towards others in her group. Her response to the rejections of Barry will reflect this established (although still emerging) selfhood. Her hesitancy in identifying the central reason for her rejection of Barry as her prince based on race may indicate a beginning sense of the impact of her actions on others and/or possibly some understanding of the "wrongness" of exclusion based on race. In response to Anne's questions concerning her choice of Barry and subsequently her failure to invite Mick to be her prince, Gayle offers several explanations of her behavior. They include a strong preference for Barry, not wanting to be alone – before admitting (in a faltering way) that it is Mick's skin color that she doesn't like and that is the basis of her exclusion. It appears that Gayle's identification of her "racially"-based value system in some way enables other "racially"-based reasons for exclusion (hair-type, skin odor) to be admitted by other children.

### *Understanding 2 – Understanding the Child as an Active Participant*

What impact will the scenario have on Mick? The foregoing socio-developmental perspective underlines how important Mick's prior experiences – particularly within his most significant attachment relationships – will be in the group. Mick's sense of self as lovable and valued will reflect the experiences he has had in those relationships and therefore how resilient he might be in the face of these challenging dynamics with his peers outlined in "The *Desirable Prince Meeting*." If Mick's experiences have nurtured his security, have facilitated a strong valuing of himself and all the characteristics that are "him" then we might expect this child to show little vulnerability to the rejections expressed in the meeting. But, resilience research underlines that even the most resilient children become vulnerable if stress is overwhelming. And his attachment figures are significantly challenged in nurturing his sense of security if they (and their cultural heritage) are not valued and/or they are alienated within the community or in the group.

### *Understanding 3 – The "Carry Forward" Possibilities*

Even the most secure, autonomous and optimistic child will be vulnerable and lose confidence in the face of ongoing, repeated rejections. Rejection within the peer group may be particularly damaging at this stage of development and later as friendships begin to develop more and more outside the direct involvement of adults. This is why terms such as "invincible" are inappropriate when discussing resilience as they imply a permanent state of invulnerability that is misleading.

We do not have details in the scenario in regards to Mick's reactions to the meeting, or more generally how his emotional and social development is proceeding in the center. It would be important for staff to use the information about children's feelings towards Mick exposed in the meeting as a catalyst to careful observation of him and his emotional wellbeing and how to best support his resilience. Rolfe (2002) has identified a number of signs that early childhood staff might use to identify that a child is feeling overwhelmed. These include: highly dependent behaviours, particularly if the child has been relatively independent in the past, poor peer relationships, regression and apathy, unhappiness, lack of initiative and/or a sense of being "lost."

*Specific Pedagogical Practices for Equity and*
*Social Justice that Derive from these Understandings*

The crux of the response to this scenario from a socio-developmental perspective does not lie solely within a focus on individuals. The quest for change sought by the teachers in this room, i.e. "to create a more equitable classroom – one where children were fair and inclusive, and questioned inequity" resides also in that part of the resilience process that relates to the "community." Masten (2001) identifies several key factors associated with resilience. These are "connections to competent and caring adults in the family and community, cognitive and self-regulation skills, positive views of self, and motivation to be effective in the environment" (p. 234). Positive relationships, new opportunities for support and positive new directions in life are all potential protective factors. Using a socio-developmental perspective to explore this scenario suggests that these are some of the dilemmas and challenges in working for social justice within the early childhood setting but that to work with these teachers will need to:

- establish, build, nurture and respect connections between the children, their families and the wider adult community as caring and competent adults in the children's life (Werner & Smith, 1992);
- provide all children with encouragement, opportunities and feedback on being effective in his environment on a daily basis (Rolfe, 2002);
- understand how best to support all children as they build and consolidate self-regulatory skills (Sroufe, 1995);
- create a community of respect for and celebration of individual differences (Howes, 1999).

A number of questions emerge that classroom teachers could use to reflect on themselves and their equity practices with young children. In particular, questions that come from a resiliency socio-cultural perspective would emphasise teacher reflection on the adults' impact on the child's sense of self-esteem and building shared community values of respect as core to working for more socially just classrooms.

*Questions for Teacher Reflection on Equity and*
*Social Justice from a Resiliency, Socio-Cultural Perspective*

- What are my understandings of how relationship experiences impact on children and in what ways do my understandings reflect my own history of relationship experiences as a child and in adult life?
- How might I support self-esteem in all children whilst at the same time encouraging honest and open expression of feelings by all?
- In what ways can I work with my early childhood community to encourage and support a shared commitment by all to respect and celebration of diversity?

## READING 2: A CRITICAL FUTURES STUDIES PERSPECTIVE ON THE YOUNG CHILD, SOCIAL CONTEXTS, THE EARLY CHILDHOOD PROFESSIONAL AND A SOCIALLY JUST EARLY CHILDHOOD CURRICULUM

The discipline of critical futures studies is concerned with developing frameworks that can respond to the dynamic reality of the constantly shifting social contexts we engage with at varying stages throughout our lives (Beare & Slaughter, 1993). When applied to education, it challenges us to consider how best to instil in children the attitudes, knowledge and outlooks needed to negotiate the future successfully as adults. Positioned at the beginning of the education system, early childhood has an important role to play in this undertaking. Early childhood teachers are optimally placed to lay foundations for children's long-term development as they move towards adulthood and come to engage increasingly with a complex and often fragmented social environment (Page, 2000).

Futures education highlights the potentially powerful role early childhood teachers have in imparting the skills, attitudes and values that are central to children's development not just in the short term, but throughout their lives (Page, 2000). On a fundamental level, the *"Desirable Prince Meeting"* underscores the importance of designing a learning environment that is anti-discriminatory. It should be an environment that will "work to ensure that young children are not discriminated against on the basis of gender, age, race, religion, language, ability, culture or national origin" (Australian Early Childhood Association, 1991, p. 4; Ministry of Education, 1996, p. 64). As this scenario highlights however, early childhood professionals also need to monitor and evaluate how such values are acted out and given meaning by the children themselves. There are four understandings that flow from critical futures studies about what early childhood professionals need to attend to in order to explore the equity meanings within the 'Desirable Prince Meeting. They are:

- Understanding 1 – the curriculum is a transmitter of culture.
- Understanding 2 – the early childhood teacher is/should be a critical pedagogist.
- Understanding 3 – the curriculum is a political and social tool.
- Understanding 4 – the early childhood curriculum is a nexus between the social concerns of individual children, the early childhood community and the outside world.

The ideas behind each of these understandings will now be discussed in turn.

### *Understanding 1 – The Curriculum is a Transmitter of Culture*

It is important for early childhood professionals to understand that the curriculum is a transmitter of culture. This understanding intersects with a key tenet of futures education, that is, the need to question the taken-for-granted truths, norms and values that underlie our pedagogical frameworks. Futures education stresses the importance of "probing beneath the surface" of the key perspectives that drive the curriculum (Slaughter, 1991, p. 34). This process helps educators to resist falling into the trap of replicating outmoded social and cultural stereotypes in their programs and to remain responsive to the social and political realities that the children bring to them. Futures education thus challenges teachers to consider the relationship between the rhetoric that drives their curricula and the reality of the lived experiences of the children in their programs. In so doing, it signals the importance of the curriculum as an instrument through which to overcome the socially and politically embedded inequality and racism which often remains unchallenged (and thus tacitly reinforced) in early childhood programs (Cannella, 1997; Lubeck, 1994; Ritchie, 1996).

## *Understanding 2 – The Early Childhood Teacher is a Critical Pedagogist*

Challenging the relationship between the rhetoric and the reality of the curriculum requires that early childhood teachers engage in a process of critical self-evaluation and act as critical pedagogues. A critical pedagogue is one who actively seeks to produce teaching and learning that is empowering, democratic and equitable (see Darder, 2002; Giroux, 1988).

The ability to design curricula that assist children to negotiate and create a more socially just world requires that early childhood teachers commit themselves to acting as a critical pedagogue (Dau, 2001; De Lair & Irwin, 2000; Diaz Soto, 2000). This requires acting with resolve to live themselves the skills, attitudes and values that they wish to see reflected in the curriculum. An internal coherence between what teacher's believe and what they seek to impart to children will be more likely when this level of self-awareness can be achieved (Campbell & Smith, 2001; Jones & Mules, 2001; MacNaughton, 1997).

## *Understanding 3 – The Curriculum is a Political and Social Tool*

Listening to children is an important means of evaluating the effectiveness of the early childhood curriculum in responding to the diverse social and cultural heritages and life experiences that are present in the early childhood community (Clark, 2000; MacNaughton, 2000; Page, 2000). The right to be heard is a fundamental premise underlying the United Nations Convention on the Rights of the Child (United Nations, 1989). By listening to children early childhood teachers can gain fresh insights into how best to build the appropriate knowledge base and skills to assist them to negotiate the social challenges they will come across in the future. It also enables professionals to tailor a curriculum with added meaning for the children as it responds to the reality of their experiences within the program (Page, 2000).

As *"The Desirable Prince Meeting"* highlights, however, this is a highly complex process. Incorporating children's voices into the curriculum can result in undermining and alienating other children and in potentially perpetuating the very values and attitudes that the educator seeks otherwise to avoid. Futures educators would argue that the curriculum is an important vehicle for counteracting such incidents (Page, 2000). The early childhood educational setting can be a safe environment in which children will rehearse and act out issues that they are exposed to in the outside world in order to make sense of them. The curriculum can thus be the means through which early childhood teachers will provide a forum for young children and adults to analyze their perceptions and convert these concerns into learning experiences. It will also provide the underpinning frameworks through which knowledge, skills and attitudes are introduced, engaged with and built so as to provide children with the conceptual frameworks needed to assess issues and reflect on them (Page, 2000).

*Understanding 4 – The Early Childhood Curriculum as a Nexus*
*Between the Social Concerns of Individual Children, the Early*
*Childhood Community and the Outside World*

The social and personal concerns children bring with them will be acted out most successfully when the curriculum acts as a nexus between the practical and theoretical dimensions of these concerns. An early childhood curriculum that seeks to remain responsive to young children's social concerns will emphasize the need to instil in individuals a sense of place in the learning environment and to facilitate in them a recognition of their connections with others. It would seek to achieve this aim by emphasizing the importance of young children developing qualities of respect and tolerance of other individuals and cultures, identifying common needs and shared interests with different cultures and individuals and developing a respect for diversity and an understanding of rights. It would further aim to encourage young children to appreciate other points of view, to cooperate and to resolve conflicts peaceably, to develop a sensitivity towards other children's needs and feelings and to develop an understanding of others regardless of gender, race, class or disability (Page, 2000). A socially responsive curriculum would also emphasise the importance of celebrating the differing knowledge and skills children bring with them into educational settings including their language, cultural heritages and life experiences to that these features become visible in the learning environment (Ministry of Education, 1996; Siraj-Blatchford & Siraj-Blatchford, 1995; United Nations, 1989). Such foci would seek to make all children and families feel they have some thing distinctive and valuable to contribute to the early childhood community and set the stage for teachers and families to discuss issues so to create a meaningful and responsive learning environment (Page, 2000). In this manner, the early childhood curriculum provides a strong foundation for children and teachers to engage with broader social concerns as it is constructed as a series of multi-layered values that serve to reinforce each other though their shared concerns.

Futures educators would also stress the importance of instilling in young children the ability to critically engage with ideas and formulate a series of alternative views. From a futures perspective, these skills are an important means of assessing problems, and then of thinking through the consequences and implications of ideas. By thinking through a number of options, children can begin to see and question the social frameworks that order, and at times, delimit the parameters of life (Page, 2000). Such an understanding helps to build in individuals an ability to recognize and assess personal issues against their broader social significance. These skills will render the curriculum more responsive and relevant to the social concerns and realities that the children bring with them into the program. Futures educators would also caution that the success of these initiatives hinge on the added ability of early childhood teachers to address these issues in a way that is sensitive to the developmental concerns of the children, a consideration that has been addressed more fully in this chapter (Page, 2000).

*"The Desirable Prince Meeting"* brings to light the raw reality and complexity of issues that are played out in the early childhood curriculum. Futures education responds to this by providing some critical frameworks through which early childhood teachers can explore their role in helping foster values that would encourage the creation of a more tolerant and responsible future society for young children.

## Specific Pedagogical Practices for Equity and Social Justice that Derive from these Understandings

A response to the *"Desirable Prince Meeting"* from a critical futures studies perspective lies in the early childhood professional taking the time to reflect on the values that underpin their work with young children (Page, 2000). Specifically, it challenges early childhood professionals to:

- view the curriculum as a vehicle through which important foundations for children's long-term development are laid (Aboud & Doyle, 1996; Black-Gutman & Hickson, 1996; Lubeck, 1994; MacNaughton, 2001; Page, 2000; Schweinhart, 2000);
- consider how best to instil in children the attitudes, knowledge, outlooks and skills that will assist them to successfully negotiate their futures (Page, 2000; Pierce, 1980; Shane & Shane, 1974; Toda, 1993);
- assess how best to instil in children the attitudes, knowledge, outlooks and skills will assist them to create a more socially just world (Aboud & Doyle, 1996; Black-Gutman & Hickson, 1996; MacNaughton, 2001);
- critically evaluate the relationship between their philosophy and the lived experiences of the children in their programs (Cannella, 1997; Lubeck, 1994; Page, 2000; Silin, 1988).

The questions for early childhood teachers that emerge from these challenges centre on the teacher critically examining the content of their programs for young children.

*Questions for Critical Reflection on Equity and*
*Social Justice from a Critical Futures Studies Perspective*

- What values, attitudes and knowledge are being shaped and modelled in early childhood programs?
- To what extent do these values and attitudes reflect and respond to the diversity of concerns and life experiences of the children attending the program?
- How might these values and attitudes resonate with the early childhood professional's intended curriculum?
- Will these values, attitudes and knowledge assist children to negotiate their other social worlds now and in the future?

## READING 3: A FEMINIST POSTSTRUCTURALIST PERSPECTIVE ON THE CHILD, SOCIAL CONTEXTS, THE EARLY CHILDHOOD PROFESSIONAL AND A SOCIALLY JUST EARLY CHILDHOOD CURRICULUM

The scenario presented raises several intersecting and complex questions from a feminist poststructuralist perspective. These questions focus on how we recognise and understand the power effects of what occurred for each of the key players (teachers and children) of the discourses (frameworks for understanding and being in the world) that were spoken into existence in this scenario. Poststructuralists share a belief that we learn through taking up and using discourse and that how we do this is linked to our subjectivity and to power (Davies, 1989; Weedon, 1997). Feminist poststructuralists have focused on individual children's subjective experiences of gendered power, challenging ideas that children's play choices are natural, or simply a result of socialization (Davies, 1988). Davies, contrasted these understandings as follows:

> In socialization theory, the focus is on the process of shaping the individual that is undertaken by others. In poststructuralist theory the focus is on the way each person actively takes up the discourses through which they and others speak/write the world into existence as if they were their own (Davies, 1993, p. 11).

From this position, Davies has argued that we need to find ways to make visible to children and educators the ways in which gendered power operates in early childhood services and seek ways to create new possibilities through it. This for Davies is at the heart of the feminist poststructuralist endeavor:

> Feminist poststructuralist theorizing, in particular, has focused on the possibilities opened up when dominant language practices are made visible and revisable (Davies, 2001, p. 179).

Feminist poststructuralist theories have diverse origins, but French social theorist, Michel Foucault is a foundational poststructuralist scholar. Foucault (e.g., 1980) was interested in systems of social thought and how we come to think in a particular way at a particular point in time. He argued that modern academic disciplines such as psychology and sociology have imposed their own desires and needs on how we view the world and given us a "will to truth," rather than a "will to knowledge" (MacNaughton, 2003). Gore explained how Foucault used these terms:

> [Foucault saw] . . . the will to knowledge as the general desire to know, and the will to truth as the desire to know the difference between truth and falsity in particular disciplines or discourses (Gore, 1999, p. 10).

The implications of this for how we understand children has been explained by MacNaughton as follows:

> For Foucault, the will to truth is highly problematic because (like other postmodern thinkers) he believed that there is no such thing as truth. He argued that what we regard as the truth about (for example) child development is subjective, incomplete, multiple, contradictory and politically charged. In contrast, the 'will to knowledge' is potentially productive yet dangerous in that all knowledge has an intimate relationship with power. The 'will to know' draws us to search beyond truth. Foucault talked of this search as an 'ordeal' (Miller, 1994, p. 280) because it was 'work done at the limit of ourselves' (Foucault, 1983, p. 47) but if done well, it places us in 'the position of beginning again' (Foucault, 1983, p. 47; MacNaughton, 2003, pp. 83–84).

Hence, reading the scenario using a feminist poststructuralist perspective requires us to find strategies for beginning again our understandings of what happened by looking for the subjective, incomplete, multiple, contradictory and politically charged in the scenario.

### Reading the Scenario from a Feminist Poststructuralist Perspective

To begin again a feminist poststructuralist reading of the scenario requires that we explore how discourse, power and subjectivity operated and what the power effects of this were for the key players. To do this requires four key poststructuralist understandings. They are as follows:

- Understanding 1: discourses are more than language, they are frameworks for understanding and being in the world.
- Understanding 2: patriarchal discourses influence how teachers understand children's play.
- Understanding 3: teachers own discursive desires and investments produce specific understandings of the child.
- Understanding 4: feminist poststructuralist ways of thinking expose relations of power in the classroom.

*Understanding 1: Discourses are More than Language,*
*they are Frameworks for Understanding and Being in the World*

In everyday usage, "discourse" refers to what is said and/or what is written. Poststructuralist theorists recast discourse to refer to the historically and culturally specific categories through which we give meaning to our lives, practice our lives, invest emotionally in our lives and construct our social structures. Thus, within poststructuralism, discourse is recast to include the emotional, social and institutional frameworks and practices through which we make meanings in our lives (MacNaughton, 2001). Identifying the different frameworks (discourses) through which we understand children and pedagogy is the beginning point for a feminist poststructuralist reading of the scenario.

However, the point for feminist poststructuralists is not just to note the different discourses at play within a specific teaching and learning moment, or within this scenario, but to reflect on how specific discourses distort, privilege and silence meanings. For Foucault as a poststructuralist, it is only once this occurs that we can understand why some meanings are produced and others are silenced and therefore begin work to bring the silenced and marginalised meanings to the center (Foucault, 1982; MacNaughton, 2001; Weedon, 1997). For feminist poststructuralists the point is to assess the ways in which discourses are politically charged and have political effects for equity and social justice, especially for gender equity and justice. By understanding the politically charged and its effects for equity and social justice in early childhood classrooms teachers can begin to search for ways to build teaching and learning relationships that make the inequitable and unjust distortions, silences and patterns of privilege less likely (MacNaughton, 2003).

The operation of discourse and their political charge and effects was evident from the moment Sheralyn was welcomed into Spider Room bringing questions about whether the concept of a "social justice disposition" was useful for building greater fairness between children in their play and relationships. Sheralyn and the teachers used cycles of collaborative action research to audio and videotape children's play and revisit what had happened. Their revisiting conversations used feminist poststructural discourses to bring the politically charged to light by challenging their images of how fairness had been part of what teachers and children said and did (e.g. Campbell, 1999). For each of them, these discussions contained moments in which they examined the power effects of discourse when a question or image exposed their own collusions in perpetuating unfairness or exclusion.

The contradictions they found in the process of revisiting their classroom had two important effects for how they understood themselves as teachers, and for their teaching practices. Firstly, they found themselves teaching from a position of uncertainty about what had happened, what it meant for those involved, and how their actions as teachers might perpetuate or disrupt unfairness or exclusion. Secondly, their uncertainty produced many more questions about the effects of privileging one account of reality over another – for example privileging a developmental view of the child over a feminist view of the child. Such privileges implied that the meanings of experience could be fixed, and that they were shared by all even as they denied and excluded the complexity of how meanings shift as they intersect with forces of gender, race, culture, class and sexuality (Lloyd, 1997).

Rather than being "frozen" by the uncertainty and complexity that they found in their discussions about Spider Room, they used their questions to attempt change. One such change involved bringing children's voices into their collaborations about how to improve their classroom. They used planned and impromptu group meetings with children to talk about how fairness and inclusion had been part of what had been said and done by people, and what they all thought should happen. They believed that these discussions could create a consensual fairness that would govern their teaching and children's play and relationships (Campbell, 2002).

Looking back Sheralyn has wondered if they were perhaps still seduced by the "modern" enticements of finding a final "Truth." They were still hoping that if they searched long enough, hard enough, in the right ways and places their uncertainty might disappear as they eventually succeeded in working out how to "do equity with young children" correctly.

Any such hopes dissolved as they exposed paradoxes in their teaching that revealed how their actions and intentions did not guarantee particular outcomes (Gore, 1993). Perhaps the most confronting of these emerged in *"The Desirable Prince Meeting."* This meeting demonstrated how they were all part of the shifting and political world of strategic voices and silences (Ellsworth, 1989; Silin, 1999).

Anne and Meg believed that a meeting with all the children about these issues would provide a forum for Barry, Gayle and others to talk about and solve the problems of exclusions for these two children. However, as *"The Desirable Prince Meeting"* showed making it possible for some children to speak about what it meant to be a boy or girl in the Prince and Princess games, also exposed the unexpected and political dimensions and effects of their play choices. These paradoxes became clearer as Anne, Meg, Leyla and Sheralyn revisited the transcript of *"The Desirable Prince Meeting"* together.

As Sheralyn and the three teachers revisited their transcript of *"The Desirable Prince Meeting"* they were investing in discourse:

> ... as powerful enough to simultaneously constitute and exclude certain possibilities of thought and action, (and opening spaces for)... examin(ing) the conditions of possibility within particular teaching and learning situations.... (Usher & Edwards, 1994, p. 91).

As action researchers their approach included looking at how discourses constituted the limitations of what was said and done, and thinking about how these might be used to change the "possibilities of thought and action" *(Ibid.)*. Foucault (1984) talked about this as a transgression made possible by the ethical and agentic subject's refusal of the normalising limitations of subjectivity – a refusal that is constituted within and through struggles to rethink the self.

For the participants as feminist researchers, their feminist poststructuralist revisiting was also a Foucauldian encounter with themselves. As Sheralyn read the text of what was said, she also re-presented the possibilities that they found when attempted to take apart the categories, practices and personal investments that constructed in and through what teachers and children said and did, and the institutional support for these discourses (MacNaughton, 1998). This representation follows using the lenses offered by feminist poststructuralism to present the reading. It emphasizes the discourses within which the teacher understood what was happening for each of the participants and illustrates how discourse can be used to read teaching and learning moments. It highlights the ways in which the categories of gender through which each of the participants understood themselves and what it means to be desirable within the gendered discourses of princes and princesses influenced what was considered reasonable and desirable for each participant.

Anne began the meeting by asking Gayle how she understood Barry's refusal to be her Prince:

> Anne: *Gayle is there a reason why you want Barry to be the Prince in your (Princess) game?*
> Gayle: *Because I always like playing Princess games ...*
> Anne: *...Do you understand why Barry doesn't want to play it?*
> Gayle: *No.*

For Anne, Gayle's pursuit of Barry only made sense if Gayle didn't understand why Barry was refusing. Anne accepted that Barry's refusal was reasonable and asked him to help Gayle see why he didn't want to be her Prince:

> Barry: ...*I just keep saying **NO** because she keeps asking me and No means (you're) bothering me.*

Barry's response traced the limits of how Gayle could be normal and desirable in his world of play – she could listen to him when he said No! and stop *bothering* him.

> Meg: *Can you just tell her... 'You're not interested in playing that game?' Next time she asks you over and over again can you just say 'Gayle I'm not interested. Maybe you should ask someone else'. And if, Gayle, your Prince needs to be a boy, there are other boys in the room you can ask.*

For Meg, Barry's desire to be left alone by a troublesome girl was also reasonable. She used two strategies to support Barry's regulation of Gayle. First she included suggestions about how Barry could justify his refusal by saying he wasn't *interested*. In Meg's approach to teaching a child's interests guided his selection of learning experiences. If Barry wasn't interested in being a Prince, then he couldn't be made to play with Gayle. Then Meg shifted the discursive boundaries that Gayle had used to choose a Desirable Prince. Meg suggested that any boy in the room could be chosen as a Prince. The category of boy-Prince became all encompassing. But Gayle understood a Desirable Prince differently:

> Gayle: *I just like Barry...*
> Anne: *That's fine to like Barry. We all like different people. We are all closer to different people than other people but what Barry is saying is that you're actually annoying him by always asking him to play that game.*

### *Understanding 2: Patriarchal Discourses Influence How Teachers Understand Children's Play*

For feminist poststructuralists patriarchal discourses produce and reproduce gender relations in which particular ways of being male and particular ways of being female are made desirable and normal. Traditional, emphasized femininity and traditional hegemonic masculinities are privileged within patriarchal discourses (MacNaughton, 2001). In classrooms seeking gender equity and gender justice finding ways to recognize and to challenge patriarchal discourses is critical. However, as we are emotionally invested in discourse shifting children's gender discourses is problematic and not achieved merely through teachers saying that girls and boys should be friends or that all girls should think or feel in a particular way.

The implications of this for Anne were that her knowledge of individuality meant she accepted that liking people differently was a natural and normal part of relationships. But these emotional (and non-rational) investments should be controlled by, rather than control, the individual. So Anne attempted to help Gayle see that if she was to be a normal (and reasonable) girl-Princess, she needed to discipline her "body, mind and emotions" (Weedon, 1997, p. 108). In Anne, Meg and Barry's patriarchal discourse, being a girl-Princess in the right way meant Gayle needed to be obedient, and docilely accept Barry's refusal to play. Her desires should submit themselves to the wishes of her boy-Prince. But Gayle continued to resist by using the teacher's intentions that all children felt included in Spider Room. Gayle gave another reasonable interpretation of her actions. Other children were excluding her:

> Gayle: *I'm but just asking because I'm always left alone . . .*

Gayle's understandable explanation of wanting to be included rather than left alone raised questions about whether Barry's refusal to play was fair. But Meg and Anne knew Barry as an easy-going and usually fair person. His exclusion of Gayle had been uncharacteristic – so they believed that Gayle's actions were the problem. Meg reminded Gayle about a time when she had refused Mick's offer to play – an offer that would have meant she was not left alone. This was evidence that it was Gayle not Barry who needed to be fixed:

> Meg: *But Gayle I remember . . . one day when Barry said he didn't want to play, Mick said he would play and you said 'No'.*
> Gayle: *It's always a bit too hard for me to play with him . . . because I always want to play with Barry.*

Using Meg's gendered discursive perspective, Gayle's isolation was self imposed and resulted from her unreasonable refusal to play with other boys. But Gayle continued to resist being the unreasonable problem. Instead, she claimed the natural and normal attractions between individuals that Anne had described earlier. This meant playing with boys like Mick was too hard because she was attracted to and desired boys like Barry more than boys like Mick. So Anne asked her to trace the limits of her category of Desirable Prince.

> Anne: *Gayle? . . . Can you tell me why you don't ask Mick to play your (Princess) games?*
> Gayle: *Because he – I like Barry.*
> Anne: *Yeah and that's ok but why is it that you choose not to play with Mick?*
> Gayle: *Because I don't, I don't (like) people that are black I – only white people.*

Other children expanded on Mick's difference:

Kaarin: His hair is curly
268. Fiona: *And cos I don't (like curly) either . . . I like only straight . . .*
Gayle: *Because sometimes I um I smell his skin and its it smells horrible.*

Gendered discourses intersect in this moment with discourses of "race" and class to position Mick as undesirable.

### Understanding 3: Teachers Own Discursive Desires and Investments Produce Specific Understandings of the Child

Discourses (frameworks for understanding ourselves in the world) do not just exist. They are spoken into existence by us in and through language and they produce understandings of what it means to be normal, desirable and acceptable to others. Some ways of understanding ourselves in the world carry more power because they are institutionally articulated and privileged and thus come to be seen as right and proper ways to understand ourselves and others. Discourses thus produce and express desires and emotional investments.

In the *"The Desirable Prince Meeting."* Gayle's personal desires and investments were exposed in a heterosexist, middle class, racist, Western discourse that other children supported. Desirable boy-Princes did not have dark skin, curly hair or smell. Anne and Meg's words and silences connected with, normalized and regulated her discourse of girl-Princess, even as they naturalised racist and classist categories of boy-Prince that made Barry Prince-like and Mick unlike a Prince.

For Anne and Meg, their beliefs in their early childhood knowledges and practices began to unravel in the context of *"The Desirable Prince Meeting."* Leyla and Sheralyn experienced a similar disillusionment when she joined with Anne and Meg to look at the transcript of *"The Desirable Prince Meeting."*

From a feminist poststructuralist perspective, *"The Desirable Prince Meeting"* exposed the play of relations of power-knowledge in these discourses at what Foucault (1980, p. 6) described as "the extremities, in its ultimate destinations, (at) those points where it becomes capillary . . . in its regional and local forms and institutions . . . ." The emotional desires and investments of the teachers and the children in specific ways of seeing and desiring expressed in *"The Desirable Prince Meeting."* express the extremities and local forms of the operation of discourses or "race," class and gender.

The meetings of Anne and Meg with children had built on visions of individuals who were empowered by reason to make choices and decisions free from the constraints and politics of identity – thus "masking the effects of gender, class and cultural knowledge" (Cannella, 1997, p. 38). Seeing Gayle as a pre-formed individual who could be socialised and empowered by reason to become the model and democratic citizen (Derman-Sparks et al., 1989) focused their attempts to fix the problems of inclusion on the individual and her thinking – in this case Gayle. Gayle was the problem because her actions had disrupted Barry's characteristic and desirable easy-going nature.

For Anne and Meg it seemed that if Gayle could just be made to see the unreason of her thoughts and actions, the problems of inclusion for and by Gayle, would be solved. Their investments in an objective form of reason and rationality (Cannella, 1997) centred on Gayle separating, individualising and personalising her exclusions.

*Understanding 4 – Feminist Poststructuralist Ways of Thinking*
*Expose Relations of Power in the Classroom*

Using feminist poststructuralisms to re-visit how what had happened revealed how in the teachers' classroom meetings with children ways of thinking, speaking and acting continued a "regime of truth" (Gore, 1993) that privileged some children and marginalised others. This means that what they said and did became an exercise of power used to tame and silence the (non-rational) desires and pleasures associated with particular ways of practicing gender as a girl-Princess.

Foucault (1980) talked about this constitution of the individual as an effect of power in which certain bodies, certain gestures, certain discourses, certain desires come to be identified and constituted as individuals. So, from a feminist poststructuralist perspective, rather than working with children to fix the problems of inclusion, the collaborative meetings individualised, constrained and deregulated some voices. They produced spaces in which some children were able to constitute heterosexist, classist and racist boundaries for being a normal and desirable boy-Prince or girl-Princess.

The teachers' voices colluded with, rather than disrupted these discourses of what it was to be a normal and desirable girl-Princess, and boy-Prince. In thinking about the paradoxes of regulation and freedom in their voices, Sheralyn now wonders about a question that Cherryholmes poses to critical educators:

> ... which forms of domination (coercion, constraint) are justified in furthering which forms of emancipation? (Cherryholmes, 1988, p. 165).

Their revisiting of "The *Desirable Prince Meeting*" drew out similar questions about how they might disrupt gendered relations of power-knowledge, even as they recognised the competing interests that such disruptions might serve. For example, Sheralyn used feminist concerns to ask:

> Sheralyn: ... *how do we help (Gayle) imagine (Mick) as the Prince and are we doing her a service in helping her to imagine him as the Prince, or would we do better in helping her to imagine herself as a Prince?*

Yet when they looked at how race and class and culture and sexuality intersected with these questions they continued to struggle over many other paradoxes that were constituted by what they, Gayle and others had said. But their questions had to move beyond an individual child like Gayle, or Mick, or Barry as a problem to be fixed. As Anne, Meg, Leyla and Sheralyn talked they each (in different ways) recognized in Gayle's words, our own contradictions, bias, investments and collusions, and the institutional support for these in the wider social and historical context. As Anne and Sheralyn reflected:

> Sheralyn: ... *no-one said: Mick is beautiful, Mick's my idea of a Prince, I just love the way he looks ... I can imagine him as my Prince ... Its about who we are consciously and unconsciously. And we're contradictory. We're not these unitary nice neat people who (are always) fair ... I know I'm not. For me, I had trouble imagining Mick as a Prince too ... its not as if I'm exempt from this. I have had very ethnocentric narrow view of those children.*
> Anne: ... *(you said) you didn't see Mick as your Prince ... and I'm thinking 'Well, yeah. I'm not racist and you know I don't see that either ... but yeah I think there's issues there for me that ... —— ...*

The understandings that build from feminist poststructuralist perspectives on pedagogies and power lead to a number of specific enjoinders for pedagogical practices that intend equity and social justice.

### *Specific Pedagogical Practices for Equity and Social Justice that Derive from these Understandings*

The crux of the pedagogical response to this scenario from a feminist poststructuralist perspective lies with a focus on exposing the operation of power in and through discourse for the children in the scenario. For the teacher, it is important to call all players to account for how power operates in and through their ways of understanding and being (their discourses). It is important in calling all players to account to seek alternative and oppositional discourses that highlight the operation of "racialized," gendered, sexualised and classed power within and through the actors in the scenario. To do this, the teacher will need to seek to know the scenario through knowing "other" to the usually dominant and privileged discourses of child development that silence issues of power. Silin (1995, p. 32) tains about the stranger "who calls us to account (and) offers a possibility of redemption through acceptance of otherness."

Sheralyn drawing from feminist poststructuralist readings of this meeting believes that thinking about the strangeness of Mick within the discourse of *Desirable Prince* called the key players all to account. It also challenged them to go further towards creating changes to the regimes of truth that constitute their teaching, their practice and their selves. In order to take up "alternative and possibly oppositional discourses where there are other meanings and subject positionings" (Usher & Edwards, 1994, p. 99) it is necessary to trace and transgress the boundaries of our discursive selves using Foucault's (1983, p. 237) three axis:

- the axis of truth through which we "constitute ourselves as subjects of knowledge";
- the axis of power through which we "constitute ourselves as subjects acting on others";
- the axis of ethics through which "we constitute ourselves as moral agents."

To trace and transgress these ourselves and our effects on others in the classroom we must look for new ways to see and understand ourselves and others by troubling the knowledge power relations of the classroom.

In Spider Room the teachers attempted to find new subject positions by troubling relations of power-knowledge in their classroom. They did this by critically examining:

- the limits and possibilities of what they think, say and do as teachers by asking what limits what I know about this child, this pedagogical practice and myself and by asking what are the possibilities for knowing these differently. For instance, what do I know about the racialisation of the child and what practices enable or challenge it?
- the personal and institutional support for these ways of knowing and practicing their teaching by asking where does this knowledge come from and in whose interests is it to understand what happened in the ways that I do. For instance, what do I consider natural and normal ways of being a boy and to what extent do they benefit racist ways of knowing and being in the world?
- the politics and effects of how their knowledge and practices are played out in their classroom by asking who benefits and how from what I know and do. What are the racial politics and their effects in this classroom?
- the interests served by continuing their investments in these ways of knowing and acting by asking in whose interests do I act here. For instance, whose interests are served by seeing children as asexual, non-racialized and naturally gendered?

In Spider Room, they continue their uncertain journey as critical friends, teaching from the paradoxes and asking themselves and each other Leyla's disruptive question:

Leyla: . . . *who gains from defending what you're doing?*

This question lies at the heart of troubling knowledge power relations in early childhood classrooms.

*Questions for Teacher Reflection on Equity and Social Justice
from a Feminist Poststructuralist Perspective*

The points for critical examination of knowledge-power relations in their teaching by the teachers in Spider Room also offer points for critical reflection on the ways in which knowledge constructs equity and social justice in early childhood classrooms. Such questions would include:

• What are the discourses of "race," gender and class through which you understand the children and the children understand themselves and each other?
• What are the equity limits and possibilities of what we as early childhood professionals think, say and do as teachers because of the discourses through which we understand the children and ourselves?
• What is personal and institutional support for specific discourses of the child and ways of knowing and practicing teaching?
• What are the politics and effects of how our early childhood knowledge and practices and discourses of gender, "race" and class are played out in our classroom?
• Whose interests were served by continuing our investments in these ways of knowing and acting?

## AN OVERVIEW OF THE PERSPECTIVES' "READINGS" OF THE *"DESIRABLE PRINCE MEETING"*

Table 1 provides a summary overview for the reader of the different ways in which each perspective approaches the process of giving meaning to and deriving pedagogical understandings and implications from the "*Desirable Prince Meeting.*" It shows that each perspective differs in the emphasis given to:

• "individual" child;
• socio-cultural contexts;
• issues of power and its effects.

*Table 1.* An Overview of the Perspectives' "Readings" of the "Desirable Prince Meeting."

| Area of Focus | Socio-Developmental Perspectives | Critical Futures Studies Perspectives | Feminist Poststructuralist Perspectives |
| --- | --- | --- | --- |
| Key understandings | The need to situate the child developmentally<br>Understanding the child as an active participant<br>The "carry forward" possibilities | (1) The curriculum is a transmitter of culture<br>(2) The early childhood teacher is/should be a critical pedagogist<br>(3) The curriculum is a political and social tool<br>(4) The early childhood curriculum is a nexus between the social concerns of individual children, the early childhood community and the outside world | Discourses are more than language, they are frameworks for understanding and being in the world<br>Patriarchal discourses influence how teachers understand children's play<br>Teachers own discursive desires and investments produce specific understandings of the child<br>Feminist poststructuralist ways of thinking expose relations of power in the classroom |
| Specific pedagogical practices | Challenges early childhood professionals to<br>• Establish, build, nurture and respect connections between children, their family and the wider adult community as caring and competent adults in children's lives<br>• Provide all children with encouragement, opportunities and feedback on being effective in their environment on a daily basis<br>• Understand how best to support all children as they build and consolidate self-regulatory skills | Challenges early childhood professionals to<br>• View the curriculum as a vehicle through which important foundations for children's long-term development are laid<br>• Consider how best to instil in children the attitudes, knowledge, outlooks and skills that will assist them to successfully negotiate their futures<br>• Assess how best to instil in children the attitudes, knowledge, outlooks and skills will assist them to create a more socially just world | Challenges early childhood professionals to<br>• Seek alternative and oppositional discourses and subject positions<br>• Trouble the knowledge power relations of the classroom |

| | | | |
|---|---|---|---|
| | • Create a community of respect for individual differences | • Critically evaluate the relationship between their philosophy and the lived experiences of the children in their programs | What values, attitudes and knowledge are being shaped and modelled in early childhood programs? To what extent do these values and attitudes reflect and respond to the diversity of concerns and life experiences of the children attending the program? How might these values and attitudes resonate with the early childhood professional's intended curriculum? Will these values, attitudes and knowledge assist children to negotiate their other social worlds now and in the future? |
| Questions for critical reflection | What are my understandings of how relationship experiences impact on children and in what ways do my understandings reflect my own history of relationship experiences as a child and in adult life? How might I support self-esteem in all children whilst at the same time encouraging honest and open expression of feelings by all? In what ways can I work with my early childhood community to encourage and support a shared commitment by all to respect and celebration of diversity? | | What are the discourses of 'race', gender and class through which you understand the children and the children understand themselves and each other? What are the equity limits and possibilities of what we as early childhood professionals think, say and do as teachers because of the discourses through which we understand the children and ourselves? What is personal and institutional support for specific discourses of the child and ways of knowing and practicing teaching? What are the politics and effects of how our early childhood knowledge and practices and discourses of gender, 'race' and class are played out in our classroom? Whose interests were served by continuing our investments in these ways of knowing and acting? |

However, each perspective does attend to the child, the teacher and the social and political contexts and effects that live in daily teaching and learning moments in early childhood classrooms.

The intention in bringing forth multiple perspectives to analyze the *"Desirable Prince Meeting"* was not to finally arbitrate on which perspective is most "true" or "right" in terms of equity and social justice praxis in the early childhood classroom. Instead, it was to highlight four understandings that we believe are central to building powerful and utilitarian understandings of how equity might be achieved in early childhood classrooms. Those understandings are that:

- There is no single right or true theory or perspective that can guide equity praxis in early childhood classrooms.
- Classroom life is complex and multifaceted and thus we need complexity and multifaceted perspectives to guide actions within it.
- Each perspective we bring to bear on understanding equity in classroom life is limited by what it can't say.
- Using different perspectives that highlight similar and contradictory points for reflection on teaching and learning can act as sustenance for critical reflection.

To explain each in turn.

## *There is No Single Right or True Theory or Perspective that Can Guide Equity Praxis in Early Childhood Classrooms*

Bringing forth multiple perspectives each of which has strong foundations in theory and in research highlight the complexity of establishing one "true" way to understand children and classroom life. Their co-existence challenges the idea that one perspective can or should claim the right to be called the "right" or "true" perspective on what happens in classroom life. Each instead offers a perspective that may be more or less productive for pedagogical action towards equity in the classroom and combined they allow a richness of possibilities for action to be explored.

## *Classroom Life is Complex and Multifaceted and Thus we Need Complexity and Multifaceted Perspectives to Guide Actions Within It*

By offering multiple perspectives on the same moment in classroom life it is possible to honour the complexities, contradictions and challenges that permeate early childhood classrooms as teachers attempt to work for social justice and equity. Teachers are often working with multiple and sometimes competing and contradictory perspectives as they search for ways forward in their work with young children. Presenting that multiplicity as something to be celebrated and worked with rather is an effort to have multiplicity seen as reality rather than as a negative effect of teacher's eclecticism.

### *Each Perspective We Bring to Bear on Understanding Equity in Classroom Life is Limited by What it Can't Say*

In juxtaposing each of the selected perspectives and their understandings about classroom life it becomes possible to highlight the possibilities and limits to each as a source of pedagogical action and change. Each is limited by the very existence of another perspective that can say what it can't. Yet, each perspective offers possibilities for strategic action for teachers confronted with the issues raised in the *"The Desirable Prince Meeting."* How should teachers decide from amongst this diversity? Should teachers who are confronted with the issues that daily classroom life brings test what the effects of acting from within each perspective will be for equity in their classrooms? What might be gained in doing so?

### *Using Different Perspectives that Highlight Similar and Contradictory Understandings Can Drive Critical Reflection on Teaching and Learning*

Generating multiple theoretical perspectives on the child in a pedagogical and social context can provide a powerful resource through which early childhood professionals can critically reflect on the challenges and possibilities of achieving social justice and equity in early childhood classrooms. Each disciplinary perspective acts as a pedagogical resource by pointing to specific pedagogical practices that derive from its understandings of the child in a social and pedagogical context and by offering questions from within each perspective that can be used for critical reflection on pedagogical practices. In part, this is because each perspective views the child within a social and pedagogical context and has well-developed arguments within it to attend to how the social world touches children's lives and the equity effects of this and their implications for the early childhood professional.

## CONCLUDING COMMENTS

At this point in the generation of knowledge within early childhood education it is critical to explore the possibilities within diverse perspectives for advancing thinking and practice for equity in early childhood classrooms. Whilst, diversity should be encouraged, not all available perspectives may be equally productive for equity. For instance, MacNaughton (2001) has shown the traditional theories of early childhood education to be lacking when it comes to gender equity. She highlighted in her research into gender equity in early childhood classrooms in Australia those individual teachers who understood and practised teaching from within traditional discourses struggled with gender equity across several dimensions. They struggled to see gender equity as an issue, they struggled to see how to practise it and they struggled to find allies in their work for it. Their struggles exposed the myths that constrain work for gender equity in early childhood. They showed how these myths were intimately connected to their "truths" about the developing child and about what and how the developing child could and should learn. These "truths" were regularly constructed at these sites through:

- the teacher's pedagogical gaze
- the teacher's reading of the child
- the teacher's strategies, including organization of space and materials
- the colleague's gaze
- the academy's gaze
- the parents' gaze
- the teachers' self gaze.

If early childhood pedagogies are to be reformed with feminist equity intent then their reformation must take place at each of these sites (MacNaughton, 2001).

The explorations in this chapter suggest that those perspectives that see the child and the teacher as engaged in and produced through their social, political and cultural contexts are those that are generative for equitable pedagogical praxis. However, research in classrooms with children and teachers will remain critical to determine which perspectives or which combination from within or between perspectives might be most productive in specific classrooms at specific points in time and in specific cultural contexts. In making judgements about which perspectives to use MacNaughton (2001) would argue that the following questions might provide a beginning basis for decision. Does the perspective or combination of perspectives selected:

- allow the teacher to see equity issues such as gender, "race," class and sexuality in the lives of the children in their classrooms?
- expand their readings of how equity issues are being understood and practiced in their classrooms?
- assist teachers to rethink the implications of how pedagogic space and materials are organized and the equity effects of that organization?

- enable teachers to intervene in unjust moments between children?
- challenge teachers to be activists for equity and social justice with children, parents and colleagues?
- challenge the idea that there is one single way, understanding or technique that will produce equity and social justice in early childhood classrooms.

These questions push us to the limits of believing that a single truth about the child, its contexts and pedagogical practices for equity are possible. They push us to seek multiple perspectives to inform our readings of classroom praxis and in doing so to seek complex and diverse ways to understand and practice with equity intent in early childhood classrooms. In enjoining readers to multiplicity, diversity and complexity in our readings of classroom life we align ourselves with a generation of early childhood academics and practitioners who draw on critical, feminist (e.g. Goldstein, 1997; MacNaughton, 2000), postmodern, (e.g. Dahlberg et al., 1999; Jipson & Johnson, 2001) postcolonial (e.g. MacNaughton & Davis, 2001; Viruru & Cannella, 2001) and queer theories (e.g. Silin, 1995; Theilheimer & Cahill, 2001) to inform their thinking and their practice. Central to this work has been a renewed interest in research that explores the theory and practice of assuring children's rights and improving equity and social justice in and through early education. Specific concerns include:

- building a critical evaluation of the relationships between social, personal and political values and philosophies in determining the goals, practices and understandings in early years settings (e.g. Dahlberg et al., 1999; Ryan & Ochsner, 1999);
- exploring the implications of current thinking and practice about child development, learning and teaching, and curriculum for equity and social justice in early childhood (e.g. Grieshaber & Cannella, 2001; Jipson & Johnson, 2001; MacNaughton, 2000; Silin, 1995);
- documenting exemplars of excellence and equity in the early childhood curriculum (e.g., Bertram et al., 2002).

We believe that using multiple perspectives to produce contrasting readings of children and pedagogies provides an important contribution to taking this work forward.

# REFERENCES

Aboud, F., & Doyle, A. (1996). Does talk of 'race' foster prejudice or tolerance in children? *Canadian Journal of Behavioural Science, 28*(3), 161–170.

Australian Early Childhood Association (1991). The Australian Early Childhood Association Code of Ethics. *Australian Journal of Early Childhood 16*(1), 3–6.

Beare, H., & Slaughter, R. A. (1993). *Education for the twenty-first century.* London: Routledge.

Berk, L. (2000). *Child development* (5th ed.). Boston: Allyn and Bacon.

Bertram, T., Pascal, C., Bokhair, S., Gasper, M., & Holterman, S. (2002). *Early excellence centre pilot programme, second annual evaluation report 2000–2001.* Birmingham, UK: Centre for Research in Early Childhood & Department for Education & Skills, UK.

Black-Gutman, D., & Hickson, F. (1996). The relationship between 'racial' attitudes and social-cognitive development in children: An Australian study. *Developmental Psychology, 32*(3), 448–456.

Bowlby, J. (1997). *Attachment and loss* (Vol. 1), *Attachment* (2nd ed.). London: Pimlico (original work published in 1969).

Campbell, S. (1999). Making the political pedagogical in early childhood education. *Australian Journal of Early Childhood, 24*(4), 21–26.

Campbell, S. (2002). *A social justice disposition in young children.* Unpublished doctoral thesis, The University of Melbourne.

Campbell, S., & Smith, K. (2001). Equity observation and images of fairness. In: S. Grieshaber & G. S. Cannella (Eds), *Embracing Identities in Early Childhood Education: Diversity and Possibilities* (pp. 89–102). New York: Teachers College Press.

Cannella, G. S. (1997). *Deconstructing early childhood education: Social justice and revolution.* New York: Peter Lang.

Cherryholmes, C. H. (1988). *Power and criticism: Poststructural investigations in education.* New York: Teachers College Press.

Clark, A. (2000). Listening to young children: Perspectives, possibilities and problems. Paper presented at the 10th European Conference on Quality in Early Childhood Education, Insitute of Education, London, August 29–September 1.

Clarke, A. D. B., & Clarke, A. M. (Eds) (1976). *Early experience: Myth and evidence.* London, NT: Free Press.

Clarke, A. D. B., & Clarke, A. M. (Eds) (2000). *Early experience and the life path.* London, NT: Jessica Kingsley.

Clarke, A. D. B., & Clarke, A. M. (Eds) (2003). *Human resilience: A fifty year quest.* London, NT: Jessica Kingsley.

Dahlberg, G., Moss, P., & Pence, A. (1999). *Beyond quality in early childhood education.* London: Falmer Press.

Darder, A. (Ed.) (2002). *Reinventing Paulo Friere: A pedagogy of love.* Boulder, CO: Westview Press.

Dau, E. (Ed.) (2001). *The anti-bias approach in early childhood.* Sydney: Prentice-Hall.

De Lair, H. A., & Irwin, E. (2000). Working perspectives within feminism and early childhood education. *Contemporary Issues in Early Childhood, 1*(2), 153–170.

Derman Sparks, L., & The ABC Taskforce (1989). *Anti-bias curriculum: Tools for empowering young children.* Washington, DC: NAEYC.

Diaz Soto, L. (2000). An early childhood dreamspace for social justice and equity. In: L. Diaz Soto (Ed.), *The Politics of Early Childhood Education* (pp. 197–208). New York: Peter Lang Publishers.

Ellsworth, E. (1989). Why doesn't this feel empowering? Working through the repressive myths of critical pedagogy. *Harvard Educational Review, 59*(3), 297–324.

Erikson, E. (1963). *Childhood and society* (2nd ed.). New York: Norton.

Foucault, M. (1980). Two lectures. In: C. Gordon (Ed.), *Power/Knowledge: Selected Interviews and Other Writings 1972–1977* (pp. 78–108). New York: Pantheon Books.

Foucault, M. (1983). On the genealogy of ethics: An overview of work in progress. In: H. Dreyfus & P. Rabinow (Eds), *Michel Foucault: Beyond Structuralism and Hermeneutics* (2nd ed., pp. 229–252) Chicago: University of Chicago Press.

Foucault, M. (1984). Michel Foucault: The ethic of care for the self as a practice of freedom. An interview translated by J. D. Giathier In: J. Bernaur & D. Rasmussen (Eds) (1987), *The Final Foucault* (pp. 1–20). Cambridge, MA: MIT Press.

Garmezy, N. (1993). Children in poverty: Resilience despite risk. *Psychiatry, 56*, 127–136.

Giroux, H. (1988). *Teachers as intellectuals: Toward a critical pedagogy of learning.* Massachusetts: Bergin and Garvey Publishers.

Goldberg, S. (2000). *Attachment and development.* London: Arnold.

Goldstein, L. (1997). *Teaching with love: A feminist approach to early childhood education.* New York: Peter Lang Publishers.

Gore, J. (1993). *The struggle for pedagogies: Critical and feminist discourses as regimes of truth.* New York: Routledge.

Grieshaber, S., & Cannella, G. (Eds) (2001). *Embracing identities in early childhood education: Diversity and possibilities.* New York: Teachers College Press.

Howes, C. (1999). Attachment relationships in the context of multiple caregivers. In: J. Cassidy & P. R. Shaver (Eds), *Handbook of Attachment: Theory, Research and Clinical Applications* (pp. 671–687). New York: Guilford Press.

Jipson, J., & Johnson, R. (Eds) (2001). *Representation and resistance in early childhood research, theory and practice.* New York: Peter Lang Publishers.

Jones, K., & Mules, R. (2001). Developing critical thinking and activism. In: E. Dau (Ed.), *The Anti-Bias Approach in Early Childhood* (pp. 192–209). Frenchs Forrest, NSW, Australia: Pearson Education.

Lloyd, M. (1997). 'Care of the self': Some implications for feminist politics. In: C. O'Farrell (Ed.), *Foucault: The Legacy* (pp. 288–297). Kelvin Grove: Queensland University of Technology.

Lubeck, S. (1994). The politics of culture, class and curriculum. In: B. L. Mallory & R. S. New (Eds), *Diversity and Developmentally Appropriate Practices: Challenges for Early Childhood Education,* New York, Teachers College Press.

MacNaughton, G. (1997). Feminist praxis and the gaze in the early childhood curriculum. *Gender and Education,* 1–22

MacNaughton, G. (1998). Improving our gender equity tools: A case for discourse analysis. In: N. Yelland (Ed.), *Gender in Early Childhood.* London: Routledge.

MacNaughton, G. (2000). *Rethinking gender in early childhood.* Sydney: Allen & Unwin; London: Paul Chapman Publications; New York: Sage.

MacNaughton, G. (2001). 'Blushes and birthday parties': Telling silences in young children's constructions of "race". *Journal for Australian Research in Early Childhood Education, 8*(1), 41–51.

MacNaughton, G. (2003). *Shaping early childhood: Learners, curriculum and contexts.* London: Open University Press.

MacNaughton, G., & Davis, K. (2001). Beyond 'othering': rethinking approaches to teaching young Anglo-Australian children about indigenous Australians. *Contemporary Issues in Early Childhood, 2*(1), 83–93.

Masten, A. S. (2001). Ordinary magic: Resilience processes in development. *American Psychologist, 56*(3), 227–238.

Ministry of Education (1996). Te Whāriki he Whārike Mātauranga mó Ngā Mokopuna o Aoteara Early Childhood Curriculum, Wellington: Learning Media Ltd.

Page, J. (2000). *Reframing the early childhood curriculum. Educational imperatives for the future.* London: Routledge/Falmer

Piaget, J. (1952). *The origins of intelligence in children.* New York: International Universities Press (Original work published in 1936).

Pierce, C. M. (1980). The Pre-Schooler and the Future. In: L. Jennings & S. Cornish (Eds), *Education and the Future.* Bethesda: World Future Society.

Ritchie, J. (1996). The bicultural imperative within the New Zealand draft curriculum guidelines for early childhood education, 'Te Whariki'. *Australian Journal of Early Childhood, 21*(3), 28–32.

Rolfe, S. A. (2002). *Promoting resilience in young children.* Research into Practice Series, Canberra: AECA.

Rutter, M., & O'Conner, T. G. (1999). Implications of attachment theory for child care policies. In: J. Cassidy & P. R. Shaver (Eds), *Handbook of Attachment: Theory, Research and Clinical Applications* (pp. 823–844). New York: Guilford Press.

Ryan, S., & Ochsner, M. (1999). Traditional practices, new possibilities: Transforming dominant images of early childhood teachers. *Australian Journal of Early Childhood, 24*, 14–20.

Schore, A. N. (1994). *Affect regulation and the origin of the self: The neurobiology of emotional development.* Hillsday, NJ: Erlbaum.

Schweinhart, L. (2000). The high/scope Perry preschool study: A case in random assignment. *Evaluation and Research in Education, 14*(3–4), 136–147.

Seifer, R., Schiller, M., Sameroff, A., Resnick, S., & Riordan, K. (1996). Attachment, maternal sensitivity, and infant temperament during the first years of life. *Developmental Psychology, 32*, 12–25.

Shane, H. G., & Shane, J. G. (1974). Educating the youngest for tomorrow. In: A. Toffler (Ed.), *Learning for Tomorrow: The Role of the Future in Education.* New York: Random House.

Silin, J. (1995). *Sex death and the education of children: Our passion for ignorance in the age of AIDS.* New York: Teachers College Press.

Silin, J. (1999). Speaking up for silence. *Australian Journal of Early Childhood, 24*(4), 41–45.

Silin, J. G. (1988). On becoming knowledgable professionals. In: O. N. Saracho & D. L. Peters (Eds), *Professionalism and the Early Childhood Practitioner.* New York: Teachers College Press.

Siraj-Blatchford, J., & Siraj-Blachford, L. (1995). Cross-curricula skills, themes and dimensions: An introduction. In: J. Siraj-Blatchford & I. Siraj-Blatchford (Eds), *Educating the Whole Child. Cross Curricular Skills, Themes and Dimensions.* Buckingham: Open University Press.

Slaughter, R. (1991). *Futures concepts and powerful ideas.* Melbourne: Futures Study Centre.

Sroufe, L. A. (1995). *Emotional development: The organisation of emotional life in the early years.* Cambridge: Cambridge University Press.

Theilheimer, R., & Cahill, B. (2001). A messy closet in the early childhood classroom. In: S. Grieshaber & G. Cannella (Eds), *Embracing Identities in Early Childhood Education: Diversity and Possibilities* (pp. 103–113). New York: Teachers College Press.

Toda, M. (1993). Future time perspective and human cognition: An evolutional view. *International Journal of Psychology, 18*, 351–364.

United Nations (1989). *United Nations convention on the rights of the child.*

Usher, R., & Edwards, R. (1994). *Postmodernism and education.* London: Routledge.

Viruru, R., & Cannella, G. (2001). Postcolonial ethnography, young children and voice. In: S. Grieshaber & G. Cannella (Eds), *Embracing Identities in Early Childhood Education: Diversity and Possibilities* (pp. 158–173). New York: Teachers College Press.

Weedon, C. (1997). *Feminist practice and post structuralist theory* (2nd ed.). Oxford: Blackwell.
Werner, E. (1989). Children of the garden Island. *Scientific American, 260,* 2–6.
Werner, E., & Smith, R. S. (1992). *Overcoming the odds: High risk children from birth to adulthood.* New York: Cornell University Press.
Werner, E. E. (1985). Stress and protective factors in children's lives. In: A. R. Nicol (Ed.), *Studies in Child Psychology and Psychiatry.* London.

# BETWEEN A ROCK AND A HARD PLACE: TEACHERS' EXPERIENCES IN MEETING THE *ABBOTT* MANDATE

Debra J. Ackerman

## ABSTRACT

*Because teacher training is an important component of high-quality early care and education (ECE), states are employing various efforts to increase the credentials of teachers in private ECE centers. In New Jersey, teachers who serve disadvantaged students in the state's community-based* Abbott *preschools are under a court mandate to obtain a Bachelor's degree and Preschool – Grade 3 certification by September 2004 or lose their jobs. This chapter describes a phenomenological study of five teachers' experiences in attempting to meet that mandate, and offers implications for policymakers to consider when evaluating the overall success of this reform effort.*

A significant research base supports the positive benefits of quality early care and education (ECE) in regard to later developmental and academic outcomes, particularly for lower-income children (Barnett, 1995, 1998, 2002; Schweinhart & Weikart, 1997). Although recent research efforts have detailed the importance of informal teacher training in providing quality ECE for young children (Cassidy et al., 1995, 1998; Horm-Wingerd et al., 1997), teachers with bachelor's (B.A.) degrees not only seem to have higher quality ECE classrooms overall (Cost, Quality, and Outcomes Study Team, 1995; Henderson et al., 1999), but also have

Social Contexts of Early Education, and Reconceptualizing Play (II)
Advances in Early Education and Day Care, Volume 13, 93–136
Copyright © 2004 by Elsevier Ltd.
All rights of reproduction in any form reserved
ISSN: 0270-4021/doi:10.1016/S0270-4021(04)13004-8

been shown to have stronger beliefs about developmentally appropriate practice (McMullen & Alat, 2002). In addition, those who complete coursework and training specifically related to early childhood education display more positive interactions with the young children they care for and educate each day (Arnett, 1989; Burchinal et al., 2002; Honig & Hirallal, 1998), and thus contribute towards a key component of ECE quality. Despite this research base, however, of the 39 states that offer state-financed preKindergarten, just over half require teachers in these programs to have a B.A. degree in Early Childhood or another subject. Furthermore, only 18 states require teachers in private ECE settings to undergo any pre-service training, much less hold a degree in early childhood education (Ackerman, 2004).

As a result of the link between teacher training and ECE quality, however, there are various efforts underway throughout the United States to encourage those who teach and care for our youngest children to increase their credentials and knowledge of early childhood practice (Ackerman, 2004). New Jersey's initiative to improve the qualifications of teachers who work in a specific cohort of private ECE centers presents a unique case within the context of these overall efforts. Because of the long running *Abbott vs. Burke* lawsuit, the state is not only providing free preschool to three- and four-year olds in its 30 special-needs, *Abbott* school districts, but has mandated that teachers who work in community-based *Abbott* preschools must obtain a B.A. and Preschool through Grade 3 (P-3) certification by 2004 or lose their jobs. To be sure, studies have documented the urgent need for improved quality in *Abbott* preschool classrooms (Barnett et al., 2001; Klayman et al., 2001). Despite the critical role that teachers play in providing quality ECE, however, little attention has been paid to the experiences of the women in *Abbott*-contracting, community-based centers who have not only been working as minimally-educated ECE teachers, but now are deadline-imposed college students, as well, placing these women very much between a rock and a hard place. Perhaps just as importantly, although these teachers can be considered the linchpins in this groundbreaking endeavor, there has been even less opportunity for them to provide feedback regarding the ease or difficulty in actually meeting the Court's mandate, and thus inform both New Jersey's and other states' efforts to improve teachers' qualifications.

Using a phenomenological lens in order to give voice to "the meaning of the lived experience" (Creswell, 1998, p. 51) of the teachers who are affected by New Jersey's new teacher licensure policy, this chapter reports on a study regarding the experiences of five women who are teachers in community-based *Abbott* preschools and are working towards meeting the Court's mandate. Thus after situating the study within the literature on quality ECE, I begin with a discussion regarding the context within New Jersey. I then follow with a review of ECE as a profession, and the constraints facing ECE teachers as both adult learners and policy implementers. The women's narratives are then grouped according to the study's research questions, which are as follows: (a) As nontraditional, adult students with various responsibilities and commitments, how are these women coping with teaching on a full-time basis, taking classes, and fulfilling their family obligations? (b) What types of support systems and mentorship are in place to assist these women? (c) What are their reactions to being told that despite their experience, they must attend college to keep their jobs?, and (d) From the women's perspectives, how does participating in the overall *Abbott* effort influence the quality of their activities in the preschool classroom? The chapter then concludes with a discussion of the implications of New Jersey's efforts, not only from a practical standpoint, but for the quality of the state's *Abbott* preschools, as well.

# THE CHALLENGES OF OBTAINING A COURT-MANDATED EDUCATION

Before I review the conceptual framework guiding this study, it is important to recognize the overall context that frames these women's experiences, including the *Abbott* decision and New Jersey's differing licensure policies for teachers of young children, and the challenges those working in ECE face as teachers, adult learners, and policy implementers. Because the goal of the Court's mandate is to provide high-quality preschool for the state's most disadvantaged children, however, I begin with a brief overview of the literature regarding quality ECE.

## *Quality Early Care and Education*

Children who experience high-quality ECE – and in particular, disadvantaged children – have shown increased social, cognitive, and academic outcomes in their post-ECE schooling (Barnett, 1995, 1998, 2002; Campbell & Ramey, 1994; Peisner-Feinberg et al., 1999; Ramey et al., 2000; Reynolds et al., 2001; Schweinhart & Weikart, 1997). Although Essa and Burnham (2001) rightfully assert that the impact of overall quality is embedded within a context of community, family, and children's characteristics, quality is frequently measured according to structural variables, such as child-teacher ratios and the number of children in a classroom (Abbott-Shim et al., 2000; Cost, Quality, and Child Outcomes Study Team, 1995; Cryer et al., 1999; Helburn & Howes, 1996; Howes & Brown, 2000; Saluja et al., 2002). As quantifiable variables, these aspects of quality are often addressed through state licensing regulations (Azer et al., 2002; Cryer, 1999).

Quality in ECE settings is also affected, however, by process variables, including caregiving behaviors, interactions between teachers and children, and the types of activities available in an early care and education setting (Bowman et al., 2001; Holloway et al., 2001; Phillips et al., 2000; Shonkoff & Phillips, 2000). Because these interactions and activities are more dependent on a teacher's experience and knowledge base, process quality is present more often when preschool teachers have received education and training specifically related to early childhood (Arnett, 1989; Bowman et al., 2001; Burchinal et al., 2002; Honig & Hirallal, 1998; Howes, 1997; Whitebook et al., 1990). Indeed, "teacher expertise" is considered to be "the crucial ingredient" (Dwyer et al., 2000, p. 6) in a high-quality early childhood environment. Given both this research base and the fact that the Court had also addressed various structural quality variables in regard to the *Abbott* preschools – including requiring a teacher and an aide in each classroom of no more than 15 students – it is perhaps not surprising, then, that the Court additionally mandated that teachers in the *Abbott* preschools must have a BA and P-3 certification, as well (*Abbott v. Burke*, 2000).

Abbott v. Burke *and Its Ramifications for New Jersey's*
*Pre-service ECE Teaching Requirements*

New Jersey's current focus on providing quality ECE and ensuring that teachers in its *Abbott* preschools could potentially contribute to that quality is the result of a long-running court battle that actually began over two decades ago. In 1981, the Education Law Center in Newark filed suit on behalf of Raymond Abbott and other students living in several urban school districts against then New Jersey State Education Commissioner, Fred G. Burke. This original *Abbott vs. Burke* suit charged that the Public School Education Act of 1975 violated the State constitution's guarantee for a "thorough and efficient education," as reliance on local property taxes to fund schools meant "the poorer the district and the greater its need, the less money available, and the worse the education" (*Abbott v. Burke*, 575 N.J. 359, 1990). Since that initial lawsuit, the "*Abbott* districts" have been defined as those that are not only urban, but serve a preponderance of children who meet the criteria for the state Department of Education's lowest socioeconomic category, as well. Subsequent *Abbott* decisions have arguably brought about an "unprecedented series of entitlements" for children in the 30 *Abbott* school districts (Education Law Center, 2003, para. 23), including extra funding to implement whole school reform and improve facilities, and as previously discussed, provide full-day preschool for three- and four-year olds (*Abbott v. Burke*, 1998). The preschool mandate utilizes private, community-based centers, Head Starts, and public schools, however. Thus in order to ensure that children would have access to the same quality of teaching no matter what the setting, the Court also mandated that all *Abbott* preschool teachers must have a minimum of a B.A., as well as P-3 certification (*Abbott v. Burke*, 2000).

For public school preschool teachers who were already required to hold a minimum of a B.A. to be licensed and certified by the state's Department of Education – whether in an *Abbott* district or not – obtaining the state-mandated P-3 certification involves successfully completing between 13–22 credits at one of the colleges which offers an endorsement program. Although there are 30 *Abbott* districts, however, only four districts run their *Abbott* preschool program exclusively through their public school system. Of the remaining 26 districts, 19 contract with private, community-based centers and/or Head Starts to provide part of their program, and an additional seven districts rely exclusively on non-public school settings. As a result, of the approximately 2,000 teachers in New Jersey's *Abbott* preschool classrooms, over 68% of them work in settings that prior to the *Abbott* mandate could hire teachers with only a minimum of six credits in Early Childhood Education and a Child Development Associate (CDA) credential in order to be considered an official "group teacher." Although non-certified teachers in the *Abbott* community-based centers currently have permission to continue teaching, if they wish to retain their jobs, they must not only obtain a B.A., but also successfully complete the new P-3 certification by September 2004.

### *Early Care and Education as a Profession: Educational Requirements, Salary, and Status*

In 2001, researchers (Barnett et al., 2001; Klayman et al., 2001) compiled data on the *Abbott* preschools. Although the studies had slightly different findings regarding classroom quality, each noted that in relation to district-run, public school preschool programs, many of the teachers in the community-based centers did not have B.A. degrees. This particular finding was not surprising, as teachers in New Jersey's private, non-*Abbott* ECE centers have only needed to meet the requirements of the state's Department of Human Services. As previously discussed, these requirements are less stringent than the educational qualifications necessary when working under the jurisdiction of the Department of Education (Division of Youth and Family Services, 1998; Education Law Center, 2001). The findings were also not inconsistent with Saluja, Early, and Clifford's (2002) nationwide study, which showed that only 50% of ECE teachers who work in nonprofit settings have an Associate's (AA) or B.A. degree.

The "two-tier" system specifying the educational background one needs in order to teach young children is not unique to New Jersey, either. With the exception of Rhode Island, the pre-service requirements for teachers in private ECE settings are consistently lower than the requirements for teachers in state-financed PreKs (Ackerman, 2004). It should be noted, however, that although anyone designated as a "teacher" in Rhode Island must have a B.A., teaching assistants may also be in charge of a group of children in private ECE settings. The minimum requirements for this latter group are attainment of a high school diploma and a "history of regular participation in an ongoing early childhood staff development program" (Rhode Island Department of Children, Youth and Families, 1993, p. 12). In the end, the existence of these two-tier systems suggests that no matter where private ECE centers are located, teachers in those settings will most likely not be expected to have the same level of education as their state-financed PreK colleagues. Combined with the "folk belief" (Genishi et al., 2001, p. 1183) that one merely needs to possess maternal qualities to be "qualified," the ECE field has thus been an easy place for many women to find employment.

It is also important to note, however, that although many of the staff in ECE centers may realize the correlation between additional teacher training and quality of care, ECE is a profession that often pays less than what one would earn pumping gas, trimming trees, or serving food (Laverty et al., 2001; Whitebook et al., 2001). Because of the low hourly wage – which in 2002 ranged from $9.21 to $11.38 for a teacher with a CDA in one of New Jersey's most affluent counties (Laverty et al., 2002) – researchers have characterized those holding these jobs as "the working poor" (Whitebook & Phillips, 1999, p. 1), and residing in a "new low-wage ghetto" (Burbank, 1994, para. 2). ECE has also been characterized as having a "higher concentration of poverty-level jobs than almost any other occupation in the United States" (Laverty et al., 2001, p. 3). Inadequate pay, minimal benefits, and energy-demanding days not only translate into a staff turnover that averages about one-third each year, but offer little incentive to assume additional professional development costs, as well (National Center for Early Development & Learning, 1997; Phillips et al., 1991; Whitebook et al., 2001).

As a gendered, low-paying job, what also may not be surprising is the less-than-positive status affiliated with both out-of-home child care and caregiving as a profession. Many would argue that a misleading distinction has arisen between ECE and "real" education (Bowman et al., 2001; Laverty et al., 2001). Nelson (2001) contends that because raising children is seen as the type of natural thing that women just "do," any job related to child care is considered to be a low-skill occupation. Despite the fact that over 60% of American preschoolers are cared for by someone other than their parents much of the workweek (Bureau of Labor Statistics, 1999), out-of-home ECE by other women is still viewed by some parents, educators, and policymakers as something not quite as important as the type of education that Americans demand for their children once they reach kindergarten age.

## *Efforts in Increasing ECE Teachers' Credentials*

Despite these constraints, there are currently many efforts underway throughout the United States to increase the training and qualifications of those who teach and care for our youngest children. Over 20 states employ variations on the Teacher Education and Compensation Helps (T.E.A.C.H.) initiative, which not only provides scholarships for ECE staff to obtain their CDA credential, AA, or B.A. degree, but also provides bonuses or raises when staff complete a specific number of credits. Other states are utilizing a combination of voluntary career lattices, counselors, and coursework available at local two-year colleges to encourage an upgrading of minimum competencies for all of their ECE teachers. Still others are providing trainings in languages other than English, in an attempt to acknowledge the culturally diverse learning needs of teachers (Ackerman, 2004; Montilla et al., 2001; Vecchiotti, 2001).

New Jersey, however, is currently the only state which *mandates* that a certain group of previously minimally-educated teachers obtain a B.A. by a specific deadline or lose their jobs. Aslanian and Brickell (1980) argue that being forced to obtain additional education can be akin to "running faster to stay in the same place" (p. 69). Furthermore, this type of "mandated continuing education" (Cross, 1981, p. 40) most often takes place in jobs that are highly technical or competitive, or are linked to professional license renewal. As previously discussed, teaching in an ECE setting has traditionally not been considered "highly technical," nor had a license renewal requirement. To the contrary, although many ECE teachers have an obvious concern and love for children, the lack of educational requirements for working in an ECE setting has been precisely *why* working in such a setting can be appealing to adults who do not have – or wish to obtain – post-secondary educational qualifications.

## *Constraints Adult Learners Face*

In addition to the unique nature of this mandated education, there are problems and constraints just from being an adult learner, including one's ongoing personal and professional responsibilities, and logistical hurdles that can make it difficult to actually attend class (Carp et al., 1974; Cross, 1981). Given that the average ECE teacher is 39 years old (Saluja et al., 2002) and effective educational change requires that teachers perceive that the goals of such change are both worthwhile and "realizable" (Fullan, 2001), these issues form the context for the first research question guiding this study: how are these women – as nontraditional, adult students with various responsibilities and commitments – coping with teaching full-time, caring for their own children, and taking classes in their off hours?

Horn and Carroll (1996) argue that not only is there an "obvious negative association between degree attainment and the presence of any nontraditional characteristics," such as delayed enrollment in college, part-time attendance, concurrent full-time employment, and non-spousal dependents, but that the "family and work responsibilities" of older women students, in particular, often makes it difficult to find enough time to complete individual course requirements (pp. 25, 2). Indeed, teacher preparation programs across the U.S. have found that one of the biggest challenges in increasing the qualifications of ECE teachers are the "competing work or family related responsibilities" of their students (Early & Winton, 2001, p. 297). Even when not enrolled in a teacher preparation program, one of the most daunting barriers for adult learners "seem[s] to relate to the factor of time" (Carp et al., 1974, p. 48). When one adds transportation, child care, and accessibility issues to the equation, this daily "juggling act" also serves as a primary source of stress for many adult women students (Darkenwald & Merriam, 1982; White, 2001).

## Constraints New Jersey's ECE Teachers Face

Through a collaboration with the New Jersey Professional Development Center for Early Care and Education (NJPDCECE), New Jersey is offsetting the barrier of teachers' minimal paychecks by offering $5,000 yearly scholarships to those who teach in *Abbott* community-based centers. There have been logistical problems within the state's teacher preparation programs, however, including a lack of uniform articulation agreements regarding transferring community college credits to four-year institutions. Coursework related to preschool teacher preparation has been limited due to the lack of qualified early childhood teaching staff, as New Jersey had previously discontinued its freestanding degree in early childhood in 1985 (New Jersey Professional Development Center for Early Care and Education, 2000, 2001).

In addition, although the community-based centers are located throughout the state, only one of the colleges that offers the P-3 has a main campus located in the southern half of New Jersey. Other colleges offer evening P-3 classes, but early childhood classes are only offered during the day. Rutgers University, New Jersey's flagship institute of higher education, does not even offer a B.A. in Early Childhood, despite being located in New Brunswick, a large *Abbott* district. Furthermore, Rutgers only offers a P-3 endorsement for those who already hold some type of certification. Of the 14 colleges that offer the P-3 endorsement and/or certification, there are eight completely different programs, ranging from BA with initial certification to a graduate specialized alternate route track. None of the programs have articulation agreements with other schools, so even if a non-certified *Abbott* teacher wanted to take one of Rutgers' P-3 courses, for example, it would not transfer towards her degree or P-3 endorsement at another college. Perhaps not surprisingly, these access issues have created much confusion regarding the most efficient way to meet the Court's mandate within the required time frame.

## *The Role of Mentors and Other Advisors*

This type of confusion can be especially acute for those teachers who are not only nontraditional students, but are without an "in-the-know," contact person, as well. Successful first-time college students often employ "scaling down" techniques as a way to navigate the higher education system (Richardson & Skinner, 1992). This strategy utilizes instructors, mentors, advisors, and peers to reduce the maze of confusion in regard to registering, classwork expectations, and receiving academic assistance. The use of mentors is thus especially important for first-generation and/or nontraditional students, who may come to college without "pave-the-way" role models, but also with an accompanying sense of insecurity about their academic abilities (Jones & Watson, 1990; Padron, 1992; Richardson & Skinner, 1992). Fullan (2001) also contends that a key factor in the implementation of educational reform efforts is the support received by teachers from both their school's leadership and the immediate community. These issues, then, lead to the second research question guiding this study: given the difficulties nontraditional students face, what types of support systems and mentorship are in place to assist these women? I also wanted to know if these women received advice or support from their fellow staff members and/or administration of their preschool, as well as what role the Department of Education-placed master teacher in their *Abbott* district – who is supposed to be providing mentoring and support – played in facilitating their college and teaching experiences.

## *Constraints ECE Teachers-as-Policy Implementers Face*

In addition to the barriers adult learners can face, Gallagher and Clifford (2000) speak of the resentment than can ensue when policy implementers – such as the ECE teachers affected by the *Abbott* mandate – are not consulted during the policy-making phase. Fullan (2001) also says that in order for teachers to be motivated to participate in educational reform efforts, they need to develop a sense of meaning about the efforts, and not just be at the receiving end of a top-down mandate. Meaning, however, is "hard to come by when two different worlds have limited interaction" (Fullan, 2001, p. 87). Perhaps because ECE has traditionally been thought of as inconsequential, low-status, women's work, some would argue there has been a tendency for policymakers to only speak for teachers, rather than with them, as if early childhood teachers are thoughtless and without a voice (Ayers, 1992), or without effective leadership skills (Whitebook, 1997). Clark (1992) and others (Fleet & Patterson, 2001) argue that "professional development" often implies "a process done to teachers" (Clark, 1992, p. 75). However, Ayers (1992) asserts that the professional growth and development of early childhood teachers cannot truly occur unless they are empowered through an opportunity to share their perspectives about learning and teaching.

These concepts lead to my third research question: given the traditional lack of status, educational requirements, and a living wage for those in the child care profession, what are these women's reactions to being told that despite their experience, they must attend college and obtain a BA degree or lose their jobs? Fullan (2001) says that in order for the implementation of educational reform to be successful, not only must the change itself not be too complex, but teachers must view the need for change as a good fit with their current needs and situation, as well. As I explain in the next section, the role of relevancy plays a key role in adult learning also.

## The Role of Relevancy

Knowles and Associates (1984) note that "courses [which] are seen by participants as directly related to their work [will] result in increased motivation and attention to learning" (p. 53). Adult learners often seek a connection between their "current competence and new learnings" (Knox, 1977, p. 433), or the opportunity to immediately apply what they have learned (Darkenwald & Merriam, 1982). The National Commission on Teaching and America's Future (1996) also argues that teachers need professional development opportunities that are linked to the current teaching and learning activities in their classroom. The importance of relevancy for adult learning, then, leads to the fourth research question for this study: from the women's perspectives, how does participating in the overall *Abbott* effort influence the quality of their activities in the preschool classroom?

Because of the research base that says educational change is dependent on the thoughts, actions, and commitment of teachers involved in any new effort (Fullan, 1993; Leithwood et al., 1999; Sikes, 1992), I wanted to know if these women were not only taking coursework that was relevant to their jobs, but if their participation in the entire *Abbott* effort was perceived as being relevant to reaching the mandate's goal of creating a quality classroom environment for the children they taught and cared for each day, as well. This question – as well as the others guiding this study – could not be answered, however, unless teachers were given the opportunity to relate their experiences.

## CONCEPTUAL FRAMEWORK

Before proceeding to both the methodology used and the women's narratives, it will be helpful to review the conceptual framework (see Fig. 1) for this study. First, in looking at the factors that are indicated at the bottom of the framework, this study is framed by its overall context not only within the *Abbott* decision, but also within the research base regarding quality ECE and the role of teacher training. The overall context also includes the conflicting policies from New Jersey's Department of Human Services (DHS) and Department of Education (DOE) regarding educational requirements for ECE teachers, the historically low wages and status of child care workers and importance given to child care, and the difficulties ECE teachers can face as both policy implementers and as nontraditional students with various other commitments. Accordingly, then, these elements not only formed the basis of the conceptual framework that guided this research (Miles & Huberman, 1984), but also led to the research questions guiding this study.

Secondly, however, as a phenomenological study, the central focus was the experiences of five women who must attain their B.A. and P-3 certification by September, 2004, if they wish to continue working as teachers in their community-based *Abbott* preschool classrooms after that date. Thus in order to answer the study's research questions, I was interested to learn of their experiences related to six key areas. To begin, since the implementation of educational reform is dependent on teachers viewing the effort as a "good fit" with their current needs, I wondered how these women were reconciling their past teaching experience with the fact that they now needed to obtain a B.A. and P-3 in order to keep their jobs. Next, because of the literature stressing the importance of role models and advisors for nontraditional students, I wanted to know what types of guidance, support, or mentoring they were receiving from their administrators, fellow staff members, and district master teacher. On a related subject, I was also interested to know about their experiences in navigating various college logistics, including accessing coursework and the special *Abbott* scholarship. Given the various family and professional constraints facing adult nontraditional students, I also wondered how successful they were in coping with their family obligations and completing

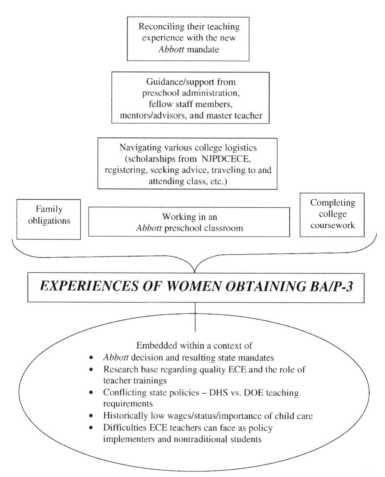

*Fig. 1.* Conceptual Framework for a Phenomenological Study of Women Early Care and Education Teachers' Experiences in Attending College and Working Towards P-3 Certification.

their college coursework, including keeping up with the workload and studying for tests. Finally, I also wanted to know about their experiences working as a teacher in an *Abbott* preschool classroom. This last area of focus received particular attention, as I was also interested in learning their perceptions of how participating in this reform effort was affecting the quality of education they were providing to their young students. If the overall goal of the Court's mandate is to improve the quality of preschool offered to New Jersey's neediest three- and four-year olds, these teachers needed to be given the opportunity to tell policymakers what effect their state-mandated education seemed to have on their daily work.

# METHODOLOGY

## *Philosophical Perspective*

Given the link between teachers' educational backgrounds and early childhood classroom quality, one might be tempted to assume that the success or failure of New Jersey's new *Abbott* policy can be measured strictly through the numbers of teachers who obtain their B.A. and P-3 by 2004. Kagan and Wechsler (1999) argue, however, that the changing realities of today's social policies demand we rely less on purely quantitative research methods, and instead incorporate qualitative methodologies that help determine whether "strategies are producing the intended results" (p. 65). Given the minimal educational starting points of most ECE teachers, the constraints facing many adult learners, and the number of states that are also attempting to increase teachers' credentials in order to improve classroom quality, then, teachers involved in New Jersey's effort need the opportunity to provide feedback regarding whether or not the underlying mechanics and strategies of the B.A./P-3 policy are, indeed, "working."

Use of a phenomenological perspective provides teachers with that opportunity. Due to its association with various branches of the social sciences, "phenomenology" can admittedly have many different meanings (Patton, 2002). For the purposes of this study, I have utilized a Husserlian (Husserl, 1958/1913, 1989, 1999) approach. For Husserl (1989), "the actual surrounding world of any person whatsoever is not physical reality pure and simple and without qualification . . . [but] is the world that is perceived *by the person* (emphasis in the original)" (p. 195). Thus this approach gives priority to the subjective knowledge derived from participants' experiences, rather than a researcher's preconceived "knowledge," or the type of information that can be gleaned from a positivistically-oriented, quantitative study. A phenomenological perspective, seeks not only to provide a way to "understand experience profoundly and authentically" (Pinar et al., 1996, p. 405) from the perspective of someone in the midst of an experience, but through heavy reliance on a participant's own words, attempts to describe the individual meaning of that lived experience in relation to a phenomenon, as well (Cohen & Omery, 1994; Creswell, 1998; Patton, 1990; Polkinghorne, 1989). In our case, the phenomenon is New Jersey's Court-mandated policy regarding necessary educational qualifications for teachers who work in the state's community-based *Abbott* preschools. Although the quantitative policy "reality" may include, for example, the fact that P-3 coursework is available at various four-year colleges and universities, phenomenological inquiry provides a way to investigate the success of the policy by allowing teachers' voices about accessing that coursework to supersede our presuppositions about reality. Without this philosophical perspective – and corresponding narratives – one might falsely attribute any failures of the B.A./P-3 policy to such things as inadequate teacher motivation or desire to improve their credentials.

## Settings

The settings for this study were two *Abbott* community-based centers in separate counties within central New Jersey, and were chosen based on the large proportion of teachers in each who were affected by the B.A./P-3 mandate, and permission of the directors to allow their staff to participate in the study. The first center was in a predominantly African-American district that only utilizes community-based centers to provide their Court-mandated preschool program (District 1). The second center was in a district which offers their program through public schools and community-based centers, and has both a large Hispanic and African-American population (District 2). I was somewhat familiar with District 1 because of my previous employment as the coordinator of CDA and professional development trainings at the county's child care resource and referral agency.

Located in a self-contained, downtown facility near a New Jersey Transit bus and rail station, the center in District 1 has five *Abbott* and two non-*Abbott* classrooms. At the time of the study, the directors – one of whom has an early childhood teaching background – hoped to gain accreditation for their center from the National Association for the Education of Young Children (NAEYC). NAEYC accreditation is considered to be a benchmark for early childhood quality (Whitebook et al., 1997). The center in District 2 serves a large Hispanic immigrant population, and is housed in the educational wing of a downtown church – also relatively close to a New Jersey Transit train station – and has five *Abbott* classrooms, as well as a multi-age, kindergarten classroom with a few *Abbott*-eligible four-year olds. In my initial discussions with the directors of both centers, my willingness to travel to their sites for interviews during naptime helped facilitate cooperation from their staff, as two of the participants did not drive, and all had very busy schedules.

## Participants

A phenomenological perspective is not possible unless the subjective reality is obtained from those who are directly experiencing a phenomenon (Giorgi, 1985).

***Table 1.*** Sample Demographics at Time of Study.

| Teacher | Age | Years of Experience | Cultural Background | Age(s) of Child(ren) | Educational Background |
|---------|-----|---------------------|---------------------|----------------------|------------------------|
| Ann | 37 | 6 | European-American | 10 | CDA; < 20 college credits; Liberal Arts major at a community college |
| Ellen | 33 | 6 | European-American | 8 | CDA; < 45 college credits; Liberal Arts major at a community college |
| Luisa | 31 | 6 | Hispanic-American | 3, 5 | CDA; 60+ college credits; Psychology major at a 4-year university |
| Nancy | 35 | 12 | European-American | 10 | CDA; < 30 college credits; Liberal Arts major at a community college |
| Rosa | 24 | 5 | Hispanic-American | 2 | CDA; Associate's degree in Accounting; Undecided as to which 4-year college/university to transfer to |

*Note:* KEY: CDA – Child Development Associate Credential.

Thus, I asked the directors of the centers that served as settings for this study to suggest possible candidates, based on the criteria of working full-time in an *Abbott* classroom, attending school part-time because of the *Abbott* mandate, and being the primary caretaker of at least one young child. As a result, the sample is composed of five teachers – Ann, Ellen, Luisa, Nancy, and Rosa – with three teachers from District 1 and two from District 2 (see Table 1). Ellen was actually a recently-hired assistant teacher in her center, but because she had six years of experience working as a teacher in another community-based *Abbott* preschool and met all the other criteria, I decided to include her in the sample, as well.

As can be seen in Table 1, the women who participated in this study are similar in many respects, yet different in others. All but one of the women was in her thirties, and their children ranged in age from two- to ten-years old. Three of the women were European-American, and two were bilingual, Hispanic-American. Their experience working with young children ranged from 5 to 12 years, and given the high turnover in ECE settings, it is surprising to note that only one teacher – Ellen – had recently left a previous center to work in her present location. It should be noted that the average age (32) and years of experience (7) of these participants are somewhat similar to the findings of Saluja, Early, and Clifford (2002) regarding the demographics of preschool teachers in the U.S., who on average are 39 years old and have been working as ECE teachers for almost seven years.

In addition, all five participants in this study worked full-time in a three- or four-year old *Abbott* preschool classroom during the day, and were taking college-level coursework in the evenings because of the Court's mandate. At the time of the study, the number of college credits they had already obtained ranged from less than 20 to over 60. Because of time and transportation constraints and their concern with obtaining a B.A. in the most efficient manner possible, however, none of the teachers were enrolled in teacher preparation programs. Instead, Ann, Ellen, and Nancy were all liberal arts majors at their local community college, and Rosa had just obtained her AA in Accounting at another community college. Only Luisa was enrolled in a four-year university, but as a Psychology major, as she had accumulated a significant number of credits towards that degree prior to the Court's decision in 2000.

*Data Collection*

The data regarding these women's experiences was gathered in their respective preschools over the course of two to four interviews during the children's naptime, between the months of February and June, 2002. Because phenomenological inquiry requires conversation that is "participatory, collaborative, and aesthetically rich" (Morrissette, 1999, para. 11) in order to discover and describe each individual's reality (Giorgi, 1985; Merleau-Ponty, 1970; Moustakas, 1994), I utilized a type of interview protocol that Denzin (1989) has termed the "Nonschedule Standardized Interview" (p. 105), and Patton (1990) the "Interview Guide" Approach (p. 283). Similarly designed, each of these less-formal, open-ended interview protocols uses a list of desired information, but allows the interviewer to change the order and phrasing of the questions within each individual conversation to best fit the participant and situation. My list of desired information was not haphazard, however, as each category of interview questioning was tied to one of my research questions. All interviews were tape-recorded using a Sony microcassette-corder, and transcribed verbatim by me.

After my first interview with three of the participants, I found Glesne and Peshkin's (1992) description of this type of interviewing to be quite fitting. They suggest that interviewing is not so much a call-and-response type of interaction, but instead similar to pitching a "wordball," and subsequently "getting words to fly . . . in every corner of your data park" (p. 63). Indeed, an inquiry about one of my participant's work hours soon turned into a discussion about getting homework done during lunch hour, working extra hours to qualify for a scholarship, and after-school care and its cost. I would not have obtained all of that rich information by merely asking a straightforward question. Denzin (2001) argues the resulting "thick descriptions" not only help readers "imagine [their] way into the life experiences of another" (p. 99), but connect personal issues with larger public issues, as well. Because the purpose of a phenomenological study is to "describe the meaning of the lived experience for individuals" (Creswell, 1998, p. 51) in relation to a particular phenomenon, this style of interviewing seemed especially appropriate both in theory and practice.

Although my interview style was consistent with the "generally broad and open-ended" approach advocated by Giorgi (1997, para. 27), I was concerned, nonetheless, about adequate organization of the teachers' narratives. Thus, I kept track of whether each teacher addressed a particular topic through the use of a data accounting sheet (see Appendix A), as suggested by Miles and Huberman (1994). By writing in notations regarding dates of conversations on a particular topic, as well as tape and transcription numbers, this tool not only gave me a quick reference about which cassette tape and transcription contained dialogue about a topic with a specific teacher, but also which topics still needed to be addressed. "Being organized" was especially critical, because I did not ask identical questions or use a specific sequence of questioning with the participants. The data accounting sheet was also useful in generating memos to myself about specific areas of a category that happened to come up in conversation, and seemed worthy of either a follow-up discussion with the initial teacher, or additional conversations with the other four participants, as well. The memos also included ideas about future questions or possible emerging themes, as advocated by Miles and Huberman (1984, 1994). In addition, each of the categories were also tied to one of my four research questions, as indicated on the left side of the data accounting sheet. This type of narrative organization helped keep me focused on the overall reasoning for discussing the various topics.

*Data Analysis Procedures*

*Coding*
The use of coding, was particularly helpful for categorizing and retrieving the information I collected in this study. Coding allows a researcher to sort information into appropriate areas of interest, much like one could categorize children's blocks by color, shape, or size. As suggested by Miles and Huberman (1994), my initial coding system (see Appendix B) was deductively derived from the six "bins" found in my conceptual framework (see Fig. 1). As previously discussed, these bins formed the descriptive categories of each woman's experience in working

towards her B.A. and P-3 certification. Thus, as I examined each transcript, I looked for chunks of text that could literally be deposited into a Microsoft Word file that represented each bin.

As the interviews progressed and I had the opportunity to notice recurring themes, I then took each bin and broke it down even further into more specific categorical codes (Miles & Huberman, 1984). This style of inductive coding provided a way to highlight the emerging findings regarding each woman's experience and their relationship not only to the original deductive "bin," but to the literature guiding the study, as well – what Wolcott (1994) has termed "progressive focusing," or a zooming "from the broad context to the particulars" (p. 18). For example, I could determine whether the experiences of the participants mirrored any of the various types of constraints that Cross (1981) argues are often barriers for adult learners, as previously discussed. In addition, all five women talked at length about problems with the scholarships and book stipends, and I soon realized that what at first glance seemed to be a generous, state-provided incentive is actually a source of stress and concern for these women. Most importantly, however, each coding category helped address my four overall research questions. The combination of interview style and coding also helped me provide the type of thick, rich description that is so essential to providing a credible narrative (Creswell, 1998; Creswell & Miller, 2000).

### *Data Verification Procedures*

Although the narrative of this study will help establish the credibility of my findings, as a researcher I engaged in other important data verification procedures. First, both my interview style and quantity of interviews allowed me to spend significant time with each of the teachers. The "give-and-take" (Denzin, 2001, p. 66) nature of our conversations allowed me to both gather and exchange information with the women in this study, and considerable rapport and trust was built up on both sides (Creswell, 1998; Creswell & Miller, 2000; Glesne & Peshkin, 1992). Part of that trust, I believe, came not only from providing each teacher with a transcript of our individual conversations as a means of "member checking" (Creswell, 1998; Creswell & Miller, 2000), but also from the assurance that they had the final authority to exclude anything they said from this study.

In addition, each teacher received a copy of the entire study in draft form, and again, in order to ensure that the findings accurately portrayed their experiences, each was encouraged to not only read the draft, but to comment on anything that wasn't quite "right," as well. As a phenomenological study, "findings" are meaningless if the participants' words have been skewed. None of the women disputed my interpretations or asked to have any narrative removed from the study, and in fact often characterized the opportunity to articulate their thoughts regarding the B.A./P-3 initiative as "therapy." They also seemed to find reading their own words and knowing that others would read them, too, as empowering. As we were discussing one of her transcripts, Ann commented, "I didn't realize I had so much to say."

Perhaps the most important aspect of verifying a phenomenological study is through disclosure of any possible research bias (Creswell, 1998; Creswell & Miller, 2000; Patton, 1990). To be sure, setting aside any empathetic notions I have about what it is like to work with young children by day, attend class at night, and take care of one's own children was difficult for me. I am a nontraditional student myself, and my personal and professional experience makes me familiar with the context of this study on various levels. Patton (1990) asserts, however, that "the final step in phenomenological analysis is the development . . . of the true meanings of the individuals" (p. 409) that have participated in a study. Thus, because this overriding goal was important to me, I have deliberately attempted to bracket out my assumptions about participating in the entire B.A./P-3 process and let these women's narratives speak for themselves. This is important for two reasons: first, as Theilheimer (1999) argues, the experiences of students who are not part of traditional teacher education programs are often left out of the literature regarding effective preparation. Thus by focusing on the reality of these women's efforts to comply with the Court mandate while they teach our most disadvantaged children, we can hopefully learn from their experience and inform larger policy issues, particularly as the U.S. grapples with the idea of improving access to high-quality early care and education. More importantly, however, I wanted this study to give voice to these women, whose traditional voice, as Maxine Greene (1988) has so aptly described, has most definitely been "submerged in cultures of silence [and] overwhelmed by official declamation [and] technical talk" (p. xi). We would not have been able to hear them if my assumptions got in the way.

## FINDINGS AND DISCUSSION

The data regarding these women's experiences in meeting the *Abbott* initiative speaks to all four of this study's research questions, which are addressed next. However, one overarching finding emerged: one the one hand, requiring minimally-educated child care teachers to obtain a B.A. and P-3 certification in order to improve the quality of early care and education in New Jersey is arguably a necessary and laudable goal. The mandate of having to obtain these new qualifications by 2004 has been quite a challenge, however, and has placed these women – as the title of the study suggests – very much "between a rock and a hard place," and in very significant ways.

### How are these Women Coping with Teaching Full-time, Taking Classes, and Fulfilling Their Family Obligations?

My first research question asked how each woman was coping with the type of barriers that could serve as impediments to completing her degree. Perhaps not surprisingly, although all were "coping," the concept of "not enough time" was a frequent theme:

> You could do so much more in a classroom and bring so much more into your classroom if you had time. But because the little bit of time you do have is spent on trying to get through school, you can't bring in all these wonderful things that you're capable of into the classroom, because you just don't have time (Luisa, Interview II).

White (2001) argues that "a primary challenge and source of stress for adult women students comes from the multiple and sometimes conflicting roles they must play in their daily lives" (p. 1). This description is certainly apt for the women in this study. What were especially poignant, however, were their "juggling act" stories regarding their determination to fit all three aspects of their lives – teacher, mother, and student – into one 24-hour period, particularly when it came to ensuring that their own children were cared for as they coped with all the demands on their time. In order to qualify for the *Abbott* scholarship – and be able to take classes towards her mandatory degree – Nancy was told she had to increase her hours from 30 to 35 each week. This involved changing her quitting time from 3 p.m. to 4 p.m. However, because the after-school program at her son's school was already booked and she only made $9 an hour, she found herself in a double bind regarding after-school care for her own child:

> He's 10 and some people say he's old enough to stay alone, but I personally don't feel that he is. When he feels secure enough himself, and I think you know as a parent when your child is ready. Some people say you're just overprotective, but I know my child, and when we're in the house, he doesn't even like to be upstairs alone when I'm downstairs, so he is not ready be in an house that's totally empty for an hour until I come home . . . My husband and I had to choose – work the extra hour or be jobless . . . But I couldn't figure out what to do with him after school, because I couldn't afford it . . . By the time I started to work my hours, the after-school program was booked (Nancy, Interview I).

Despite Nancy's quandary regarding after-school care, evening child care was often the biggest dilemma for these women – they did not receive any release time to attend class during the workday, and thus went to school during their off hours. The community college several of the women attended had a special child care class for students, but utilizing this facility had its own drawbacks:

> I have class tonight, but no babysitter... They do have a class there that you can take your children to in the evenings, but I don't get out until 9 something. And it's going to be a late night, and there's school tomorrow [for him], and they don't even show up to open that classroom until *after* my class starts (Nancy, Interview I).

Other women, such as Rosa and Luisa, utilized a well-organized system of babysitters, the center where they worked, fathers, and grandparents to care of their children while they both worked and went to school. Ellen describes the important role family members play in watching her eight-year old son so that she could work and attend class two nights a week:

> I moved back in with my dad in the house I grew up in . . . so it's actually me and my son, my dad, my grandfather who's 92, and my brother . . . My brother bartends so he works at night, so he's able to pick him up from school, which is at 2:45, and he stays with him until I get home [when I don't go to class] ... I'm in school Tuesday nights from 7 to [9:40], so his grandmother – his father's mom – picks him up every Tuesday, and then he just sleeps over there and then they'll bring him to school Wednesday morning. And Thursdays I'm in class from 6 to [8:40], and same thing – his father will watch him and sometimes he'll just sleep over there, and sometimes he'll come home on Thursday night (Ellen, Interview I).

Attending class and completing their coursework was an equally difficult aspect of their juggling act. Cross (1981) cites "not enough time" as one of the biggest situational barriers for adult learners. All of the participants in the study mentioned their difficulty in finding enough time to attend class after working all day with three- and four-year olds, do their homework, and meet their family obligations. Rosa – who worked 40 hours a week – could not do her homework until after her two-year old was asleep at 10 p.m. (Interview II). Sometimes the women were able to use naptime to study for tests or complete their reading, but the lack of windows in the classroom made naptime "too dark" for Luisa (Interview I). This strategy did not always work out as planned for those with adequate light, either:

> I can study sometimes during naptime, if I don't have a lot of prep work that day, then, yes, I can study. But if I do – if I do have a lot of things to do, then no, I can't study. It depends upon what kind of day . . . And then the night of the test, I'm like, "Oh, my God, I didn't study!" . . . I've been finding out real fast – not wanting to – but that I'm doing better on these tests by cramming, so if it's gonna work, it's gonna work. I just get a little nervous . . . (Ann, Interview I).

The period between after school care and evening classes could also be hectic – Nancy described a typical afternoon of getting off work and picking up her son, only to head back out for a 6 p.m. class:

> I worked yesterday until 4, and by the time I tried to call a parent on my way out – I had a child with a 102 fever here – so I made the phone call to the parent and it took me 15 to 20 minutes to get through. So I'm leaving here at 4:20 now – ran home, picked up my son, I went over to [my friend's] and got her dogs out, ran home, picked up a frozen microwave meal for my son from Foodtown, fed him, and off to school . . . I have to leave my house at 5:30 to get [to school] at 5:45, because [the professor] won't let us in to take the test if we're late. So you're under even MORE pressure. He tells us "If you're late, you can't take the test" (Nancy, Interviews I & II).

In addition, because they worked between 37 and 42 hours each week, weekends at home presented a difficult choice for these women, as well. They often struggled to reconcile the demands of completing coursework with their desire to spend time with their families:

> I'm taking two classes now, and it's really killing me to go home and still care for one child. It's like I have no time, or my days I don't go to school, I have to do homework or study for tests, so you're constantly doing something, and then you're like "Wait a minute – I still need to spend time with my son." I don't want to push him off, but then you still need to do your schoolwork, so what do you do? I don't know (Ann, Interview I).

"Not enough time," however, had additional connotations for these women in regard to their status as an *Abbott* college student. First, none of the women expressed a perception of insufficient academic ability to receive a *passing* grade in any of their classes. Adding to the pressures of the 2004 deadline, however, was the fact that *Abbott* teachers have been told they must get a minimum of a B in all their classes to continue in the program (Ann, Interview I; Luisa, Interview II; Nancy, Interview III). Several of the women in the study mentioned that they needed to take as many classes as possible each term to meet the long-term 2004 deadline, but they worried if they would have enough short-term time each week to do the work necessary to receive a B in each class. Three of the women dropped a class because they didn't think they had enough time to devote to their coursework and thus ensure they would receive at least a B, setting them back even further.

Secondly, the state of New Jersey first mandated that teachers in *Abbott* preschools must have a B.A. and P-3 in 2000, but only gave teachers without degrees and certification four years to meet the new qualifications. Thus the issue of "not enough time" influenced all these women's choices regarding which college and degree program to enroll in. For a preschool teacher "starting from scratch," so to speak, attending a teacher preparation program would not only seem to be appropriate, but would appear to be the most efficient way to obtain both a B.A. and P-3, as well. At the time of the study there were six colleges in New Jersey that offered a B.A. in Early Childhood, but none of the campuses were located in the counties where District 1 or 2 are located (Ackerman & Mangin, 2002). This issue was a moot point for Luisa, as she had already attained a significant amount of credits towards a B.A. in Psychology, and viewed continuation of that program as the fastest way to meet the Court's mandate. Had Ann, Ellen, Nancy, or Rosa elected to enroll in the closest teacher preparation program that led to a B.A. and P-3, however, it would have involved a 40 to 70 mile round-trip commute in the evenings after work, and two of these women do not even drive. For these two particular women, although both of the centers that formed the settings for this study are close to New Jersey Transit train stations, the train lines in Districts 1 and 2 do not stop within walking distance of the college that offered this teacher preparation program, and would have involved additional travel time on a bus. The issue of "not enough time," therefore, essentially precluded all five of these women from enrolling in a four-year teacher preparation program that would allow them to graduate with both a B.A. and P-3 certification.

Lastly, because all of the women in the study still had between a full two and three-and-a-half year's worth of classes left to take in order to obtain a B.A. and P-3, they knew that if they continued to take only two classes a term, they would not meet that goal. Between their work and family obligations and lack of release time to attend class, however, taking on additional credits was not feasible. As I explain in the next section, the problems with lack of time were further compounded by the financial "support" these teachers received from the state.

### *What Types of Support Systems are in Place to Assist These Teachers?*

Most of the women in the study felt they were receiving competent advice from their college counselors regarding which classes would "count" for transfer to a four-year program or towards a degree. When I initially asked each teacher about the types of support they received from their fellow staff members at their centers, I envisioned something like weekly study sessions between all the women who were attending school, or informal advice around the coffee urn. In reality, none of the women participated in a study group. I also thought that perhaps the master teacher or someone else in their districts played a mentoring role. Only Luisa had a role model, who also was a personal friend (Interview II). Queries regarding the master teacher's role in supporting their academic efforts brought about responses such as "I can't tell you the last time I saw her" (Ann & Ellen, Interview II).

Fullan (2001) notes that local and community support are key factors in the implementation of educational reform efforts. The interpretation of the idea of "support" for some of these women, however, was often something much more basic than study groups or mentors. When they found their motivation lagging, they relied heavily on each other for emotional support. In addition, Nancy – who had to increase her hours to qualify for the scholarship, but then had trouble paying for afterschool care for her own son – related the way her directors stepped in to help her:

I possibly couldn't qualify for the scholarship money if I couldn't increase my hours, so [one of the center directors] is actually helping me pay for my after-school care . . . [She] offered to pay, so we rotate weeks for payment, which is nice because that's the one good thing about the two of them – they are usually willing to work with you. They weren't willing to work with me when it came to the hours – they just said, "That's it. You don't have a choice." But when I had this problem, they were at least willing to help me solve it . . . We're lucky here, because a lot of directors wouldn't do that (Nancy, Interview I & II).

The costs associated with going to college can dictate both where someone attends school and the number of credits they undertake per semester. The scholarship provided by the state of New Jersey and administered by the New Jersey Professional Development Center for Early Care and Education (NJPDCECE) at Kean University is designed to eliminate one of the biggest situational barriers facing adult learners: the cost of going to college. The scholarship itself offers up to $5,000 each year for coursework, as well as a $50 stipend for each class. Although the women in this study would arguably be hard-pressed to pay for the cost of tuition without the support of the scholarship, the program has proven to have some barriers of its own. The following account is from a conversation with Nancy halfway into the Spring term:

Recently, I had to call the Professional Development Center . . . I received a letter from [school] that I was being sued . . . [They're] suing me and they're suing Ann for this semester's tuition. The lawyer sent us a letter saying it was already in collections [for] Spring 2002 . . . Well, we faxed our scholarship, our registration form, and submitted the bill that [school] gives us when we register to the Professional Development Center . . . and we hadn't heard a thing, so we figured everything was fine . . . Well, then we received the letter from the lawyer, stating that we were going to be taken to court because the payment hasn't been made, and this was last week. So I called Professional Development last Wednesday, and they said, "Oh, here's your application right here." They never even looked at it. They didn't do anything to it. It sat there since the beginning of January (Nancy, Interview II).

In addition to being sued by their school for nonpayment, Ann and Nancy had been dropped from their classes in previous terms because of late scholarship payments (Interview II & III). Rosa – who attended a different college – came to class one evening after eight weeks of attendance, and because of nonpayment by the NJPDCECE, was told she had to leave:

[The Professional Development Center] didn't pay the classes on time. The teachers, one time they didn't let us go in, because they say we didn't pay the class . . . We couldn't stay there – we have to pay it if we want to stay in the class (Rosa, Interview I).

Luisa had never been dropped, but received "a late notice every single semester," and has thus paid her school's late fee out of her own pocket (Interview I). Unraveling the "nightmare," however, involved trips to Kean during the workday, because the NJPDCECE was only open the same hours the women worked in their centers:

You have no idea how many times I've had to leave work to go to Kean . . . for them to sign papers – it is a nightmare. And every time I leave here, I don't get paid. So I'm leaving here, losing money, or using up my personal days that I can save for emergency reasons – I do have two children at home – to go there and deal with them (Luisa, Interview I).

In addition to the potential for miscommunication between the NJPDCECE and the schools, there was also a lot of confusion and embarrassment regarding the proper way to let their colleges know that their tuition bills would be paid by a third party:

After you register for classes you have to go to the cashier part to pay your tuition – so we have to go in there and it's kind of embarrassing, because we have to stand there and say, "Well, we're part of the *Abbott* program and we're on scholarship, so what do we do now?" And they're like, "Well, we'll put you on, but you have to fax these papers away and we need proof." They kind of degrade you, and I'm just thinking that there should be some way that the people on our scholarship – they should already know that, or give us a paper or something, instead of feeling . . . it was a really no-good feeling that you have (Ann, Interview II).

NJPDCECE also provides each scholarship recipient with a $50 stipend per class, which can be used for books, child care, or transportation costs. At first glance, this amount might seem generous. For the women in the study, however, $50 did not begin to cover their incidental expenses, and the stipend itself did not arrive until the term was almost over. Nancy had to borrow money from the center's directors in order to buy her Spring term books, because the term started shortly after both the December holidays and her son's birthday, and she found herself short of funds (Interview III). Ann had an even worse dilemma:

One book is $85 for one class. Do you see? I have bills at home that didn't change – I can't just shell out $85 for a book – I make $10 an hour . . . When I'm going to school, my circumstances at home didn't change. I live paycheck to paycheck. So for me to shell out $85 for a book – it's a lot. I could be taking that $85 and buying food or paying a bill . . . and then that's only one class, do you see? Because you have another class – in Anthropology you need a textbook and a workbook. That's another $90. So that's two classes with books almost $100 each, and they're giving us $50 a class. That doesn't help me (Ann, Interview II).

She continues with what happened when she went to buy her books at the beginning of the Spring term:

Last time we bought books for this semester . . . [we all] drove over there . . . and I said I have two classes I need books for. Well, when he said $85 for one book, I liked to die. I said, "Nancy, forget it." She's like, "Ann, you need the book – what are you going to do?" I said, "Nancy, they're going to turn off my electricity – I need to pay that before I pay $85 for a textbook." I said, "Let me copy yours or something." I can't put out $85 for a book (Ann, Interview II).

The previous term she had the same dilemma:

Last semester I did the same thing, because I was copying somebody's book every chapter – I would copy . . . Nancy bought the book and I was making copies every chapter. I told her that when I get my check, I'll give her half of the difference of the book. I can't just shell out that money for that. And for them to just give us $50 – they know the books are going to be well over that, and they kind of got us, because we need the book . . . so you know what I mean? (Ann, Interview II).

Ellen – who earned $9 an hour at the time of the study – lent her opinion regarding the scholarship and stipend:

And then you have to get the notebook and all that other little supply stuff. And for women that don't have family members to watch their children, they have to pay a babysitter, I'm sure, when they go to school. So, it's definitely not like we're getting a free ride here at all. It sounds good and looks good on paper – saying that they're going to pay for you to go to school – but you're really still shelling out some cash (Ellen, Interview II).

It is clear from these initial findings regarding the scholarship and book stipend that although this type of financial support is crucial, there are perhaps some kinks in the system that need to be addressed if the state hopes these teachers will continue in their studies.

### What are These Women's Reactions to Being Told That Despite Their Experience, They Must Increase Their Credentials or Lose Their Jobs?

Being a college student and getting at least a B in a wide array of liberal arts courses was not easy for the women in this study. Indeed, in the first two years of the program, it was difficult for some teachers to even get started, as the NJPDCECE reported that about one-fourth of those who applied for the *Abbott* scholarships were not eligible because they could not pass the required literacy test (New Jersey Professional Development Center for Early Care and Education, 2000, 2001). Others – like Ann and Nancy – passed the literacy test, but then "hit a snag" when they took one of the placement tests at their community college:

It's very hard to get used to, because I'm 37 years old – I'm not college age . . . We just took our basic skills test for college. We'd been putting it off, and we had to take the test . . . The test was Algebra. First of all, I never took Algebra in high school – I didn't have to – I took a business course and didn't need to take Algebra. Only the people in the college prep took Algebra. How am I ever going to answer these questions if I never learned it? And another thing was the fractions – I learned that but I forgot! So Nancy and I took it together, and we were like, "Wow! You don't realize how long it's been since you've been in High School and you learned how to do this!" You forget. Needless to say, we both failed – both math . . . (Ann, Interview I).

Teachers who did not pass the placements tests administered by their colleges have had to take remedial courses in order to work up to the classes that will actually count towards their degree. Going back to school was even difficult for the three women in this study who had taken some college courses immediately after high school, as they had been out of school for at least ten years. All five women in this study had been working as teachers in ECE centers for at least five years, and Ellen, Luisa, Nancy, and Rosa have been in this role much of their adult lives.

Despite their lack of a college degree, these years of experience have given the women in this study a unique perspective regarding New Jersey's efforts to improve the early care and education of its most disadvantaged students, particularly in regard to the skills and attributes one needs to teach young children. However, because there were insufficient numbers of certified teachers in New Jersey who were willing to work in preschool settings when the *Abbott* program began, in 2001 Acting-Governor DiFrancesco announced The Governor's *Abbott* Preschool Teacher Recruitment Program. This program provided salary incentives between $3,500–$6,000 and a laptop computer to anyone with a B.A. who could qualify for a Certificate of Eligibility under the Alternate Route to Certification guidelines, and would teach in an *Abbott* preschool (New Jersey Department of Education, 2001). As a result, at the time of the study there had been a recent influx of new teachers into the community-based *Abbott* preschools, including one of the settings for this study. These "alternate route" teachers, however, may have been college graduates, but did not always have experience either teaching or working in an early childhood setting. The presence of the alternate route teachers was particularly "belittling" to the women in that center, as not only did these new, inexperienced teachers earn a much higher salary, but their lack of experience spoke volumes regarding the state's preference for a degree over practical knowledge, as well. Perhaps the biggest irony for the women in this study was that as experienced teachers who were no longer considered "good enough" to teach – and had no mentors or role models themselves – they were often called upon to act as role models to the teachers who had no experience, but had a degree:

> I see people coming in who have their degree, but they don't have their P-3 yet, with no experience whatsoever in preschool. And they don't have the slightest idea what to do. I actually have been asked at the beginning of a new teacher's stay, "Oh, can you show them the way? Can you help them? Can you do this with them or that with them? Or maybe you can help them set up their classroom." And it doesn't happen for long – usually I wean myself away, because I have all my own stuff to do. But that has happened a few times ... And then I find myself feeling resentful ... because you go to yourself, "Why am I good enough to help this person, but I'm not good enough to make the same kind of money?" Or good enough to say, "Well, all these years of experience count for something," when it only counts to benefit certain people, or certain reasons (Nancy, Interview IV).

Despite the state's undervaluing of their experience, however, these women have continued to perform their jobs with a sense of dignity and resolution. In the meantime, because there did not seem to be any office or person that was dedicated solely to helping them with their own educational experiences, they attempted to comply with the new rules and straighten out the scholarship and registration snafus on their own. During an interview, however, Ann ruefully commented on the certainty of a particular office when their allotted time to finish school runs out in 2004:

> Oh, but you know what they'll have a person for? They're going to have a person in 2004 to know all of us who didn't make our degree, and they will be right here to take our jobs. They'll have a person for that. Watch. They will. I know it. They will be right here taking my job (Ann, Interview II).

One additional ironic point for three of the women in this study is that the Court mandated that *Abbott* preschool teachers must have a B.A. and P-3 in 2000, but the master teacher in their district spent the previous school year conducting mandatory, non-credit CDA classes for them. Now their CDA was worthless as far as keeping their jobs or increasing their pay, and they "lost" a whole year that could have been spent taking for-credit classes towards their B.A. Although the language is decidedly non-scholarly, it is safe to say that these women felt as if they had been thoroughly "raked over the coals" more than once by the state. As I explain in the next section, this feeling extended to their work in their classrooms, as well.

### *From the Women's Perspectives, How Does Participating in the Overall* Abbott *Effort Influence the Quality of Their Activities in the Preschool Classroom?*

As discussed earlier, the New Jersey Supreme Court mandated the new B.A./P-3 teaching credential for teachers in the state's *Abbott* preschools because of the literature base linking high-quality ECE to teacher training. Given the role of relevancy in adult learning, however, I wondered whether the teachers perceived that the mandate was "working" in terms of reaching the goal of high-quality preschool classrooms. Since all of the teachers in this study faced the very real threat of losing their jobs if they did not meet the 2004 deadline, their focus was on accumulating credits towards a B.A. – in anything – in the most efficient way possible, rather than on specific coursework. As a result, the three teachers who were in AA programs were advised to be Liberal Arts majors, which would hopefully enable them to transfer most of their credits into a four-year teacher preparation program. The two remaining teachers already had some college credits before the *Abbott* mandate, and thus they were advised to continue with their previous degree programs: accounting and psychology. Perhaps because none of their coursework was related to early childhood, then, Ellen's thoughts were similar to the feelings of the other teachers in this study:

> I think in other people's eyes [going to school] legitimizes us more, because that's what they're telling us we have to do, but as far as I'm concerned, I know that going to school is not going to give me more insight into my job than I already have. Especially since a lot of the stuff I'm taking has NOTHING – nothing to do with – a lot of the required classes have nothing to do with this. Like Human Geography – what does that have to do with being in the classroom all day? (Ellen, Interview III).

In addition to feeling as if their coursework had little relevance to their jobs, the teachers in this study felt the mandate had other negative consequences for their daily work. Indeed, Goffin et al. (1997) contend that although public policies are an attempt by the government to solve problems, these same policies can "hinder the ways in which early childhood educators can educate and care for young children" (p. 20). For the women in this study, being a part of the *Abbott* effort meant that they not only had to take classes that seemed to have little relevancy to their teaching, but because they did not receive any release time to take their college classes, their energy levels were severely taxed, as well. At the time of the interviews, Nancy had been sick for over seven months with upper respiratory infections, walking pneumonia, and mononucleosis (Interview IV). Ann spoke of being "exhausted all the time" and without "the patience even with yourself to deal with the problems" one encounters in a three-year old classroom (Interview IV). Ellen was "definitely a lot more tired," and found, much to her chagrin, that she had to smoke more often since she started taking classes (Interview III). The difficulty in juggling "too many things" left Rosa "not even feeling like coming into work anymore" (Interview II). Luisa talked of the "pressure" of being told "you have to go to school or lose your job," and added that spending time taking classes such as "Psychology of Death and Dying" may have counted towards her B.A., but offered little immediate payoff in terms of her daily work in the classroom (Interview II).

Perhaps most importantly for these teachers, participating in the overall *Abbott* effort sometimes meant their current classroom activities bore little resemblance to their pre-*Abbott* classrooms, as all *Abbott* preschools have had to develop or choose a specific curriculum model which should "revolve around children's strengths, experiences, and inclinations" (New Jersey Department of Education, 2002, p. 1.1). At the time of the study, one of the centers used a combination of both a Scholastic curriculum and *Creative Curriculum* (Dodge et al., 2002). Although using both frameworks sometimes entailed "more work" (Rosa, Interview I), the teachers found the curriculums to be helpful, particularly in how *Creative Curriculum* helped set up a "better learning environment" (Luisa, Interview II).

The other setting for this study utilized *Curiosity Corner* (Success for All Foundation, 2001), which is produced by the Success for All Foundation, and is a scripted, weekly-theme based curriculum that dictates exactly which books should be read for each theme and how the teacher should "facilitate." Although the teachers did not use the words "developmentally inappropriate" when discussing this curriculum, compared to their past experiences in the classroom, they intuitively sensed that that something was amiss in its effect on their teaching. They also felt discouraged by the no-input-required, robot-like role assigned to them as a result:

> I just want to do things the way I think I should do them, but we can't . . . You yourself know what's best for your class . . . and you know when they're bored, because this curriculum has us reading the same book four times a week, and they're tired of it. You know when they're not going to grasp something and maybe you could do it your way, which they would get it better. But no, you can't – you have to do it the way they're telling you to do it (Ann, Interview III).

The teachers also felt that using *Curiosity Corner* (Success for All Foundation, 2001) gave them little leeway to follow the children's interests:

> This one time we were doing some kind of theme, and my coach came in from *Curiosity Corner*. Well, here my kids had gotten the tablecloth off the table – I was watching them – but they got the tablecloth and spread it out on the floor, they went and got all the dishes and the food, spread it all on the floor, and they ran over to writing and were writing invitations to a picnic, sat down, had a picnic. They just were playing so nicely. I'm just observing what was going on and didn't say anything to them. Well, [the *Curiosity Corner* curriculum coach] came in, she observed what was going on in the middle of it, and then went back [to the directors] and said, "Well, Ann's kids are in there having a picnic, and that wasn't part of the theme" (Ann, Interview III).

Nancy talked about her fears of "being caught" not following the theme:

> I used to function well with spur of the moment kinds of things. If I saw one of them [and] they were dancing in a certain way, I knew it was okay to turn on music that fit in and we just had fun for fifteen or twenty minutes . . . I've been told you can add to the curriculum, but you can't add to it in a way that you can be that spontaneous, so it makes a difference in someone that's so used to being able to do that . . . We can still do that, but it's not the same. You're afraid, or you're not sure. Or you're thinking, "Oh, God, do I have to stop and go make a phone call and make sure this is okay?" Well, you've lost the moment at that point (Nancy, Interview III).

Admittedly, although each of the women in this study had her CDA, because none of them were in teacher preparation programs, none of them had taken more than a few early childhood classes at the time of the study, either. Based on their experiences just with their coursework so far – and in some cases, their preschool classroom curriculum, as well – however, all were skeptical that merely taking their eventual four or five P-3 certification classes would positively influence the quality of their teaching activities in the preschool classroom. In the meantime, they also continued to feel very much "stuck" in "no-win" situation.

# IMPLICATIONS

The intent of this study was to both discover five ECE teachers' experiences in working towards their B.A. and P-3, and inform New Jersey's policy regarding this effort. Although a study focusing on only five women from two different districts leaves much left to learn about the experiences of the many other teachers in New Jersey's community-based *Abbott* preschools, these women's narratives shed light on some important issues, nonetheless. Based on the preceding findings and discussion, this section addresses both the practical and quality-related implications that may need to be considered when evaluating the overall success of the policy.

### *Administrative Implications*

As previously stated, the state's goal of having well-educated teachers in its *Abbott* preschool classrooms – and offering to pay for that education – is laudable. Given the financial constraints facing most ECE teachers, however, having a scholarship program that "sounds" better than it actually operates has the potential to undermine the entire program. To be dropped from one's classes because of payment miscommunication, or sent letters saying that a school is suing for nonpayment were clearly unneeded aggravations for these women. They also expressed exasperation with not getting any release time to take care of their "school-related business," nor having access to anyone who might help them when they experienced school-related difficulties. The scholarship problems were so discouraging to the women in this study that they often felt like giving up.

   In addition, the provision of $50 per class for the incidental expenses incurred while enrolled in a degree program is arguably better than receiving nothing. Given that the goal of the mandate is well-educated teachers, however, participants should not have to choose between purchasing textbooks and paying their utility bill. At the very least, this study suggests that the state needs to rethink its policy regarding the $50 per class stipend, and more importantly, revisit the administration of the entire New Jersey Early Childhood Scholarship Program.

### *Implications for Staffing*

This study also sheds light on staffing issues related to the *Abbott* mandate. The 2004 deadline looms large for these women – they continually expressed anxiety about what will happen when the deadline for finishing their degrees arrives. In addition, because they were not given any release time from their jobs in order to attend classes, they also expressed frustration at being asked to work full-time and complete as much as four year's worth of schooling on a part-time basis. Of the five teachers in this study, as of March, 2003, only Luisa anticipated receiving her B.A. in 2004, but in December – rather than September – and then would still need to obtain her P-3 certification through an alternate route program. Rosa knew she would still be working towards her B.A. in 2004, despite having already completed coursework for her AA degree. The remaining three teachers – Ann, Ellen, and Nancy – will still be working on their AA degrees when the deadline arrives, but hoped the state would give them an extension to finish their coursework, and at the same time not ask them to step down as teachers. Nancy, however, said the impending deadline – without any talk of a possible extension – was seriously affecting her and other teachers' motivation to remain in school:

> We're not going to make it anyway, so why should we stress ourselves and our families [by going to school]? If [the state] gave us an extension, we might push harder to meet the goal, but why continue to kill ourselves if we're only going to lose our classrooms anyway? (Personal conversation, March 19, 2003).

It will be interesting to see not only if New Jersey's Department of Education will ask the Court to extend or revise that deadline because of teachers like Ann, Ellen, Luisa, Nancy, and Rosa, but if the Court will grant an extension, as well. If they are unable to remain in their jobs as teachers, these centers are going to lose experienced staff who are knowledgeable about the communities they serve and truly care about the young children in their care. This is especially tragic for the children and families who have come to depend on their bilingual ECE teachers, who – like Rosa and Luisa – can serve as "model[s] of acculturation" and facilitate Spanish-speaking children's "entrance into an American world" (Eggers-Piérola, 2002).

There is an additional staffing implication from this study, however. The new *Abbott* licensure requirement may paradoxically decrease the number of qualified teachers in community-based centers by decimating the ranks of experienced ECE teachers who leave for other teaching or administrative jobs once they obtain their degrees. Even if granted an extension, none of the women in this study expected to remain in their centers once they obtain their degrees. In a large scale study of New Jersey's *Abbott* preschool teachers, Ryan and Ackerman (2004) found that 33% of teachers who are currently enrolled in for-credit coursework – the majority of whom work in community-based centers – do not anticipate remaining in their current jobs once they obtain their degrees or certification, either. When asked why they did not plan on remaining after completing their degrees, the top reason cited in their study was the higher pay and benefits available to public school teachers. Nancy echoed this sentiment:

> Once I do have my bachelor's, I'm not going to continue to stay here, for just the hassle and the aggravation. And the same feeling I feel now – I don't see that changing. That's not changing at all. Why am I going to want to spend all that time in school and get my education just to work in a preschool and not have the same benefits as public school teachers? That would be stupidity. I'm sorry . . . As I'm fighting and struggling so hard for that, I want to see something in return later on (Nancy, who has twelve years of experience, Interview IV).

This is not a new problem for the preschools that serve New Jersey's disadvantaged children. In the Court's 2002 *Abbott* ruling (*Abbott v. Burke*, 2002), the justices commented on reports that Head Start programs in the *Abbott* districts had lost more than 125 certified teachers due to the higher compensation packages offered by school districts. District preschool programs offer a six-hour, 180-day work year, plus paid holidays, higher salaries, and greater benefits. Programs in community-based preschools run all-day and year-round, and if centers are closed for a holiday, the women are often not paid.

If this trend continues, New Jersey may very well find itself without qualified preschool teachers in its community-based *Abbott* preschools once again. Given the difficulties New Jersey has already faced in recruiting qualified preschool teachers, the state will need to consider the ramifications that losing these teachers – both before and after they increase their credentials – will have on the state's ability to fulfill the Court's mandate. This study also suggests, however, that although the use of a mandate may effectively serve as the "stick" to force teachers to obtain higher qualifications, the offering of a "carrot" of truly comparable pay and benefits in order to alleviate teacher recruitment and retention problems is probably necessary.

### Implications for ECE Quality

This study also has several implications regarding the quality of ECE that is being offered to the state's most disadvantaged three- and four-year olds. First, the problem of teacher retention has another important dimension, as although staff with a B.A. degree and P-3 certification may be an essential part of a high-quality ECE setting, so is a stable, low-turnover workforce (Howes & Hamilton, 1993; Whitebook et al., 1990; Whitebook et al., 1998). Secondly, quality in ECE settings is also affected by the interactions between children and teachers, and Howes and Smith (1995) found that children's positive social interactions with teachers play a key role in their cognitive activity. Given the educational starting points of the teachers in this study, the limited time allowed to complete their degrees, and the absence of release time to attend class, one wonders how the resulting lack of energy and increased pressure described by the teachers affects their daily interactions in the classroom. Although the teachers' sense of being tired and stressed is understandable, if it results in lower-quality interactions with the children, the *Abbott* mandate is "backfiring" in a sense. This study suggests the need to keep the overall goal of quality ECE in mind, and in so doing, consider what supports teachers might need in order to be both successful educators and students.

In addition to these considerations, the study presents some implications in regard to the whole B.A./P-3 effort and its effect on ECE quality. On the one hand, the Court's mandate of a B.A. and P-3 mirrors the educational pre-service background advocated by NAEYC (2001) and the *Eager To Learn* Committee on Early Childhood Pedagogy (Bowman et al., 2001). The Committee's recommendations also emphasized, however, that the professional development of early childhood teachers should include high-quality, specialized training that provides a strong knowledge base regarding appropriate teaching practices and child development. In addition, early childhood teachers need access to regular, ongoing feedback and experience-specific (rather than "one-size-fits-all") training from leaders and specialists in their field.

As previously discussed, all the teachers in this study were enrolled in coursework that would lead to a B.A. Because of the 2004 deadline, however, their enrollment choices were based on convenience and expediency, rather than early childhood teacher preparation. Perhaps not surprisingly, they continually expressed frustration at being asked to spend so much time and effort on coursework that seemed to have no relevance to their daily work in the classroom. Given the link between specialized training and high-quality ECE, then, one wonders if the type of process quality that is so closely tied to teacher training will actually be realized in all of the *Abbott* preschool classrooms, particularly if the state continues to promote and value attainment of a B.A. over early childhood training and/or experience. Luisa, who has six years of experience, is working towards a B.A. in Psychology, and then will work as an Alternate Route teacher herself, echoed the thoughts of all the women in the study when she commented on the specific P-3 coursework by saying, "I can't imagine what five courses in education could possibly teach me that I don't already know" (Interview II). Perhaps Luisa's attitude is understandable, given her lack of exposure to early childhood courses. Considering all five of these teachers' educational backgrounds and current college majors, however, perhaps the more appropriate question is whether four or five courses in education are *sufficient* for providing teachers with the "specific foundational knowledge of the development of children's social and affective behavior, thinking, and language" that is necessary for a thorough grounding in "what is optimal pedagogically for children's learning and development" (Bowman et al., 2001, pp. 11, 10).

None of the teachers in this study expressed an awareness of *Eager to Learn* (Bowman et al., 2001) or its recommendations. This study suggests, however, that if teachers were given the opportunity to focus on high-quality teacher preparation coursework – rather than a deadline – they might not only come to understand why expanding their knowledge base is important, but actually begin to modify their pedagogical approaches in order to improve process quality in their classrooms, as well. In addition, if this coursework was linked to activities in their classrooms and these teachers also had access to feedback from early childhood specialists, districts might not have to rely on didactic curriculums that emphasize "sticking to the script," rather than children's needs and interests. If the overall motivation for increasing teachers' credentials is higher-quality ECE classrooms, what seems to be needed is a "backward mapping" approach (Elmore, 1980) so that preschool teachers might have access to the types of coursework, mentoring, and support that will positively impact their teaching beliefs and practices.

The women in this study have articulate and intelligent ideas about the kinds of education and professional development that would best help their daily work, as well as insights into the types of policies that could improve actual practice. If a state like New Jersey really wants to improve the quality of early care and education for its most disadvantaged children, perhaps rather than continuing to place these teachers between a rock and hard place, it is time for all of us to listen to what they have to say.

## ACKNOWLEDGMENTS

The author wishes to gratefully acknowledge and thank the teachers who participated in this study. Without their willingness to be open and honest about their experiences in attempting to meet the *Abbott* mandate, this study would not have been possible. Thanks are also extended to Maureen Taylor, Stuart Reifel, and the anonymous reviewers of this chapter. Their thoughtful comments and suggestions on earlier drafts of the manuscript are greatly appreciated. Finally, a special thank you is extended to Sharon Ryan for her support and encouragement, and especially for her commitment to the early childhood field.

## REFERENCES

*Abbott v. Burke*, 575 N.J. 359 (1990).
*Abbott v. Burke*, 153 N.J. 480 (1998).
*Abbott v. Burke*, 163 N.J. 95 (2000).
*Abbott v. Burke*, 170 N.J. 537 (2002).
Abbott-Shim, M., Lambert, R., & McCarty, F. (2000). Structural model of Head Start classroom quality. *Early Childhood Research Quarterly, 15*, 115–134.

Ackerman, D. J. (2004). States' efforts in improving the qualifications of early care and education teachers. *Educational Policy, 18*, 311–337.

Ackerman, D. J., & Mangin, M. (2002). *Examining the feasibility of extending the* Abbott *preschool teachers' educational requirements to all early care and education teaching staff in New Jersey's* Abbott *and ECPA districts.* Unpublished manuscript.

Arnett, J. (1989). Caregivers in day-care centers: Does training matter? *Journal of Applied Developmental Psychology, 10*, 541–552.

Aslanian, C. B., & Brickell, H. M. (1980). *Americans in transition: Life changes as reasons for adult learning.* New York: College Entrance Examination Board.

Ayers, W. (1992). Disturbances from the field: Recovering the voice of the early childhood teacher. In: S. A. Kessler & B. B. Swadener (Eds), *Reconceptualizing the Early Childhood Curriculum: Beginning the Dialogue* (pp. 256–266). New York: Teachers College Press.

Azer, S., LeMoine, S., Morgan, G., Clifford, R., & Crawford, G. M. (2002). Regulation of child care. *Early Childhood Research & Policy Briefs, 2*(1), 1–6. Available at http://www.fpg. unc.edu/~ncedl/PDFs/RegBrief.pdf.

Barnett, W. S. (1995). Long-term effects of early childhood programs on cognitive and school outcomes. *The Future of Children, 5*(3), 25–50.

Barnett, W. S. (1998). Long-term effects on cognitive development and school success. In: W. S. Barnett & S. S. Boocock (Eds), *Early Care and Education for Children in Poverty* (pp. 11–44). Albany: State University of New York Press.

Barnett, W. S. (2002). Early childhood education. In: A. Molnar (Ed.), *School Reform Proposals: The Research Evidence* (pp. 1–26). Greenwich, CT: Information Age Publishing.

Barnett, W. S., Tarr, J. E., Lamy, C. E., & Frede, E. C. (2001). *Fragile lives, shattered dreams: A report on implementation of preschool education in New Jersey's* Abbott *districts.* New Brunswick, NJ: Center for Early Education Research.

Bowman, B. T., Donovan, M. S., & Burns, M. S. (Eds) (2001). *Eager to learn: Educating our preschoolers.* Washington, DC: National Academy Press.

Burbank, J. R. (1994). *Moving beyond the market: A proposal for education linked state subsidies for child care workers' wages* [Website]. Seattle: Economic Opportunity Institute. Retrieved November 17, 2001, from http://www.econop.org/ECE-1994Proposal-print.htm.

Burchinal, M. R., Cryer, D., Clifford, R. M., & Howes, C. (2002). Careqiver training and classroom quality in child care centers. *Applied Developmental Science, 6*, 2–11.

Bureau of Labor Statistics (1999). *Labor force participation of fathers and mothers varies with children's ages* [Website]. Retrieved November 19, 2001, from http://www.bls.gov/ opub/ted/1999/Jun/wk1/art03.htm.

Campbell, F. A., & Ramey, C. T. (1994). Effects of early intervention on intellectual and academic achievement: A follow-up study of children from low-income families. *Child Development, 65*, 684–698.

Carp, A., Peterson, R., & Roelfs, P. (1974). Adult learning interests and experiences. In: K. P. Cross, J. R. Valley & Associates (Eds), *Planning Non-Traditional Programs: An Analysis of the Issues for Postsecondary Education* (pp. 11–52). San Francisco: Jossey-Bass.

Cassidy, D. J., Buell, M. J., Pugh-Hoese, S., & Russell, S. (1995). The effect of education on child care teachers' beliefs and classroom quality: Year one evaluation of the TEACH Early Childhood Associate Degree Scholarship Program. *Early Childhood Research Quarterly, 10*, 171–183.

Cassidy, D. J., Hicks, S. A., Hall, A. H., Farran, D. C., & Gray, J. (1998). The North Carolina Child Care Corps: The role of National Service in child care. *Early Childhood Research Quarterly, 13*, 589–602.

Clark, C. M. (1992). Teachers as designers in self-directed professional development. In: A. Hargreaves & M. G. Fullan (Eds), *Understanding Teacher Development* (pp. 75–84). New York: Teachers College Press.

Cohen, M. Z., & Omery, A. (1994). Schools of phenomenology: Implications for research. In: J. Morse (Ed.), *Critical Issues in Qualitative Research Methods* (pp. 136–156). Thousand Oaks, CA: Sage.

Cost, Quality and Child Outcomes Study Team (1995). *Cost, quality and child outcomes in child care centers, technical report.* Denver: University of Colorado at Denver.

Creswell, J. W. (1998). *Qualitative inquiry and research design: Choosing among five traditions.* Thousand Oaks, CA: Sage.

Creswell, J. W., & Miller, D. L. (2000). Determining validity in qualitative inquiry. *Theory into Practice, 39*, 124–130.

Cross, K. P. (1981). *Adults as learners.* San Francisco: Jossey-Bass.

Cryer, D. (1999). Defining and assessing early childhood program quality. *Annals of the American Academy of Political and Social Sciences, 563*, 39–55.

Cryer, D., Tietze, W., Burchinal, M., Leal, T., & Palacios, J. (1999). Predicting process quality from structural quality in preschool programs: A cross-country comparison. *Early Childhood Research Quarterly, 14*, 339–361.

Darkenwald, G. G., & Merriam, S. B. (1982). *Adult education: Foundations of practice.* New York: Harper & Row.

Denzin, N. (1989). *The research act: A theoretical introduction to sociological methods.* Englewood Cliffs, NJ: Prentice-Hall.

Denzin, N. (2001). *Interpretive interactionism.* Thousand Oaks, CA: Sage.

Division of Youth and Family Services (DYFS), Department of Human Services, State of New Jersey (1998). *Manual of requirements for child care centers.* Trenton, NJ: Bureau of Licensing.

Dodge, D. T., Colker, L., & Heroman, C. (2002). *The creative curriculum for preschool* (4th ed.). Washington, DC: Teaching Strategies.

Dwyer, M. C., Chait, R., & McKee, P. (2000). *Building strong foundations for early learning: Guide to high-quality early childhood education programs.* Washington, DC: U.S. Department of Education, Planning and Evaluation Service. Available at http://www.ed.gov/offices/OUS/PES/early_learning/Foundations.doc.

Early, D. M., & Winton, P. J. (2001). Preparing the workforce: Early childhood teacher preparation at 2- and 4-year institutions of higher education. *Early Childhood Research Quarterly, 16*, 285–306.

Education Law Center (2001). *Comparison of* Abbott *preschool requirements:* Abbott*, DHS childcare, and deficiencies of DHS regulations* [Website]. Retrieved March 8, 2002, from http://www.edlawcenter.org/pubic_html/preschool-long.htm.

Education Law Center (2003). *History of Abbott: Progress toward equal educational opportunity for urban students in New Jersey* [Website]. Retrieved March 24, 2003, from http://www.edlawcenter.org/ELCPublic/AbbottvBurke/AbbottHistory.htm.

Eggers-Piérola, C. (2002). *Connections and commitments: A Latino-based framework for early childhood educators.* Newton, MA: Education Development Center.

Elmore, R. (1980). Backward mapping: Implementation research and policy decisions. *Political Science Quarterly, 94*, 601–616.

Essa, E. L., & Burnham, M. M. (2001). Child care quality: A model for examining relevant variables. In: S. Reifel & M. H. Brown (Eds), *Advances in Early Education and Day Care: Early Education and Care, and Reconceptualizing Play* (Vol. 11, pp. 59–113). Amsterdam: JAI Press.

Fleet, A., & Patterson, C. (2001). Professional growth reconceptualized: Early childhood staff search for meaning. *Early Childhood Research & Practice*, *3*(2), online journal available at http://ecrp.uiuc.edu/v3n2/fleet.html.

Fullan, M. G. (1993). *Change forces: Probing the depths of educational reform*. London: Falmer Press.

Fullan, M. (2001). *The new meaning of educational change* (3rd ed.). New York: Teachers College Press.

Gallagher, J., & Clifford, R. (2000). The missing support infrastructure in early childhood. *Early Childhood Research & Practice*, *2*(1), online journal available at http://ecrp.uiuc.edu.v2n1/gallagher.html.

Genishi, C., Ryan, S., Ochsner, M., & Yarnall, M. M. (2001). Teaching in early childhood education: Understanding practices through research and theory. In: V. Richardson (Ed.), *Handbook of Research on Teaching* (4th ed., pp. 1175–1210). Washington, DC: American Educational Research Association.

Giorgi, A. (1985). Sketch of a psychological phenomenological method. In: A. Giorgi (Ed.), *Phenomenology and Psychological Research* (pp. 8–22). Pittsburgh: Duquesne University Press.

Giorgi, A. (1997). The theory, practice, and evaluation of the phenomenological method as a qualitative research procedure. *Journal of Phenomenological Psychology*, *28*, 235–261.

Glesne, C., & Peshkin, A. (1992). *Becoming qualitative researchers: An introduction*. White Plains, NY: Longman.

Goffin, S. G., Wilson, C., Hill, J., & McAninch, S. (1997). Policies of the early childhood field and its public: Seeking to support young children and their families. In: J. P. Isenberg & M. R. Jalongo (Eds), *Major Trends and Issues in Early Childhood Education: Challenges, Controversies, and Insights* (pp. 13–28). New York: Teachers College Press.

Greene, M. (1988). *The dialectic of freedom*. New York: Teachers College Press.

Helburn, S. W., & Howes, C. (1996). Child care cost and quality. *The Future of Children*, *6*(2), 62–82.

Henderson, L. W., Basile, K. C., & Henry, G. T. (1999). *Prekindergarten longitudinal study, 1997–1998 school year: Annual report*. Atlanta: Georgia State University Applied Research Center School of Policy Studies. Available at http://www.arc.gsu.edu/prek/report/prek9798Long.pdf.

Holloway, S. D., Kagan, S. L., Fuller, B., Tsou, L., & Carroll, J. (2001). Assessing child-care quality with a telephone interview. *Early Childhood Research Quarterly*, *16*, 165–189.

Honig, A. S., & Hirallal, A. (1998). Which counts more for excellence in childcare staff: Years in service, education level or ECE coursework? Paper presented at the Annual Quality Infant/Toddler Caregiving Workshop, June 15–19, Syracuse, NY.

Horm-Wingerd, D., Caruso, D. A., Gomes-Atwood, S., & Golas, J. (1997). Head Start Teaching Center: Evaluation of a new approach to Head Start staff development. *Early Childhood Research Quarterly*, *12*, 407–424.

Horn, L. J., & Carroll, C. D. (1996). *Nontraditional undergraduates: Trends in enrollment from 1986 to 1992 and persistence in attainment among 1989–90 beginning postsecondary students*. Washington, DC: National Center for Education Statistics, U.S. Department of Education, Office of Educational Research and Improvement. Available at http://www.nces.ed.gov/pubs/97578.pdf.

Howes, C. (1997). Children's experiences in center-based child care as a function of teacher background and adult:child ratio. *Merrill-Palmer Quarterly*, *43*, 404–425.

Howes, C., & Brown, J. (2000). Improving child care quality: A guide for Proposition 10 commissions. In: N. Halfon, E. Shulman, M. Shannon & M. Hochstein (Eds), *Building Community Systems for Young Children* (pp. 1–24). Los Angeles: UCLA Center for Healthier Children, Families and Communities.

Howes, C., & Hamilton, C. E. (1993). The changing experience of child care: Changes in teachers and in teacher-child relationships and children's social competence with peers. *Early Childhood Research Quarterly, 8,* 15–32.

Howes, C., & Smith, E. W. (1995). Relations among child care quality, teacher behavior, children's play activities, emotional security, and cognitive activity in child care. *Early Childhood Research Quarterly, 10,* 381–404.

Husserl, E. (1958/1913). *Ideas: General introduction to pure phenomenology* (W. R. B. Gibson, Trans.). London: George Allen & Unwin.

Husserl, E. (1989). *Ideas pertaining to a pure phenomenology and to a phenomenological philosophy* (R. Rojcewicz & A. Schuwer, Trans.). Dordrecht, The Netherlands: Kluwer.

Husserl, E. (1999). *The idea of phenomenology: A translation of "Die Idee der Phanomenologie" Husserliana II* (L. Hardy, Trans.). Dordrecht, The Netherlands: Kluwer.

Jones, D. J., & Watson, B. C. (1990). "High risk" students in higher education: Future trends. In: *ERIC Digest, ED325033.* Washington, DC: ERIC Clearinghouse on Higher Education.

Kagan, S. L., & Wechsler, S. (1999). Changing realities – Changing research. In: S. Reifel (Ed.), *Advances in Early Education and Day Care: Foundations, Adult Dynamics, Teacher Education and Play* (Vol. 10, pp. 41–67). Stamford, CT: JAI Press.

Klayman, D., McKey, R. H., & Resnick, G. (2001). *Evaluation of early childhood programming in the 30* Abbott *school districts: Phase I report.* Rockville, MD: Westat.

Knowles, M. S., & Associates (1984). *Andragogy in action.* San Francisco: Jossey-Bass.

Knox, A. B. (1977). *Adult development and learning.* San Francisco: Jossey-Bass.

Laverty, K., Burton, A., Whitebook, M., & Bellm, D. (2001). *Current data on child care salaries and benefits in the United States: March 2001.* Washington, DC: Center for the Child Care Workforce.

Laverty, K., Siepak, K., Burton, A., Whitebook, M., & Bellm, D. (2002). *Current data on child care salaries and benefits in the United States: March 2002.* Washington, DC: Center for the Child Care Workforce.

Leithwood, K., Jantzi, D., & Steinbach, R. (1999). *Changing leadership for changing times.* Buckingham, UK: Open University Press.

McMullen, M. B., & Alat, K. (2002). Education matters in the nurturing of the beliefs of preschool caregivers and teachers. *Early Childhood Research & Practice, 4*(2), online journal available at http://ecrp.uiuc.edu/v4n2/mcmullen.html.

Merleau-Ponty, M. (1970). *Phenomenology of perception.* New York: Humanities Press.

Miles, M. B., & Huberman, A. M. (1984). Drawing valid meaning from qualitative data: Toward a shared craft. *Educational Researcher, 13*(5), 20–30.

Miles, M. B., & Huberman, A. M. (1994). *Qualitative data analysis.* Thousand Oaks, CA: Sage.

Montilla, M. D., Twombly, E. C., & De Vita, C. J. (2001). *Models for increasing child care worker compensation.* Washington, DC: Urban Institute. Available at http://www.urban.org/periodcl/cnp/cnp_8.PDF.

Morrissette, P. J. (1999). Phenomenological data analysis: A proposed model for counsellors. *Guidance & Counseling, 15,* 2–7.

Moustakas, C. (1994). *Phenomenological research methods.* Thousand Oaks, CA: Sage.

National Association for the Education of Young Children (2001). *NAEYC standards for early childhood professional preparation: Baccalaureate or initial licensure level.* Washington, DC: NAEYC.

National Center for Early Development & Learning (NCEDL) (1997). Quality in child care centers. *Early Childhood Research & Policy Briefs, 1*(1).

National Commission on Teaching & America's Future (1996). *What matters most: Teaching for America's future.* New York: Author. Available at http://www.tc.columbia.edu/~teachcomm/WhatMattersMost.pdf.

Nelson, J. A. (2001). *Why are early care and education wages so low?* New York: Foundation for Child Development. Available at http://ffcd.org/nelson/pdf.

New Jersey Department of Education, Office of Innovative Programs and Practices (2001). *Governor's Abbott district preschool teacher recruitment program* [Website]. Trenton: Author. Retrieved October 4, 2001, from http://www.state.nj.us/njded/clear/Abbott/.

New Jersey Department of Education (2002). *Early childhood education curriculum framework (PTM#1502–98).* Trenton: New Jersey Department of Education. Retrieved October 22, 2002, from http://www.state.nj.us/njded/ece/framework/doc/doc.pdf.

New Jersey Professional Development Center for Early Care and Education (2000). *A position statement on articulation: Background, barriers, and objectives.* Union, NJ: Articulation Working Committee, Kean University.

New Jersey Professional Development Center for Early Care and Education (2001). *Early childhood teacher preparation symposium, February 9, 2001, summary report.* Union, NJ: Office of Professional Standards and Articulation, Kean University.

Padron, E. J. (1992). The challenge of first-generation college students: A Miami-Dade perspective. In: L. S. Zwerling & H. B. London (Eds), *First Generation Students: Confronting the Cultural Issues* (Vol. 80, pp. 71–80). San Francisco: Jossey-Bass.

Patton, M. Q. (1990). *Qualitative evaluation and research methods.* Newbury Park, CA: Sage.

Patton, M. Q. (2002). *Qualitative research & evaluation methods.* Thousand Oaks, CA: Sage.

Peisner-Feinberg, E. S., Burchinal, M. R., Clifford, R. M., Culkin, M. L., Howes, C., Kagan, S. L., Yazejian, J., Byler, P., Rustici, J., & Zelazo, J. (1999). *The children of the cost, quality, and outcomes study go to school: Executive summary.* Chapel Hill: University of North Carolina at Chapel Hill, Frank Porter Graham Child Development Center. Available at http://www.fpg.unc.edu/ncedl/PDFs/CQO-es.pdf.

Phillips, D., Howes, C., & Whitebook, M. (1991). Child care as an adult work environment. *Journal of Social Issues, 47*(2), 49–70.

Phillips, D., Mekos, D., Scarr, S., McCartney, K., & Abbott-Shim, M. (2000). Within and beyond the classroom door: Assessing quality in child care centers. *Early Childhood Research Quarterly, 15,* 475–496.

Pinar, W. F., Reynolds, W. M., Slattery, P., & Taubman, P. M. (1996). *Understanding curriculum: An introduction to the study of historical and contemporary curriculum discourses.* New York: Peter Lang Publishing.

Polkinghorne, D. E. (1989). Phenomenological research methods. In: R. S. Valle & S. Halling (Eds), *Existential-Phenomenological Perspectives in Psychology: Exploring the Breadth of Human Experience* (pp. 41–60). New York: Plenum Press.

Ramey, C. T., Campbell, F. A., Burchinal, M. R., Skinner, M. L., Gardner, D. M., & Ramey, S. L. (2000). Persistent effects of early childhood education on high-risk children and their mothers. *Applied Developmental Science, 4,* 2–14.

Reynolds, A. J., Temple, J. A., Robertson, D. L., & Mann, E. A. (2001). Long-term effects of an early childhood intervention on educational achievement and juvenile arrest. *Journal of the American Medical Association, 285,* 2339–2346.

Rhode Island Department of Children, Youth and Families (1993). *Child day care center regulations for licensure.* Providence, RI: Author. Available at http://www.dcyf.state.ri.us/docs/center_regs.pdf.

Richardson, R. C., Jr., & Skinner, E. F. (1992). Helping first-generation minority students achieve degrees. In: L. S. Zwerling & H. B. London (Eds), *First Generation Students: Confronting the Cultural Issues* (Vol. 80, pp. 29–44). San Francisco: Jossey-Bass.

Ryan, S., & Ackerman, D. J. (2004). Getting qualified: A report on the effects of preschool teachers in New Jersey; Abbott districts to improve their qualifications. New Brunswick, NJ: National Institute for Early Education Research.

Saluja, G., Early, D. M., & Clifford, R. M. (2002). Demographic characteristics of early childhood teachers and structural elements of early care and education in the United States. *Early Childhood Research & Practice, 4*(1), online journal available at http://ecrp.uiuc.edu/v4n1/saluja.html.

Schweinhart, L. J., & Weikart, D. P. (1997). The High/Scope preschool curriculum comparison study through age 23. *Early Childhood Research Quarterly, 12*, 117–143.

Shonkoff, J. P., & Phillips, D. A. (Eds) (2000). *From neurons to neighborhoods: The science of early childhood development*. Washington, DC: National Academy Press.

Sikes, P. J. (1992). Imposed change and the experienced teacher. In: M. Fullan & A. Hargreaves (Eds), *Teacher Development and Educational Change* (pp. 36–55). London: Falmer Press.

Success for All Foundation (2001). *Curiosity Corner teacher's manual*. Baltimore: Author.

Theilheimer, R. (1999). Helping things come out much better: Understanding the student's perspective in an early childhood vocational education program. In: S. Reifel (Ed.), *Advances in Early Education and Day Care: Foundations, Adult Dynamics, Teacher Education and Play* (Vol. 10, pp. 71–113). Stamford, CT: JAI Press.

Vecchiotti, S. (2001). *Career development and universal prekindergarten: What now? What next?* New York: Foundation for Child Development. Available at http://www.ffcd.org/vecchiotti.pdf.

White, J. (2001). Adult women in community colleges. *ERIC Digest, EDO-JC-01–01*. Available at http://www.gseis.ucla.edu/ERIC/digests/dig0101.html.

Whitebook, M. (1997). Who's missing at the table? Leadership opportunities and barriers for teachers and providers. In: S. Kagan & B. T. Bowman (Eds), *Rethinking Leadership in Early Childhood and Education*. Washington, DC: National Association for the Education of Young Children. Available at http://www.ccw.org/tpp/pubs/whosmissing.pdf.

Whitebook, M., Howes, C., & Phillips, D. (1990). *Who cares? Child care teachers and the quality of care in America: Final report, National child care staffing study*. Washington, DC: Center for the Child Care Workforce.

Whitebook, M., Howes, C., & Phillips, D. (1998). *Worthy work, unlivable wages: The national child care staffing study, 1988–1997*. Washington, DC: Center for the Child Care Workforce.

Whitebook, M., & Phillips, D. (1999). *Child care employment: Implications for women's self sufficiency and for child development*. New York: Foundation for Child Development. Available at http://www.ffcd.org/ourwork.htm.

Whitebook, M., Sakai, L., Gerber, E., & Howes, C. (2001). *Then & now: Changes in child care staffing, 1994–2000*. Washington, DC: Center for the Child Care Workforce.

Whitebook, M., Sakai, L., & Howes, C. (1997). *NAEYC accreditation as a strategy for improving child care quality*. Washington, DC: National Center for the Early Childhood Workforce.

Wolcott, H. F. (1994). *Transforming qualitative data: Description, analysis and interpretation*. Thousand Oaks, CA: Sage.

# APPENDIX A

## *Data Accounting Sheet*

| | Topic | Ann | Ellen | Luisa | Nancy | Rosa |
|---|---|---|---|---|---|---|
| Coping | Job schedule | | | | | |
| | Number, ages of children at home | | | | | |
| | Transportation to class | | | | | |
| | Completing classwork | | | | | |
| Reactions to being told they must obtain a B.A. & P-3 or lose their jobs | Feelings reg. being told must get degree/lose job | | | | | |
| | Experience in ECE setting | | | | | |
| | Motivation for choosing employment | | | | | |
| | Previous academic exp., perceptions of ability | | | | | |
| | Present percept. of ability, feelings of belonging in college | | | | | |
| | Future career plans | | | | | |
| Support | Experiences with scholarships and book stipends | | | | | |
| | Registering for classes | | | | | |
| | College advisement | | | | | |
| | Advice, support from fellow staff and administrators | | | | | |
| | Mentor/role model? | | | | | |
| How does being part of this effort influence the quality of their activities in the preschool classroom? | Teaching in *Abbott* classroom | | | | | |
| | Impact on all of the above on their work as a teacher | | | | | |
| | Connections between college/ECE classroom | | | | | |

# APPENDIX B

*Coding Scheme for Study*

The following list details the *initial deductive codes* (indicated by •) that were derived from the six "bins" that are part of each participant's experience in working full-time in an *Abbott* community-based center and working towards her B.A., as well as the *subcodes* (under each initial code) that spoke to the overall experience category:

• Reconciling their teaching experience with the new *Abbott* mandate
  Motivation for employment in     Salary disparities – degree vs. non-degree
    field
  Years of experience              Insult of alternate route teachers
  Dealing with mandate on an
    emotional/psychological level

• Guidance/support from preschool administration, fellow staff members, mentors/advisors, and master teacher
  Fellow staff          Financial support
  Family workers        Emotional support
  Directors
  Master Teacher
  Role models

• Navigating various college logistics (scholarships from New Jersey Professional Development Center, registering, seeking advice, traveling to and attending class, etc.)
  Usefulness of advise from
    college counselors
  Choosing classes
  Registering for classes
  NJPDCECE scholarships          Problems with scholarships
  Cost of books vs. book stipends
  Transportation to class

• Family obligations
  After school care
  Evening care
  Weekends

Getting child to school or other
    activities
Being a mom                              Balancing mom vs. student vs. teacher

- Working in an *Abbott* preschool classroom
Job schedule
Curriculum
Connections with college and
    preschool – is it relevant?
Future career plans
Status as teacher pre-*Abbott* vs.
    current status
Energy level as a result of all of
    the above experiences

- Completing college coursework
Studying/Time Management              Time conflicts: attendance, deadline, "B"
Previous academic experience
    and perceptions of ability
Present perceptions of academic
    ability

# LESSONS FROM HOME: A LOOK AT CULTURE AND DEVELOPMENT

Irma Cantú Woods

## ABSTRACT

*Given the considerable interest currently in the field of early childhood on ways culture influences children's development, in this chapter I present findings from an ethnographic study I conducted over a six-month period that looks at cultural influences on children's development. The study looks at 20 Mexican-American children living in a low-income neighborhood in a South Texas community. The children and their families were studied in three specific settings: the children's homes, the neighborhood surrounding the children's homes, and the Head Start Center the children attended which was located in the neighborhood. The children ranged in age from 3 to 5 years. Research methodology involved participant observation, informal interviewing, formal interviewing, and document analysis. The theories of Bronfenbrenner and Ogbu provide the framework for considering the cultural perspective in looking at children's development. Numerous possible themes of cultural aspects as uniquely influencing children's development emerged from the study's data collection. The theme I address in this chapter is the adults' use of names when addressing children. The findings of the study are also compared to the criterion of cultural diversity in* Developmentally Appropriate Practice in Early Childhood Programs *(Bredekamp & Copple, 1997). Implications for future research and early childhood practice are also*

Social Contexts of Early Education, and Reconceptualizing Play (II)
Advances in Early Education and Day Care, Volume 13, 137–161
ISSN: 0270-4021/doi:10.1016/S0270-4021(04)13005-X

*presented. Finally, I suggest a new metaphor for looking at culture and its influence on child development.*


During the past ten years there has been considerable increased interest in the cultural and contextual processes of child development (Bruner, 1990; Cole, 1996; Goodnow, Miller, & Kessel, 1995; Greenfield, 1997; Jessor, Colby & Shweder, 1996; Rogoff, 1990; Shore, 1996). This interest across a variety of disciplines can be attributed in part to the limitations of the developmental perspective which has long dominated our view of how children grow and develop. The developmental perspective focuses on universal sequences of development which primarily reflect Piagetian theory. For scholars and practitioners in the field of child development and early childhood education, the dominance of the developmental perspective was further supported by the publication of a document titled *Developmentally Appropriate Practice in Early Childhood Programs Serving Children From Birth Through Age 8* (hereafter called DAP) (Bredekamp, 1987).

The DAP guidelines were published by the National Association for the Education of Young Children (NAEYC), the largest professional organization representing early childhood education in the United States and were designed to reflect what early childhood professionals considered to be developmentally appropriate for the care of young children in group settings. The DAP guidelines are based on two principles: age appropriateness and individual appropriateness. The first principle is concerned with age-related levels of development in young children and clearly reflects developmental Piagetian theory that looks at children as active learners who construct their own knowledge by manipulating the environment organized by the adult world. The second principle is concerned with the individual needs of children in the areas of language, intellect, culture, and physical development.

The DAP guidelines of 1987 generated a host of critics (Fowell & Lawton, 1992; Jipson, 1991; Kessler, 1991; Lubeck, 1994; New & Mallory, 1994; O'Loughlin, 1991; Spodek, 1991; Walsh, 1991) who questioned the heavy emphasis of the guidelines on a developmental theoretical perspective, thereby excluding other theoretical alternatives and views that would help explain the development of children. Clearly absent from the DAP guidelines was the cultural perspective in influencing development. The implication was that a child develops as an individual "... determined by the universal nature of man, and that it is beyond culture" (Bruner, 1986, p. 85). By omitting a clear cultural perspective, the DAP guidelines reflected the dominate culture in the U.S. (Delpit, 1988), steeped in Western thought.

In response to the critics' responses to the DAP guidelines, Bredekamp (1991, 1993) affirmed the developmentalist perspective in DAP. Bredekamp argued that DAP's principle on individual appropriateness addressed the cultural dimension but the argument failed to place the child as an individual within a cultural context of group dynamics. In a continued effort to address the critics' concern, a position statement on curriculum and assessment (Bredekamp & Rosegrant, 1992) was published seeking to correct "misinterpretations of developmentally appropriate practice" (p. 4). This position statement presented a wider view of theoretical perspectives, including the cultural perspective in understanding child development. A second position statement on linguistics and cultural diversity (NAEYC, 1996) challenged early childhood educators "to become more knowledgeable about how to relate to children and families whose linguistic or cultural background is different from their own" (p. 6).

One of the concerns addressed by the position statements was the tendency of early childhood programs to promote a "tourist approach" (Derman-Sparks, 1989) to culture instead of an authentic view of culture as reflected in the everyday life of children and their families. A tourist approach to culture emphasizes the visible aspects of culture such as music, food, holidays, dress, and language. The invisible aspects of culture are those which govern behavior based on the beliefs and values of a given social group. Erikson (1997) points out the difference between visible culture and invisible culture as explicit and implicit. The implicit aspects of culture are those which even the persons of a given culture are not aware those cultural aspects exist. "Much of culture is not only held outside conscious awareness but is also learned and taught outside awareness" (Erikson, 1997, p. 40). McLoyd (1999) is concerned with cultural validity as necessary "to identify the rules that regulate conduct and the rules that define various practices and institutions" (p. 131). According to McLoyd (1999) these rules form the cultural framework needed to understand culture and to identify cultural differences.

In 1997 the DAP guidelines (Bredekamp & Copple) were revised in response to the critiques that challenged the Piagetian theoretical framework. The revised guidelines emphasize the importance of gaining knowledge "of the social and cultural contexts in which children live" (p. 9). However, while affirming that development and learning take place within multiple social and cultural contexts, the revised DAP guidelines state:

> The teachers should learn about the culture of the majority of the children they serve if that culture differs from their own. However, recognizing that development and learning are influenced by social and cultural contexts does not require teachers to understand all the nuances of every cultural group they may encounter in their practice; this would be an impossible task. Rather, this fundamental recognition sensitizes teachers to the need to acknowledge how their own cultural experience shapes their perspective and to realize that multiple perspectives

in addition to their own, must be considered in decisions about children's development and
learning (p. 12).

Is it enough to simply be sensitive to multiple perspectives without knowing
what those perspectives are? Being sensitive to cultural differences does not
provide a knowledge base in understanding how culture influences development.
If Erikson (1997) is correct in his assertion that much of culture is ". . . learned
and taught outside awareness" (p. 40), how does one even become aware of
those invisible aspects of culture that would help teachers make decisions about
children's development and learning? Rogoff and Morelli (1989) point out that the
understanding of human development requires more than simply acknowledging
multiple perspectives need to be considered when looking at development. Without
knowledge of the invisible or implicit aspects of culture, one is left with the visible
or tourist approach to culture. Such an approach not only limits the understanding
of how culture influences development but can also lead to stereotyping a particular
culture. Such stereotyping only serves to perpetuate ignorance of the role of culture
in human development.

The concept of culture as a social context has long been addressed in the fields of
anthropology and sociology. Seldom has it been addressed with depth in the field
of child development. Knowledge of cultural processes as they influence children's
development is becoming more and more critical if we are to understand how to
address social issues in the U.S. It is no longer enough to appropriate the visible
aspects of a culture such as food and music or to give lip service to a language
by learning a few words or phrases. It is all too common today for people to
learn and use each others visible aspects of culture without truly understanding,
accepting, and valuing those aspects of culture that help to explain difference
in human development. In this chapter I seek to show how culture influences
development. I first present some definitions of culture. I then present an overview
of an ethnographic study I conducted over a six-months period. From that study
I present one theme that emerged from the data to illustrate how implicit aspects
of culture influence development. Finally, I compare my findings to the criterion
on cultural diversity in *Developmentally Appropriate Practice in Early Childhood
Programs* (Bredekamp & Copple, 1997).

## DEFINITIONS OF CULTURE

Culture is a term that can be defined in a variety of ways. Often culture is
conceptualized as a metaphor to help define its complexity. Erikson (1997) uses
the metaphor of a human toolkit to illustrate how culture enables people to produce

activity. In defining culture for this study I use Tylor's (1958 [1873]) definition as "that complex whole which includes language, knowledge, belief, art, morals, law, custom, and other capabilities and habits acquired by man as a member of society" (p. 1).

## OVERVIEW OF STUDY

This ethnographic study looks at a group of 20 Mexican-American children and their families living in a low-income neighborhood in a South Texas community. The children and their families were studied in three specific settings: the children's homes, the neighborhood surrounding the children's homes, and the Head Start Center the children attended which was located in the neighborhood. The children ranged in age from 3 to 5 years. The study was conducted over a period of six months during which time I lived in the neighborhood to facilitate the gathering of data.

Two theoretical perspectives guided my thinking and formed the framework for the study. Bronfenbrenner's (1979) ecological theory provides notions of multiple systems in society that influence children's development. Ogbu's (1981) cultural-ecological theory provides specific notions about cultural discontinuity, which are not found in Bronfenbrenner's theory. These two theories complement one another and offer a strong base for affirming the role of culture in children's development.

The ecological theory of human development proposed by Bronfenbrenner (1979) looks at the complex interaction between the developing person and the environment. Bronfenbrenner (1979) defines environment as "a set of nested structures, each inside the next, like a set of Russian dolls" (p. 3). The developing child is embedded in several environmental systems, ranging from immediate settings, such as the family, to more remote contexts, such as the broader culture. Each of the systems interacts with the others and with the individual child to influence development in complex ways.

Bronfenbrenner's innermost environmental structure, or microsystem, consists of the immediate contexts that the child actually experiences. For example, a young infant's microsystem may be limited to the home and family. As the child matures and is exposed to child care, the neighborhood, playgrounds, peers, and teachers, this structure becomes more complex. According to the theory, not only are children influenced by the microsystem environment, but they influence the people present in the environment as well.

The next environmental layer, or mesosystem refers to the links or interrelationships among microsystems. According to Bronfenbrenner, children's development is likely to be optimized by strong, supportive links between microsystems. For example, children's development is enhanced for children participating in home and school environments where interconnections are "characterized by more frequent interaction between parents and school personnel, a greater number of persons known in common by members of the two settings, and more frequent communications between home and school . . ." (Bronfenbrenner, 1979, p. 218).

Bronfenbrenner's third environmental layer, or exosystem, consists of settings that children never experience directly but that may still affect their development. For instance, the materials in the classroom and curricula taught there are shaped by school boards and economic circumstance. Children's emotional well-being may be influenced by how well the parents get along with their boss.

Finally, Bronfenbrenner stresses that development always takes place in a macrosystem, that is, a cultural context in which microsystems, mesosystems, and exosystems are embedded. Cultural values differ from culture to culture and can greatly influence the kinds of experiences children have in their homes, neighborhoods, schools, and all other contexts that affect them directly or indirectly (Shaffer, 1993). The incidence of child abuse in families, for example, is much higher in those culture that sanction physical force and violence (Belsky, 1980).

One of the key propositions in Bronfenbrenner's ecological theory is that only by observing the transactions between developing children and their ever-changing natural settings will we understand how individuals influence and are influenced by their environments (Shaffer, 1993). Bloch and Pellegrini (1989) point out that Bronfenbrenner's theory places much emphasis on the bidirectional influence of children and environment, and the dynamic and interactive linkages of different ecological systems on each other. These linkages between settings become important in terms of the child's developmental potential. Powell (1989) asserts that "the least favorable condition for development is where between-setting links are nonsupportive or completely absent" (p. 41). The ecological approach, then, provides a strong base for looking at social issues that affect children and their development.

The cultural-ecological theory proposed by Ogbu (1981) emphasizes cultural, subcultural theories of success and child rearing that are affected by the larger cultural ecological environment, and that, in turn, affect child rearing techniques, child activities, and development. His theory is concerned "with the problem of developing an appropriate model for cross-cultural research in child rearing and development, particularly for studying minority children in the United States" (p. 413). Ogbu calls for research conducted on a diversity of groups and rejects a monolithic mentality by looking at patterns of child rearing and development of different groups of societies in their respective contexts.

The central concept in Ogbu's theory is the origin of human competencies. Ogbu defines competence as "a set of functional or instrumental skills" (Ogbu, 1981, p. 414) which address child rearing techniques embedded in culturally defined adult tasks. The child develops the competencies necessary to function well in the culture surrounding the child.

Also central to Ogbu's theory is the native theory of child rearing which focuses on people's beliefs about proper ways to raise children. Ogbu (1982b) explains that the competencies or attributes fostered in children depend on the requirements of their positions in the wider social and economic systems. The way people organize their subsistence activities influences how they organize the up-bringing of their children. Ogbu maintains that the continuing disproportion of school failure among minority groups can be attributed to the alternative competencies children develop as an adaptation to the limited opportunity available to them to benefit from their education (Ogbu, 1974).

Ogbu (1982a) discusses the cultural discontinuity concept to explain why some minority children do so poorly in school. Ogbu suggests some minorities experience discontinuity in school because their cultural features often have developed in response to their treatment by the dominant group. Ogbu's theory has been used by researchers as a basis for studying minority students success, or lack thereof, in formal school settings (Fordham & Ogbu, 1986; Fox, 1990; Hays, 1992; Valentine & Andrew, 1989). However, Ogbu's theory of instrumental competencies and cultural discontinuity has not been studied in early childhood settings. Prior to Ogbu's theory, Cardenas and Cardenas (1973) proposed the theory of incompatibilities to help explain the poor performance of Mexican-American children in the American public school system. I did not find any references to the theory of incompatibilities used in studies of early childhood settings. My study identifies some of the instrumental competencies children develop within the context of the family and reflected in the cultural diversity found within child care practices in terms of developmentally appropriate practices.

The theories of Bronfenbrenner and Ogbu provide a framework for considering the cultural perspective in looking at children's development. Bronfenbrenner offers a description of environmental systems which constitute natural settings for young children. By observing the transactions between the developing child and the systems, one can gain a better understanding of the cultural influences on children's development. Bronfenbrenner also focuses on the linkage between the systems which, in this study, focuses on the cultural context (macrosystem) and child care practices in terms of developmentally appropriate practice in a Head Start center (microsystem and mesosystem).

Ogbu presents a unique way to look at children's development by considering the link between parents subsistence activities (i.e. a mesosystem, in Bronfenbrenner's terms) and the child-rearing practices (a macrosystem) they use. Subsistence activities may, by necessity, involve interacting with groups outside the parents' immediate family settings and culture and which often involves the dominant group in society. The relationship between the parents and these groups, then, influences how parents bring up their children in the acquisition of instrumental competencies. Another dimension in Ogbu's theory is the cultural discontinuity when the instrumental competencies a child brings to different settings, such as the school setting, do not match with the competencies required in the different settings (a mismatch between micro and macrosystems). This study looks at these two dimensions of Ogbu's theory by focusing on the instrumental competencies of children, or cultural diversity, and the cultural discontinuity that may exist in terms of developmentally appropriate practice. Developmentally appropriate practice (DAP) has been criticized as perhaps appropriate only for the white, middle class populations in the U.S. A combination of Bronfenbrenner's and Ogbu's theoretical frameworks provides an opportunity to address that criticism by looking at continuities and discontinuities between environmental systems.

Research methodology involved participant observation, informal interviewing, formal interviewing, and document analysis. As part of the participant observation, I rented a small wood frame house close to the housing project where the majority of the children and their families lived. I also volunteered one day per week in the Head Start classroom where the 20 preschool children were enrolled. By living in the same neighborhood as the children, I was able to more accurately observe and record information about the children's multiple environments. As a native ethnographer, my entry into the neighborhood was facilitated by my ability to speak Spanish and by being identified by the people in the neighborhood as "*una de nuestra gente*" (one of our people). My acceptance by the community allowed me to participate in the daily, ordinary life of the people while maintaining my research focus.

Numerous possible themes of implicit cultural aspects as uniquely influencing children's development emerged from the study's data collection. The theme I address in this chapter is the adults' use of names when addressing children. On the surface this theme may appear to be an obvious cultural aspect of child-rearing practices among Mexican-American families. A closer look will reveal important implications in understanding the development of children growing up in Mexican-American communities.

## THE USE OF NAMES

Many years ago I was visiting a child care center on an evaluation visit when I was approached by a teacher with whom I was on friendly terms. "You know," she began, "I have been wanting to ask you a question for some time. In your culture, why do you call your children 'mom' and 'dad'? Puzzled, I replied, "What do you mean?" "You know," the teacher said. "You call children *'mama'* and *'papa'*. Why?" I thought about the teacher's question for a few seconds. The teacher was correct. We often use the words *'mama'* and *'papa'* when addressing children. I looked at the teacher and said, "I don't know why. We just do." But the question haunted me for a long time. (Author's personal recollection.)

# THE HOME ENVIRONMENT

The housing project and the surrounding neighborhood where I conducted the study can be conceptualized as a village for two reasons. First, life in a housing project necessitates the proximity of the people living there. Secondly, many elements of the housing project are designed to be shared by the residents: the playgrounds, the recreation room, the parking spaces, and the gardening tools. In the immediate surrounding neighborhood, the grocery store, bus stops, laundromat, restaurant, houses of worship, and the Head Start program are all available for use by the neighborhood community. During my visits with the children's families and daily interactions with them at the Head Start Center, the bus stop, the grocery store, or trips to the mall, a consistent pattern emerged of how parents addressed their children.

In the children's homes and within family activities, parents or other adult relatives used the children's given names when giving commands or directions to the children. When visiting with Mrs. Naranjo one day, I commented about this observation to her. Mrs. Narango explained it by saying:

> If I want Valerie to do something I use her name because she knows I mean it. I mean, if I just say "pick up your toys" she thinks I don't mean it or I'm just playing. But when I tell her to do something, I say "Valerie" and she does it. Well, most of the time, anyway. Or I'll say it in Spanish, "*¡Valeria!*" and then she knows I really mean it.

Other parents echoed Mrs. Naranjo's sentiment. "If I want Ana to do something, I say 'Ana, get your sweater' or 'Ana, get in the car,' " said Mrs. Olivares. Mr. Soliz put it rather succinctly, "Just tell them what you want them to do. Plain and simple. And when I say, 'Eric,' he knows it's him I'm talking to."

Parents also used the diminutive forms of their children's given names. The name *Elena* became *Elenita* and the name *Fernando* became *Fernandito*. Ms. Lopez stated the use of the diminutive form of a name was a way to show "*ternura a los niños*" (tenderness to children). Ms. Lopez further explained.

> *Cuando digo "Elenita" se oye más suave, con más dulcura. Se oye más cariñoso cuando decimos los nombres de los niños así. Y es una manera para que los niños se sientan mejor y se porten bien. Pero yo he notado que ahora muchos padres les dan nombres en inglés a sus hijos que no se pueden decir con cariño. Ashley, por ejemplo. Sólo podemos decir Ashley. Ya las cosas van cambiando.*

When I say "*Elenita*" it sounds softer, with more sweetness. I sounds more affectionate when
we say children's names like that. And it is a way for children to feel better and behave well.
But I have noticed many parents give their children English names which cannot be said with
affection. Ashley, for example. We can only say Ashley. Things are changing.

Mrs. Lopez introduced an important aspect in the form parents used their children's
names – the use of affection. By using the diminutive form of a name (not found
in the English language) Ms. Lopez emphasized the value of using affection or
"*ternura*" (tenderness) when addressing children. She lamented the fact English
names could not be converted to the diminutive form with the implication that by
using the diminutive form a child would feel better and thus be more cooperative
with the parents' requests.

I was visiting one afternoon with Mrs. Tovar in her home. In between following
a "*novela*" (Spanish soap opera) on television, we chatted about the children and
daily happenings. Five-year-old Cassandra, Mrs. Tovar's daughter, was playing
on the floor with a set of small stuffed toy bears. Mrs. Tovar's two-year-old son
was sleeping on Mrs. Tovar's bed in the next room "*Cassandra, anda ver si tu
hermanito todavía está dormido*" (Cassandra, go check if your little brother is still
asleep), Mrs. Tovar told Cassandra. Cassandra did not move from her play. After a
few moments, Mrs. Tovar again repeated her request, "*Cassandra, tu hermanito.*"
(Cassandra, your little brother.) Again, Cassandra ignored her mother. Finally, in
an exasperated tone, Mrs. Tovar said, "*¡Cassandra, deja tu juego. Andaa vera tu
hermanito!*" (Cassandra, leave your play. Go check on your little brother!) This
time, Cassandra got up quickly and went to the next room and returned, said,
"*todavía está dormido.*" (He is still asleep). Mrs. Tovar motioned Cassandra over
to her and putting her arm around Cassandra told her, "*Mi hijita, cuando te digo
algo, me tienes que oír y obedecer, ¿Mamita, me entiendes?*" (My dear daughter,
when I tell you something, you have to listen to me and obey. Dear mama, do you
understand me?) Cassandra simply nodded her head and returned to her play.

Like other parents in the study, Mrs. Tovar used her daughter's name in
connection with a specific command. Mrs. Tovar commanded Cassandra to check
on her little brother three times and each time she used her daughter's name. But
when giving advice to Cassandra about listening and obeying, Mrs. Tovar used
the terms "*mi hijita*" and "*mamita*" to address Cassandra. These terms and other
similar ones I refer to as "*nombres de cariño*" or names of endearment. Families
used the *nombres de cariño* in very specific instances: to give advice, to show
concern, to comfort, to console, and to show affection.

Ernesto enjoyed climbing on his mom's lap whenever I visited with Ms. Vela.
When he smiled, his missing two front upper teeth created an irresistible instant
liking of him. Ms. Vela hugged Ernesto, often interrupting our chatting to talk with
Ernesto: "*Mi'jito, qué lindo mi'jito. ¿Por qué te quiero tanto?*" (My dear son, my

wonderful dear son. Why do I love you so much?) Ernesto would nestle his head on Ms. Vela's shoulder and Ms. Vela would hold him closer to her saying, "*Mi'jito, mi'jito.*" Little else needed to be said about the bond of affection between mother and child.

Ms. Soliz was volunteering one afternoon in Ms. Sandoval's classroom in the Head Start Center. The children were getting ready for naptime and the children were going by turn to get their naptime covers and pillows from their cubbies. Ms. Soliz's four-year-old son Sergio was lying on his cot without a cover and pillow. Ms. Sandoval turned off the classroom light and as children were settling down, Sergio began crying, saying, "I don't have a blanket and pillow." Ms. Soliz comforted him by stroking his head saying, "*Ay, mi hijo lindo.* It's O.K. Don't cry, *papacito.* I'll go ask Ms. Arriola if she has one. It's O.K. *mi'jito.*" Ms. Soliz obtained a blanket from Ms. Arriola (one of the teachers) and returning to her son, covered him with a blanket saying, "There, you see, *mi'jito,* you're O.K. now."

The *nombres de cariño* were also commonly used by parents at arrival and departure times at home and at the Head Start Center. "Bye, *mi hijo* or *mi hija*" was a common departing phrase and "Hi, *mama*" or "Hi, *papacito*" was a common greeting at the end of the day. Often, parents used the plural "*mamas*" or "*papas*" when addressing a single child. Parents also used the *nombres de cariño* not just with their own children, but with all the children in the classroom, greeting children with "Hi, *mi'ja*" or "How you doing, *mi'jo?*"

Ms. Garcia explained her use of *nombres de cariño* with children:

> If I see kids are going to get hurt, like running out in the street with cars coming I say, "Francisco, watch out." Because I don't want him to get hurt. I mean, I don't want no kid to get hurt. I don't want my kids to get hurt. So if somebody tells my kids to watch out, I'm glad. But if the kids are fighting or if a bigger kid is picking on a little kid, I go out and say, "Hey, *mi'jo*, don't do that."

I asked Ms. García why she used *nombres de cariño* in the second situation.

> Well, I don't know. I mean, it sounds better to say "*mi'jo.*" It's, it's more soft, like you're not mad. "*Mi'jo,*" I mean, that's what we say. I don't know why. It's just something we say. And the kids pay attention. They listen better when we call them like that.

Mrs. Ruiz spoke of her reasons for using *nombres de cariño*.

> I grew up hearing "*mi'ja*" and "*mama*". And now I use it with my kids. I don't speak a lot of Spanish, but I use those words. It always made me feel good when my mom called me "*mi'ja*" or "*mi'jita.*" It's like she really cared about me. I want my kids to know I love them. I mean, I tell them, "I love you." But when I say "I love you, *mi'jo,*" it means more. I don't know why. I just does.

Mrs. Pérez shared a moving story when she was growing up in a single parent household.

I remember one day me and my mom went to J. C. Penny to buy me some clothes for school. When we came back, when we got off the bus, a block from our house, we saw a bunch of people down the street. Then we heard fire trucks. Our house was on fire. We ran to our house and watched as the firemen put out the fire. My mother didn't say nothing. She just held me close to her saying over and over, "It's O.K., *mi'jita*. It's gonna be O.K." When it was over, she hugged me real tight and said, "*Mamita*, it's O.K. We didn't get hurt. And you still have new clothes to wear to school." I never forgot that day. What I remember most is how safe I felt with my mom holding me and saying "It's O.K. *mi'jita*. It's O.K." So I use those words with my children, *mi'jo* and *mi'ja*. I want them to feel safe and loved.

Mr. Ramos had very strong feelings about his use of *mi hijo* and *mi'jito*.

He, he's my son. His grandma calls him *mi'jo*. We're family. My mother still calls me "*mi'jito*" and I'm a grown man. My son is *mi'jo* to me. Sure I call him *Rogelio*. But it's just him and me. I'm his dad and he's *mi'jo*.

## THE NEIGHBORHOOD ENVIRONMENT

One Saturday morning I went to the neighborhood supermarket to do my grocery shopping. I found most of the items I needed and proceeded to the check-out lanes to pay. There was one "quick-check" lane opened and three regular lanes. The three regular lanes were quite long, about six or seven people waiting in each line. As I waited in line, Dalia, a cashier, began to push aside a display case which served to close off the lane. Dalia then picked up the hand microphone and announced, "Two cashiers needed, number five and number six!" I quickly stepped out of the lane where I was and entered the newly opened lane. As Dalia began scanning my groceries, she looked up at me and asked, "Did you find everything you needed, *mi'ja?*" I assured her that I had, noting she was about my age. As I was writing out the check to pay for my groceries, Dalia picked up the microphone again and said, "Cashiers, I need you. Number five and number six. Come on, *mamacitas*."

I had a chance to later talk with Dalia. I asked her why she used *nombres de cariño* with the customers and the employees. She looked surprised at my question and was silent for a moment. She then chuckled and said,

You got to be kidding! I just use them. I don't know why. I mean, that's what I say at home to my kids. With the customers I guess it's to be friendly, make them feel at home. When people say "*mi'ja*" to me, it makes me feel like they know me. And "*mamacitas*," gosh I don't know how to explain. It's just what we say. Why is it important to understand? That's just what we say. *Así nos criamos*. (That's how we were raised.)

The daily life in the neighborhood involved the use of the *nombres de cariño*. The use of "*mi hijo*" and "*mi hija*" were more pronounced in the neighborhood because they became the common way adults used to address people – children and adults alike. At the neighborhood restaurant, the servers used *nombres de cariño* with the customers. Age was not a determinant of who was called *"mi hija"* or *"mi hijo."* Servers who were at least thirty years younger than some of the customers addressed the customers using *nombres de cariño*. The environment in the restaurant became in a sense, a familial environment.

Many of the people in the housing project and surrounding neighborhood attended Santa Catarina Catholic Church. The parish priest Father Serna used the term *"mis hermanos y hermanas,"* (my brothers and sisters) when addressing the general congregation. When addressing the children and referring to the children, Father Serna used the term *"los hijitos"* (the dear children). One of Father Serna's sermons in particular emphasized the significance and importance in using *nombres de cariño* in child-rearing practices.

The sermon one Sunday in November focused on service to others and teaching children how to be kind to one another and how to live the gospel. Father Serna told the congregation, *"Les voy a demonstrar como enseñar a sus hijos."* (I am going to demonstrate how to teach your children.) Father Serna then called a child about six years old from the congregation to join him at the altar. The child stood next to Father Serna who looked at the child, then looked out to the congregation saying, *"Esta es la manera de hablar con sus hijitos."* (This is the way to speak with your dear children.) Father Serna got down to the child's level and putting his arm around the child said, *"Mira, mi hijita. Tu y tu hermanito pelean mucho. ¿Por qué? ¿Que está pasando?"* (Look, my dear daughter. You and your little brother fight a lot. Why? What is happening?) Having demonstrated his point, Father Serna hugged the child and then motioned to the child to return to her place. Turning once again to the congregation, Father Serna continued.

> *Ensenen a sus hijitos como servir a otros por medio de su ejemplo. Hablen con ellos con ternura, con cariño. Uno puede ser firme a la vez de ser respetuoso. No es necesario gritarles a sus hijos. Usen esos nombres de cariño: mi hijito, mi hijita. Porque todos somos los hijos de Díos, los hijitos de Díos.*

> Teach your dear children how to serve others by your example. Speak with them with tenderness, with love. One can be firm and respectful at the same time. It is not necessary to yell at your children. Use those names of endearment: my dear son, my dear daughter. Because we are all children of God, the dear children of God.

I later spoke with Father Serna about his sermon and asked him why the *nombres de cariño* were so common among the people of the neighborhood. His reply was similar to what others had said, but he placed the *nombres de cariño* within a religious context.

> Well, it's so much a part of our culture. I think we don't even think about it. But thinking about it now, maybe we can trace the roots to the *Virgen de Guadalupe, tan querida por la gente*

*mexicana* (the Virgin of Guadalupe, so loved by the Mexican people). *Cuando la Virgen se le aparesió a Juan Diego en Tepeyac in 1531, le llamó "mi hijito." Le preguntó, "¿Juan Diego, mi hijito, a dónde vas?"* (When the Virgin appeared to Juan Diego on Tepeyac in 1531, she called him "my dear son." She asked him, "Juan Diego, my dear son, where are you going?") Maybe that's where it originated. I don't know. They are so much a part of who we are and how we relate to others. Those words help to establish a special relationship among us. It is not like one person is higher than another. It's more like we are related to one another as family.

The concept of relationships in the use of *nombres de cariño* was echoed by Tomas Rendon, professor of ethnic studies at the local university.

To say *mi hijito* or *mi hijita, mama* or *mamacita* is to talk about a relationship. When you give somebody a name, that's his only kind of thing. You're baptizing him into the world of independence. But the idea of *mi hijito, mamacita*, even though we are not related, that creates the cultural ties, the dependent ties, and there's a sense of warmth that you get from the group, from the family, and from everybody. When you say *mi hijito, mama, papacito*, that is family to a child. We are family-oriented as a culture. And so, of course, we are going to use family names to refer to the children and to somebody else's children. It still helps to create bonds by using our own family titles for them.

## THE CLASSROOM ENVIRONMENT

During the summer months of the six-month period I lived in the neighborhood, I taught one summer course at the local community college to help finance my research study. One day I found a note on my office desk from one of my colleagues concerning a mutual student and a discussion my colleague and the student had about the use of nicknames with young children. The note read: "We discussed. She was confused about the use of nicknames. I told her that I believe the best advice is to not use them; names are always O.K. and show more respect, I think."

The use of the children's names was a consistent practice in the Head Start classroom. As each child arrived in he morning, the parent or adult accompanying the child signed the child in and then assisted the child in putting on his/her name tag. The child's full name was printed on the name tag which was worn all day until the child went home. The teachers and assistant teachers also wore name tags.

Another consistent practice was the morning roll call after breakfast during circle time. The child's full name was called to which each child was expected to respond if present, "I'm here today." The children's full names were also used to label the naptime cots, cubbies for personal storage, display folders for each child's art work and projects, and the name chart used for the group management system.

Mrs. Medina was the classroom teacher and we discussed the emphasis the Head Start program placed on the use of the children's names in very audible and visual ways. Mrs. Medina explained by saying:

> Well, it has to do with self-esteem. I mean some parents call their children nicknames like *"Güero"* or *"Gordo"* and that's not very nice. We think it's important for children to know what their real name is. When they go to school their teachers will call them by their real names so they need to know. That's why we use the children's first and last names. Also, the name tags help the children learn to read their names. Many of the children learn to read each other's names because of the name tags. Also, the name tags help us to know who should be at the center.

In September the twenty children in the study moved from Mrs. Medina's classroom to Mrs. Sandoval's classroom. Mrs. Sandoval also commented on using the children's names.

> We are supposed to call children by their real names. The teachers at the college tell us that helps children develop a good self-concept and that it's better for them. You know, feeling good about themselves. I mean, if we call children by nicknames, sometimes nicknames are negative. But calling children by their names teaches children to know what their name is. And we call children by their real names. Like if a child's name is Armando, we call the child "Armando," not "Mando." At trainings we go to, they tell us the same thing.

The teachers consistently called children by their names and the children's printed names were visible throughout the classrooms. Nicknames defined as variations of the children's names, such as Letty for Leticia, were not used by the teachers, as Ms. Sandoval had explained. Nicknames that described physical characteristics of the children were not used because of the negative connotation attributed to those nicknames. For example, *"gordo"* and *"flaco"* as descriptors of a child who was fat or thin were not used as nicknames to address children. However, nicknames in the form of *nombres de cariño* were used by some of the teachers at the center.

I asked Mrs. Medina why she used the *nombres de cariño* with the children.

> I don't know. That's the way I was raised. My mom still calls me *"mi'jita,"* even at my age. I mean, I know we're supposed to use the children's real names and I do. But sometimes *mi hijo* or *mama* works best, especially if the child doesn't feel good. I think it makes a child feel loved, like they're at home. Sometimes the children come in looking sad and if I just say, "What's wrong, *mi'jito?*" everything just seems to come out. I don't know. I never thought of them as nicknames. They're just names we use in the family. I guess I shouldn't use them. They tell us not to use nicknames, but I forget. The teachers at the college. They teach nicknames are not appropriate and we should only use the children's names.

Ms. Sandoval did not use the *nombres de cariño* with the children in the classroom. Instead, she used the terms "Sir" and "Ma'am" regularly. The use of those terms fall under another theme of the study which I do not present in this chapter.

Ms. Arriola, Ms. Sandoval's assistant teacher used the *nombres de cariño* during daily interactions with the children. Ms. Arriola talked about the use of the terms.

> I never really thought about it. I mean about saying *"mama"* or *"mi hijo, mi hija"* with the children. I just use them. I guess I just grew up hearing those words and my parents using them. I don't even think about it; I just use them. I guess they're just loving words, words we use in the family with the children. But we use them with grown-ups, too. I don't know. In a way those words bring us closer together and in a way, they help me feel people understand when they use those words. I know I should only use the children's names in the classroom. But sometimes *mi hijo* or *mi hija* is better to say.

My interactions with the staff at the Head Start Center were primarily limited to the teachers and assistant teachers working in the classroom with the twenty children in my study. One day I was going into Mrs. Medina's classroom when I hear Mrs. Lawrence, an African-American teacher, talking with a child outside her classroom door. Mrs. Lawrence was down at the child's level and holding the child's hands. The child was crying softly, almost trying to hold in her sobs. I heard Mrs. Lawrence say, "What's wrong, *mi'jita*? You look so sad this morning. Come here, *mi'ja*." Mrs. Lawrence opened her arms and the child went to her immediately, burying her head on Mrs. Lawrence' shoulder and began crying audibly. Mrs. Lawrence held the child will quietly comforting her.

Mrs. Lawrence later shared with me her reasons for using *nombres de cariño*.

> I grew up around Hispanic kids and I heard *mi 'jo* and *mi'ja* used a lot by their parents but I never paid much attention to it. It was later when I began working here that I began to see how the children reacted. They'd come looking sad or scared, like at the beginning of school and when I greeted them with, "Hi, *mi'ja*," they would look up at me and smile, a shy smile, but I knew it meant something to them. So I now use those words not just with the children here at the Head Start Center, but with my own kids and my youngest is a teenager. But when she comes in looking down or like that, I just say, *"Mi'ja*, you O.K.?" and everything begins pouring out of her. I don't really know why those words work like that, but they sure help.

## ANALYSIS

The early childhood literature emphasizes the use of the children's names as a means of promoting children's positive self-esteem (Gestwicki, 1995; Hildebrand, 1997; NAEYC, 1991). Self-esteem may be defined as the evaluative component of the self or the positive or negative manner in which a person judges herself or himself (Page & Page, 1992). Self-esteem is but one aspect of self. Lewis and Brooks-Gunn (1979) present two aspects of self: the self as subject (I) which is the active, knowing, experiential self or what is called self-concept, the ability to describe self. The second aspect of self is the object (Me) and is one's awareness and evaluation or what we call self-esteem. Together these two aspects help to answer the question "Who am I?" and are concerned with the search of self or what Erikson (1959) called the quest for identity. According to Erikson (1959), identity is "a conscious sense of individual identity" (p. 102). Erikson went beyond the self in defining identity and proposed that identity involves "a maintenance of an inner solidarity with a group's ideals and identity" (1959, p. 102). Identity or the answer to the question "Who am I?" involves understanding and accepting self and one's society (Miller, 1993).

Concern with the development of self goes back to the late 1800s with the work of Baldwin (1987), followed by Cooley (1902), and Mead (1925). All of them addressed the importance of social interaction as the foundation in the development of self knowledge and understanding (Grusec & Lytton, 1988). The concept that knowledge of self develops only in a social context is widely accepted today in the early childhood field. Social interaction in the practice of teachers calling children by their names is an example of how children develop self-concept. The beginning of the development of self-concept can be noted when the infant "first recognizes his mother and first feels recognized by her, when her voice tells him he is somebody with a name and he's good" (Evans, 1967, p. 35). The emerging self-concept can also be seen in the social interactions among young children which usually begin by the children telling each other their names (Berger & Thompson, 1996).

Self-esteem is the second component of the self and is concerned with how I feel about who I am in the form of the descriptive self. My self-concept tells me I am a Mexican-American woman, mother of three children, a grandmother, a daughter, a sister, a wife, and so on. My self-esteem tells me how I feel about being a Mexican-American woman, mother, and each of the roles I have. Self-esteem is concerned with feelings and emotions and positive self-esteem is the foundation of positive emotional well-being (Page & Page, 1992).

The teachers at the Head Start Center called children by their names because it "helps children develop a good self-concept, feel good about themselves." The children wore name tags throughout the day as a means of identification. Wearing a name tag helps to initiate social interaction which in turn helps to develop self-concept. The teachers also talked about the emphasis trainers and college instructors place on using the children's names. Ms. Sandoval discussed the importance of using the child's correct name, for example, Armando, not "Mando." (It is important to note here that calling a child by name does not necessarily mean promoting positive self-esteem or self-concept. If a person dislikes his/her given name, as I discovered among some of the people in the neighborhood, using his/her name may not help the person feel good about self.)

The revised DAP guidelines (Bredekamp & Copple, 1997) address the need for young children "to develop a positive self-identity" (p. 8) and give as an important task for parents and teachers of young children to support "children's developing self-concept and sense of positive self-esteem" (p. 115). The guidelines identify as an example of appropriate practice the promotion of children's development of language and literacy through meaningful experiences such as recognizing their names and the names of their friends. Mrs. Medina echoed this practice in her use of the children's names because the children "learn to read their name and the names of the other children." The guidelines clearly support children's development of positive self-identity, but offer no specific connection between the use of children's names and the development of a positive sense of self. The guidelines do not seek to "issue a prescriptive set of practices but to encourage educators to reflect on their practice" (Bredekamp & Copple, 1997, p. 123). By omitting specific mention in the use of names to promote a positive sense of self in developmentally appropriate practice, educators must rely on other sources, namely their own reflection, training workshops, books, and courses in early childhood education.

One of the resources is the *Early Childhood Classroom Observation* (NAEYC, 1991), the instrument used by early childhood educators to validate quality of care in early childhood programs. This instrument specifically states that staff "call children by name" (p. 5) and gives as an example of fostering positive self-concept the use of "children's names in songs, games" (p. 10). The instrument does not address the issue of nicknames, inferring only the use of the children's names is appropriate. Mrs. Medina and Ms. Sandoval viewed the use of nicknames based on physical characteristics as "negative" and inappropriate. My college colleague was clear in her advice to a student that nicknames not be used. Names and nicknames that negatively shape a child's self-perception will less likely help a child feel worthwhile and capable (Harter, 1983). Positive exchanges of feelings between adults and children are necessary for social interaction and the development of the inner sense of emotional well-being (Emde, 1989). The issue is whether the use of nicknames is always negative.

The *nombres de cariño* used in the three contexts of the child care center, the children's homes, and the neighborhood are all rooted within the context of the family. *"Mi hijo," "mi hija," "mi hijita," "mi hijito," "mamacita,"* and *"papacito"* are terms that help create bonds not just between family members but between members in the community. The people of the neighborhood could not explain why they use the terms. People "just use them." They "grew up hearing those words." A common refrain among the people was "I don't think about it. I just use them." Dalia laughed at the idea of my asking why she used the terms with her customers. Her explanation was *"Así nos criamos"* (That's how we were raised). Mr. Lozano summarized the sentiments of the people in using *nombres de cariño* as "the feeling of being family."

Noam Chomsky (1965) has proposed a theory of language which involves generative grammar with the "implicit ability to understand indefinitely many sentences" (p. 15). Some sentences are "kernel sentences" (p. 17), simple sentences that play little or no role in the generation of sentences. According to Chomsky, kernel sentences have "intuitive significance" (p. 18), an embedded sense that cannot be changed. When *nombres de cariño* are used, they are, in a sense, the kernels in the sentence. The meaning of the terms is so tight that they cannot be changed without losing their meaning. The meaning is so embedded in the culture that the people of the neighborhood cannot explain why they use the terms. The *nombres de cariño* are nicknames based on relationships initially formed within the family. The relationships, through the use of nicknames, are extended outside the family, into the neighborhood, and the community. These relationships help the child and adults develop a sense of self, not just as an inner self awareness, but as the "understanding and acceptance of both the self and one's society" (Erikson, 1959, p. 102).

Kaomea (2003) presents the concept of "excavation" to explain the need to uncover or peel away hidden perspectives on familiar practices. By looking deeper into a familiar practice, such as the use of *nombres de cariño* in Mexican-American communities, one can gain a better understanding of how community and culture influence children's development. This study forced me to uncover for myself the layers covering the significance of *nombres de cariño* not only as they help to explain a child's development of self and community, but also the implications for practices in educational systems.

The revised DAP guidelines (Bredekamp & Copple, 1997) stress the importance of the child's development of positive self-identity, but raise the issue of using the children's names in the development of language and literacy. The *Early Childhood Classroom Observation* (NAEYC, 1991) connect the development of a positive self-esteem with the use of the children's names. The implication is that nick-names of any type are not appropriate.

*Nombres de cariño* are, as Tomas Rendon noted, family titles that support relationships among people. In this study, the use of the *nombres de cariño* was at the core of the social interactions between adults and children. Murillo (1971) emphasized the importance of the family in the Mexican-American community, often taking priority over the identification of the self. This study appears to show that some nicknames are not only positive but necessary for children's emotional well-being. John Dewey in his now classic *The Child and the Curriculum* (1902) addressed this issue of different theoretical perspectives:

> Profound differences in theory are never gratuitous or invented. They grow out of conflicting
> elements in a genuine people – a problem which is genuine just because the elements, taken

as they stand, are conflicting. Solution comes only by getting away from the meaning of terms that is already fixed upon and coming to see the conditions from another point of view, and hence a fresh light.

The early childhood profession, as reflected by the DAP guidelines (Bredekamp & Copple, 1997) asserts the importance of promoting children's positive development of self. The early childhood literature supports the use of the children's names as one way to promote the development of self. However, as Zahan (1979) points out, "to define self, we separate it from the other" (p. 9). This study indicates that the use of *nombres de cariño* helps to bind the people together, to unite them in a relationship of family. This unity helps in establishing social and emotional ties which are essential in the development of self. Dewey's words suggest that the meaning of positive self-concept can allow other positive ways of calling children. The use of *nombres de cariño* in this study is "another point of view" that can help shed "a fresh light" on the development of a positive self-concept and self-esteem in young children.

# IMPLICATIONS FOR FUTURE RESEARCH

This study was limited to twenty children and their families and the contexts of the Head Start Center, the children's homes, and the community. The data included in this study reflects a bias because it is my social construction of the lives of the people living in the neighborhood. The ethnographic research methods can be replicated, but any results may differ substantially. Therefore, every diverse community needs to be examined in light of its particular contexts. This study also suggests that the environmental systems proposed by Bronfenbrenner (1979) may not be necessarily nested but linked in various ways. Research from the perspective of linkages may shed new light on Bronfenbrenner's theory. Ogbu's (1981) theory of instrumental competencies has been applied to school-age children, primarily to help explain why minority children fail in school. Research that looks at the development of instrumental competencies in young children during the formative years may provide new insights in the development of minority children and the strengths they bring to the formal school system. These new insights may offer new ways to look at the education of minority children. Another area of research this study suggests is cultural appropriations within a given group that generate adapted cultural practices. The use of nicknames as an appropriate means to address children is not part of the early childhood literature and research in this area would be helpful in understanding diverse communities. Finally, future research on how poor communities protect their children through effective strategies generated from within their culture can strengthen and affirm parents and families. Research studies should lead to new understandings of practice and I now turn to the implications of this study on early childhood practice.

## IMPLICATIONS FOR EARLY CHILDHOOD PRACTICE

The DAP guidelines (Bredekamp & Copple, 1997) reflect what is considered the best practice in the field of early childhood education today. The DAP guidelines support and affirm the importance of culture and context in the development of children. How this support and affirmation should be reflected in actual practice remains vague. The use of nicknames is not addressed in the DAP guidelines. However, in the children's homes, community, and Head Start Center, the use of nicknames in the form of *nombres de cariño* is an integral part of forming connections, not just among family members but with people within the community. The practice of only using the children's names to promote a positive self-identity needs to be reconsidered. The *nombres de cariño* help to establish a group identity which is also part of self-identity. Every community, undoubtedly, uses some positive forms of nicknames. Putting this knowledge into practice would demonstrate cultural sensitivity, even if it is simply understanding and acceptance.

## CONCLUSION

Through the years metaphors have been proposed to aid our understanding of human development. Metaphors are useful because they help to conceptualize a phenomenon. However, all metaphors ultimately fail, creating a need to rethink and reconceptualize ideas.

Froebel's metaphor of kindergarten, or a garden of children, presents children as seeds who need to be planted in rich and fertile soil and tended with appropriate care in order to grow and develop well. The metaphor suggests development is simply a maturation process of internal growth. The seed is "prepacked" with everything it needs to begin the process of life. This metaphor suggests that only one environment – the garden – is needed for growth and development to take place. Outside elements of sun and water are needed, but these are added to the garden with no other needed interaction. Perhaps Froebel's metaphor needs to be extended to suggest different contexts for different parts of the garden and as the roots of plants extend beyond their immediate area, connections are made to all parts of the garden.

Bronfenbrenner's (1979) metaphor of nested Russian dolls helps to describe the ecological theory of nested systems. The metaphor does not help to describe the

interaction among the systems which is central to the theory. This study suggests
the ecological systems are linked in different ways, but not necessarily nested.
This linkage is an important part in understanding how the systems interact with
one another to bring about growth and development.

NAEYC's metaphor of the torch helps to explain the influence the DAP
guidelines have on informing the early childhood profession of what is considered
appropriate practices. The DAP guidelines are voluntary and thus can only
illuminate or inform early childhood practices. Practitioners in the field have to
incorporate the DAP guidelines into their system of what they believe is good for
children in varying communities.

By looking at culture and context, a new metaphor may help to explain the growth
and development of children. I suggest it is time to break new ground and consider a
new garden with a unique system of interaction – the cornfield (*la milpa*). *La milpa*
by definition is a small cornfield usually small enough to be tended by a family.
Multiple rows of corn need to be planted for cross-pollination to take place. Without
cross-pollination, a corn seed will produce the corn stalk but will not bear fruit.
Bronfenbrenner's (1979) ecological systems are like the multiple rows of corn,
but rather than being nested, the systems are linked one to another much like the
process of cross-pollination links the multiple rows of corn in different directions.
The cross-pollination carries the elements of the culture and context, such as the
use of nicknames, to multiple rows of corn and helps to explain the growth and
development of children. By examining *la milpa* metaphor and relating it to the
ecological systems, we can perhaps gain a better understanding of the cultural
perspective in explaining children's development. How does a garden of children
grow and develop? This study attempts to answer that question by proposing that
we examine children's experiences within their culture and context. This idea is not
new. John Dewey (1938) suggested it more than 60 years ago. This study suggests
the garden is not a universal garden where the rules and norms of development
apply equally. Rather, the garden is *la milpa*, a small cornfield representing an
individual community. There are many *milpas* and each *milpa* needs to be studied
individually in order to understand culture and context. By looking at a child's
total experiences, a picture of the child's development will emerge. If we look at
the picture with an open mind, discerning eyes, and an accepting heart, we will
see the strengths of the developing child.

# REFERENCES

Baldwin, J. M. (1987). *Social and ethical interpretations in mental development: A study in social
psychology*. New York: Macmillan.

Belsky, J. (1980). Child maltreatment: An ecological integration. *Developmental Psychology, 17,* 3–23.

Berger, K. S., & Thompson, R. A. (1996). *The developing person through childhood.* New York: Worth Publishers.

Bloch, M. N., & Pellegrini, A. D. (1989). *The ecological context of children's play.* Norwood, NJ: Ablex.

Bredekamp, S. (Ed.) (1987). *Developmentally appropriate practice in early childhood programs serving children from birth through age 8* (exp. ed.). Washington, DC: NAEYC.

Bredekamp, S. (1991). Redeveloping early childhood education: A response to Kessler. *Early Childhood Research Quarterly, 6,* 199–209.

Bredekamp, S. (1993). Myths about developmentally appropriate practice: A response to Fowell and Lawton. *Early Childhood Research Quarterly, 8,* 117–119.

Bredekamp, S., & Copple, C. (Eds) (1997). *Developmentally appropriate practice in early childhood programs* (Rev. ed.). Washington, DC: NAEYC.

Bredekamp, S., & Rosegrant, T. (Eds) (1992). *Reaching potentials: Appropriate curriculum and assessment for young children* (Vol. 1). Washington, DC: NAEYC.

Bronfenbrenner, U. (1979). *The ecology of human development.* Cambridge, MA: Harvard University Press.

Bruner, J. S. (1990). *Acts of meaning.* Cambridge, MA: Harvard University Press.

Cardenas, B., & Cardenas, J. A. (1973). Chicano – bright-eyed, bilingual, brown, and beautiful. *Today's Education, 62*(2), 49–51.

Chomsky, N. (1965). *Aspects of the theory of syntax.* Cambridge, MA: MIT Press.

Cole, M. (1996). *Cultural psychology: A once and future discipline.* Cambridge, MA: Harvard University Press.

Cooley, C. H. (1902). *Human nature and the social order.* New York: Charles Scribners.

Delpit, L. (1988). The silenced dialogue: Power and pedagogy in educating other people's children. *Harvard Educational Review, 58*(3), 280–298.

Derman-Sparks, L. (1989). *Anti-bias curriculum.* Washington, DC: NAEYC.

Dewey, J. (1902). *The child and the curriculum.* Chicago: University of Chicago Press.

Emde, R. (1989). The prerepresentational self and its affective core. *Psychoanalytic Study of the Child, 38,* 165–192.

Erikson, E. (1959). Identity and the life cycle. *Psychological Issues,* Monograph 1. New York: International Universities Press.

Erikson, F. (1997). Culture in society and in educational practices. In: J. A. Banks & C. A. M. Banks (Eds), *Multicultural Education: Issues and Perspectives* (pp. 31–60). Needham Heights, MA: Allyn & Bacon.

Evans, R. I. (1967). *Dialogue with Erik Erikson.* New York: Harper & Row.

Fordham, S., & Ogbu, J. U. (1986). Black students' school success: Coping with the burden of "acting white". *The Urban Review, 18,* 176–206.

Fowell, N., & Lawton, J. (1992). An alternative view of appropriate practice in early childhood education. *Early Childhood Research Quarterly, 7,* 53–73.

Fox, T. (1990). Basic writing as cultural conflict. *Journal of Education, 172*(1), 65–83.

Gestwicki, C. (1995). *Developmentally appropriate practice: Curriculum and development in early education.* Albany, NY: Delmar Publishers.

Goodnow, J., Miller, P., & Kessel, F. (1995). *New directions for child development: Cultural practices as contexts for development.* San Francisco: Jossey-Bass.

Greenfield, P. (1997). Culture as process: Empirical methodology for cultural psychology. In: J. W. Berry, Y. H. Poortinga & J. Pandey (Eds), *Handbook of Cross-Cultural Psychology: Vol. 1. Theory and Method.* Boston: Allyn & Bacon.

Harter, S. (1983). Developmental perspectives on self-esteem. In: E. M. Hetherington (Ed.), *Hankdbook of Child Psychology: Socialization, Personality, and Social Development* (Vol. 4). New York: Wiley.

Hays, K. G. (1992). Attitudes toward education: Voluntary and involuntary immigrants from the same families. *Anthropology and Education Quarterly, 23*, 250–267.

Hildebrand, V. (1997). *Introduction to early childhood education* (6th ed.). Upper Saddle River, NJ: Prentice-Hall.

Jessor, R., Colby, A., & Shweder, R. A. (1996). *Ethnography and human development: Context and meaning in social inquiry.* Chicago: University of Chicago Press.

Jipson, J. (1991). Developmentally appropriate practice: Culture, curriculum, connections. *Early Education and Development, 2*(2), 120–136.

Kaomea, J. (2003). Reading erasures and making the familiar strange: Defamiliarizing methods for research in formerly colonized and historically oppressed communities. *Educational Researcher, 32*(2), 14–25.

Kessler, S. A. (1991). Early childhood education as development: Critique of the metaphor. *Early Education and Development, 2*, 137–152.

Lewis, M., & Brooks-Gunn, J. (1979). *Social cognition and the acquisition of self.* New York: Plenum Press.

Lubeck, S. (1994). The politics of developmentally appropriate practice. In: B. L. Mallory & R. S. New (Eds), *Diveristy and Developmentally Appropriate Practices* (pp. 17–43). New York: Teachers College Press.

McLoyd, V. C. (1999). Cultural influences in a multicultural society: Conceptual and methodological issues. In: A. S. Masten (Ed.), *Cultural Processes in Child Development: The Minnesota Symposia on Child Development* (pp. 123–135). Mahwah, NJ: Lawrence Erlbaum.

Mead, G. H. (1925). The genesis of the self and social control. *International Journal of Ethics, 35*(3), 251–273.

Miller, P. H. (1993). *Theories of developmental psychology* (3rd ed.). New York: W. H. Freeman.

Murillo, N. (1971). The Mexican American family. In: N. N. Wagner & M. J. Haug (Eds), *Chicanos: Social and Psychological Perspectives* (pp. 97–108). St. Louis, MO: C. V. Mosby.

National Association for the Education of Young Children (1991). *Early childhood classroom observation.* Washington, DC: Author.

National Association for the Education of Young Children (1996). NAEYC Position Statement: Responding to linguistic and cultural diversity – recommendations for effective early childhood education. *Young Children, 51*(2), 4–12.

New, R. S., & Mallory, B. L. (1994). Introduction: The ethic of inclusion. In: B. L. Mallory & R. S. New (Eds), *Diversity and Developmentally Appropriate Practices* (pp. 1–13). New York: Teachers College Press.

Ogbu, J. U. (1974). *The next generation: An ethongraphy of education in an urban neighborhood.* New York: Academic Press.

Ogbu, J. U. (1981). Origins of human competence: A cultural-ecological perspective. *Child Development, 52*, 413–429.

Ogbu, J. U. (1982a). Cultural discontinuities and schooling. *Anthropology and Education Quarterly, 13*, 290–307.

Ogbu, J. U. (1982b) Socialization: A cultural ecological approach. In: K. Borman (Ed.), *The Social Life of Children in a Changing Society* (pp. 253–267). Hillsdale, NJ: Lawrence Erlbaum.

O'Loughlin, M. (1991, October). Rethinking early childhood education: A socio-cultural perspective. Paper presented at Conference on Reconceptualizing Research In Early Childhood Education, Madison, WI.

Page, R. M., & Page, T. S. (1992). *Fostering emotional well-being in the classroom*. Boston: Jones & Bartlett.

Powell, D. R. (1989). *Families and early childhood programs*. Washington, DC: National Association for the Education of Young Children.

Rogoff, B. (1990). *Apprenticeship in thinking: Cognitive development in social context*. New York: Oxford Univeristy Press.

Rogoff, B., & Morelli, G. (1989). Perspectives on children's development from cultural psychology. *American Psychologist, 44*, 343–348.

Shaffer, D. R. (1993). *Developmental psychology: Childhood and adolescence*. Pacific Grove, CA: Brooks/Cole.

Shore, B. (1996). *Culture in mind: Culture, cognition and the problem of meaning*. New York: Oxford University Press.

Spodek, B. (1991). Early childhood curriculum and cultural definitions of knowledge. In: B. Spodek & O. N. Saracho (Eds), *Issues in Early Childhood Curriculum* (pp. 1–20). New York: Teachers College Press.

Tylor, E. (1958). *Primitive culture*. New York: Harper (original work published in 1873).

Valentine, P., & Andrew, L. (1989, March). Living in Franklin Square: An exploration of Black culture. Paper presented at the annual meeting of the American Educational Research Association, San Francisco.

Walsh, D. J. (1991). Extending the discourse on developmental appropriateness: A developmental perspecive. *Early Care and Development, 2*(2), 109–119.

Zahan, D. (1979). *The religion, spirituality, and thought of traditional Africa*. Chicago: University of Chicago Press.

# PART II:
# RECONCEPTUALIZING
# PLAY (II)

# BEYOND FUN AND GAMES TOWARDS A MEANINGFUL THEORY OF PLAY: CAN A HERMENEUTIC PERSPECTIVE CONTRIBUTE?

Karen VanderVen

## ABSTRACT

*In a postmodern context this paper proposes that analogical scholarship in which one conceptual schema is used to view another in order to generate new perspectives, be used to view play. Hermeneutic philosophy specifically is used in a process modelling hermeneutic inquiry. Included are a review of play, hermeneutic philosophy, and the outcomes of the juxtaposition of hermeneutic concepts against play. Resultant perspectives on key issues in play, such as the meaning of play, play in meaning making, the binaries of play, play and practice, and play in the reconceptualizing movement in early childhood education, follow.*

Play is something we all recognize. We know when somebody is being "playful." Being concerned with early childhood education we can and do take a position on play, present our own perspectives and theories, and implement our practices based on these. Yet over the years, despite both our implicit and explicit investment in play's role in early childhood education, we continue to have questions: What is play? What does play mean? How do children benefit from playing? How can we improve our practices around play?

Social Contexts of Early Education, and Reconceptualizing Play (II)
Advances in Early Education and Day Care, Volume 13, 165–205
ISSN: 0270-4021/doi:10.1016/S0270-4021(04)13006-1

Thus play, perhaps as much as any area or concept in early childhood development and education, has for years been the subject of both lively debate and multidisciplinary study, with attempts to define its purpose, identifying characteristics, practices, and role in human development (e.g. Pellegrini, 1995; Schwartzman, 1978; Sutton-Smith, 1997). The very energy and effort that has been devoted to trying to understand play suggests that there is value in continuing to study it.

The rationale for a new review of play is further supported by the contention that "alternative theoretical paradigms are needed to understand early childhood experiences" (Frost et al., 2001, p. 35). Issues of theory and practice in early childhood education have traditionally been examined from disciplines within and closely related to it, e.g. child development and developmental psychology (Bloch, 1992). The advent of the reconceptualizing movement in early childhood, with its emphasis in viewing at the field through new lenses supports a fresh look at the nature of early childhood's driving values, theories, research methodologies, and practices. Thus a viewing of play through an external perspective, hermeneutic philosophy, is the purpose of this paper.

Hermeneutics is a branch of European philosophy concerned with human understanding, meaning making and interpretation (e.g. Mallery et al., 1986; Nakkula & Ravitch, 1998). There are several reasons for bringing a hermeneutic perspective to play. Hermeneutics, like play, has a long and evolving history as a body of thought. Hermeneutic philosophers and scholars of hermeneutics have accorded play a place in their formulations. Hermeneutics is increasingly being seen as a theory with practice applications for human service professions such as applied child and youth development (Nakkula & Ravitch, 1998). There could be hermeneutic implications for "understanding" play in all its complexity, both in terms of theory and practice.

Within hermeneutics and the early childhood reconceptualizing movement is the notion of *interpretivist* method of inquiry. An interpretivist approach recognizes that we try to "make sense" of circumstances "within a cultural framework of socially constructed and shared meanings" and that we "create and re-create our social world as a dynamic meaning system, that is, a system that changes over time" (MacNaughton, Rolfe & Siraj-Blatchford, 2001, p. 35). Interpretivist methodology thus involves trying to "understand socially constructed and shared meanings and re-present them as theories of human behavior" (p. 36). Thus in this paper the focus of inquiry is the relationship between play (as one aspect or construction of human behavior) and hermeneutics, with an emphasis on the perspectives and insights hermeneutics might generate when used as a lens for viewing some current conceptions of play. The interpretivist approach recognizes, as is the case here, that the selection and expression of ideas and concepts and how they are re-constructed is determined by an author's values, background, and available resources.

Packer and Addison's *Entering the circle: Hermeneutic investigation in psychology*, is organized in a way that "reflects three phases that can be distinguished in interpretive inquiry" (1989, p. 3) and can be used as a format for organizing this investigation. The three phases follow:

I. "*Discovering an appropriate workable perspective from which interpretation can proceed.*" In this phase, there will be a more specific rationale for the selection of hermeneutics as a lens for viewing play, including how the activity relates to the current reconceptualizing movement in early childhood education.

II. "*Conduct of inquiry within that perspective.*" The perspective having been articulated, herein there will be a review of both play and hermeneutics. For play, a synopsis of an array of contemporary viewpoints and theories of play will be presented to establish the grounding for the hermeneutic review. For hermeneutics, a more detailed consideration of major tenets of hermeneutics and hermeneuticists' treatment of play will be given.

III. "*Critical reflection upon and evaluation of the interpretive account that is the outcome of inquiry*" (p. 3). In this last phase, the material in phases I and II, play and hermeneutics, will be viewed with an interpretivist slant. That is, the concepts of hermeneutics as a lens will be juxtaposed against those in play, to see then what interpretation might be made, what insights about play might thus emerge, and what the implications are for the role of play in reconceptualizing early childhood education, and in play related practices.

# PHASE I – APPROACHING THE STUDY OF PLAY AND HERMENEUTICS: ESTABLISHING A PERSPECTIVE

The act of *establishing a perspective within which to undertake interpretivist inquiry* can serve as a forestructure – a hermeneutic concept derived from Martin Heidegger (Nakkula & Ravitch, 1998; Packer & Addison, 1989). A forestructure is essentially the knowledge and experience we bring to a subject when we encounter it. To set the stage for the more detailed exposition in Phase II the forestructure set out here will address the reconceptualizing movement in early childhood education. analogical scholarship, play and hermeneutics as "fuzzy" constructs, and issues of theory and practice. These will serve to frame subsequent discussion.

## *The Reconceptualizing Early Childhood Education Movement*

The reconceptualizing movement in early childhood has been underway for more than a decade. Reconceptualizers are taking a critical look at the common assumptions that have come from within the field of early childhood education for years and have dominated both theory and practice. In general, a postmodern perspective embracing issues of race, class and gender as they affect values and practices in early childhood eduction has been a focal point of reconceptualist thinking.

*Reconceptualizing and Postmodernism*
The postmodernist perspective challenges the assumptions about truth of the "modern" age in which there was a striving to establish absolute truth, using methods of rational-empiricist science, and the use of the findings to attain predictability and control. The social sciences such as psychology to which early childhood education is closely related, for many years were dominated by the "modernist" paradigm (e.g. Fishman, 1999).

A number of early childhood reconceptualizers specifically describe the postmodern frame that situates their thinking (e.g. Bloch, 1988; Dahlberg et al., 1999; Tobin, 1997). Grieshaber and Cannella state it as:

> Concern about . . . belief in universal truths and the imposition of these truths on all humanity"
> . . . while postmodern perspectives could expand our ways of understanding each other and
> appreciating our differences, postmodernism is also undefinable and multidirectional and
> presents challenges to universal truths. The complexity, ambiguity, and certainly the challenge
> to truth are disturbing to many (Grieshaber & Cannella, 2001, p. 9).

As Bloch (in Swadener & Kessler, 1992) puts it, " The terms 'critical theory,' 'interpretivist or symbolic research,' or 'post-modern' are rarely heard in seminar rooms, publications, or conferences focusing on early childhood education." Bloch gives several reasons for the "lack of recognition or acceptance of alternative theoretical and methodological perspectives in early childhood education." One is the "domination of psychological and child development perspectives" (p. 3). Another is that early childhood education, separate from elementary education, was not influenced by the "post-modern paradigms" (p. 4) in schools of education, and thus remained "tied to . . . largely positivist and empirical-analytic paradigms in theory and method" (p. 4).

Among the areas that post-modern thought, and the reconceptualizers, encourage new perspectives are power and hegemony. Following Foucault, in whose theory of power (Kelly, 1998) the discourse representing the language that contains these themes; truth may mean different things to people of various cultural backgrounds; and knowledge must be viewed in terms of its context and with reference to issues of diversity.

Certainly child development and early childhood education have been bounded fields; that is, they have drawn from within themselves for content, direction, and practice. In contrast he reconceptualizers look outside traditional or mainstream early childhood education and have composed an agenda featuring interpretivist science, critical theory, and post-modernism to bring the early childhood education table – a new menu indeed. These perspectives have encouraged a good deal of questioning of the theoretical and practice foundations of the field. All of it has implications for the theories that the field embraces and the practices it implements. Such theories and their mode of generation come under the scrutiny of the emancipatory aspect of reconceptualizing. They are considered dominant viewpoints. Similarly traditional dichotomies, such as the "good" and "bad" teacher (Ryan et al., 2001) reign in the early childhood field and await being deconstructed or reframed.

Deconstruction, referring to Derrida's concept, occurs when a text or concept is taken apart, so to speak, to examine the values and biases that generated it (Boyne, 1990; Grieshaber & Cannella, 2001). For example, developmentally appropriate practice has been considered a dominant discourse in early childhood education. A discourse in postmodernism is a socially created, value laden and hence linguistic system that can imply power or superiority (Ryan et al., 2001). Developmentally appropriate practice thus has come under scrutiny, i.e. been deconstructed to reveal the theories and empirically derived knowledge that has contributed to it.

Other postmodern concepts are structuralism and poststructuralism. Structuralism is a modernist concept in which preset and existent structures are used as frames for viewing a particular phenomenon. Grieshaber and Cannella (2001) for example, cite Piagetian theory of cognition as an example of structuralism. Piaget's concepts of learning are assumed to be universal, to apply to everybody, thus making Piagetian theory a structuralist theory. Poststructuralism in the postmodern orientation, then challenges "pre-existing systems of meaning" and as applied to cognitive development, "challenges child development and other scientific claims to universal cognitive structures" (p. 12).

This perspective certainly opens one of the most predominant and debated discourses in early childhood education – play – to new ways of looking at it, or reconceptualizing it. While the reconceptualizers don't exclusively confine their viewpoint to a cultural, emancipatory, and gender based agenda, these issues seem to be the major focus now.

*Reconceptualizers and Play*
That there can be new perspectives on play, and play's place in Developmentally Appropriate practice is underscored by Hyun in *Making Sense of Developmentally Appropriate Practice (DCAP) in Early Childhood Education* (1998) in which she points out that how we interpret play differs across cultures, as does even the conception of what is considered to be play. Certainly play seems an ideal

representative of a postmodern inquiry; Henricks (In Reifel, 2001), quotes Kuchler (a German literary theorist) as saying that we "have reached the end of modernity and the beginning of play" (p. 51). Henricks makes an important comparison between modern and postmodern play. Modern play is more goal oriented, rational, and less valued than work. Modern play is a way for "people to manipulate their environments in ways that give them pleasure" and "learn boundaries of the possible" (p. 66) although the realm of possibility is also embraced in postmodern play. Work is a primarily a function of adults; play is for children and is more "childish." Play for postmodernists is not a escape from the reality of life but rather a response to its indeterminacy and discontinuousness. There is the reflexive notion of being "played with" as well as being the "player": the modernist notion of play giving the "subject" the player – an autonomous sense of control. Thus play is more dialogic and interactive. Perhaps the most salient feature of play in Henrick's account is play's sheer elusiveness. Play doesn't rest in the subject; rather, it is boundless and like the world in which it exists. In this notion of play there is nothing about how to encourage play, what might be "good" play – a developmentalist or educator's concern, and what developmental outcomes might be attained by children at play. These of course could be seen as modernist concerns.

King (1992) points out that with the reconceptualizers' focus on race, class and gender, attention to *context* variables continues to be ignored even though "no behavior has meaning apart from the context in which it occurs" (p. 44). She continues to say that in the case of play, especially, the very "definition requires attention to aspects of the context." A prime example is that when adults direct children's activity, even though it might be pleasurable, they perceive it as work, whereas if children choose the activity and select their own participation they consider it play. Other classroom contexts, including the children's personal histories, the social context, the curricular context – all shape children's play, meaning that play is "never, simply, the free expression of children" (p. 47). Even though play is inevitably shaped by its contexts, play (paradoxically) according to King "is about the deconstruction of context the escape from contexts; in fact, one of play's major purposes is to make context irrelevant" (p. 58).

Gender issues in play, not surprisingly, have also been addressed by re-conceptualizers (Davies, 1997; Hughes & MacNaughton, 2001; MacNaughton et al., 2001). MacNaughton et al. (2001) point that complexity in construction of gender is a complex process and that play, because it can reflect nuances, can be a valuable research approach for studying it. Davies discusses the construction of gendered identity through play, and contends that more recent analyses of boy and girl play behavior shows that the way in which gender "is established and maintained, highly problematic." This "begins to reconceptualize the individual/social interface in children's play" (p. 117). Davies makes the interesting point that children in the future will need to understand their "power" to create a complex social world in their play and to "take responsibility for the social efffects of taking up one discursive practice rather than another, of finding different ways of being male or female, or neither" (p. 123). While discussing the notion of children's freedom in play, Davies indicates that there is no way adults are not involved in and influential in children's play. Adults can help children have a sense of the possible, as enabled through play, and to find different ways of being male and female, and to imagine different futures. Because only play seems to surface the nuances of such a process, it thus has utility as a research method addressing such issues.

The reconceptualizers, by stating that there must be consideration of perspectives from outside the established boundaries of child development and developmental psychology as they have provided the underpinnings for early childhood education, thus pave the way for utilization of analogical scholarship in early childhood issues.

### Analogical Scholarship

The viewing of play through an external theory or conceptual schema i.e. a hermeneutic lens is an act of analogical scholarship. In analogical scholarship one conceptual schema or theory is juxtaposed against another, to see what new ideas and thoughts emerge. To cognitive scientists, analogy making is central to cognition and knowledge generation – "analogy is *everything*," according to Hofstadter (2001, p. 499). To Gentner et al. (2001) analogy is central to human cognition, and to view it as the human ability to "think about relational patterns" (p. 2). Hopefully the conjoint viewing of play and hermeneutics will not only further illuminate our understanding of play, but also perhaps shift the relational patterns we see "within" play.

The case for taking an analogical approach a subject is further underscored by Gergen (1995) in his description of a "scholarship of dislodgment," one that "loosens the grip on the conventional" (p. 58). Gergen, whose social constructivist approach to knowledge challenges modern notions of science (in line with postmodernism), states, "in the claim to content, scientists have also made a strong distinction between a literal language (reflecting the world) and a metaphoric one (altering the reflection in artistic ways; again the literal is privileged over the metaphor. Yet, if a literal language is removed from the field, then the entire scientific corpus is open to analysis as metaphor" (p. 41). Certainly the reconceptualizing movement in early childhood education might be viewed as looking for ways to release the field from traditional or conventional values and practices, in which case analogical scholarship is a way of do so.

## Play and Hermeneutics as "Fuzzy" Constructs

The very existence of dozens of definitions, theories, and perspectives on play places it in an interesting category as a concept. Play is not a static or convergent concept. Play does not have just one meaning to all. As the positivists might desire, there is no "operational" definition of play that is universally accepted. If there were, there would be little to be learned by interpretivist scholarship. Rather, play is not only divergent and open-ended, but also it has other features that support its suitability for interpretivist study. Play is a mode rather than a category of activity meaning that it is amenable to examination over time according to Schwartzman (1978). Play can be considered a "fuzzy" concept (p. 323). The notion of fuzziness of some concepts has been further confirmed in subsequent formulations of fuzzy thinking and fuzzy logic e.g. Kosko (1993). The important point is that being fuzzy does not mean that a concept doesn't exist or that it can't be reasoned with or about. Similarly as will be seen, hermeneutics is as open-ended as play. In fact, because it is a philosophy with multiple proponents, typologies, schools, and concepts, it is like play, not only fuzzy but complex. As with play, despite its fuzzy aspects and multiple perspectives subsumed within the notion of hermeneutics, there are still, as a hermeneuticist would say, common understandings that can be stated.

## Theory and Practice

Because hermeneutics concerns itself with the relationship between theory and practice, it can be useful at this point to look at these concepts in more detail. Human services such as early childhood education are concerned with practices – informed actions that can alter the lives of clients. A common expression thus is "theory-to-practice." Theory is seen as comprising a body of knowledge from which practice might be deduced, or that might inform or shape practice, but is not "directly linked to it" (Bloch, 1992, p. 5). This implies a relationship but one in which the movement from theory to practice might be considered a quantum leap rather than a sequential progression. When the possibility is considered that there can be different types and levels of theory, a clearer and perhaps more useful relationship between theory and practice is possible, encouraging more congruence between theoretical constructs and practice premises.

Walker and Avant in the field of nursing proposed four levels of theory accordiing to VanderVen (1994). These are *meta-theory*, concerned with the kinds of theory a field needs and how to construct it, *grand theory*, abstract formulations de signed to give overall perspective to the structure and content of a field; *middle range theory*, a more "workable" level of theory with conceptual aspects but more visible links to practice, and *practice theory*, in which practice itself is reviewed and reflected upon to generate theoretical concepts – somewhat akin to Glaser and Strauss' grounded theory (1967). There can be a dynamic relationship among these different levels of theory: one level informs the other in a continuing interactive cycle.

Crucial to the arguments of this paper is that theory can serve as a "lens" through which to view, understand, and draw practice implications (Frost et al., 2001). Applying the lens concept, a theory based look at play may, however, be more sharply focused if we are clear as to what levels and kinds of theory we are using as our both our telescope and microscope. In sum, the concepts of reconceptualizing early childhood education, analogical scholarship, play and hermeneutics as fuzzy constructs, and theory and practice issues, comprise the rationale or justification for the inquiry into the relationship of play and hermeneutics, and the implications of hermeneutics for understanding play in theory and in practice. This leads to conducting the inquiry.

## PHASE II: CONDUCTING THE INQUIRY

To conduct this inquiry each body of knowledge (play as the subject of the inquiry and hermeneutics as the lens for viewing) must somehow be represented and organized for purposes of communicating with the reader. As was mentioned before this is interpretive: a selective process as a function of an author's own forestructure, background and resources.

Still it must be stressed that this review is undertaken with some degree of trepidation. Schwartzman, in *Transformations* (1978), as she embarked on the study of various sources of play theory, warned about the threats to play of definitions, classifications and metaphorical transformations, which, while having value, can result in "a reduction of play to some other phenomenon" (p. 7). She suggests that this can be avoided by not "forgetting the intrinsically playful, 'as if' quality of theorizing." Bearing this in mind along with the hermeneutic notion of "thrownness" (Nakkula & Ravitch, 1998, p. 3) in which one feels uncomfortable when facing a new or challenging situation, the inquiry will proceed.

### Play: Rhetorics, Theories, Binaries

Texts for analysis were selected with a focus on those authors who have obviously drawn on multiple resources to derive and configure their own perspectives. This approach is somewhat reminiscent of that pioneered by the famous trend analyst, John Naisbitt (1982) who needed a means to codify the vast amounts of data that are continually generated that might be used to predict trends. On the premise that journalists selecting material choose that which is the most significant and reflective of reality, used journalistic accounts and the qualitative method of content analysis to identify salient themes, patterns and frequencies.

Sutton-Smith's question, "Is there any future for play theory?" (1995, p. 275) suggests that play theory is a worthy question to pursue. Because hermeneutics as the lens might be or is considered a meta-theory that can lead to better understanding of other more specific theories (Nakkula & Ravitch, 1998), then "some" meta-level play theory would be needed. So play literature that is theoretically oriented (and reflects syntheses of other theory and research) was selected. Recency was also taken into consideration, but if an older source were frequently referred to then it was consulted directly as well.

A comment by Frost et al. (p. v) sets the format for the presentation of various levels of theory: "Values and beliefs must be articulated and aligned with relevant play theories." Since in postmodernism, there is attention given to the belief systems and values that underlie a particular theory, Sutton-Smith's "seven rhetorics of play" (Sutton-Smith, 1995, 1997) can be considered an articulation of values and beliefs. Similarly, Johnson et al. (1999) offer "four metaphors for play" that they consider are "influenced by modern theory" (p. 19). Then an array of theories can be examined to see how they relate to the rhetorics (and metaphors). Do they reflect them, or do they offer differing perspectives?

These discourses were derived by Sutton-Smith acknowledging the "complex value system" of those who promulgate them (1995, p. 277) and thus might be considered meta-theory. If one looks at Sutton-Smith's extensive and life long effort to study play theories through the lens of the trend analysis method, one might assume that his premises reflect a great deal of analysis and synthesis – another reason for beginning with them.

The question then arises: what types of conceptions of play should be presented, so that there is not only sufficient coverage but also some organizational format to bring at least minimal coherence into the review. Here again, a hermeneutic perspective offers a possibility. Crusius (1991) underscores the role of both rhetoric and dialectics in philosophical hermeneutics. Rhetoric is intended to offer a possible truth, although it cannot be verified; and like hermeneutics is concerned with interpretation. Dialectics are a crucial aspect of hermeneutic inquiry, with its dialogic and reciprocal aspects. Dialectics lead to ongoing questioning. However, it seems that in play there are binary opposites rather than dialectics. These are often considered in the literature but done so more implicitly as part of a larger discussion. Because the bulk of knowledge of play is subsumed under play theory (in many cases with supportive empirical research) these predominant or common binaries might also need to be considered.

Thus following the presentation of the rhetorics and metaphors will be a synthesis of grand or major play theories arranged in a loosely ecological framework that allows cultural and macro-factors to be considered as well as the interactions among levels of play functions; and then a consideration of commonly seen binaries.

*The Rhetorics of Play*
Sutton-Smith proposes four major rhetorics: play as progress, play as power, play as fantasy and the self in play. In later work (Sutton-Smith, 1997) he proposes three more: play and identity, play and fate, and play as frivolity. A brief description of these rhetorics follows.

*Play as progress.* The "play as progress" rhetoric in general reflects well accepted premise that there is valuable learning for children attained through play, such as social, emotional and cognitive skills. This reflects the common premise that "play is the child's work" (p. 279). There are other perspectives subsumed here as well. One is the contention that play enables children to adapt to their world. In the "progress" schema, too, children and adults are highly separated; only children play and there is no playful aspect to adult activity. There is a purist aspect to this perspective on play: power strivings and confrontative or assertive forms of play (e.g. capture-escape) are omitted. However, adults' commitment to the value of play for children's development justifies their efforts to organize and guide it.

*Play as power.* A scrutiny of play reveals that play, despite its benign connotation, can embrace power relationships and enact power differentials. Power themes are salient in adult activities, one example being the modern national obsession with contact sports whose structures and purposes reflect power relationships. In this context, the power theme is not surprisingly seen as representing a masculine perspective, i.e. "maledom" (p. 287) thus embracing a gender hierarchy. Again the separation of children and adults in belief systems about play is apparent, as Sutton-Smith comments that the "discourse of power is not typically found in child psychology and education" (p. 284).

*Play as fantasy.* Play as fantasy is concerned with the "make believe," pretense, and imaginative aspect of play. Sutton-Smith makes the point that such play is actually less free range so than we might think; the imagination is mediated by the very cultural frames it might be seen as transcending. In contrast to play as power, fantasy play is more likely seen as a female pursuit.

*Play of the self.* In the rhetoric of the play of the self lies the notion that play offers an optimal, chosen, pleasurable even "peak" experience to the player. Phenomenological notions of play, related to a search for meaning, a way of understanding one's own experience of the world through the "individual subjective experience" (p. 288) afforded by play, are subsumed in this rhetoric as is as play as performance or as a means of improvisation.

*Play as fate.* This rhetoric is hard to describe in a few sentences; as well Sutton-Smith (1997) makes the point that this is a more ancient rhetoric and less attended to as some of the more modern rhetorics. It refers to luck, chance (and is embodied in games of chance) and is perhaps the most dialectally opposed to the "progress" rhetoric.

*Play and identity.* In this notion, play is seen as situated in a social context, reflecting and being reflected by, membership in a community. This rhetoric is closely allied with that of play as power, in that this community identity is generated by sports and other kinds of contests (Sutton-Smith, 1997).

*Play as frivolity.* This refers to play conceived as trivial, meaningless and a waste of time. While Sutton-Smith accords says the concept of play as frivolity is one of the ancient rhetorics, it could be seen as having a very modern cast, as he himself refers to educators (Sutton-Smith in Pellegrini, 1995) who feel that play is indeed a non-learning activity and show this by their pedagogical approaches and endorsement of such practices as eliminating art, music, physical education and recess.

*Metaphors of Play*
While rhetoric and metaphor do not have an identical meaning, each in its way is an attempt to pull together specific theoretical perspectives into a larger perspective. Johnson et al. (1999) propose four metaphors that they see as "influenced by modern theory" and that have "practical implications" (p. 19).

*Play as transformation.* Play as transformation refers to primarily to the symbolic aspect of play in which children use objects to represent something else. There are different kinds of transformations, depending on what theme the child is enacting and what s/he is using to represent its pretend aspects.

*Play as performance.* In play as performance, the authors refer to Sutton-Smith's notion of the quadralogue, in which play involves not only players and co-players, but also directors, producers and an audience. These can be real or imagined and thus play is a "staged event" (p. 21).

*Play as script.* Script theory views players using play as a means of intereipreting their own experience. They call forth children's concepts or scripts representing their recall of common experiences. There are various levels of scripts, ranging from the simple to more complex, seen as story lines or narratives, involving making connections among scripts and connecting events to larger goals.

*Play as metacommunication.* In the play as metacommunication metaphor, the context or frame in which play occurs is key; play is integrally connected to the setting in which it occurs and the messages offered by that setting. Within a play episode or frame, there is communication among the players to identify the nature of the play event, including its beginning and ending. Play paradoxically is pretend within a frame, but yet is inexorably tied to reality; the continued interchange between the two (reality and fantasy) reflects the metacommunication aspect. There are continued messages at multiple levels.

*Theories of Play*
The theories of play summarized here are those most frequently encountered in both scholarly works (specifically concerned with theories) and those concerned with practice, but providing a theoretical justification for it (praxis). Bronfenbrenner's ecological hierarchy, beginning with the self and internal processes and moving outwards towards the environment, the broader context and larger, more embracing concepts is loosely used to order the categories. Ecology is a credible construct, and has been previously applied to play (e.g. Bloch & Pellegrini, 1989). In an ecological configuration, the hierarchy is not hegemonic; rather it is dynamic – one level is related to another, up and down, and there can be and is interaction among them.

*Play as engagement.* The notion of play as engagement refers to the energizing aspect of play that encourages the player to engage, or interact with the environment. This concept is not a major feature of some theories, but the significance of emotion as energizing feature of play pertains here (e.g. Landreth & Homeyer, 1998) as does contemporary arousal-modulation theory (Johnson et al., 1999) proposing that play emerges by a need to keep an optimal level of arousal in our central nervous system. Herein is also included the notion of "playfulness" or a "disposition" to play (Dodd et al., 2001) that could increase the likelihood of play occuring given a particular environment or situation.

*Play as construction.* The concept of "constructivism" so prevalent in contemporary early childhood education as the predominant approach to how young children learn (e.g. Fosnot, 1996) is of course fundamental here. Constructivist theory implies that the player builds something through the processes of play. This category embraces those concepts of play as it encourages learning about the self through absorbing information from the environment and changing one's mental model and hence actions on the environment in response to it, as in Piaget's processes of assimilation and accommodation (1962) and Vygotsky's zone of proximal development (Fromberg, 2002; Frost et al., 2001; Wertsch, 1985). The theories of both Piaget and Vygotsky are central in constructivist theory (Fosnot, 1996). In constructivism, the socio-cultural aspect as was especially emphasized by Vygotsky, is supported in "negotiated meaning" between children and others (p. 19).

There is also the form of play known as "constructive" (Smilansky, 1990) in which the child proactively utilizes material to make a "creation" (p. 2). This play emphasizes the interactive aspect of construction – the child in dialective interaction with the environment. The child takes in information, processes it in line with his/her mental structures, and then acts on the environment by construction of meaningful objects that reflect internally situated interests and goals.

"Play as construction" is probably the most akin to Sutton-Smith's "play as progress" rhetoric. Erikson's (1977) description of play as mastery – enabling the recreation through play of a disequilibrious situation to lead to better understanding similarly can be subsumed under the rubric of play as construction.

*Play as imagination.* That play enables and serves to develop imagination is so integral to most play theories (e.g. Singer & Singer, 1998) that it commands a major category, just as play as fantasy is one of Sutton-Smith's major rhetorics and play as performance is one of the metaphors of play (Johnson et al., 1999). Sociodramatic play (Smilansky, 1990) with its research base relating children's participation in this particular form of pretend or imaginative play with the ability to develop symbolic representation, is a major example of theory showing the role imagination in play. A pretend or imaginative play story line might be viewed as a narrative and thus contribute to the creation of meaning (Bruner, 1990). Another form of imagination might be play as improvisation (Nachmanovitch, 1990) which involves combining various available elements to create a performance. Imagination is the internal organizer of such improvisation.

Also germane is the relationship between play and theory of mind. Theory of mind refers to children's ability to know that others are capable of thinking, as well as to their own sense of what thinking capacities they have. It is concerned with what degree do children understand pretense, that is, whether something indeed stands for something else that is not there (Fein & Wiltz, 1998; Lillard, 2001). When they do, then such a theory of mind may serve to further shape and generate play. Play as pretense also enables a forward-looking stance: imagination allows the child to project a vision of the future.

*Play as meaning.* The notion that children play to "make sense" of their world, to understand the meaning of their experience, is salient in contemporary play theory (e.g. Bruner, 1990; Fromberg, 2002). Play as meaning making thus deserves a category of its own even though it could be considered an aspect of constructivism, bearing in mind von Glasersfeld's (1996) contention that children construct meaning through social interaction and that the language over a period of time accommodates at least to the individual meanings constructed by others. According to Bruner (1990) "the central concept of a human psychology is *meaning* and the processes and transactions involved in the construction of meanings" (p. 33) and the "quest for meaning(s) within culture are the proper causes of human action" (p. 20). There is a major implication: that children construct knowledge, rather than having it transmitted by teachers, who need then to provide opportunities for such construction to occur. To Bruner, too, meaning is communicated through narratives that serve to organize experience. The *expressive* function of play: that is, that play enables both the expression of feelings and emotions as well as acquiring better understanding of one's own feelings and those of others (e.g. Landreth & Homeyer, 1998), can enable children to make meaning. There is the idea of play as *representation*, in which children utilize their senses to bring forth an external reflection of these (Eisner, 1994). Representation could be somewhat akin to constructive play, as it is a way of conceiving the world and showing its meaning externally through any number of sensory-appealing media. Certainly play is a mode that enables children to represent their internal worlds; to some degree the concept of representation overlaps Erikson's (1977) concept of play as mastery.

*Play as connection.* Play enables children to make connections among various elements of their experiences, or to some theorists, *integrate* their experiences (e.g. Fromberg, 2002). As Fromberg states, "Play is a powerful integrator of experience and can support the growth of connections, not only with other people and other experiencees in the environment, but play also creates stronger structural connections and pathways within the brain" (p. 29). Enriched environments stimulate the development of these connections. Vygotsky's notion of the *mediating* function of play (Karpov & Haywood, 1998) (an important concept not heard as often as the zone of proximal development and scaffolding) is also in line with the notion of play serving to help children make connections among diverse experiences. That play enables children to create meaning can occur because it is integrally connected to their (children's) everyday experiences" (Isenberg, 1998, p. 493). One might say that play enables the connection to be made between the inner world of the player and his or her interaction with the external world and that meaning "means" the understanding of the child's *relationship* with that world. In a non-linear dynamical systems perspective (VanderVen, 1998), play enables children to use play to "connect various elements of experience" and to "make meaning out of their experience as they combine various aspects into larger configurations" (p. 22). Similarly, meaning making is "a dynamic process" (Fromberg, 2002, p. 11).

*Play and context.* That play is shaped by the context in which it occurs is emphasized by almost all play scholars. This of course is the function of play that is the focus of the ecological-cultural approach (Bloch & Pellegrini, 1989) and stressed in the reconceptualist view of play (King, 1992). As was stated before, the role accorded to context is a matter of degree. Some theories, more likely middle-range ones, certainly accord attention to the environment, usually the immediate environment, e.g. a classroom as to how it both shapes and allows play. Grand and synthesizing theories accord the context, in terms of culturally defined belief systems that shape all levels of activity a major focus in play. The context shapes the belief systems and social structures through which children learn (through play) both implicitly and explicitly the ways of their culture and society. The very playthings and accompanying language are contextually shaped. The issue of play and identity may fit in here, since even though identity is "constructed" by the self, in interaction with internally evolving mental structures and interaction with the environment in a transactional process, context is extremely crucial in identity formation, as shown by a theorist such as Erikson (1950) whose neo-Freudian theory gave direct accord to the role of the social context; and by the reconceptualist theorists who draw specific attention to how cultures situate identity formation in their construction of race, ethnicity, and gender.

In its broadest sense play serves as communication – in fact, as meta-communication according to Bateson. Meta-communicative messages serve as "frames" (Schwartzman, 1978) showing how another message shold be interpreted. In order to understand an action as play, it must be framed by the contextual message, "this is play" (p. 218). As Bateson himself puts it in *Mind and Nature.* "What is characteristic of play is that this is a name for contexts in which the constituent acts have a different sort of relevance and organization from that which they would have had in non-play. It may even be that the essence of play lies in a partial denial of the meanings that the actions would have had in other situations" (1979, p. 125).

*Play as power.* Play as power is one of Sutton-Smith's rhetorics and is also a theme seen across theories. Play can enable the powerless (small children) to feel powerful and more in control (e.g. Erikson, 1950, 1977). At the same time, as has been pointed, there are power themes and power struggles within play (e.g. Davies, 1997; Schwartzman, 1978) that possibly never enable a child to experience a complete sense of power. Power needs to be sought and is not always attained, although successful strategies might be affirmed – an important learning. There is a paradoxical aspect to power and play. Play can help a player feel both powerful through the act of playing, yet oppressed through roles and places in play that consign the player to a diminished or uneffective position in the play.

*Play as transformation.* The notion of play as transformation was pioneered by Schwartzman (1976) and fits in well with the organizational schema presented here. While it is obviously difficult to hierarchize these different play categories, somehow the notion of play as transformation might be considered the most embracing if one considers that there are multiple levels of transformation and that transformation is a continually evolving process. In the metaphor of Johnson et al., transformation refers primarily to the pretend and fantasy aspects of play in which the players transform the meaning of objects, scenes and actions (1999). This is akin to one aspect of Schwartzman's (1978) concept of transformation – that children can transform objects by making them stand for whatever they want them to. At another level of transformation, play itself can be viewed as an agent for change. Play itself "plays" an active role in changing and transforming an environment. This notion of play as affecting the environment in which the play takes place does not seem to be as manifest in play theories as does the notion of how the context of the player affects the play. However, if one applies a transactional or recursive approach to viewing play (VanderVen, 1998) and the act of play is considered an active agent, then play is a complex dynamic system continually exchanging information from the environment over time. This contributes to the transformation of the player and of the environment.

*The Binaries of Play*

Many writers on play implicitly and often explicitly discuss the binary or dichotomous aspects of play, (e.g. Davies, 1997; Monighan-Nourot, 1998; Schwartzman, 1978; Sutton-Smith, 1995). Monighan-Nourot supports the inclusion of a review of some of the dichotomous references to play. She discusses "binary oppositions" actually observed in children's play and states that, "bipolar tensions" encourage numerous functions of play (1998, p. 383). Similarly Fromberg (1999) points out the learning possibilities offered to children in dialectic activity. Just as tensions then enable children to develop insight into their worlds, so also might recognition of the "bipolar tensions" in play lead play theorists to an expanded understanding. Since dichotomies often seem to reflect common-sense or stereotyped thinking, an examination may set the stage for a hermeneutic dialectic reframing.

*Fantasy and reality.* Play is often seen as primarily involving fantasy; yet it is often discussed in terms of its ability to reflect and create reality. That there is a salient imaginary or fantasy aspect to play seems almost universally accepted, and viewed as an escape from reality in which children can in a sense create their own through the fantasy of play. However, fantasy can also be viewed as ways for children to understand and construct their reality through play. Some philosophers would say that we can never truly understand reality, that we can certainly construct and share meanings through communication, but that an aspect of any reality is fantasy, and that reality must by necessity be integrated into any fantasy.

*Work and play.* This binary is perhaps the most frequently referred to in all of the discussion of and discourses about, play (e.g. Davies, 1997). There is a tendency for the concepts to be seen as oppositional: there may be a desire for children to work when they are "just playing" although there is the trite saying that "play is children's work." The fact that there is research showing that children can differentiate between work (when their activity is directed by an adult), and play (when they choose their activity) even though there may be great similarity between the activity itself (King, 1992) has interesting implications for deconstructing or reframing this dichotomy. This is especially so when it is considered that the children found equivalent pleasure in the activity whether or not they thought it work or play.

*Process and product.* A very common affirmation for children's playing is that it enables them to experience a process without emphasis on outcome or product and thus experience more freedom and sense of power. In fact, the process argument is often used as a justification for adults' detachment from children's play. Yet, that there might be outcomes from play – learning a particular concept, developing a different sense of meaning, and that even having "made something" can also lead to a sense of empowerment, is less often considered. The product notion does reflect the premises of Sutton-Smith's (1997) "progress" rhetoric.

*Pleasurable and serious.* One of the most prevalent notions about play that is considered an indicator that play is occurring, is the fact that it is fun or pleasurable. In fact, the title referring to "fun and games" stereotyped expression reflecting Sutton-Smith's frivolity rhetoric, was selected to show that there is much more to play, a much more profound side, than that. The well documented therapeutic use of play is an example. The expression and the scenarios created by children dealing with traumatic and puzzling situations through play with a serious intent might not be pleasurable. Certainly the play of children during the Holocaust would be a prime example (King, 1992).

*Rule based and free flowing.* Some researchers claim that play is rule based, even though the rule structure may be hard to detect (e.g. Fromberg, 2002; Monighan-Nourot, 1998). Conversely there is the idea that play enables the transcendence of rules; by playing, one can step out of the strictures and requirements imposed by rules. Thus play is more "free flowing," unrestrained by rules for its conduct.

*Choice and requirement.* There is a notion that play is "freely chosen" by children, thus making the activity play; and that if participation in an activity is required that it is not play. Rather as the children themselves would concur the adult directed activity is work. However, little considered is the possibility that among children, work can be fun; that children are engaged by attention from adults who are requiring their participation, and that in the dialectic and oscillating nature of play (Fromberg, 2001), work can be embedded in play, and conversely there can be a playful aspect to work. The concept of context too can reframe this dichotomy. It has been made quite clear that context, on many levels, shapes and can even determine the content and process of play. So an activity in one context may seem to be work, while the same activity in another context would seem to be play.

*Freedom and constraint.* Play is viewed as freeing children from the restrictions felt in their everyday lives as they can imaginatively create scenarios that they may freely choose and experience as liberating; yet the contexts of play and the implicit power relationships that can exist in play act as constraint, even if a child may not always recognize this.

*Past and future.* While Erikson (1950) discussed play's ability to enable children to integrate past, present, and future, others have focused more on how the past shapes play e.g. Freud (Frost et al., 2001) whereas that play enables projection into the future enables children to be able to consider the issue of "what-if" (Isenberg, 1998).

Three organizational schemes reflecting current conceptions of play: play rhetorics, play themes (as synthesized from contemporary theories) and binaries of play have been presented. This might be considered a snapshot rather than a movie indicating that it is a statement at this point of time, subject to continued change over time. A postmodern frame situates this review of play as a text, just as play itself is a text (Schwartzman, 1978). It is not required to claim truth, and is subject always to further interpretation. In a similar orientation the exposition of hermeneutics follows.

## Hermeneutics

As has been stated hermeneutics, like play, is a complex and multi-faceted theory whose numerous divergent and subtle thought lines are difficult to describe in limited space. What is presented is an interpretation of the resources encountered, with an eye towards identifying the common themes or as hermeneuticists themselves would say, common understandings that emerge when looking at the hermeneutics across its various proponents and interpreters.

### Nature of Hermeneutics

Hermeneutics is strongly situated in contemporary post-modern thought (Gergen, 1994; Packer & Addison, 1989). Postmodernism and hermeneutics challenge both the rational (formal logic, hypothetical deductive approach to knowledge) and the empirical (factual and data based approach to knowledge) characteristic of the modern or industrial-scientific era of the earlier 20th century (Packer & Addison, 1988). Hermeneuticists along with postmodernists eschew the notion of absolute truth, focus on how we interpret our experience, are concerned with the social construction of language and meaning, and promulgate a reframing of power differentials. Thus hermeneutic philosophy appears to be situated as well within the early childhood reconceptualizing movement.

In today's global and complex world, how we interpret the messages we constantly receive and how others interpret those we send is crucial. While hermeneutics is thus a philosophy for the times, its origins are old, harking back centuries where the focus was on interpretation of Biblical nexts. Named for Hermes, the messenger to the Greek gods and from the gods to humans (Packer & Addison, 1989); hermeneutics is thus concerned with communication, the significance of messages, the translation of complex messages and their interpretation (Nakkula & Ravitch, 1998). Despite the importance of interpretation there is in the tradition of Hermes, a "tricky" side to messages – they can easily be misinterpreted and our preformed prejudices that are like the messages sent, shaped by the past and by cultural frames we do not completely understand (Packer & Addison, 1989).

*Culture* is a fundamental concept in hermeneutics. Crusius (1991) indicates that the main function of interpretation might be, "How shall we receive – understand and evaluate – our own cultural heritage?" (1991, p. ix) Communications are situated in the cultural context in which they are produced; in line with the definition of hermeneutics as "the systematic application of understanding to the (a) text, (that) reconstructs the world in which the text was produced and places the text in that world" (Mallery et al., 1994, p. 1).

*Texts* are any production, oral, written, performed; a text can be art work, an interaction, a conversation. Texts thereby are culturally influenced and interpreted in line with forestructures that are also culturally influenced. In line with the earlier discussion of hermeneutic research, hermeneutics is intended to deduce specific meanings of texts using everyday judgement rather than scientific method and proof (Mallery et al., 1994). As with many schools of thought, there are different schools or kinds of hermeneutics. Classical hermeneutics refers to the historical approach of hermeneutics, particularly as it evolved to aid in the interpretation of Biblical texts.

Methodological hermeneutics focused on finding a scientific interpretation by "situating a text in the context of its production" (Mallery et al., 1994, p. 1). More recently, three major hermeneutic approaches, with their representative authors, have emerged and it is a consideration of these that will situate the discussion of the relationship between hermeneutics and play theory.

One of these is *philosophical hermeneutics*. Philosophical hermeneutics draws upon the existential psychology of Martin Heidegger and this perspective is reflected in the hermeneutic philosophy oriented towards "existential understanding" (Mallery et al., p. 7) of Hans Georg Gadamer, who is known for expanding on Heideggerian ideas (Nakkula & Ravitch, 1998). Gadamer's hermeneutics encourages the reconsideration of the relationship between philosophy and science and the role of language as the means of constituting our "being in the world" (Bleicher, 1980, p. 128). In fact Gadamer views language as "functioning like forms of play" (Nakkula & Ravitch, 1998). Philosophical hermeneutics views text as comprising a dialogue between interpreter and text rather than with the original intent of the sender; thus reflecting a mediating function.

Juergen Habermas is representative of *critical hermeneutics* (e.g. Thompson, 1981), which is concerned with the social foundations of discourse. His views contrast with those of Gadamer who contends that communication involves power and can be used to subjugate. Without specific action such communication perpetuates misunderstanding. However, Habermas believes that "common truth" can be established through interaction in a community, a process referred to as the "theory of communicative action" (Crusius, 1991; Mallery et al., 1994; Nakkula & Ravitch, 1998). In critical hermeneutics, language can only be understood by considering the practical ways in which people use it. The contrasting viewpoints of Gadamer and Habermas are embodied by the Habermas-Gadamer debate (e.g. Mallery et al., 1994). Habermas (putting it somewhat simply) contends that a "self-reflective" approach with analysis using inputs from several sources can overcome prejudice, and as stated already, reduce misunderstanding. Gadamer however would then contend that these analyses would still be governed by culturally determined factors that shape how the interpretation proceeds and thus not really be freed from the constraints of language as being socially constructed and shaped by the social fabric of its culture.

Then, there is *phenomenological hermeneutics* as represented by Paul Ricouer (Bleicher, 1980; Mallery et al., 1986). In phenomenological hermeneutics, texts are deconstructed to attend to the socio-cultural influences in their generation, a different process than Gadamer's seeking of understanding through continued dialogue. Since Ricouer attends to notions of play in his hermeneutics, his work will be included here.

### Some Hermeneutic Concepts

The notions of *meaning making*, *interpretation* and *text* as central in hermeneutics have already been described as an entrypoint into this discussion of hermeneutics. Other fundamental concepts or constructs include *forestructure*, the *hermeneutic circle*, hermeneutic perspectives on *power*, *prejudice*, *language*, *communication*, *context* and *praxis*.

*Meaning making and interpretation.* Hermeneutics is concerned with meaning making and interpretation of experience.

It is "the theory or art of explication, of interpretation" (Gadamer, 1991, p. 88). Meaning making is intended to extend *understanding* (Nakkula & Ravitch, 1998; Packer & Addison, 1988) Hermeneutics extends the distinction between *explanation* (the function of the rational-empiricist approach) and *understanding* (a dynamic and overtly subjective knowing that is situated in the person and which can change over time as the person and the context inevitably change). Nakkula and Ravitch add the notion of *articulation* – that part of the process of knowing is to be able to articulate one's understanding or interpretation.

In hermeneutics the meaning of various phenomena is constructed by the human who experiences them. This has strong roots in Heidegger's contention that . . . the most "pressing question of all knowing (is) the question of the 'meaning of being,' in particular, the meaning – making essence of being human." Truth is not scientific reality; rather it is our evolving understanding of, or the meaning we make, of our ongoing experience in the world through our relationships with people, "with work, with play" (Nakkula & Ravitch, 1998, pp. 89–90).

*Forestructure and the hermeneutic circle.* In hermeneutics, our understanding of any text is shaped by our *forestructure* – the particular background that we bring to viewing it and interpreting it. Forestructure is shaped by our culture, background, experience and expectations. At the outset of undertaking to interpret a text, we both understand and misunderstand something (Packer & Addison, 1989).

Thus forestructure determines entrance into the *hermeneutic circle*. The hermeneutic circle, in Gadamer's formulations, "clarifies the relationships between the interpreter and what is to be interpreted or understood" (p. 79). The hermeneutic circle is the process of increasingly informative interpretive inquiry; it usually begins with everyday understanding as a text. The inquiry then enters a *circular* process by which understanding is increased as layers of meaning are increasingly uncovered with the continuing of the process of investigation. As this process goes forward, we inevitably encounter the unfamiliar and integrate it into our current understanding yielding *expansion of horizons* (Nakkula & Ravitch, 1998, p. 8) or *appropriation of meaning* (Ricouer, 1981, p. 182). This is making one's own what was previously alien or unknown. The hermeneutic circle enables relationships between parts and wholes to be seen (Steinsholt & Traasdahl, 2001). Understanding then leads to explanation, and then explanation to further understanding in the continuous circular process (Ricouer, 1981). Attaining greater understanding is more than the linear process of acquiring factual knowledge; such understanding can be ambiguous, in line with Slattery's (1995) contention that ambiguity is characteristic of postmodern hermeneutics because it is the reality of both the "human condition and the natural world" (p. 106). Similarly, the hermeneutic way of knowing is consonant with the notions of chaos theory, which accepts the unpredictable and imprecise nature of the world, and of "fuzzy concepts" as earlier described.

*Hermeneutics, power and prejudice.* Our forestucture is inevitably reflective of prejudice. We encounter a new situation with the biases of our past experience as we have heretofore constructed it. As post-modernism contends, and in this application of hermeneutics, knowledge and activity should be emancipatory rather than hegemonic: no particular knowledge source is superior to or should hold sway over another. Thus in hermeneutics, power of knowing is shared. In a modern relationship the perspective of an authority figure such as a teacher or a therapist, even though biased, would predominate. In applied hermeneutics uncovering prejudice is a mutual process in such a relationship, leading to *reciprocal transformation* (Nakkula & Ravitch, 1998). One party alone doesn't change at the behest of the other. Rather both do in a dialectic and dynamic process of interaction over time moving towards increased understanding of each person by the other. Such interaction, in applied work, is *ethical*. Since the work involves the well being of other people, the uncovering of prejudice in the practitioner (e.g. early childhood teacher, child or youth worker, teacher, therapist), at least serves to prevent the unwitting and perhaps unhealthy imposition of a dominant perspective on a vulnerable recipient.

*Hermeneutics, language and communication.* Given that any text can be the subject of hermeneutic intepretation, language then plays a key role in hermeneutics. To Gadamer, "all understanding is made possible by language" and language is "the constituting force in human development and human being" (Nakkula & Ravitch, 1998, pp. 25–26). Language of course is then subjective. It is the symbol system used to express meaning and by which people subjectively construct the meaning of their lives and through which they communicate meaning to others who interpret it through their own linguistic framework. Play comes in in Gadamer's conception of the significance of language in development: "the language game" develops in the same way as does play, through interaction with others and having language stand for or represent something else.

Similarly, to Habermas language is key. Language "is the medium by which meaning is shared" (1968, p. 157) and is not surprisingly the basis of *communication* among people. "Understanding is a communicative experience" (p. 181). To Habermas, "a primary role for hermeneutics is as a method for fostering clearer communication among individuals" (Nakkula & Ravitch, 1998, p. 26). This notion is made more explicit in his "theory of communicative action" (Habermas, 1971; Mallery et al., 1994) in which communication, integrated through an ongoing process of "self-reflection" and interaction, can relate to more rational action among a larger group.

*Human development in the context of everyday lived experience.* Without literally referring to hermeneutic theory, the famous developmentalist Robert Kegan, espouses a hermeneutically sympathetic view of human development in, *The Evolving Self* in which he was "proposing a view of human being as meaning-making and exploring the inner experience and outer contours of our transformations in consciousness throughout the lifespan" (Kegan, 1995, pp. 1–2). This statement certainly has a strong hermeneutic flavor.

Hermeneutics is concerned with context. People can only be understood in the context in which they conduct their daily lives and the meanings of these lives that they linguistically construct out of their experiences and interactions with others. Central to this process are the fundamental hermeneutic activities of interpretation and articulation. Given this conception, then hermeneutics today is considered to be a "theory for understanding life or human *being* . . . a theory of living . . . a natural theory of life" (Nakkula & Ravitch, 1998, p. 4). The interconnectedness of people and events is stressed in hermeneutics as well as a temporal factor. In applied developmental hermeneutics, tranformative processes occur over an extended time span in the contexts in which they occur and which influence them.

*Hermeneutics and praxis.* Hermeneutics offers a new and much-needed perspective on the theory – practice breach. To Gadamer, "Hermeneutics is primarily practice, the art of understanding and making things understandable to others" (Steinsholt & Traasdahl, 2001, p. 75). Gadamer himself, writing in *Reason in the Age of Science* (1993) says, "Today practice tends to be defined by a kind of opposition to theory" and suggest that "the opposed concept, the concept of theory, has become something different in our time. It suggests nothing of what *theoria* was to the eye disciplined enough to discern the visibly structured order of . . . human society (p. 69). Gadamer defines *praxis* (not necessarily in the way we consider professional "practice") as "choosing, or deciding for something and against something else, and in doing this a practical reflection is effective, which is in itself dialectical in the highest measure" (p. 81). As Steinsholt and Traasdahl (2001, p. 75) state, to Gadamer, "practice comes first." He . . . has always been concerned with not getting lost in a veritable wilderness of theoretical and methodological constructs. This suggests that the dichotomy can be reframed with implications for educational, developmental and psychological "applied" activities, including play.

## Play and hermeneutics

For Gadamer, play is not just 'mere' play (Madison, 1991, p. 135).

This section focuses on how hermeneuticists have treated play in their philosophies; play occupies a significant role in the work of the three major hermeneuticists considered here, although Gadamer seems to be the one who has accorded play the most significant place in his thinking.

*Play and text.* While play and a play frame or context could be a text there is also reference to the "playful" aspect of reading a text. The significance of playfulness is considered by Ricouer (1981) who discusses the relationship of a reader with text as governed by playfulness and refers to this as "being able to read between the lines." "To accomplish this one needs more than anything else to be aware of the forms of play in texts" (p. 224). These include variations in meaning. A reader can have fun by discovering something an author did not mean to be seen. Taking such a stance enables a reading from "odd angles" (Steele, 1989, p. 224) and one might suspect, then being able not only to take a critical stance towards the text, as the author contends, but also to perhaps discover some really meaningful aspect or a surprise element. Such is a feature of both play and of hermeneutic inquiry.

*Play, understanding, and meaning-making.* Gadamer emphasized the relationship between play and understanding saying that "understanding permeates our very existence but is not an activity separate from our other activities" (Steinsholt & Traasdahl, 2001, p. 74). Play in this context of understanding is a "mode of existence." Understanding is not a "scientific comprehension of a detail; rather it is a practical understanding of our lives and possibilities" (p. 75). Thus for example the playing child at school or day care must be seen in the context of his or her whole life situation.

To Gadamer, play is fundamental in the hermeneutic intent of meaning-making and understanding. Play is referred to as a metaphor for the "understanding process"; the meaning of play lies in "the enhanced self-understanding the player receives as a result of play" (Madison, 1999, p. 134). Edelschick (1998) extends this notion saying that play is a "necessary component of growth and meaning making . . . for an experience to be most meaningful, we must lose ourselves in the play of the experience" (p. 284).

*Play and context.* In hermeneutic considerations of play, the relationship of play to the context of "world" of the player, figures largely. To Gadamer,

> The experiences of a child in its cultural everyday world thus create the underpinnings for play . . . There can be no play in a vacuum . . . Play cannot be divorced from concrete life" . . . Play is a part of the whole, the life situation or context in which it occurs". Thus a child in a care situation must be viewed, or 'understood' in context, or "total life situation (Steinsholt & Traasdahl, 2001, p. 78).

There is a close connection between play and context, or "world," and the hermeneutic circle as it enables part-whole relationships to be uncovered. The hermeneutic circle allows ever increasing understanding of one's surround or context. We are cast into the world and are thus pressed to have to interpret and try to understand that world. As we gain new experiences, our *horizons of understanding* expand, and hence our greater understanding of our context.

*Play and language.* Language and play are intertwined: "Language . . . comes into *play* . . ." (Gadamer, 1981, p. 4) wherever people engage in a reciprocal, dialectic conversation. "Language is nothing other but the universal medium of our experience of the world, the form in which the *play of experience* realizes itself (Madison, 1991, p. 133). From these statements we can recognize that these hermeneuticists see language as fundamental to the process of making meaning out of experience, and that this can be seen as a playful process.

More pragmatically, in their explication of hermeneutics in applied development, Nakkula and Ravitch (1998) stress the role of language as a tool and play as a way of encouraging it. Furthermore, language addresses the issue of power and reframing of power for vulnerable populations, e.g. children and youth. Linguistic competence is needed for participation in the major institutions of society, and as it develops through playful experiences and activities, thus confers greater effectance and power. Further drawing on Gadamer et al. (1998) comment on Gadamer's position that language is learned as a "language game" that progresses as the child learns symbolic representation. This "game" continues to be reiterated in life as the "as we confront new activities with their own set of governing rules" (p. 250). Games also "play" a major role in discovering what is truth. Gadamer's notions as to what is truth are enlightened by his utilization of game and play (Teigas, 1995) in which he likens play and games to the aesthetic experiences offered by art. To Gadamer, there is a close relationship between play and experiencing art (Steinsholt & Traasdahl, 2001). Games have clear rules and behavioral expectations that shape the players' actions and thus hold "authority" over the players; this is so likewise for works of art which exert a kind of authority over their viewers. Similarly, a play "extends its authority not only to its actors but also to its audience. Thus, through this authority, the play transfers to its audience what it represents or what it is about" (Teigas, 1995, p. 75). Ultimately art can represent "truth" by presenting other points of view and challenging things people take for granted. Art does not directly copy reality, but rather can extract what is significant from what might on the surface seem inessential, and thus "recover" truth (p. 76).

*Play as a dialectic transformational process.* Play is *transformational* in the view of both Gadamer and Ricouer. In "playful encounters" with others in dialogue, in a dialectic "to-and-fro" process (Ricouer, 1981, p. 186), one discovers greater possibilities for being and acting, and *self realization* (Madison, 1991, p. 134). Thus play transforms those who participate in it. This to Ricouer is accomplished through play's paradoxical aspects. It enables the abolishment of "everyday reality, yet everyone becomes himself" (p. 187). By stepping aside from the constraints of reality, to "assume different voices" new perspectives and creative perceptions can occur. Yet, while doing this, one grows into his or her own self.

A central concept in Ricouer's attention to play is *appropriation*, a notion that further extends our understanding as to how transformation can occur through play. *Appropriation* is the transforming relationship a reader has with a text on the premise that an encounter with any text engages readers they bring their experience to it. Play of course, enables an appropriative relationship to a situation or text. This is in contrast to *distanciation* (Ricouer, 1981) which reflects the attempt to bring objectivity to the reading of a text.

The relationship of play, identity and self is considered by Gadamer. The player can abandon the self, but yet can find the self in play, still maintaining an inner concept of self while pretending to be someone else (Steinsholt & Traasdahl, 2001). There is a paradoxical aspect: "in forgetting himself, the child finds himself" (p. 86) and thus play contributes towards the creation of identity.

*Play and life.* As was discussed earlier, hermeneutics is concerned with aspects of "everydayness" of life and according to Gadamer (Steinsholt & Traasdahl, 2001) thus is a mode of existence, not separate from our other activities. Play offers a "practical understanding of our lives and possibilities" (p. 75). Play is a part of the whole, the life situation or context in which it occurs. Lives are "linguistic constructions" people build from the range of, or from the texts of their experiences. In fact, such construction is the source of life direction, according to Ricouer (1981). Ricouer goes so far as to say that individual construction of experience, rather than internalization of early parental relationships, is what really governs the developmental process. Thus we might say that Ricouer's notion of construction is akin to the constructivist theories in early childhood education (e.g. Fosnot, 1996); and to the constructivist concepts of life span development (e.g. Kegan, 1994).

# PHASE III: CRITICAL REFLECTION ON THE INTERPRETIVE ACCOUNT

The "critical reflection and evaluation of the interpretive account that is the outcome of inquiry" (Packer & Addison, 1989, p. 3) is the last phase of this work. The reflection will be based on both the *process* of creating the account as inquiry, and on the *content* – the specific descriptions and concepts of play and hermeneutics that were presented. Having presented various perspectives on play theories, and some essential concepts and tenets of hermeneutics, the emphasis now is the *relationship* between hermeneutics and play.

## Process of the Inquiry

### Hermeneutic Aspects

Perhaps the first reflective comment to made is to emphasize that as the process gets underway, that the entire activity of recording the inquiry was in itself hermeneutic. What has emerged is a text that embodies the hermeneutic notion of there being no absolute truth. This is in line with Crusius' (1991) comment that the process of writing is akin to a hermeneutic circle. As we continue to reflect in the entire writing process, there is the ongoing potential for alteration of the forestructure we bring to it and thus what we actually say. What readers "see" in this paper will have a hermeneutic flavor: They will bring their own forestructures to the reading, hopefully "playfully" interact with the text (Ricouer, 1981) and construct their own understanding, meaning and interpretation of it.

By necessity the task of this paper has required organization and categorization of ideas as a function of how material consulted was selected, interpreted and understood by the author. As the conjoint viewing of play and hermeneutics is set out, utilizing an organizational framework and categories, there will need to be a distinct attempt to maintain Schwartzman's "as-if" and playful stance. Care will need to be taken not to reduce play to something it isn't. Schwartzman (1978) mentioned also how "classifications" . . . have frequently been formulated by researchers "to make sense" out of the range of materials that they have actually collected (p. 7). This is what admittedly has been done in this paper. A hermeneutic perspective suggests that a pejorative frame does not have to be assigned to this activity. Like a hermeneutic circle, the reflective process that goes into an organizational schema can still lead to a re-drawing of boundaries that in turn can lead to new ideas, new directions for inquiry and ultimately greater understanding.

Schwartzman continues to say that "all too frequently a classification scheme is formulated and that is all" (p. 7). Using some kind of organizing schema *doesn't* have to be all. Play continues to be the fascinating concept that others in the past have confirmed. Play is something we all recognize, sense its power, hope to utilize in our work, and continue to explore and document its dynamic growth and change over time – very much in the hermeneutic sense. Perhaps an insight as well is that play like many constructs and concepts, will never totally be captured, totally "explained." How we view play, how we construct it, will continue to be situated in perspectives generated by our experiences, our times, and our culture. Play, in line with Schwartzman's cautions, will be seen not as "is," which has a ring of the final, but rather, "as" or "and" – still open to new reframings, understandings and interpretations.

So hermeneutics endorses the ongoing effort to bring new ways of studying play to the fore, but feeling safe that there is no need to come up with a final statement. As Gergen (1995) states, "To the extent that any reality becomes objectified or taken for granted, relationships are frozen, options sealed off, and voices unheard" (p. 58). With play viewed through a hermeneutic lens, and undoubtedly other lenses to come in the future, there does not seem much danger of that.

## Analogical Issues
A strong rationale for the use of analogy in a hermeneutic inquiry was made earlier. However, when the act of juxtaposing one complex theory or schema up against

another actually takes place to conceive and certainly describe this process is difficult. Indeed, *how* does one juxtapose one theory against another, even though scholars refer to this process? What will emerge or be seen by aligning the two perspectives together?

There seem to be fundamental similarities among the "fuzzy" constructs and concepts of play and of hermeneutics, and yet the match isn't exact. In fact, it is quite impossible to bring hermeneutics and play into "structural alignment." Still, hermeneutically, one can *launch* into the attempt. A visual metaphor for the juxtaposition playfully comes to mind. The juxtaposition suggests many commonalities that are almost congruent with each other, but with some aspects of each that "stick out around the edges." It is viewed as rather like the sun. The area of congruence is like a sun, and the area of difference – what radiates out around the periphery, is the rays, with differing lengths of color and ray for play and for hermeneutics. The sun is not static. One can imagine the rays moving and changing colors. When one juxtaposes two open-ended, dynamic concepts, the result obviously would not be quiescent. Nor with the characteristics of these two open ended complex constructs would the "findings" necessarily be able to reflect everything that was set forth in the earlier exposition since there seems to be no set template for such an effort. To try to compose and use one could be an artificial imposition with an attempt to be "scientific" that is not in the hermeneutic tradition. This is not necessarily a limitation; the text then leaves questions open for others, in interaction with it, to make their own interpretations.

## Content of the Account

There will be comments on the three formats for the play exposition: play and rhetoric, play theories, and the binaries of play.

### Play and Rhetoric

There is a close relationship between hermeneutics and rhetoric, with both similarities and differences. Rhetoric is designed to convince, hermeneutics to interpret. Yet each "holds open a notion of truth that is neither self-evident nor reducible to methodological verification" (Crusius, 1991, p. 9). With the hermeneutic framework in mind, one can revisit Sutton-Smith's rhetorics. Now they might be viewed as a forestructure people have used to try to understand and codify or categorize perspectives on play. In the light of the notion of a hermeneutic circle, and extending inquiry over time, it could be useful for play scholars to continue to examine the rhetorics to see if there might be different emphases or if the boundaries might be redrawn and the rhetorics renamed. This could lead to greater understanding and a continuation of the viewing of theories through a rhetorical framework while not committing the proposals to scientific validation.

Hermeneutics and rhetoric tells us it is important to examine the values and belief systems that shape our discourses. At the same time, hermeneutics might suggest that in evaluating these discourses we are careful not to imply that by being a discourse it has to be negative. So we are continually challenged hermeneutically to reflect on the nature of our rhetoric.

Such a reflection can be made on the rhetoric of "play as progress." Can there be a consideration of how play, in all its multiple aspects and open boundedness, might serve as "progress" – to help children be prepared for the chaotic, unpredictable, interconnected and rapidly changing world of the future (e.g. Handy, 1989)? A formulation of what attributes they "might" need, includes the abilities to self-regulate, maintain one's center; function as a contributing and adaptive member of a system, create new combinations, view phenomena as emergent and changing over time, construct one's own life and meaning; to recognize the paradox inherent in ordinary situations, and others (VanderVen, 1998). A hermeneutic perspective on play similarly suggests that play can support development of these attributes. There is no one pathway to "play as progress." Rather progress will be as varied as the way it is constructed by culture and individuals, and by the play activities that may contribute to it. Only time, of course, will tell.

We can hermeneutically challenge too the rhetoric of play as frivolity. If play is as central to human development, to the construction of meaning, it can hardly be frivolous, except as some frivolity and playfulness then is part of these actions. Similarly, hermeneutics might challenge us to ask, "Who is to say that frivolity might not be a good thing?"

## Play Theories

There seem to be so many "common understandings" between play theories and hermeneutics that one could almost say that play "is" hermeneutics, or that hermeneutics "is" play. However, this would be to fall into the very trap against which Schwartzman has warned. So where there seem to be close overlappings, the terminology "as" rather than "is" will be used.

*Play as engagement.* In the theoretical section, there was a category called "play and engagement," to refer to the child's entry into play situations with the comment that many theorists don't give as much attention to this aspect of play as they do for others. Hermeneutics, with the concepts of "thrownness," and of "launching ourselves" into the world as a child "launches into play" (Steinsholt & Traasdahl, p. 81) gives more credence to this aspect of play.

*Play and self.* The role of play in construction of self and identity is a common denominator in both play theory and hermeneutics. In play – in the continued making meaning of experience, the self is constructed. The process, hermeneuticists would emphasize, is a dialectic one. Aspects of the self are lost in an act of play depending on the nature and the context of the play, but new aspects of the self are "found" and constructed as well as the play evolves.

*Play as meaning making.* If the major concern in hermeneutics is how people interpret and make meaning of their experiences, then there is great congruence between this notion and the play theorists' contention that play enables one to make meaning from one's ongoing experiences in daily life in line with the observation that the notion of meaning making is central in both play theories and in hermeneutics. That children use play to interpret and make meaning out of their daily experiences is directly supported by a hermeneutic perspective. In that meaning is socially constructed, play involving others enables such meaning to be negotiated. Perspectives may be changed in interaction and contribute to more harmonious interaction.

*Play as text.* Play theorists in general have not considered play as a text in the way hermeneuticists consider various productions and expressions to be texts. Applying the notion of text to play, any act of play is a text, used for interpretation and subject to interpretation. This certainly supports those ways that early childhood educators consider play to enable one to have a window on the world of a child. Play as text also supports the concept of play as performance and improvisation. A play act engages an audience that interacts with the messages of the play.

*Play, language, and constructivism.* There are parallels between the well-accepted theory that children learn and develop meaning through a constructivist process. While there is acceptance of the ways in which play contribute to language development in children, perhaps a hermeneutic approach deepens this recognition. In a hermeneutic view of language, language constitutes the symbol system used to construct and to make meaning of experience. Play in Gadamer's concept of the "language game" certainly seems to serve this function.

*Play and imagination.* The word "imagination" interestingly was not a major aspect of the hermeneutic texts consulted for this paper. In comparison with the literature on play in which imagination is a focus, there seems much less attention to imagination as a concept or category as there is with others. Yet as is presented here, many components or aspects of imagination are embraced by hermeneutic theory, including those of meaning making and interpretation. How might a text be interpreted and responded to without some degree of imagination from the reader?

*Play and context.* Context is a major notion in both play and hermeneutics. If one considers both rhetorics and play theories, then the notion of immediate and more far reaching contexts of play is embraced. Many play theorists tend to consider the immediate context or play settings rather than the value and belief systems and the wider elements of an ecological hierarchy, however. Hermeneutics encourages more attention to the wider context of values and culturally determined values as they situate and shape play, and should be considered when interpreting any children's play activity.

*Play as transformation.* As play as transformation is well-established in play theory, so is it supported by hermeneutics, both in the notion of enabling object representation and in the more embracing concept of reciprocal transformation (Nakkula & Ravitch, 1998) in which in interaction with others on a non-hegemonic plane, both parties are changed or transformed as prejudicial forestructures are challenged and mutual understanding develops. In reciprocal transformation experience and reflective processes in interaction with others transform each party's interpersonal perceptions, above and beyond objects. Furthermore there is inherent reciprocity in the playful interaction involved in artistic and performance activities.

*Play and communication.* Almost directly allied to the relationship of play to language and constructivism is the role of play in communication. Play in that it embraces language is a medium along with language for making meaning and communicating this meaning to others. Play can be a means of enacting Habermas' "communicative action"; ongoing engagement in play can situate a dialogic process that increasingly brings to light and affirms common understandings. To some extent, perhaps, the implicit rule structure in play and games may be likened to "communicative action" – players must understand the common structures and perform within their boundaries.

*Play and connection.* A hermeneutic conception of play emphasizes the contention of play theorists as to play's ability to enable children to make connections. The hermeneutic circle concept extends a sense of how this happens. As inquiry through the means of play continues, new experiences are encountered and the horizon of understanding is extended. The connectionist notion of play as a "lymphatic system" (Fromberg, 2002) allowing children to integrate diverse aspects of their experience, is thus hermeneutically supported.

*Play and time.* While time may be an implicit aspect of play theories, especially those that propose developmental stages or phases of play, the role of time is more explicit in hermeneutics. The time factor in the hermeneutic circle, likened to an extended play sequence, is salient as increased understanding is generated in the time extended process of uncovering layers of meaning. There is a notion of "becoming" over time (Nakkula & Ravitch, 1998) which supports the premise that play enables children to project the future.

*Play, forestructure and the hermeneutic circle.* Children bring their past experiences to a play situation, and as hermeneuticists may enter a "circle of play" through the onlooker aspect of play. Undertaking play, and as any play proceeds over time, all of the reciprocal, contextual, connectionist and constructive aspects of play enable ever more complex understanding and meaning to be experienced, over time.

The emphasis in Gadamer's hermeneutics on circular processes can contribute to issues in how to represent and organize various perspectives on play. Sutton-Smith's rhetorics were presented in linear form. So was the synthesis of grand and middle-range play theories, which didn't really quite fit into an ecological framework even when considered as a hierachized series of steps or phases leading towards greater complexity and contextualization. It could be possible that various play attributes are best expressed and connected in some kind of *circular* form, in which a player enters play and dialectically and recursively moves through the various "as" functions of play. with the context both shaping and being affected by the changes of and actions of the player. This process would actually be akin to a hermeneutic circle, in which continuation in a process of inquiry and exploration and uncovering increasingly leads to greater complexity – and greater understanding.

*Play and power.* Even though play as power is a rhetoric, in general there has been little discussion of power in mainstream play theory (although this is changing in light of the reconceptualists' studies of play). In a hermeneutic perspective, particularly the applied hermeneutics of Nakkula and Ravitch (1998) the reciprocal aspects of reframed relationships allow a child participants a greater sense of power by being respected and having an attempt made to respect the particular background and perspectives they bring to the relationship. An asset of play is its ability to enable a player to feel powerful and effective. Articulated in this paper is the notion that within play there can be oppressing power differentials, especially in the gendered aspects of play. Play can be emancipatory, but it can have hidden aspects of oppression waiting to be uncovered.

Perhaps a consideration of power aspects of play can help in the ongoing reframing of the play-work binary. When children's play is directed by adults, they may consider this a loss of power and thus identify it with "work" – an adult activity as they might construct it. When children organize their own play, they may feel more implicit empowerment, and thus consider it with the childhood associated construction, "play." The issue is not simple, however. The hermeneutic notion of reciprocal transformation (Nakkula & Ravitch, 1998) introduces an ethical aspect. It is ethical for professionals (e.g. teachers, therapists, caregivers) to continually reflect upon and review their interaction with children to be open to messages as to how their contribution is received and as to how sensitive it is to their unique background and experience. Heretofore, there seems to have been little discussion with reference to ethical aspects of play and the adult role in play. For example, when adults sense the imposition of a disempowered position to a child in play, do they intervene?

*Play as life.* The absolute significance of play as an essence of living, of human life, seems affirmed in the juxtaposition of play and hermeneutics. As play theorists adumbrate the numerous functions of play: to develop a sense of self and identity, to construct knowledge through language, to create meaning, to connect experiences, to communicate with others and to interpret others' communications, to understand one's particular immediate and cultural context, to represent one's world and to imagine alternative scenarios, they elaborate upon what it means to be human. These conceptions resonate highly with the tenets of hermeneutics.

In reviewing the consideration of the relationship between play and hermeneutics here there seem to be no great surprises. There is no emergent insight that is so startling and profound that it is stunning. Rather in many ways preexisting premises are supported. Still the resonance between the language of play and the language of hermeneutics can be empowering and serve the hermeneutic process of interpretation turning into *articulation*. What emerges may actually have more heuristic value for early childhood education and the role of play in it. Hermeneutics obviously embraces play. That such a longstanding and continuously evolving school of philosophy should not only support play but also accords play such a central position in its formulations can be quite heartening to those in early childhood education continually have to justify or defend play in the face of its possible demise or displacement in favor of "academic" activity (Elkind, 1990). Indeed, the hermeneutic perspective on play offers a meta-message that should be welcomed by early childhood educators who have to fight the current wave of resistance to play in neighborhoods and educational settings. When there is external confirmation of play theorists' contention all along: that play holds a centrality in child and human development, that play leads towards greater understanding of self and others, that play is a powerful way of learning; more support for the significance of play is provided.

## The Binaries of Play

Hermeneutics can encourage a reframing of the ubiquitous binaries of play through recasting them as dialectics. A hermeneutic perspective, with its acceptance of the paradoxical, encourages binaries to be seen as dynamic and interactive, rather than as oppositional. So, in a reframing, there can be reality and fantasy, for example. A player can fantasize about reality in and represent reality in play. In representing reality, a player can add elements of fantasy, and vice versa. There can be freedom and free choice in play, but hermeneutically, one might contend, not completely.

In fact, the issue of how to organize a view of play or view play holistically – to understand as in a hermeneutic circle both the whole and the parts, is addressed by a reframing of the binaries. There could be a *nested* aspect to play in relationship to other structures and concepts against which it is aligned oppositionally. There can be play in work. There can be work in play. There can be past, present and future in one play frame or episode. Children bring their past into play, represent it in the present, and use these scenarios to project themselves into the future.

## Hermeneutics, Play and Reconceptualizing Early Childhood Education

In the first phase of this inquiry (discovering a perspective to serve as an entrypoint) the reconceptualizing movement in early childhood education was discussed as providing a strong rationale. This can be revisited at this final juncture. At this point it appears that three major contributions of hermeneutics to reconceptualist thought are its emancipatory aspects, its core consideration of culture and context, its encouragement of the reframing of binaries, especially those that embed power differentials; and its overall conception of the nature of and the signficance of play.

With its support of addressing hegemonic practices, with an approach addressing the existence of prejudice, applied developmental hermeneutics "argues for a hermeneutic approach colored by race, class and gender" sensitivity (Nakkula & Ravitch, 1998, p. 21). Describing their eclectic hermeneutic framework that by "integrating (a) white European male canon with ideas that represent the practical and political challenges of our time, we have developed a hermeneutic framework designed to meet the interpretive demands of everyday life in a diverse and complex society" (p. 21). Such an approach resonates with the hermeneutic notion of culturally determined perspectives that figure into the ongoing construction of meaning through language and the cultural situatedness of activity. As the reconceptualizing movement grows, it might continue to allow, even encourage, the kind of analogical scholarship that enables the uncovering of those hegemonic and prejudicial value systems that serve to make some theories and practices of early childhood education insensitive to issues of diversity, culture, and context.

In general hermeneutics supports the dialogic and interactive, postmodern conceptions of play. The dialectic contribution of hermeneutics enables support for the reconceptualizers' notion of play and player – that one plays and is played with, for example. A dialectic view of play and work reframes the "modern" conception of play as of lesser value than work. As the reconceptualizing movement grows, it might continue to allow, even encourage, the kind of analogical scholarship that enables the uncovering of those hegemonic and prejudicial value systems that serve to make some theories and practices of early childhood education insensitive to issues of diversity and power differentials.

As to play itself, the overall hermeneutic conception of play seems quite supportive of the reconceptualizers' (and the chaos theorists') view of play as boundless, a response to the uncertainty in the world but a way to explore what the possibilities are.

## Hermeneutics, Play, Theory and Praxis

A review of an array of play theories loosely categorized as meta, grand and middle-range theories was presented in this paper. On one hand this typology was more helpful than lumping everything into a larger category of "theory." On the other hand was the hope that a hermeneutic lens might then offer even more integration of the concepts of theory and practice. Indeed it has. It offers new possibilities for reframing of the theory-practice dichotomy. In the future, and with the encouragement of Gadamer's concept of theory and practice, as he says, "*theoria* itself is a practice" (Gadamer, 1981, p. 90) then the question arises, "How can that be?" One possibility would be that the integration of theory and practice actually exists in the *mental model* or *working model* of the practitioner. A practitioner holds a current internal conception or judgement based on past experience and knowledge of what needs to be said or done at a particular moment. This governs what the practitioner then actually does. If the relationship between the mental model and direct practice exists, then there is real utility for the self-reflective stance encouraged in a hermeneutic approach. Such reflection on practice comprises a complex dynamic system of the mind, in which there is a constant dialectic between information generated in practice, the processing of that information, and the interpretation of it. This embodies the notion of the hermeneutic circle, in which ever increasing pursuit of and acquisition of information leads to greater understanding. There could be great implications for preparation of early childhood practitioners through both training and education. Passive transmission of information through didactic presentations might certainly have greater impact on practice with the inclusion of a reflective process. Similarly, it would seem as if much more reflection on the part of children might be encouraged. This would enhance both knowledge and understanding, in line with the hermeneutic notion of *articulation*, being able to articulate one's interpretation. A hermeneutic approach could be brought to the reflection by removing the right-wrong aspect, and simply requesting comment on the child's understanding.

The hermeneutic circle can be used to frame some issues in the nature of the professionalization of early childhood education. Reifel (1997) has stated that we

> need to confront the challenges created by our evolving size, knowledge bases, and diversity of the field. We need to recognize not only the many pieces of the field, but also the larger whole that the pieces create. Without such efforts we may lose our identity and power as a community (7).

Recognizing the many pieces as part of a whole is reflective of the intent of the hermeneutic circle, to enable through the process of successive uncovering, a greater awareness of both. A hermeneutic inquiry undertaken by the early childhood field into the issues posed by Reifel could be intriguing and valuable.

The applied developmental hermeneutics of Nakkula and Ravitch (1998) were formulated and utilized with the focus on work with youth (adolescents). With the integrated hermeneutic notion of theory and practice in mind, there might then be some consideration of adapting such an applied developmental hermeneutics to early childhood education, taking into account of course, the unique context of early childhood.

The title of this paper "Beyond Fun and Games: Towards a Meaningful Theory of Play: Can a Hermeneutic Perspective Contribute" began it and can serve to close it. Indeed there is more, much more, to play than fun and games, although these are certainly significant aspects of it. Because in hermeneutic inquiry there is no final closure or absolute truth, "towards" becomes a significant sign. Perhaps by reviewing a variety of conceptions of play in the context of hermeneutics, there has been movement towards a meaningful theory that hermeneutically speaking would have implications for praxis and be constantly open to revision. That remains for the future, and since in hermeneutics evolution over time enables greater understanding and meaning to emerge, there are infinite possibilities. As the title asked, "Can a hermeneutic perspective contribute?"

# REFERENCES

Bateson, G. (1979). *Mind and nature: A necessary unity*. New York: G. P. Dutton.
Bleicher, J. (1980). *Contemporary hermeneutics*. London: Routledge & Kegan Paul.
Bloch, M. (1992). Critical perspectives on the historical relationship between child development and early childhood research. In: S. Kessler & B. Swadener (Eds), *Reconceptualizing the Early Childhood Curriculum: Beginning the Dialogue* (pp. 3–20). New York: Teachers College Press.
Bloch, M., & Pellegrini, A. (1989). Children, context and play. In: M. Bloch & A. Pellegrini (Eds), *The Ecological Context of Children's Play* (pp. 1–15). Norwood, NJ: Ablex.
Bruner, J. (1990). *Acts of meaning*. Cambridge, MA: Harvard University Press.
Crusius, T. (1991). *A teacher's introduction to philosophical hermeneutics*. Urbana, IL: National Council of Teachers of English.
Dahlberg, G., Moss, P., & Pence, A. (1999). *Beyond quality in early childhood education: Postmodern perspectives*. Philadelphia: Falmer.
Davies, B. (1997). The construction of gendered identity through play. In: B. Davies & D. Corson (Eds), *Encyclopedia of Language and Education: Oral Discourse and Education* (Vol. 3, pp. 116–124). Dordrecht: Kluwer.
Dodd, A., Rogers, C., & Wilson, J. (2001). Effects of situational context on playful behaviors. In: S. Reifel (Ed.), *Theory in Context and Out* (Vol. 3, pp. 367–389). Westport, CT: Ablex.
Edelschick, T. (1998). Entering play: Lessons of grief, joy, and growth. In: M. Nakkula & S. Ravitch (Eds), *Matters of Interpretation* (pp. 276–290). San Francisco: Jossey-Bass.
Eisner, E. (1994). *Cognition and curriculum reconsidered* (2nd ed.). New York: Teachers College Press.
Elkind, D. (1990). Academic pressures – Too much, too soon: The demise of play. In: E. Klugman & S. Smilansky (Eds), *Children, Play and Learning: Perspectives and Policy Implications* (pp. 2–17). New York: Columbia University Press.
Erikson, E. (1950). *Childhood and society*. New York: W. W. Norton.
Erikson, E. (1977). *Toys and reasons*. New York: W. W. Norton.
Fein, G., & Wiltz, N. (1998). Play as children see it. In: D. Fromberg & D. Bergen (Eds), *Play from Birth to Twelve and Beyond. Contexts, Perspectives and Meanings* (pp. 37–49). New York: Garland.
Fishman, D. B. (1999). *The case for pragmatic psychology*. New York: New York University Press.
Fosnot, C. T. (Ed.) (1996). *Constructivism: Theory, perspectives, and practice*. New York: Teachers College Press.
Fromberg, D. (2002). *Play and meaning in early childhood education*. Needham, MA: Allyn & Bacon.
Frost, J., Wortham, S., & Reifel, S. (2001). *Play and child development*. Upper Saddle River, NJ: Merrill/Prentice-Hall.
Gadamer, H.-G. (1993). *Reason in the age of science*. Cambridge, MA: MIT Press.
Gentner, D., Holyoak, K., & Kokinov, B. (Eds) (2001). *The analogical mind. Perspectives from cognitive science*. Cambridge, MA: MIT Press.
Gergen, K. (1994). *Realities and relationships: Soundings in social construction*. Cambridge, MA: Harvard University Press.
Glaser, B. & Strauss, A. (1967). *The discovery of grounded theory: Strategies for qualitative research*. Chicago: Aldine.
Grieshaber, S., & Cannella, G. (Eds) (2001). *Embracing identities in early childhood education: Diversity and possibilities*. New York: Teachers College Press.
Habermas, J. (1968). *Knowledge and human interests*. Boston: Beacon Press.
Handy, C. (1989). *The age of unreason*. Cambridge: Harvard University Press.

Henricks, T. (2001). Play and postmodernism. In: S. Reifel (Ed.), *Theory in Context and Out* (Vol. 3, pp. 51–71). Westport, CT: Ablex.

Hofstadter, D. (2001). Epilogue: Analogy as the core of cognition. In: D. Gentner, K. Holyoak & B. Kokinov (Eds), *The Analogical Mind: Perspectives from Cognitive Science* (pp. 499–538). Cambridge, MA: MIT Press.

Hughes, P., & MacNaughton, G. (2001). Fractured or manufactured: Gendered identities and culture in the early years. In: S. Grieshaber & G. Cannella (Eds), *Embracing Identities in Early Childhood Education: Diversity and Possibilities* (pp. 114–132). New York: Teachers College Press.

Hyun, E. (1998). *Making sense of developmentally and culturally appropriate practice (DCAP) in early childhood education.* New York: Peter Lang.

Isenberg, J. (1998). Play among education professionals. In: D. Fromberg & D. Bergen (Eds), *Play from Birth to Twelve and Beyond: Contexts, Perspectives and Meanings* (pp. 493–498). New York: Garland.

Johnson, J., Christie, J., & Yawkey, T. (1999). *Play and early childhood development.* New York: Addison Wesley/Longman.

Karpov, Y., & Haywood, C. (1998). Two ways to elaborate Vygotsky's concept of mediation. Implications for instruction. *American Psychologist, 53*(1), 27–36.

Kegan, R. (1994). *In over our heads: The mental demands of modern life.* Cambridge, MA: Harvard University Press.

King, N. (1992). The impact of context on the play of young children. In: S. Kessler & B. Swadener (Eds), *Reconceptualizing the Early Childhood Curriculum: Beginning the Dialogue* (pp. 43–61). New York: Teachers College Press.

Kosko, B. (1993). *Fuzzy thinking: The new science of fuzzy logic.* New York: Hyperion.

Landreth, G. & Homeyer, L. (1998). Play as the language of children's feelings. In: D. Fromberg & D. Bergen (Eds), *Play from Birth to Twelve and Beyond: Contexts, Perspectives and Meanings* (pp. 193–196). New York: Garland.

Lillard, A. (2001). Explaining the connection. Pretend play and theory of mind. In: S. Reifel (Ed.), *Theory in Context and Out* (Vol. 3, pp. 173–177). Westport, CT: Ablex.

MacNaughton, G., Rolfe, S., & Siraj-Blatchford, I. (2001). *Doing early childhood research. International perspectives on theory and practice.* Buckingham, UK: Open University Press.

Madison, G. (1991). Beyond seriousness and frivolity: A Gadamerian response to deconstruction. In: H. Silverman (Ed.), *Gadamer and Hermeneutics* (pp. 119–135). New York: Routledge.

Mallery, J. C., Hurwitz, R., & Duffy, G. (1994). Hermeneutics: From textual explication to computer understanding? In: S. Shapiro (Ed.), *The Encyclopedia of Artificial Intelligence.* New York: Wiley, 1987. Paper posted, 1994 and found at http:www.ai.mit.edu/people/jcma/papers/1986-ai-memo-871/memo.html.

Monighan-Nourot, P. (1998). Sociodramatic play. Pretending together. In: D. Bergen & D. Fromberg (Eds), *Play from Birth to Twelve and Beyond: Contexts, Perspectives and Meanings* (pp. 378–391). New York: Garland.

Nachmanovitch, S. (1990). *Free play: Improvisation in life and art.* Los Angeles: Jeremy P. Tarcher.

Naisbitt, J. (1982). *Megatrends.* New York: Warner Books.

Nakkula, M., & Ravitch, S. (1998). *Matters of interpretation: Reciprocal transformation in therapeutic and developmental relationships with youth.* San Francisco: Jossey-Bass.

Packer, R., & Addison, R. (Eds) (1989). *Entering the circle: Hermeneutic investigation in psychology.* Albany: State University of New York Press.

Pellegrini, A. (Ed.) (1995). *The future of play theory: A multidisciplinary inquiry into the contributions of Brian Sutton-Smith.* New York: State University of New York Press.

Piaget, J. (1962). *Play, dreams and imitation in childhood.* New York: W. W. Norton.

Reifel, S. (1997). A changing early childhood community. Where next? *Journal of Early Childhood Teacher Education, 18*(3), 1–9.

Ricouer, P. (1981). *Hermeneutics and human sciences.* Cambridge, UK: Cambridge University Press.

Ryan, S., Ochsner, M., & Genishi, C. (2001). Miss Nelson is missing! Teacher sightings in research on teaching. In: S. Grieshaber & G. Cannella (Eds), *Embracing Identities in Early Childhood Education. Diversity and Possibilities* (pp. 45–59). New York: Teachers College Press.

Schwartzman, R. (1978). *Transformations: The anthropology of children's play.* New York: Plenum Press.

Singer, D., & Singer, J. (1998). Fantasy and imagination. In: D. Fromberg & D. Bergen (Eds), *Play from Birth to Twelve and Beyond. Contexts, Perspectives and Meanings* (pp. 313–318). New York: Garland.

Slattery, P. (1995). *Curriculum development in the postmodern era.* New York: Garland.

Steele, R. (1989). A critical hermeneutics for psychology. Beyond positivism to an exploration of the textual unconscious. In: R. Packer & R. Addison (Eds), *Entering the Circle: Hermeneutic Investigation in Psychology* (pp. 223–238). Albany: State University of New York Press.

Steinsholt, K., & Traasdahl, E. (2001). The concept of play in Hans-Georg Gadamer's hermeneutics: An educational approach. In: S. Reifel (Ed.), *Theory in Context and Out* (Vol. 3, pp. 73–96). Westport, CT: Ablex.

Sutton-Smith, B. (1997). *The ambiguity of play.* Cambridge: Harvard University Press.

Teigas, D. (1995). *Knowledge and human understanding. A study of the Habermas-Gadamer debate.* Lewisburg, PA: Bucknell University Press.

Thompson, J. (1981). *Critical hermeneutics: A study in the thought of Paul Ricouer and Juergen Habermas.* Cambridge, UK: Cambridge University Press.

Tobin, J. (Ed.) (1997). *Making a place for pleasure in early childhood education.* New Haven, CT: Yale University Press.

VanderVen, K. (1994, August). Advancing child and youth work through integration of theory and practice. *Child & Youth Care Forum, 22*(4), 263–284.

VanderVen, K. (1998). Play, Proteus and paradox. Education for a chaotic and supersymmetric world. In: D. Fromberg & D. Bergen (Eds), *Play from Birth to Twelve and Beyond. Contexts, Perspectives, Meanings* (pp. 119–132). New York: Garland.

von Glasersfeld, E. (1996). Introduction: Aspects of constructivism. In: C. T. Fosnot (Ed.), *Constructivism: Theory, Perspectives and Practice* (pp. 3–7). New York: Teachers College Press.

Wertsch, J. (1985). *Vygotsky and the social formation of mind.* Cambridge, MA: Harvard University Press.

# FROM CONTEXT TO TEXTS: DAP, HERMENEUTICS, AND READING CLASSROOM PLAY

Stuart Reifel, Priscilla Hoke, Dianne Pape
and Debora Wisneski

## ABSTRACT

*This chapter critiques the concept of play as a part of educational practice in early childhood education. After dissecting a developmentally appropriate statement about play, we present some principles of hermeneutic analysis as an additional way to observe and think about classroom play. The issue of which narrative tale (child, children, community, curriculum, teacher, etc.) any play event might inform is presented. An illustrative case is presented, followed by suggestions for situating play inquiry's text in context.*

"Play is an important vehicle for children's social, emotional, and cognitive development, as well as a reflection of their development." (Bredekamp & Copple, 1997, p. 14).

Play has had a privileged place in early childhood education for centuries (Frost et al., 2001), and it continues to occupy a featured role in developmentally appropriate practice (DAP) (Bredekamp & Copple, 1997) and debates about early childhood theory and practice (see Grieshaber & Cannella, 2001; Reifel & Brown, 2001). While teachers may have varying views about the roles of

Social Contexts of Early Education, and Reconceptualizing Play (II)
Advances in Early Education and Day Care, Volume 13, 207–218
Copyright © 2004 by Elsevier Ltd.
All rights of reproduction in any form reserved
ISSN: 0270-4021/doi:10.1016/S0270-4021(04)13007-3

play in their classrooms (e.g. Bennett et al., 1997), there continues to be a strong belief in play as a significant part of any early childhood program. The quotation presented above is one of the National Association for the Education of Young Children's "Principles of child development and learning that inform developmentally appropriate practice" (Bredekamp & Copple, 1997, p. 9). Offered by this influential professional organization, these principles represent a foundation for the field of early education and care.

Buried in this aforementioned statement of principle is a tangle of belief, theory, and research that is simultaneously affirming and puzzling. It is affirming, in the sense that it supports those of us (including all the authors of this chapter) who believe that classroom play is in many ways important, if not vital for children, as well as their teachers. It is also puzzling that much is compacted into what we mean by play as related to development and learning in early education and care.

It is our purpose, therefore, in this chapter to examine some of our compacted ways of viewing and thinking about play. We intend to use a hermeneutic perspective, seeing play or descriptions of play as text that is in need of explication, to chart multiple ways that we need to read and think about classroom play as an avenue for learning and development. We will begin with a brief description of hermeneutics as it relates to education (see VanderVen, in this volume, for a more extensive presentation), then address play as described in the DAP guidelines. From that basis, we will look at the multiple ways that play (or descriptions of play) has been, and could be, read by early childhood teachers, teacher educators, and researchers. Our argument is that children's play actions, how we observe and think about those actions, and our knowledge base related to those actions are all separate but intersecting text narratives. Our reading of those texts and narratives needs to be clarified, based on the point of view of the observer and the contextual frameworks within which she is working.

To make our argument more meaningful, we will introduce a classroom play episode. The episode will be used to illustrate the intersecting texts of play, and some of the lenses we might use to assist our reading of the play (Frost et al., 2001).

## HERMENEUTICS: INTERPRETATION TEXT

Hermeneutics began as a way of exploring the meaning of written texts, religious texts in particular. In the latter part of the 20th century, scholars began to apply the principles of hermeneutics to texts other than sacred writings, as well as to non-written articulations such as dialogs and other enactments. With a philosophical rather than scientific agenda, scholars attempted to understand subject-object relations (i.e. objective reality); objective reality was not a concern, as was putting the meaning of texts (however identified) in their most illuminative narrative contexts. Building on such classic works as Gadamer's (1975) *Truth and Method*, scholars attempted to find meaningful ways of interpreting texts by means of deconstructing, reconstructing, reflecting, and contextualizing all sorts of texts (Mallery et al., 1987; Steinsholt & Traasdahl, 2002).

Gadamer (1975) himself was aware of play, and how the give and take of engaging in play relates to how we sort out the subjective from the objective (Sutton-Smith, 1997). Others have applied his thinking to scientific and social inquiry, refining the hermeneutic approach to the study of, for example, psychology (Packer & Addison, 1989). The hermeneutic concern in such inquiry has to do with locating a perspective for viewing texts, studying them within that perspective, and critically reflecting and evaluating the resulting meanings. We will want to return to this matter of perspective, as it is for our argument a central matter that needs attention.

Play scholars frequently present play dialog and action episodes in their efforts to describe and understand play, creating a written text to further their arguments. We turn to classic examples of this work for DAP, and for other developmental and educational discourse. Who has not been exposed to Piaget's (1962) text on symbolic play, or Vytogsky's (1978) on childhood object transformation as it relates to the zone of proximal development and mental development? What does it mean to use those scholarly play texts as a principle for early education and care? What does hermeneutics tell us about play as a vehicle for development in classrooms, or as a reflection of development?

Many have assumed that when children play, they are exploring meanings, and that their play words and actions are our entrée to those meanings (e.g. Hartley et al., 1952). In other words, some play scholars have seemingly shared assumptions with hermeneuticians about play text as a way to reconstruct a world of the child's meanings. It is these assumptions that we are elaborating in this chapter. And it is these assumptions that hermeneutics may help us clarify.

### *DAP: A Guiding Text for Early Education and Care*

Some of those assumptions are reflected in the DAP's text on the roles of play in learning and development. "Children express and represent their ideas, thoughts, and feelings when engaged in symbolic play" (Bredekamp & Copple, 1997, p. 14), suggests that play is a text where we can read children's "ideas, thoughts, and feelings." "Play gives children opportunities to understand the world" (p. 14), suggests that the activity of play is a form of meaning making, whereby children construct their texts of life (Dyson, 1989, 1997). And "Children's play gives adults insights into children's development and opportunities to support the development of new strategies" (Bredekamp & Copple, 1997, p. 14), suggests that adults can read play in ways that will allow subsequent guidance and enhancement of children's meaningful texts and learning strategies. While the DAP guidelines do not offer citations for theory or research to support these points, it is likely that a number of psychological, in particular psychoanalytic scholars provide a basis for seeing play as a form of story (i.e. text) with which a child explores life's meanings (e.g. Erikson, 1963, 1977; also Axline, 1964; Bruner, 1991; Landreth, 2002). The implication is that an adult, whether teacher, researcher, or therapist, can see play as a form of text, and that the text is meaningful to the child who creates it. The adults' ancillary challenge, then, is to observe (i.e. read) the play, interpret it in terms of its origins and trajectory, and use the resulting insight to help the child construct his meanings. Children's play creates opportunities for organizational skill building, reasoning and arguing (Wasserman, 2000). Viewed this way, teachers can observe from the sidelines and refrain from intervening, but instead learn "the art of reflective teaching" (p. 104) about the texts of children's play.

We have, then, at least two ways to think about what is going on as children play. Play as the "reflection" of children's development appears to be a text that can be read and interpreted by adults, and play as an "important vehicle" for development is a meaning-making activity for children's creation of text(s).

So, play is something to be interpreted, implying that perhaps it can be read as a text. DAP complicates this further by stating that play is "an important vehicle for social, emotional, and cognitive development" (p. 14). Now the adult must be prepared to interpret and gain insight about any play text that can have meaning for children's interactions, feelings, and mental activities, as well as how all those change over time. Any play text immediately becomes more complicated, as the meaning to be interpreted from the play text might be social, emotional, or cognitive, or some combination of them (Fein, 1989; Smilansky & Shefatya, 1990). The complication does not end there, as play is called "a highly supportive context for these developing processes" (p. 14); so the story the adult observes may be simultaneously about context, as well as development (Reifel & Yeatman, 1993). Such complications require that the teacher or classroom researcher interpret play based on setting, developmental domain, and developmental trajectory (and perhaps contextual history), all at the same time.

While DAP offers us more specific ways of considering play, it is not so clear that play is always readable as a text. When children play, DAP asserts that they may be expressing understanding of the world, control of emotions, or development of symbolic capabilities, all of which could be interpreted as texts created by individual children. Each of these suggests a different kind of text, each requiring a different knowledge base for the "reader" of play and different inferential skills directed toward individual children. Many early childhood teachers have beliefs that accord with DAP, and may be more likely to provide a program that supports play (Kemple, 2003; Kemple, David & David, 1997; Kemple & Hartle, 1997), seeking validation for play in the classroom especially with the increased academic focus of schools. When the play involves interaction with others, it provides an intersection of texts, with a text for each participant and inferences about each individual AND the group. Problem solving, literacy acquisition, skill practice, creativity, imagination, and curriculum learning involve different sorts of frameworks for reading play, including developmental and contextual knowledge, in addition to knowledge of the child. Are we to see narrative text about each child? About the child in the group? About children in a particular context? Is what we read in play a part of a narrative about a child? About the group? About the context and how children are negotiating it? About how the teacher is supporting play? About the teacher as sensitive inference maker? The interpretation of play may depend on the teacher having practice in observing play and the role of the teacher in reflecting on her "own needs and behaviors" (Wasserman, 2000, p. 104). Ward (1996) affirms that many believe that play "is under the child's domain" (p. 1), and interference by an adult may "inhibit, disrupt, or reduce the emotional benefits of play." As Cazden has recommended, "instead of confrontation, it may be more useful for teachers to go beyond their own adult egocentricity and explore the ideas that flow from the children's own premises" (1981, Foreword). If the teacher is to interpret play, she must understand the journey from non-play to play and ask, "What is meaningful to the child's journey?" The number of things about which adults can infer meanings in play is astounding, and the demands on the teacher as reader of play are accordingly great.

(We will note here a number of play-related texts that could be included in DAP's principles, but have not been: gender identity development, sex roles, cultural customs, social status, community formation and identity, personality formation, communications skills, and interests. The relatively narrow developmental bias in DAP's view of play has been discussed by Sutton-Smith [1997, 1999] and Reifel [1999]. Negative texts of play, such as bullying and discrimination – sex, ethnic, and language – are certainly not addressed. For example, Katch [2001] notes that children are exposed to violent imagery through television and videos and often use pretend play to try to make sense of what they see. She struggles with maintaining a balance between turmoil and calm with children while trying to understand their need to express their feelings about violence as they attempt to understand that others have ideas about violence as well. "One thing I have learned," she says, "is the importance of making a clear distinction between pretend violence and behavior that truly hurts or frightens children" (p. 129). Katch arrives at the conclusion that she must be willing to look at the children's anger in pretend play as well as their affection. See Riojas-Cortez and Flores (this volume); Freeman and Brown (this volume); Malloy and McMurray-Schwartz (this volume); also Campbell et al. (this volume).)

DAP gives us a great deal to consider about play, including some ideas about play as a form of text about the child. Other implied narratives that an adult might consider have to do with the context of play (social grouping, curriculum, challenges provided); the play text may be about the group, about how the group is functioning (e.g. Paley, 1992), about how the teacher is engaged in the group (e.g. Jones & Reynolds, 1992; Kemple & Hartle, 1997), or about how the teacher is reflecting on and creating her narrative of the classroom (e.g. VanHoorn et al., 2003). Since young children seldom document their own play texts, the early childhood teacher is put in the powerful position of representing children's play texts, by means of running records or other forms of documentation, as well as making inferences about those texts. We have seen an example of the power of documentation and reflection of play through the work of teacher-researcher Vivian Paley. Through systematic documentation and transcription of play and play stories of young children, Paley has been able to reflect upon the growth of an individual child (1981, 1986), the influences of sociopolitical issues such as race and gender (1979, 1995, 1997), and personal and group experiences with exclusion (1990, 1992). However, Paley's attempt to make meaning of the children's play did not end with documentation, but was extended and enhanced through diligent reflection, introspection, and dialogue with the children about play. These examples of reading text show the myriad ways in which a teacher can understand play.

How do more typical teachers relate to play? Bennett et al. (1997), in their study of British early childhood teachers, argue that teachers do not relate to children's classroom play as a text of any sort. Bits and pieces of DAP perspective appear in teachers' daily actions and in their discussion of the play that occurs in their classrooms. What teachers intended for classroom play was not always practiced by children, and when it was, the teachers' intents seemed to be to make play contribute to particular learning outcomes. Even then, teachers' notions of what children were doing as they played did not seem to take into account individual children's developmental trajectories, or the texts that might represent those trajectories. Hermeneutic analysis might give the teacher a more realistic picture of the array of ways that play can be meaningful for children, suggesting that teacher intervention needs to become much more informed.

### A Text, and Efforts to Make Meaning from It

Let us look for a moment at a discussion of a play text that was presented at a graduate seminar. The text comes from a former laboratory schoolteacher's files, collected while she observed dramatic play and interviewed children about the play stories that were being dramatized.

"Why do all your stories have to do with fighting?" I asked a group of my kindergarten boys in the spring of the year. "It seems you are always chasing and killing and fighting."

One child named Sam gives me an incredulous look, as if to wonder if I could really be so stupid. He explains slowly for me, "We're not fighting. We are *saving* in our stories." The other children nod their heads in agreement.

"Why do you have to save everyone in your stories, then?" I asked.

Once again, Seth replies to me in a tone that denotes he is stating the obvious, "Well, we have to be ready for when we grow up."

"Oh, so when you grow up you have to go around saving people?"

"Yes. See over there, Miss Debora. That's the dorms where the college students live. On the top floor live the boys and under them live the girls. Now if a robber came to get the girls one night, the boys can go down the steps and capture them and save the girls. So we have to practice to be ready when we are grown up for college," Seth illustrates.

Note the differences in perspective between the teacher, with her concern about classroom order and civility, and that of the players who have a bigger picture of the narrative where their play text fits. The sensitive teacher's first interpretation of play text was to assume that it was about fighting, but sensitive as she was, she opted to interview the players to find out the narrative within which they situated the text. And it is clear that teacher's perspective (concern about play fighting, or violence) was in a different field of meaning as the players' perspective revealed (preparation for presumed adult roles). The implied narrative of the dramatic play text as being connected to story, and thereby literacy, takes something of a back seat to the rather eye-opening narrative of gender roles, with boys seeing themselves as potential saviors of girls in distress. The elaboration of children's ideas about college life and gender relations had not appeared in the initial play text, but is brought into it by the teacher's and students' efforts to clarify the play's meaning.

Our professional literature attests to our desire to clarify and understand play and its place in the classroom. Whether reflecting on their own responses to play in the classroom (Callas et al., 1998) or examining the inconsistencies between their beliefs and practice surrounding children's play (Bennett et al., 1997), teachers continue to attempt to make meaning of children's play. It is paradoxical that "child's play" (a euphemism for something viewed as simple and easily accomplished) actually represents a complexity and ambiguity infrequently recognized outside of the early childhood profession. Certainly both teacher and children have their own perspectives about the nature of play, and both can add depth and detail to the discussion.

*Teacher, Researcher, Teacher as Researcher:*
*Finding Perspective and Play Text in the Classroom*

What inferences and conclusions do we draw from our thinking about hermeneutics and classroom play? We believe that reflective teachers are always working on a number of narratives about their work (Connelly & Clandinin, 1996); in some sense these are "sacred stories" about teaching (Clandinin & Connelly, 1995). Observation and interpretation of play serves as one basis for communicating about what is really meaningful and important about teaching in the early childhood classroom. Early childhood teachers frequently turn to play as a feature of their narrative, introducing all the potential complexity that we have been exploring here. And that complexity can create ambiguity for early childhood professionals as they look at play through different lenses, lenses that can be very intimate, personal, and cognizant of the power and immediacy of play in children's lives. Although play is indeed what often characterizes healthy children's behavior, the absence of a child playing can be telling, signaling a pathology that should be pursued (Axline, 1964; Frost et al., 2001; Landreth, 2002). Often considered insignificant in the larger scheme of the adult world, play is, nonetheless, very significant to many early childhood teachers as an avenue for children's growth and development, and an opportunity for the assessment of children's emotional, motor, cognitive, creative, and social capabilities (Bredekamp & Copple, 1997; Frost et al., 2001).

What does the hermeneutic perspective (Packer & Addison, 1989) tell us that we should identify? This perspective raises questions about who we are as observers and documenters of play. We sense that there is a profound challenge for play scholars and play-oriented teachers as they build their narratives about classroom play and the texts that comprise those narratives. First, existing play research, particularly developmental research, does not always speak to classroom play in ways that are informative to teachers (Reifel, 1999). It is worthwhile to know, developmentally, what stages each child may exhibit, but stage knowledge alone does not tell us about how children are adapting to a classroom context (VanHoorn et al., 2003). Teachers must read broadly beyond the literature on classroom play, to gain insights into the possible narratives where the contexts of play texts might have meaning for children and the class.

Second, teachers must always remind themselves that their perspective is not their students' perspective(s). Children have their own issues and points of view, which may not be on the teacher's horizon. As noted above, Katch (2001) is concerned about violent play topics that occur during play in her kindergarten classroom. She does not, however, ban the scripts she observes being played in her classroom about killing, suicide, blood and gore. Instead, she invites the children to engage in discourse with her and with each other regarding their play scripts, in hopes they will gain control over their fears and concerns. The text she interprets in play is clearly aligned with children's emotional development and needs. Teachers may be legitimately preoccupied with the demands that are placed on them as teachers, such as literacy development, but hermeneutics argues that part of that demand might be to find children's meanings in their classroom experiences. Play is certainly one possible entrée to that effort.

Third, teacher researchers have a significant task, helping to create pieces of the web of meanings that classroom play begins to weave. While academic, theoretically oriented researchers may be asking play questions that have meaning for theory (and possibly implications for classroom practice), classroom researchers have legitimate questions to ask about how play has meanings in their own classroom context. Do we see developmental progress in classroom play, when the children remain in the preoperational stage for the entire time we work with them? When groups are playing in the blocks, can we see who is building individual structures and who is building entire contexts? Probably not. But we can see and hear the process of group cohesion in play, and the manner that children increasingly share ideas and feelings as they pretend in classrooms, as Bateson (2000), Vytogsky (1978), and Reifel and Yeatman (1993) suggest. How do significant play activities relate to teacher planning, reflection, documentation, and engagement with a group? These are meaningful stories that only teacher scholars can weave from play texts.

Fourth, we need to ascertain methods for teachers to decide what is important about play. As mentioned above, children play but they do not create the documents based on their play. It is up to the teacher or teacher researcher to record play words and actions. But children play as much as they can, all the time. How do we select what to document? How do we decide when a dialog merits transcription for later reflection, or when a play story should be placed in a larger narrative? Is it interesting when a group plays house the same way every day for months, or when they begin each day playing house before going off to other play interests? How do we decide? One place to begin is with DAP, to see if the texts we are seeing/hearing tell us a larger story about children's social, emotional, cognitive, and physical development. But what do we not yet know about narratives of emotional and social development? And what other meaningful narratives might there be? At this point, the sensitive teacher is our best method for inquiring about these meaningful narratives, and a sensitive teacher that reads broadly will push our understandings in new directions.

Fifth, as our example episode suggests, a sensitive teacher will probably need multiple sources for creating and interpreting play texts. If we think there is a story of development, we will need to seek play texts at two different times. If we want to see learning or literacy acquired, then we need the text and some form of data about how that text relates to learning. Children are also important interpreters of their own play. Hermeneutics tells us that we must revisit our texts, with more perspective, more context, and more acknowledgement of relationships that provide meaning. Any play text does not stand alone; the children, and we, make sense of it. Hermeneutics reminds us that any text must be studied rigorously, acknowledging the perspectives of players and those who document play.

Related to this is the implied multi-subjectivity of the episode we presented. We acknowledge that children and teachers have perspectives to bring to a text. Having done so, we need to say that a legitimate inquiry about play text narrative can be a teacher's narrative or children's narrative(s). We want to know what play means to children, how their texts are contributing to whom they are. It is also legitimate to know about how the play text is contributing to the teacher's growing world of reflection about children and play; how does a play text help teachers think more meaningfully about play (Reynolds & Jones, 1997)? As Bennett et al. (1997) have shown us, teacher reflection is every bit as important to the meaningful use of play in the classroom as is the play itself. Hermeneutics reminds us that perspective (teacher, child, group) for viewing text is an important concern, a concern that is often not acknowledged explicitly in early childhood research.

Classroom play is unique in many ways, because of the characteristic qualities of classroom purposes (Reifel, 1999). Making meaning of play text may involve critically examining our classroom purposes and procedures. Ongoing time and space for play, documentation, discussion, reflection, and sharing, must be considered and used in our classroom practices to engage in the meaning making process. Hermeneutics reminds us to be critically reflective of what we see and hear, and how we are thinking about it.

## REFERENCES

Axline, V. (1964). *Dibs: In search of self.* Boston, MA: Houghton Mifflin.
Bateson, G. (2000). *Steps to an ecology of mind.* Chicago: University of Chicago Press.
Bennett, N., Wood, L., & Rogers, S. (1997). *Teaching through play.* Philadelphia, PA: Open University Press.
Bredekamp, S., & Copple, C. (Eds) (1997). *Developmentally appropriate practice in early childhood programs.* Washington, DC: National Association for the Education of Young Children.
Bruner, J. (1991). *Acts of meaning.* Cambridge, MA: Harvard University Press.
Cazden, C. (1981). Foreword. In: V. Paley (Ed.), *Wally's Stories.* Cambridge, MA: Harvard University Press.
Clandinin, D. J., & Connelly, F. M. (1995). *Teachers professional knowledge.* New York: Teachers College Press.

Connelly, F. M., & Clandinin, D. J. (1996). Practice: An analysis. In: J. Chafel & S. Reifel (Eds), *Advances in Early Education and Day Care: Theory and Practice in Early Childhood Teaching* (Vol. 8, pp. 91–116). Greenwich, CT: JAI Press.

Dyson, A. H. (1989). *The multiple worlds of child writers: Friends learning to write.* New York: Teachers College Press.

Dyson, A. H. (1997). *Writing superheroes: Contemporary childhood, popular culture, and classroom literacy.* New York: Teachers College Press.

Erikson, E. H. (1963). *Childhood and society* (rev. ed.). New York: W. W. Norton.

Erikson, E. H. (1977). *Toys and reasons.* New York: W. W. Norton.

Fein, G. (1989). Mind, meaning, and affect: Proposals for a theory of pretense. *Developmental Review*, *9*, 345–363.

Frost, J., Wortham, S., & Reifel, S. (2001). *Play and child development.* Columbus, OH: Merrill/Prentice-Hall.

Gadamer, H. G. (1975). *Truth and method.* New York: Seabury Press.

Grieshaber, S., & Cannella, G. S. (Eds) (2001). *Embracing identities in early childhood education: Diversity and possibilities.* New York: Teachers College Press.

Hartley, R. E., Frank, L. K., & Goldenson, R. M. (1952). *Understanding children's play.* New York: Columbia University Press.

Jones, E., & Reynolds, G. (1992). *The play's the thing: Teachers' roles in children's play.* New York: Teachers College Press.

Katch, J. (2001). *Under deadman's skin: Discovering the meaning of children's violent play.* Boston: Beacon Press.

Kemple, K. M. (2003). *Friends at school: Orchestrating social competence and inclusion for all young children.* New York: Teachers College Press.

Kemple, K., David, G., & David, C. (1997). Teachers' interventions to preschool and kindergarten children's peer interactions. *Journal of Research in Childhood Education*, *12*, 34–47.

Kemple, K., & Hartle, L. (1997). Getting along: How teachers can support children's peer relationships. *Early Childhood Education Journal*, *24*(3), 139–146.

Landreth, G.L. (2002). *Play therapy: The art of the relationship* (2nd ed.). New York: Brunner-Routledge.

Mallery, J. C., Hurwitz, R., & Duffy, G. (1987). Hermeneutics: From textual explication to computer understanding. In: S. C. Shapiro (Ed.), *Encyclopedia of Artificial Intelligence*. New York: Wiley.

Packer, M. J., & Addison, R. B. (Eds) (1989). *Entering the circle: Hermeneutic investigation in psychology.* Albany, NY: State University of New York Press.

Paley, V. (1979). *White teacher.* Cambridge, MA: Harvard University Press.

Paley, V. (1981). *Wally's stories.* Cambridge, MA: Harvard University Press.

Paley, V. (1986). *Mollie is three: Growing up in school.* Chicago, IL: University of Chicago Press.

Paley, V. (1990). *The boy who would be a helicopter.* Cambridge, MA: Harvard University Press.

Paley, V. (1992). *You can't say you can't play.* Cambridge, MA: Harvard University Press.

Paley, V. (1995). *Kwanzaa and me.* Cambridge, MA: Harvard University Press.

Paley, V. (1997). *The girl with the brown crayon.* Cambridge, MA: Harvard University Press.

Piaget, J. (1962). *Play, dreams and imitation in childhood.* New York: W. W. Norton.

Reifel, S. (1999). Play research and the early childhood profession. In: S. Reifel (Ed.), *Advances in Early Education and Day Care: Foundations, Adult Dynamics, Teacher Education and Play* (Vol. 10, pp. 201–212). Stamford, CT: JAI Press.

Reifel, S., & Brown, M. (Eds) (2001). *Early education and care, and reconceptualizing play: Advances in early education and day care* (Vol. 11). Oxford, UK: JAI Press/Elsevier.

Reifel, S., & Yeatman, J. (1993). From category to context: Reconsidering classroom play. *Early Childhood Research Quarterly, 8*, 347–367.

Reynolds, G., & Jones, E. (1997). *Master players: Learning from children at play*. New York: Teacher's College Press.

Smilansky, S., & Shefatya, L. (1990). *Facilitating play: A medium for promoting cognitive, socio-emotional and academic development in young children*. Gaithersburg, MD: Psychosocial & Educational Publications.

Steinsholt, K., & Traasdahl, E. (2002). The concept of play in Hans-Georg Gadamer's hermeneutics: An educational approach. In: S. Reifel (Ed.), *Theory in Context and Out (Play and Culture Studies)* (Vol. 3, pp. 73–96). Westport, CT: Ablex.

Sutton-Smith, B. (1997). *The ambiguity of play*. Cambridge, MA: Harvard University Press.

Sutton-Smith, B. (1999). The rhetorics of adult and child play theories. In: S. Reifel (Ed.), *Advances in Early Education and Day Care: Foundations, Adult Dynamics, Teacher Education and Play* (Vol. 10, pp. 149–162). Stamford, CT: JAI Press.

VanHoorn, J., Nourot, P., Scales, B., & Alward, K. R. (2003). *Play at the center of the curriculum* (3rd ed.). Columbus, OH: Merrill/Prentice-Hall.

Vytogsky, L. (1978). *Mind in society*. Cambridge, MA: Harvard University Press.

Ward, N. (1996). Adult intervention: Appropriate strategies for enriching the quality of children's play. *Young Children, 51*(3), 20–25.

Wasserman, S. (2000). *Serious players in the primary classroom: Empowering children through active learning experiences*. New York: Teachers College Press.

# RECONCEPTUALIZING ROUGH AND TUMBLE PLAY: BAN THE BANNING

Nancy K. Freeman and Mac H. Brown

## ABSTRACT

*Rough and tumble (R&T) play is a well-researched form of play fighting that contributes to children's academic and social success. Some continue to believe it inevitably leads to bullying and aggression, but this chapter makes that case that R&T should be reconceptualized and supported by creating settings that welcome and encourage consenting players' participation. R&T can be supported by creating an emotionally safe environment where children are empowered to choose whether or not to join in, by the provision of wide-open spaces, adequate time, and adults who will provide a physical and emotional safety net at arm's length.*

They raced across the yard. The competition was real as they tripped on their own and each other's feet, stumbled and scrambled, even body slammed each other to the ground. Then the game stopped. They collapsed in a heap, catching their breath, ready for the glace or gesture that would signal the start of the next episode. And the action resumed, with all its intensity, over and over again, until the players were utterly worn out or grown-ups came to bring it to an end.

Have you observed rough and tumble play? Were the players teenagers or toddlers? Puppies or preschoolers? What was your response? And what made you do what you did?

Rough and tumble play (R&T) was first described in professional literature over forty years ago (Harlow, 1962) and has been evidenced in educators' and neuroscientists' research agendas for more than a generation (Blurton-Jones, 1975; Panksepp, 1993). It is defined as running, pouncing, chasing and fleeing, wrestling,

Social Contexts of Early Education, and Reconceptualizing Play (II)
Advances in Early Education and Day Care, Volume 13, 219–234
© 2004 Published by Elsevier Ltd.
ISSN: 0270-4021/doi:10.1016/S0270-4021(04)13008-5

kicking, open-handed slapping, falling, and other forms of physical and verbal play fighting (Harlow, 1962; Pellegrini & Smith, 1989),[1] and has been characterized as a basic function of the mammalian brain (Panksepp, 1993). In spite of the fact R&T has been described and investigated by scholars from a variety of disciplines, it continues to be, next to sexual play, probably the most misunderstood, and most frequently censured, form of play (Johnson et al., 2001).

This chapter will describe rough and tumble play, present some of the arguments adults use in its defense, review the most frequently voiced objections to its presence in the schoolyard, and will offer possible explanations for these objections. Finally, we will advance a reconceptualized view of R&T that celebrates the contributions it makes to children's growth and development as well as their *joie de vivre*.

## WHAT IS ROUGH AND TUMBLE PLAY?

Rough and tumble, like all play, exists within a play frame – it occurs in a special "what if" space where ordinary rules governing acceptable interactions are suspended, replaced by the mutually agreed upon rules of the game (Bateson, 1972; Chick, 2001). R&T may appear markedly like aggression or violent play, but it is a highly sophisticated activity and there are specific physical markers that cue the careful observer to the differences between the two.

In R&T players always wear a "play face" which helps to create the frame in which behaviors that might ordinarily be interpreted as aggression are transformed into play. When children are engaged in R&T we see their smiles and hear their laughter. R&T episodes are sustained by skillful players rather than brought to an end by aggressive interactions. R&T is reflected in humans as well as in other primates by players' posture; eye contact; bared teeth, smile, or exaggerated grimace; and their physical bearing (Bateson, 1972). The rules of R&T include reciprocity, children are taking turns being the aggressor and the underdog, and the player who is at the bottom of the pile-up one minute is on the top of it the next (Johnson et al., 2001; Pellegrini & Smith, 1998). Not surprisingly children have been shown to be much more adept at differentiating R&T from aggression than adults (Connor, 1989; Sutton-Smith, 1988). In one illustrative study, four-to-nine-year-olds accurately labeled fighting that was playful 100% of the time, undergraduate students were 75% correct, and visiting scientists consistently mistakenly labeled R&T as aggression (Panksepp, 1993).

It is important to make clear the distinction we are making between play fighting and aggression. Habitually aggressive children become bullies on the playground and bullies' interactions with other children are neither consensual nor reciprocal.

They cause the play episode to end; adversaries are seeking domination rather than companionship. Bullying, whether carried out by individuals or gangs, is an anti-social rather than pro-social behavior. Bullying can be harmful to individual children and destructive of the classroom community effective teachers are working to establish.[2] In contrast, R&T builds community among the players.

## R&T'S DEVELOPMENTAL COURSE

R&T's developmental course has been mapped across species (Panksepp, 1993). Children's lessons in rough and tumble begin in infancy, and take years to master. Babies' first lessons in R&T are likely to be their fathers' playful roughhousing and "I'm going to get you" games of chase and capture which include tickling, laughter, and hugs (Carson et al., 1993; Clarke, 1999). This play gives babies opportunities to exercise and develop control of their large muscles as they enjoy being embraced, playfully tossed into the air, or swung in adults' arms. The physical benefits of this rough play include the sensory stimulation of escaping gravity and being weightless, if only for a moment. The emotional and cognitive benefits of playful roughhousing are more complex and involve a wide variety of developmental domains. We consider them below.

During the rough and tumble of infancy, even before they can escape by crawling away, young children show their understanding of the "what-if" pretense of the play frame. They are able to interpret others' non-literal, symbolic, playful aggression as being different from genuine anger or real-life conflict. By the time of their first birthday socially competent babies are also likely to be able to take turns, sometimes they are the pursued, and sometimes they are doing the pursuing. They are demonstrating reciprocity, another competency they need to negotiate rough and tumble with caregiving adults as well as with playmates (Clarke, 1999).

One and two-year-olds take the competencies they developed in the nursery into toddler classrooms where we are likely to see the earliest forms of peer R&T. Toddlers often follow or chase one another around the room, jostle each other as they cluster together at the top of the slide, or engage in other interactions that appear to be competitive or confrontational (Clarke, 1999). These exchanges can be interpreted as early demonstrations of associative play, children are pursuing their own interests while interacting successfully with peers when their paths cross (Parton, 1932). They are increasing their ability to negotiate the give-and-take that will eventually become R&T. It seems more than coincidental that two year olds are not only beginning to play together, but they also acquiring symbolic representation and are beginning to achieve intersubjectivity about the presence of the play frame. Both are critical milestones if they are to understand the rules of the game and to successfully sustain R&T or other forms of social play (Piaget, 1976; Vygotsky, 1976).

Beginning with these two-year olds' chase and flee games and pushing and shoving episodes, the incidence and repertoire of R&T increases gradually as children enter their preschool years. When they are three and four years old their R&T can be expected to take the form of play fighting and name-calling. At this age we begin to see evidence that there is cooperation among players, as children learn teamwork, and are becoming able to contribute to the group as both a leader and a follower (Clarke, 1999).

Rough and tumble peaks in the later primary years, between the ages of five and eight. At this stage players who have learned the rules of R&T enjoy wrestling, tackling, or chase and capture games (Clarke, 1999; Pellegrini & Smith, 1998). This playful fighting provides affiliative groups of children opportunities to coordinate their behaviors; experience the give and take of friendship and turn taking; and to limit the power of their ego, putting the needs and interests of the group ahead of their own. Among eight to ten-year-old players R&T is a way children in middle childhood establish their dominance, gauging their own and their peers' strength and status while they learn to interpret their peers' behavior, distinguishing feigned, playful challenges to their social position from genuine ones (Pellegrini & Smith, 1998). Social scientists have identified many long-term benefits of R&T, however from the players' perspectives it's just plain fun.

Spontaneous R&T on the playground wanes when youngsters enter puberty and leave behind the ways of childhood. It seems, however, to prepare some successful players to enjoy organized contact sports like football and wrestling (Clarke, 1999).

As boys become young adults vestiges of spontaneous R&T persist, however, both on and off the playing field. Rough talk may begin to replace some of young men's rough behavior. At this stage an invitation to join the game might be as subtle as a sly smile or a twinkle in the eye, and the play frame, the context for R&T, might be created simply when players hold their heads close together, as if they were "huddling up." These young adults' R&T is likely to include ribald and scatological story telling and joking, which might be accompanied by feigned boxing and good-natured arm punching.

We have seen evidence that R&T becomes increasingly symbolic as children grow older. At age five a friendly punch on the arm was an invitation to R&T and could lead instantly to a full-blown R&T episode. But at age 20 the same friendly hit is more likely to mean "remember when" and "if we were not so grown up and mature we could R&T for real" than to lead to the playful aggression of childhood.

This paper focuses primarily on physical forms of rough and tumble play. It must be said, however, that play fighting can also be verbal. *Oppositional talk* has, for example, been observed among children attending Head Start. This style of banter, sometimes called "playing the dozens" is, in fact, characteristic of many African-American communities where it is used to create a pecking order (usually with the most verbal or most physical at the top), affirm participants' mutual respect, and to express solidarity (Corsaro, 1997). It is helpful to remember that physical and verbal R&T are different versions of the same phenomenon. They are both characterized by feigned aggression, sustainability, implicit rules of engagement, reciprocity, and the role they play cementing friendships.

## ROUGH AND TUMBLE PLAY IS A CARING RELATIONSHIP

R&T is played among friends and is a major staging area or context for expressions of friendship and caring (Reed & Brown, 2000). It gives children experience sustaining the kinds of reciprocal relationships that characterize all enduring caring human interactions (Noddings, 1992). Play fighting gives children, particularly boys, what are sometimes their only opportunities to experience the give-and-take of being the care-giver as well as the cared-for when they are interacting with peers.

The importance of this give-and-take to children's social development and emotional health is apparent when we focus on the fact that sustained play requires the one-caring to become engrossed in their efforts to meet the needs of cared-for. To be successful, players need to experience the motivational shift required to put others' needs above their own (Goldstein, 1998). The motivational shift occurs when the play fighting stops long enough to give the child who had the wind knocked out of him by a nasty fall time to regain his composure, or when everyone agrees to "hold up" so the player whose shoes became untied can re-tie his laces. These experiences make particularly important contributions to boys' social development because, except under the guise of the roughhousing and feigned aggression that are the preferred interactional style of the most popular boys on the playground, males' opportunities to show caring and affection toward each other are severely limited by the mainstream's narrow definition of masculinity (Reed, 1996; Reed & Brown, 2000).

Playground roughhousing cements boys' friendships and does not disappear as children move from childhood into adolescence. It does, however, find a new outlet that lets players disguise their caring as competition. As organized sports replace spontaneous R&T boys gain opportunities to openly hug each other or pat each others' backsides without eyebrows being raised or their masculinity being challenged. The parallels between contact sports, like football and wrestling, and spontaneous rough and tumble play are, in fact, unmistakable. They create a sanctioned outlet for boys' high levels of energy while giving them opportunities to express caring and friendship in ways that are likely to be lost on the uninitiated but not on the peers who are their best friends (Pellegrini, 1994).

When boys become men opportunities to show caring and affection for each other are even more proscribed than they were during their youth. Watch two or more good friends greet each other at a comfortable social event. They are likely to exchange big smiles, hearty handshakes and slaps on the back. Notice how they stand with their heads together just as they did on the playground when they were children. Now instead of taking sides and preparing for an episode of physical R&T they are sharing a story or a joke, perhaps with a cold beer. It seems that the horseplay of the playground has moved to the sports bar where the most demonstrative displays of males' intimacy welcomed by mainstream mores are likely to appear ribald and raucous. The fact is that as they enter adulthood males' opportunities to show their caring and affection for each other are even more proscribed than they were during their youth. Their skill in, and enjoyment of, physical R&T as a demonstration of affection is expected to lie dormant until they have the chance to initiate their own children, nieces and nephews, and grandchildren to the give-and-take of playful games of chase and capture.

## ROUGH AND TUMBLE – THE FORBIDDEN FRUIT OF THE PLAYGROUND

In spite of the fact that play fighting seems to be an inevitable part of the culture of childhood, and is distinctly different in a number of documented ways from aggression (Connor, 1999; Panksepp, 1993; Periolat & Nager, 1988; Sutton-Smith, 1988), it continues to be the forbidden fruit of the playground. Both practitioners and researchers continue to consider R&T problematical, believing it inevitably gets out of control, leads to bullying, feeds aggression, and would open them up to risk of legal prosecution if a child were to be injured (Docket & Tegel, 1996; Pellegrini & Smith, 1998; Reed et al., 2000). These attitudes persist because many adults are opposed to, or are, at best, ambivalent about rambunctious physical endeavors. They resist condoning activities that are boisterous, seem to be dangerous and to break all the rules about "getting along" with their classmates.

Researchers have demonstrated, however, that not only is R&T ubiquitous, engaging, in one study, as many as 70% of the players over the course of two months of observation (Sutton-Smith, 1988), but that the ability to R&T is actually an asset rather than a liability. There are long-term benefits to helping children become adept R&T players. Children who know the rules of R&T and follow them consistently are likely to excel academically, tend to be more socially adept, and are good at solving social problems (Pellegrini, 1994).

Adults who appreciate the contributions made by R&T should not loose sight of the fact that children are likely to make any number of missteps in the process of mastering this complicated form of play. They and their peers can be expected to encounter frustrations when their actions are misinterpreted or they misjudge playmates' intentions. We know that each misstep or failed attempt to R&T is a lesson learned in the subtleties of the game and that learning to R&T is no different from learning any other social skill. Children will look to adults for encouragement and support. In the end, children who have had the freedom to explore and express their friendships through R&T should be quite good at making the distinction between play fighting and aggression by the time they leave their preschool years.

## WHO ARE THE R&T PLAYERS?

Conventional wisdom tells us that boys enjoy rough and tumble play and girls prefer to "play nice." Researchers have indicated that this is true (Aldis, 1975; Carlsson-Pagie & Levin, 1987; Costabile et al., 1992; Sutton-Smith, 1988). It should not be denied, however, that girls are often adept at R&T.[3] In their hands the games may take the form of hitting and slapping, chase and flee games, and verbal and/or physical teasing. Girls seem to generally stop short of the full body contact, tackling, and scuffling that characterizes boys' play fighting (Pellegrini & Smith, 1998).

Anecdotal observations of four-year-old girls who were identified by their teachers as active participants in R&T indicate that their participation my be dependant on boys' involvement. Several hours of observations in their preschool classrooms and on their playgrounds have revealed that they sustained R&T when boys adept at R&T participated with them.

Many differences between boys' and girls' play can be explained, no doubt, by their different socialization. From infancy on, fathers, particularly, are inclined to roughhouse with their sons, and girls are socialized to be quiet, to get along well with their playmates, and to be compliant (Pellegrini & Smith, 1998; Piaget & Inhelder, 1969). Four year old children readily differentiate "girl" and "boy" toys and behaviors, and are influenced by the implicit and explicit messages that are sent by parents, teachers and peers to conform the mainstream gender expectations (Martin et al., 1990). That means that boys are expected to be rough and boisterous (even though that behavior might get them into trouble) and girls are rewarded for being quiet, getting along well with each other, and enjoying each other's company.

It would be interesting to investigate how gender roles are being blurred by children's increased opportunities to play together as equals throughout their early childhood years. Neighborhood soccer teams, for example, are usually co-ed until children are eight to ten years old. In those settings girls are showing themselves to be at least as aggressive as boys, perhaps because of their typically-more-advanced language and social abilities. It appears that girls are seizing opportunities to R&T in organized sports, liberties they are unlikely to take during spontaneous playground play. It could be that gender equity is more of a reality on the soccer field than it is in the boardroom, or maybe the demise of pick-up neighborhood games has cast girls in a new light that removes the constraints created by traditional gender roles. Those intriguing questions remain to be answered. We hope they suggest the complexity of the issues surrounding the real and feigned aggression exhibited when children's play is active and rambunctious.

## WHO CHALLENGES R&T? SHOULD THEIR VIEW BE RECONCEPTUALIZED?

It might seem that play which offers so many documented advantages would be enthusiastically supported and promoted by teachers of young children. But that is far from the case. R&T is generally misunderstood (Reed et al., 2000). More often than not, it is censured by adults who ban "fighting" on the playground, or it is forced underground – behind the playhouse or over the hill, out of adults' sight and supervision (Sutton-Smith & Magee, 1989).

The conventional view is that rough play should always be suppressed. That prohibition fails to make a distinction, however, between aggression and R&T. Adults who consider only the observable characteristics of aggression are likely to take the position that play fighting promotes the view that "boys will be boys"; encourages male hegemony; will, inevitably, lead to bullying and possibly even gang behavior; and is just too risky in the current litigious social climate (Periolat & Nager, 1988). The research we have conducted (Reed et al., 2000) as well as anecdotal evidence we have collected over years of working in and observing playgrounds have convinced us that "No fighting on the playground" is the policy in most schools and classrooms, and is a reflection of mainstream early childhood educators' beliefs (Bredekamp & Copple, 1997).

Try as they might, adults are not likely to extinguish R&T, however. Children are experts at pursuing the activities that contribute to their efforts to resolve their current developmental crises, that give them opportunities to express their friendships and affiliations, and that invite them to refine the skills that will serve them well in the real world of childhood. Even if their actions have to be clandestine, children know how to sustain activities that nurture their friendships in spite of adults who try to scrutinize and control their play (Chevalier, 1998; Sutton-Smith & Magee, 1989).

We assert that rather than obstructing children's R&T play, adults should create settings that welcome and encourage consenting players' participation. We believe adults have a responsibility to provide a suitable physical setting as well as a safety net of informed, arms-length supervision. It is important to note that we do not abdicate our adult responsibilities to ensure all children's safety, but neither do we believe we are justified in prohibiting behavior just because some youngsters fail to understand the rules of R&T or choose not to participate.

Our view is not a popular one, however. At two international conferences where one of the authors advocated that teachers condone and, even more radically, encourage, willing players' participation in R&T, his position was vigorously challenged. We will explore some of the rationales upon which these challenges seem to have been based.

## CHALLENGES TO R&T

### *Traditional Perspectives*

Traditionalists' approach to play can be explained by considering several dimensions of the institution of school, the governance of public education, and the standards of accountability by which they will be evaluated. First, school is compulsory. Large numbers of children must attend every day, and it would be fair to assume that many children are in the classroom against their wills. When students are cast in the role of being resistant and resentful, teachers become jailors or truant officers, enforcing the system's law and order. They come to represent the *status quo*, denying the existence and expression of dissenting and diverse voices (Freire, 1997).

Second, and related to children's compulsory school attendance, is the fact that some teachers and administrators see themselves as the personification of the long arm of the law. They believe children in their charge have to be managed and their impulses need to be reined in. In these schools teachers are so powerful that they rule the everyday routines of classroom life: when and where children can talk, how they can move about the classroom and the school, when they can eat and drink, even the timing and duration of bathroom breaks.

Teachers who define their roles in these ways are likely to justify play in the curriculum by documenting the contributions time spent in carefully planned play environments can make to children's physical, cognitive, emotional and social development. They are confident play helps children acquire the knowledge and competencies required by the standards and ubiquitous high-stakes tests. This means the benefits of play flow from play environments that have been created and controlled by adults. From this perspective R&T can be seen as a threat to teachers' power and the law and order that characterize school. That is because in R&T a small number of children, typically the assertive boys, take control of a part of the playground. Educators who consider having power over children to be requisite to good teaching are likely to wonder, "What's the use of appearing to be 'in charge' if I permit children to go out on the playground and break all the rules enforced in the classroom?" What's more, rambunctious play does not appear to support the attainment of mandated curriculum standards or to contribute to children's success on high-stakes-tests used to assess teachers' and schools' effectiveness. Teachers in these kinds of settings are likely to, themselves, feel disempowered by the system and vulnerable to criticism if their students do not live up to externally set benchmarks of achievement. Viewed in this way it can be expected that they will ask, "How could I ever justify R&T to skeptical supervisors?" and, "How could I be seen to condone such aberrant behavior?"

And third, teachers are likely to forbid R&T because it is outside of the their personal experience. Our society continues to see teaching, nurturing, and raising childern as women's work. Women are apt to create classrooms that reflect and value feminine ways of interacting and behaving. Teachers who didn't R&T in their own childhoods or left chase and flee games behind in the now far removed, distant, and unexamined past are unlikely to understand its rules or the role it plays socializing its players (Johnson et al., 2001).

### Feminists' Perspective – The Story of the Water Table

A skeptical conference attendee challenged R&T on different grounds when she described this incident, which she had observed in a classroom of five-year-olds:

> A group of four girls was outside playing at the water table. A gang of boys moved over to the water table, unceremoniously stepped in front of them, took over the water table and began to play in the water. The girls simply stepped aside, eventually moving on other activities.

If we were to have observed this event first hand we likely would know more about these children's relationships: Who do they typically chose to play with, and what do they do when they have time to set their own agendas? Was this a case of bullying? Was it a demonstration of a prevalent behavior pattern that privileges masculine agendas?[4]

Since we didn't have first-hand knowledge of this scenario, our first response was to suggest that this was not R&T, for it did not include elements of reciprocity or mutual consent. But the conference attendee persisted. She seemed to be voicing the frequently made assumption that a permissive policy toward R&T is to blame for bullying and every incidence of classroom aggression. She felt that condoning such behavior reinforced male hegemony.

Perhaps part of the confusion surrounding R&T lies in the fact that this kind of play is often the staging area where affiliations and power coalitions are formed. In this case these boys' friendships might well have been forged during their past successful R&T episodes that gave them opportunities to both challenge and care for one another. Often it is not clear if the children who are not R&T players (in this instance the girls who first had control of the water table) understand the difference between rough behavior that is playful and real fighting. It could be that non-players become frightened because they interpret the roughhousing they are witnessing to be out-of-control aggression that might be turned against them. Or, alternatively, non-R&T players might recognize R&T for what it is, a stylized form of rough play. They may not feel threatened by it at all, but simply choose not to participate. Research studies have neither described non-participating peers' reactions to R&T nor its effect on non-participating classmates.

Another issue that concerned this conference participant had to do with assumptions these children seemed to be making about the appropriateness of male domination. The girls at the water table acquiesced to the boys. It could be that these girls had internalized messages about male superiority which continue to characterize today's mainstream culture or that they felt bullied or frightened by the group of children who are successful R&T players. The fact is that we lack enough information to further interpret this event.

We do not uncritically permit some groups of children to overpower their peers who either do not understand R&T or choose not to participate in play fighting. We do assert, however, that this incident at the water table deserves careful analysis and thoughtful reflection. On first blush we might think the girls were victims of boys' assertive, some would say overpowering, behavior. But, on the other hand, it could be that while these girls have appeared to willingly give up the water table they may use a less direct and more feminine approach such as bantering with the boys to subtly undermining their free reign. They might even understand and participate in play fighting, giving up their position in this coveted center only to claim ascendancy over another group of players on the other side of the playground.

There can be no question that genderized behaviors are transmitted and refined on the playground. Learning society's expectations about how to be a girl or a boy is a major developmental task for all children. However, we are certainly not suggesting that teachers of young children should be in the position of perpetuating stereotypes that are harmful, limiting, or unjust. We are recognizing, however, that adjudicating playground disputes puts the early education educator in the difficult position of trying to support each individual child's development while not perpetuating unjust stereotypes that continue to limit opportunities for self expression and self actualization for approximately half of our students.

## INTENTIONALLY WELCOMING R&T ONTO THE PLAYGROUND

Rather then banning R&T and labeling boys and girls who play rough as troublemakers we believe teachers should reconceptualize their view of reciprocal, consensual rough play. They should create environments that help all children form affiliations and friendships in the ways that fit their personal strengths and preferences. Each teacher's goal should be to help every child claim his or her personal agency. To that end children should be encouraged to step out of the stereotypes created by strict gender typing and narrowly defined gender-based expectations. A sensitive teacher knows that not all boys enjoy R&T, not all girls avoid it. The point is that every classroom should support boys and girls in their play choices, recognizing that individuals need a repertoire of interactional styles that will enable them to get along with a wide variety of peers.

All children need to understand, moreover, the differences between consensual and non-consensual rough housing. They must appreciate the rights, responsibilities and privileges that are due peers in a democratic society. We believe that making these issues of power, reciprocity and self-agency part of the explicit curriculum would empower all children, the players and the observers, boys and girls alike. It would give all children experience making decisions about joining or not joining groups of players, and would give them strategies to protect themselves from becoming victims of aggression or gang behaviors that lack the structure and rules that govern R&T players.

## SUMMARY

Our call to reconceptualize rough and tumble play should not be misinterpreted as an indication that we are indifferent to violence, aggression, or bullying among school children. These are real problems that responsible adults cannot ignore. We are, instead, making a plea to adults who are responsible for children that they inform themselves about the characteristics of R&T, the benefits that come to successful players, and the research documenting its role in children's development. We hope that they carefully reconsider their attitudes and policies related to peers' playful rough housing.

True R&T is a vehicle for children, particularly boys, to create and sustain friendships and is an expression of their caring relationship. It is a highly developed form of socialization that should be encouraged by caregiving adults.

Like all children's activities, R&T needs appropriate supervision, but it requires a special approach that gives children freedom from adult interference. First, we should create an emotionally safe environment where children are empowered to choose whether or not to join in without fear of ridicule or coercion from children or adults. Next, R&T players need a wide-open space, ideally one with soft grass or another resilient surface, so they have room to run and chase, tackle and pile-on without getting hurt. Next, they need time to play, at least a half-an-hour a day to fully develop their game into a satisfactory play episode. And finally, they need to know that adults are there, albeit at arms' length, to provide a physical and emotional safety net as needed.

We want to clearly caution readers to the potential dangers involved in putting R&T onto the "approved" list of playground activities. Adults should not over-do the attention they pay to successful R&T players. Too much supervision or regulation will destroy the play frame and ruin the game. R&T has been a vital part of childhood for a long, long time. It has never depended on adults to survive – let's be sure to leave it that way. Our children deserve to enjoy this legacy of childhood unspoiled.

## RECOMMENDATIONS

Our first-hand experiences as teachers of young children, observations in others' classrooms, research projects, and review of the literature lead us to make these recommendations to readers ready to reconceptualize their view and attitudes about R&T play.

(1) Permit both boys and girls to participate in R&T play.
(2) Create a space designed to support and reserved for R&T players.
(3) Educate teachers and parents about the characteristics of R&T, the contributions it makes to players' social development, and the differences between R&T, aggression, and bullying.
(4) Educate children about R&T play.
  (a) Make the rules of the game explicit.
  (b) Discuss issues of power, domination, and privilege.
  (c) Empower both boys and girls with strategies to join in or opt out of R&T play.

(5) Add information about R&T to teachers' preservice and in-service professional development.
(6) Conduct additional research that has the potential to put R&T into the context of theorists and practitioners who are integral to early childhood education.

## ISSUES FOR FURTHER STUDY

Does R&T limit opportunities for self actualization? *Abraham Maslow* articulates the importance of providing all students the opportunity to reach self actualization. For that to happen all members of the classroom community must feel safe – and they don't when they see R&T they don't understand. From this perspective it looks dangerous and out of control. All children need help recognizing R&T for what it is, and what it's not.

*Erik Erikson* describes the process of self-regulation which helps children learn to effectively set limits on themselves. In R&T peers enforce the rules and permit only those who abide by them into their R&T play. What are the implications of child-directed and child-regulated R&T from this perspective?

*Howard Gardner* would put R&T into the context of multiple intelligences. He would be likely to say that children who R&T are using the intelligence that is their strength – their preferred ways of knowing, which, we predict, would most likely to be bodily-kinesthetic, interpersonal, and spatial intelligences. But schools are so heavily skewed toward logical/ mathematical and linguistic intelligences that children whose strengths and interactional styles are outside these parameters are ostracized, lost, undervalued and overlooked.

In sum, we are convinced that there is a rationale for reconceptualizing rough and tumble play. It makes important contributions to children and childhood. We believe it is important and valuable in and of itself, and hope we have successfully made the case that it needs no further justification than the pleasure children derive from having the freedom to express their friendships, caring, and connection in multiple ways. The classrooms where they spend their days should welcome play that gives children opportunities to freely express themselves in ways that reflect their personal abilities, strengths and interests.

## NOTES

1. Some researchers consider physical contact a requisite part of the definition of R&T. Others include games of chase and flee, name-calling, and other non-physical play fighting within their definition of rough and tumble (Pellegrini & Smith, 1989). This paper considers both contact and non-contact forms of play fighting to be R&T.

2. We realize the uninitiated may not be able to tell the difference between R&T and aggression. This chapter is intended to help them make that distinction. We urge readers who are unsure if the episode they are watching is real fighting or play fighting to conduct a member check, that is, to ask the players if they want to be involved and if they are comfortable with the action. Answers to those questions will help adults learn to differentiate between real and feigned aggression.

3. There remains a significant gap in the literature, for descriptions of girls' rough and tumble play are noticeably absent, as are descriptions of how girls are likely to exhibit their friendship and caring in non-conventional or difficult-to-identify ways. Careful analysis might well demonstrate the girls' participation in R&T is significant, but that it manifests itself in yet-to-be-documented ways.

4. We do not condone nor are we intending to justify masculine privilege. We are simply recognizing its continued existence, in spite of efforts to make relationships between the sexes more egalitarian.

# REFERENCES

Aldis, O. (1975). *Play fighting*. New York: Academic Press.

Bateson, G. A. (1972). *Steps to an ecology of the mind*. New York: Ballentine.

Blurton-Jones, N. G. (1975). Categories of child interaction. In: N. G. Blurton Jones (Ed.), *Ethological Studies of Child Behavior* (pp. 97–129). London: Cambridge University Press.

Bredekamp, S., & Copple, C. (Eds) (1997). *Developmentally appropriate practice in early childhood programs* (Rev. ed.). Washington, DC: National Association for the Education of Young Children.

Carlsson-Pagie, N., & Levin, D. E. (1987). *The war play dilemma: Balancing needs and values in the early childhood classroom*. New York: Teachers College Press.

Carson, J., Burks, V., & Parke, R. (1993). Parent-child physical play: Determinants and consequences. In: K. MacDonald (Ed.), *Parent-Child Play: Descriptions and Implications* (pp. 197–220). Albany: State University of New York Press.

Chevalier, M. (1998). Paradoxes of social control: Children's perspectives and actions. *Journal of Research in Childhood Education, 13*, 48–55.

Chick, G. (2001). What is play for? Sexual selection and the evolution of play. In: S. Reifel (Ed.), *Theory in Context and Out: Play & Culture Studies* (Vol. 3, pp. 3–25). Stamford, CT: Ablex.

Clarke, J. L. (1999). Development reflected in chase games. In: S. Reifel (Ed.), *Play Contexts Revisited: Play & Culture* (Vol. 2).

Connor, K. (1999). Aggression: Is it in the eye of the beholder? In: S. Reifel (Ed.), *Play Contexts Revisited: Play & Culture* (Vol. 2, pp. 213–217).

Corsaro, W. A. (1997). *The sociology of childhood*. Thousand Oaks, CA: Pine Forge Press.

Costabile, A., Genta, M. L., Zucchini, E., Smith, P. K., & Harker, R. (1992). Attitudes of parents toward war play in young children. *Early Education and Development, 3*(4), 356–369.

Docket, S., & Tegel, K. (1996). Identifying dilemmas for early childhood educators. *Australian Research in Early Childhood Education (Also available as ERIC Document ED406033.), 1*, 20–27.

Freire, P. (1970/1997). *Pedagogy of the oppressed* (Revised 20th anniversary edition). New York: Continuum.

Goldstein, L. (1998). More than gentle smiles and warm hugs: Applying the ethic of care to early childhood education. *Journal of Research in Childhood Education, 12*(2), 244–261.

Johnson, J. E., Welteroth, S. J., & Corl, S. M. (2001). Attitudes of parents and teachers about play aggression in young children. In: S. Reifel (Ed.), *Theory in Context and Out, Play & Culture Studies* (Vol. 3, pp. 335–354). Stamford, CT: Ablex.

Martin, C. L., Wood, C. H., & Little, J. K. (1990). The development of gender stereotype components. *Child Development, 61*, 1891–1904.

Noddings, N. (1992). *The challenge to care in schools: An alternative approach to education.* New York: Teachers College Press.

Panksepp, J. (1993). Rough and tumble play: A fundamental brain process. In: K. MacDonald (Ed.), *Parent-Child Play: Descriptions and Implications* (pp. 147–184). Albany, NY: State University of New York Press.

Parton, M. B. (1932). Social participation among pre-school children. *The Journal of Abnormal and Social Psychology, 27*, 243–269.

Pellegrini, A. D. (1994). The rough play of adolescent boys of differing sociometric status. *International Journal of Behavioral Development, 17*(3), 525–540.

Pellegrini, A. D., & Smith, P. K. (1998). Physical activity play: The nature and function of a neglected aspect of play. *Child Development, 69*(3), 577–598.

Periolat, J., & Nager, N. (1988). The positive aspects of aggressive behavior in young children. ERIC Document 373–926.

Piaget, J. (1976). Symbolic play. In: J. S. Bruner, A. Jolly & K. Sylva (Eds), *Play – Its Role in Development and Evolution* (pp. 555–569). New York: Basic Books. Originally published in part in *Play, Dreams and Imitation in Childhood* (pp. 166–171). Routledge & Kegan Paul (1951).

Piaget, J., & Inhelder, B. (1969). *The psychology of the child.* New York: Basic Books.

Reed, T., & Brown, M. (2000). The expression of care in the rough and tumble play of boys. *Journal of Research in Childhood Education, 15*(1), 104–116.

Reed, T., Brown, M., & Roth, S. A. (2000). Friendship formation and boys' rough and tumble play: Implications for teacher education programs. *Journal of Early Childhood Teacher Education, 21*(3), 331–336.

Sutton-Smith, B. (1988). War toys and childhood aggression. *Play and Culture, 1*, 57–69.

Sutton-Smith, B., & Magee, M. A. (1989). Reversible childhood. *Play & Culture, 2*, 52–63.

Vygotsky, L. S. (1976). Play and its role in the mental development of the child. In: J. S. Bruner, A. Jolly & K. Sylva (Eds), *Play – Its Role in Development and Evolution* (pp. 535–554). New York: Basic Books. Originally published in *Soviet Psychology, 12*(6), 62–76 (1966).

# WAR PLAY, AGGRESSION AND PEER CULTURE: A REVIEW OF THE RESEARCH EXAMINING THE RELATIONSHIP BETWEEN WAR PLAY AND AGGRESSION

Heidi L. Malloy and Paula McMurray-Schwarz

## ABSTRACT

*The purpose of this paper is to review the literature on war play and aggression. The paper begins with an introduction to play and the theories of Piaget, Vygotsky, and Corsaro. This is followed by a definition of pretend aggression and the war play debate. Literature is reviewed on how violent television, war toys, and war play shapes children's imaginary play and aggressive behaviors. Attention is also given to the teacher's role in war play and the methods used to investigate war play. Suggestions are made for future approaches to the study of war play within the context of the peer culture. The paper concludes with implications for early childhood educators.*

## WAR PLAY, AGGRESSION, AND PEER CULTURE

Play represents reality with an "as if" or "what if" attitude and it connects or relates children's experiences. In play, children are actively involved in a pleasurable, intrinsically motivated, rule governed activity with emerging and shifting goals

Social Contexts of Early Education, and Reconceptualizing Play (II)
Advances in Early Education and Day Care, Volume 13, 235–265
© 2004 Published by Elsevier Ltd.
ISSN: 0270-4021/doi:10.1016/S0270-4021(04)13009-7

that children develop spontaneously (Fromberg, 1992; Frost et al., 2001). Play is the foundation of children's learning and development. Through play, children construct understandings of concepts and explore feelings (Carlsson-Paige & Levin, 1987; Piaget, 1951; Smilansky, 1968).

Traditional views of play have focused on children's ability to create mental representations. For example, Piaget (1951) theorized that children actively construct mental structures or schemas that allow them to represent objects, actions, and events in their minds. As children play, they act on their environment and transform incoming information about the world, so that it fits their current level of understanding. As representational thought is developed, children become active participants in imaginary play.

Vygotsky (1978) believed that children's ability to participate in representational play relied on their social participation with others. Children learn how to participate in imaginary play through their communications with adults and others at the interpersonal level, before they internalize the process at the individual level. Through these social interactions, children learn to act in a cognitive realm and the environment no longer dictates what they can do.

Corsaro (1985) agrees that children are active participants in the creation of their own development and imaginary play. However, children not only assimilate and internalize the process of imaginary play, they also appropriate, reinvent, and reproduce the process through their innovations and creativity. "In role-play, children do not simply imitate adult models, but rather use information acquired from observation and interactive experience with adults to reproduce social events" (Corsaro, 1985, p. 77). As children pretend they extend the ideas taken from the adult world and give them new meaning to address their own peer concerns (Corsaro, 1985, 1997). According to Corsaro (1997), children develop in an adult culture that provides them with resources and information, but because children have less experience and knowledge than adults, they may not interpret the information in the same way. Children create their own meanings based on their limited understanding of the information from the adult culture and bring these new meanings into peer culture. "Behavior and activities the children regard as important (physical aggressiveness, mobility, play with guns) become part of peer interactive events, in this sense role play is not only important for the children's development and use of social knowledge, but is also a part of peer culture" (Corsaro, 1985, p. 120).

This paper examines a specific type of imaginary play that appeals to young children, particularly boys, who create a peer culture based on heroic good guys and evil bad guys in the early childhood classroom. A review of the literature addresses violent television, war toys, and war play and how these mediums shape children's imaginary play and aggressive behaviors. Attention is also given to the teacher's role in children's war play. A reconceputalization of the relationship between play and aggression is explored, including alternative methods and approaches for examining children's aggression in play through the lens of the peer culture. The paper concludes with implications for teachers. However, we begin with a definition of pretend aggression and the theoretical debates on children's war play.

### Aggression in Imaginary Play

Pretend aggression is one component of peer culture and imaginary play that concerns parents and teachers (Carlsson-Paige & Levin, 1987, 1990) because it resembles the real aggressive behaviors that are intended to hurt or harm another person (Crick & Grotpeter, 1995; Dollard et al., 1939). Pretend aggression is an *act about* overt aggression (Frey & Hoppe-Graff, 1994). It is acting out the "harming of others through physical aggression, verbal threats, or instrumental intimidation" (Crick & Grotpeter, p. 710). Researchers have defined pretend aggression as children exhibiting aggression in the context of make-believe, that includes children or doll characters acting out roles (e.g. "I'll be Batman, you be Robin"), children pretending to transform objects into other objects (e.g. pretending a Lego is a gun), or children creating objects and imaginary people (e.g. "Let's pretend Joker's cat took the book") (Goff, 1995; Watson & Peng, 1992).

Aggression is pretend when the participants recognize that the messages within interactions represent behaviors and objects within the play realm rather than reality. When children participate in pretend aggression, they say things that they do not really mean except within pretend and often communicate about things that do not really exist. When a child points a finger and thumb at another child, the finger and thumb do not "denote" what would be "denoted" by a gun "for which it stands." The gun itself is fictional and the word "gun" cannot be used to shoot real bullets. However, the distinction between play and reality is fragile and can break down. To participate in aggressive play, children need to understand that the aggressive behaviors that are displayed in play are different in meaning from the real aggression that can occur at any time and break the play "frame." Pretend aggression can be mistaken for the real aggression of combat and pretend play may become a real battle with real injuries or hurt feelings. It may also be possible to evoke real feelings of terror within an imaginative play frame with imaginary objects, interactions, people or fantastic beings (superheroes, monsters, pirates) (adapted from Bateson, 1972). Sutton-Smith and Kelly-Byrne (1984) suggest that children use play to display aggression in ways that are more socially acceptable to the adults in their culture, but "at any time also, impulse can break through this mask into cruelty and danger" (p. 194).

## The War Play Debate

War play is a form of imaginary play that includes episodes of pretend aggression. War play involves acting out roles of violence, aggression, or war that children have witnessed or experienced in their homes, neighborhoods, or on television. Although war play can include manufactured war toys, children can also use their imaginations to turn their finger, a stick, or a pen into a powerful weapon (Nielsen & Dissanayake, 2001; Nilsson, 1989).

War play is primarily an activity that is embraced by boys (Carlsson-Paige & Levin, 1987; Dyson, 1994; Jordan & Cowan, 1995; Paley, 1984; Sutton-Smith, 1988; Wegener-Spöhring, 1989). Boys are more likely than girls to participate in real aggression (Farver, 1996; Huesmann et al., 1984; Kupersmidt et al., 1995; Sanson & Di Muccio, 1993; Wegener-Spöhring, 1989; Williams & Schaller, 1993) and pretend aggressive play with superhero and war themes (Boyatzis et al., 1995; Boyd, 1997; Carlsson-Paige & Levin, 1987, 1990; Caulfield, 2002; Costabile et al., 1992; Dyson, 1994; Jordan & Cowan, 1995; Paley, 1984; Scales & Cook-Gumperz, 1993; Sutton-Smith, 1998; Watson & Peng, 1992; Wegener-Spöhring, 1989). Boys like play themes of danger and violence that involve fighting, killing, and simulated wars (Cramer & Hogan, 1975). They are more likely than girls to play with guns (LaVoie & Adams, 1974) or war toys involving face-to-face fighting, shooting, and action figures (Wegener-Spöhring, 1989).

War play may be attractive to boys, because they identify with the stereotypical and explicit male gender roles that are evident in war play themes. The roles boys act out in war play are almost exclusively linked to strong, powerful, fearless, and aggressive male television characters who rescue the weak and helpless female victims (Carlsson-Paige & Levin, 1990). Furthermore, society expects boys to be more aggressive than girls, and war play provides boys with a socially acceptable outlet for the expression of aggressive behaviors (Carlsson-Paige & Levin, 1987).

Debates continue among researchers, theorists, and educators as to whether it is necessary for children to act out war play scenarios. Developmentalists have argued that children express what they need to work on through their play; therefore, if they are participating in war play, it must be meeting certain developmental needs (Carlsson-Paige & Levin, 1987, 1988; Kostelnik et al., 1986; Wolf, 1984). War play may meet children's needs for "curiosity; exploration; anxiety and fear reduction; self-regulation of cognitive, emotional, and physiological states; and social identity" (Goldstein, 1995, p. 141). Researchers have suggested that "war play helps children meet their needs for power, control, and mastery" (Carlsson-Paige & Levin, 1988, p. 82). Also it is a tool to help children learn to distinguish "fantasy from reality, good from bad, right from wrong, and express anger and aggression at a time when children are being asked, in real life, to gain control of them" (Carlsson-Paige & Levin, 1988, p. 82). Finally, according to the developmentalist perspective, war play is pretend; it is not connected to real world violence. Therefore, it should be viewed in terms of what it means to children which is often different from what it means to adults who bring to it their knowledge of violence in the world (Carlsson-Paige & Levin, 1988). However, developmentalist would agree that ideas for children's war play often come from real world violence. During World War II, children drew war related pictures including weapons, planes, and ships; and themes of war were common in the children's dramatic play (Bonte & Musgrove, 1943; Rautman, 1943). More recently, Levin (2003) documented how children incorporated the Oklahoma City bombing and the terrorist acts of September 11, 2001 into their play.

Sociopolitical theorists suggest that adults should discourage children from play that involves pretend aggression because it contributes to real aggression by teaching that violence is an acceptable way to interact with other people, solve problems, and display power (Carlsson-Paige & Levin, 1987, 1988). Social learning, cognitive neoassociation, and social cognitive theories support this argument by suggesting that observing and participating in aggression, even fantasy aggression, increases the likelihood that children will behave aggressively (Bandura, 1973; Berkowitz, 1984; Huesmann, 1988; Huesmann & Eron, 1984, 1989). However, proponents of cathartic theory suggest that participating in pretend aggression should decrease children's tendency to behave aggressively in the future (Dollard et al., 1939; Feshbach, 1956). Research (Berkowitz, 1964; Bushman, 2002; Mallick & McCandless, 1966) has failed to support the catharsis hypothesis. It is more likely that previous displays of aggression lead to an increase rather than a decrease in future aggression (Bushman, 2002; Bushman et al., 2001; Mallick & McCandless, 1966). However, some people believe that participating in aggression makes them feel better (Bushman et al., 2001). These perspectives on aggression have not been studied in relationship to children's imaginary play.

### Violent Television Contributes to Aggression

Many ideas for children's pretend aggression come from television programs, particularly cartoons (e.g. Carlsson-Paige & Levin, 1987; Costabile et al., 1992; Gronlund, 1992; James & McCain, 1982; Scales & Cook-Gumperz, 1993). Several reviews (e.g. Comstock, 1991; Eron et al., 1994; Huston et al., 1992;

Liebert et al., 1982) detail the overwhelming evidence that viewing aggression and violence on television can increase aggressive attitudes, values, and behaviors. Researchers have found that children imitate the aggressive behaviors of filmed models (Bandura et al., 1963). Children are also more likely to harm other children after viewing televised violence (Hapkiewicz & Stone, 1974; Liebert & Baron, 1972), including viewing aggressive cartoons (Boyatzis et al., 1995; Cameron et al., 1971; Ellis & Sekyra, 1972; Huesmann et al., 2003; Mussen & Rutherford, 1961), than viewing non-violent television programs.

In the 1980's, regulations that were used to govern children's television programming were eliminated by the Federal Communications Commission (FCC) and product based programming became legal (Brotman, 1987; Carlsson-Paige & Levin, 1987). This opened a door for children to buy more toys, including main characters, scenery, and weapons based on television programs (Carlsson-Paige & Levin, 1987). In the fall of 1987, toy companies produced 80% of all children's television shows, many of which focused on violence (Carlsson-Paige & Levin, 1990). By creating toys and television shows as packages, a lucrative relationship was established between the toy and television industries. In 1994, the sale of products linked to Power Rangers, one of the most violent children's television programs, set an industry record by surpassing one billion dollars (Levin & Carlsson-Paige, 1995).

Boyatzis et al. (1995) conducted an observational study to determine the effects of watching Power Rangers on the behaviors of 52 elementary children, ages 5–7, in an afterschool program. The children were divided into two groups. The first group's aggressive behaviors were recorded during a free play session. The second group watched a Power Rangers episode with 140 aggressive acts, then aggressive behaviors were recorded during a separate free play period. Boyatzis et al. (1995) found that the boys who watched only one episode of Power Rangers, committed seven times more aggressive acts than children who did not watch the cartoon. The boys who watched Power Rangers imitated the cartoon characters by directing flying kicks and karate chops toward their peers (Boyatzis, 1997; Boyatzis et al., 1995).

## Reports of Increased Aggression

Teachers and parents have expressed concerns about the effect of violent television on children's play and the repetition of violent acts children use in play to imitate television characters. Early childhood teachers and parents have reported an increase in aggression and a lack of creativity in children's play since the deregulation of the broadcasting industry (Carlsson-Paige & Levin, 1987, 1990).

Carlsson-Paige and Levin (1987) conducted 30 open-ended interviews with parents located in Iowa, Colorado, Canada, and Sweden. The majority of interviews were conducted with parents of boys. Many of the parents, who were interviewed, believed that the war play of their children was more aggressive and less creative than the play they had participated in as children. Additionally, parents in the late 1980s felt differently about war play, than parents only five years earlier.

Carlsson-Paige and Levin (1987) also asked parents of three- to five-year-old children, in four daycare centers, to complete questionnaires on the topic of war play. Parents of boys completed 42 of the 59 questionnaires. All but three boys participated in war play. The boys who did not participate in war play had parents who banned war play. Only five parents reported girls participating in war play, typically with boys. Parents reported that children first became interested in war play between 18 months and three years. The most common source for children's interest in war play came from television, followed by school, older siblings, and the neighborhood. Two-thirds of parents believed themes for war play came from television programs or commercials, and parents often described children's play as imitative of television images.

Costabile et al. (1992) assessed the attitudes of parents toward their children's war play by developing a questionnaire for parents based on the questionnaire created by Carlsson-Paige and Levin (1987). Teachers distributed the questionnaires to 316 Italian parents and 84 English parents of children between the ages of two and six years old. Costabile et al. suggested that the incidence of war play was low. Only 36% of the Italian parents and 57% of English parents indicated that their children participated in war play. The majority of the children were boys who participated in war play once a week to once a month. Parents reported that children were most likely to participate in weapon play, followed by war play with combat figures, and acting out war play roles. Similar to the findings of Carlsson-Paige and Levin (1987), Costabile et al. stated that the majority of parents reported that their children became interested in war play between the age of two and three years old and that their ideas for war play came from television. All parents indicated that the children who were interested in war play were most likely to participate in this activity with other children, but many also indicated that the children played war themes on their own. Parents were divided when asked whether they would discourage war play, allow war play within limits, or allow war play unconditionally. However, most parents agreed that children should not be allowed to bring war toys to school and that teachers should help children turn their war play into a more constructive activity. Both the Italian parents and the English parents were more accepting of boys playing with toy weapons and combat figures than girls. The English parents were also more accepting of boys watching violent television programs than girls.

Teachers have also reported increases in the aggression of children's play. Carlsson-Paige and Levin (1987) sent questionnaires to 16 teachers in three daycare centers. Although the majority of teachers banned war play in their classrooms, "all of the teachers reported that the children in their classroom attempted to engage in war and weapons play" (Carlsson-Paige & Levin, 1988, p. 82). Boys were more commonly engaged in war play than girls. Similar to parent responses (Carlsson-Paige & Levin, 1987; Costabile et al., 1992), the influence of television was mentioned by almost all teachers who described children's war play in detail. However, two-thirds of teachers were not happy with how they were approaching war play in their classrooms. Carlsson-Paige and Levin also interviewed 42 early childhood professionals, 83% were teachers of children between the ages of two and ten years old. The teachers reported that the children's war play was more imitative and aggressive than it had been in the past. However, this was a biased sample, because Carlsson-Paige and Levin knew that half of the early childhood professionals had concerns about children's war play prior to completing the questionnaires.

Nevertheless, Ritchie and Johnson's (1982) informal observations of a preschool laboratory program support the results of Carlsson-Paige and Levin's (1987) teacher questionnaires. They observed that over a two year period more and more of the children's play appeared to be connected to television programs and movies, particularly superhero programs. The superhero play was more aggressive than the children's other play. The conflicts in superhero play were solved through aggression that relied on physical strength or magical powers.

During the 1990's interest in children's war play was renewed when a new cartoon, more violent than its predecessors, begin to air in 1993. The television show Power Rangers showed real-life actors who, with the help of special effects, could perform acts previously limited to inanimate cartoon characters (Levin & Carlsson-Paige, 1995). To investigate the effect of the new Power Rangers program on children's war play, Levin and Carlsson-Paige distributed questionnaires to early childhood professionals in 17 states. The questionnaires were completed by 204 teachers working with 2–7-year-old children. Ninety-seven percent of the teachers were concerned about the negative effects of Power Rangers on the children in their classrooms. Similar to their findings in 1987, teachers were concerned about the increase of violence in the classroom and the children's violent, imitative, and less creative play. They also voiced concerns about children's confusion between fantasy and reality, their obsessive involvement with Power Rangers, their overwhelming desire for Power Rangers merchandise, and their identification with Power Rangers as role models for social behavior. Ninety-eight percent of the teachers were also concerned about the increase in children's violence and aggression. Teachers reported seeing aggression in the children's social interactions, artwork, stories, writing, and play both inside the classroom and out on the playground. Several teachers believed that Power Rangers desensitize children to violence and weaken their ability to successfully resolve conflicts.

Boyd (1997) questioned the accuracy of the teacher reports of "increased" aggression since deregulation of the broadcasting industry. The concerns of early childhood teachers suggest that war play is a common occurrence in the daily lives of children. Boyd conducted two preliminary studies to investigate the frequency of children's participation in war play. She collected time interval samples of 17 children, ages 3–5 years, in a laboratory preschool. During her month of observation, only two boys played superheroes and the time spent in the play accounted for less than 1% of the 300 minutes she observed in play. Similarly, Boyd observed that superhero play occurred in only 5% of the playtime at a full day child care program. Of the 16 children observed, only four boys participated in superhero play and not a single child who participated in the superhero play was hurt by another child.

Boyd (1997) suggested that teacher reports of increased aggression may not be objective. First, teachers and children have different perspectives on real and pretend aggression. Young children understand the difference between actual aggression and pretend aggressive behaviors (e.g. fighting in war play) (Engel, 1984; Wegener-Spöhring, 1989); but parents, educators, and researchers find it difficult to distinguish real acts of aggression from pretend aggressive episodes (Sutton-Smith, 1988; Wegener-Spöhring, 1989). In addition, teacher perspectives often differ from other non-teaching adults. Connor (1989) found that teachers rated children's behavior as aggressive rather than playful more often than did other non-teaching adults. Boyd suggested that the responsibility of teachers to keep children safe causes them to be overly sensitive to play that might lead to potential disruptions or injury. Although Boyd's findings support Costabile's et al. (1992) parent reports of children's infrequent participation in war play, Boyd did not report on the frequency of either real aggression or pretend aggression in the war play activities that were observed.

## *Do War Toys Contribute to Aggression?*

Longitudinal studies have not been conducted to investigate the long-term effects that playing with war toys may have on children's development, but researchers have tried to uncover the immediate relationship between war toy play and children's aggressive behavior. Prior to 1990, the majority of researchers found that boys' behavior became more aggressive when they played with violent toys as opposed to nonviolent toys (Potts et al., 1986; Turner & Goldsmith, 1976; Wolff, 1976). However, Sutton-Smith (1988) concluded, after reviewing eight experimental studies on war toys, that no conclusive relationship could be drawn between war toys and aggressive behaviors. Aggressive behaviors that were exhibited by boys in experimental settings did not carry over to play in classrooms (Wolff, 1976). Furthermore, only one of the eight experimental studies reviewed by Sutton-Smith reported girls responding to war toys with aggressive behaviors (Mendoza, 1972). Sutton-Smith (1988) also argued that the findings were not conclusive, because early researchers failed to either measure pre-existing levels of the children's aggression (LaVoie & Adams, 1974; Mendoza, 1972; Potts et al., 1986; Turner & Goldsmith, 1976) or discriminate between real and pretend aggression (Mendoza, 1972; Wolff, 1976).

Researchers in the 1990's, corrected for these methodological problems (Connor, 1991; Goff, 1995; Watson & Peng, 1992), but the findings are still inconclusive. For example, Connor discriminated between children's real and pretend aggression in a study on children's play with toys. Eight children (five boys, three girls), four and five years old, were divided into three groups based on their previously determined levels of aggression (i.e. high, moderate, low). Each group was exposed to three sets of toys: regular toys, micro war toys, and macro war toys. Micro war toys consisted of action figures and their corresponding accessories (e.g. G. I. Joe, Princess of Power). Macro toys consisted of child size accessories (e.g. guns, knives, and grenades) that children could use to act out war themes in play. The toys were presented in 20–30 minute sessions over a span of four weeks. The toys were presented to the children in the following order: rapport session with toys from own classroom, regular toys, micro war toys, macro war toys, regular war toys, micro and macro war toys, and all three sets of toys. Connor also collected qualitative data on children's play styles (i.e. interactive or solitary), play talk, play action, play themes, and choice of toys. Connor found that real aggression was only observed when children had disputes over toys. The least interactive play and most solitary play occurred when children played with the micro war toys. When children played with macro toys, observers recorded the most interactive play, dramatic play, and pretend aggression, but no real aggression was observed. The children were able to control the aggression in their play by calling out phrases like "time out," "I'm dead," or "you can't do that kick."

Watson and Peng (1992) also measured pre-existing levels of aggression and distinguished between real and pretend aggression in their war toy study. They distributed questionnaires to the parents of 36 boys and girls, aged 3–5 years, to gather information pertaining to demographics, the number of toy guns in the home, the frequency of toy gun play, the children's preferred television programs, the children's preferred toys, and the forms of discipline the children received from their parents. Naturalistic observations of the children's free play were conducted at their daycare centers. Children were randomly videotaped for 15 minutes each.

Then, a second 15 minutes of videotape was recorded of the children playing with toys that included some war toys that the researcher brought to the center. Real and pretend aggression were coded as well as the duration of rough and tumble play and pretend play. Finally, story completion was used to assess pretend aggression.

Watson and Peng (1992) found that children who played with toy guns were more likely to exhibit real aggression and less likely to participate in nonaggressive pretend play than children who did not participate in toy gun play. However, toy gun play was not the most important predictor of children's aggression. The strongest predictor of real aggression was parental physical punishment. Parent's physical punishment was also related to less imaginative play and having more toy guns. In contrast, pretend aggression was predicted by the aggression level in the television programs children viewed, not parental punishment. Watson and Peng found that boys preferred aggressive television more than girls did, and boys were more likely to participate in pretend aggression than girls. In addition, children who participated in toy gun play and preferred aggressive toys to nonaggressive toys were more likely than other children to participate in pretend aggression.

Goff (1995) suggested that Watson and Peng's (1992) analysis of the data may not be accurate. According to Goff, Watson and Peng should have performed a square root transformation on their correlation data and considered how the children in the free play sessions affected each other's play behavior. Goff set out to replicate Watson and Peng's (1992) study, but correct for the problems in their analysis.

Similar to Watson and Peng (1992), Goff (1995) investigated the effect of playing with violent toys on the behaviors and attitudes of 36 children, aged 3–5 years. She collected data through parent questionnaires and experimental play sessions. However, in the experimental condition, the children were divided into 12 groups of three children. The children participated in a 50 minute play session with both violent and nonviolent toys. The children's aggressive behavior was coded in regard to the context of real play or pretend play. Goff reported that when children played with the violent toys, as opposed to the nonviolent toys, the amount of real, pretend, and total aggression increased. Similar to Watson and Peng, Goff also found that boys rather than girls preferred violent television and violent toys. In addition, the children who preferred more violent toys and television shows had parents who possessed a more positive attitude toward spanking than the parents of children with less violent preferences. This finding provides some support for the relationship Watson and Peng found between parental punishment and childhood aggression. Goff suggested that these findings support Berkowitz's (1964) aggressive cue hypothesis that children are more likely to be aggressive when toys they associate with aggression are present.

Since the deregulation of the broadcasting industry in 1984, the television industry and toy industry have worked together to create several television programs with corresponding merchandise. Parents and early childhood educators have expressed concerns regarding the effect that this link between violent television programs and single purpose war toys has upon children's war play (Carlsson-Paige & Levin, 1987). Sanson and Di Muccio (1993) investigated the effect of watching cartoons and playing with toys associated with the cartoon. They divided 30 working-class children and 30 middle-class children, aged 3–5 years, into three groups. A base line rate of the children's aggressive behaviors and prosocial behaviors was established in a 15 minute free play session. Then, one group of children watched "Voltron" an aggressive cartoon, the second group watched "Gummi Bears" a neutral cartoon, and the third group did not watch a cartoon. After watching the cartoons, the children played with robots from the "Voltron" cartoon or bears and dragons from the "Gummi Bears" cartoon. The three groups were divided into six groups to balance the order of toy presentation. Children's behaviors were observed and coded for aggression and prosocial behaviors for 15 minutes when they played with one set of toys, followed by a second 15 minute play session with the other set of toys. Although the observers coded both real and pretend aggression, the overall rate of behaviors was so low that the total across all categories of aggression was used in the final analysis.

Sanson and Di Muccio (1993) found that "viewing aggressive cartoons and then playing with the associated aggressive toys would lead to more aggression and less prosocial behavior than viewing the neutral cartoon and playing with it's associated toys" (p. 98). However, the effect of toys on aggression was not as consistent as the effect of toys on prosocial behaviors. When the effect of toys was examined without participants previously watching a cartoon, children from working-class families displayed more aggression and prosocial behaviors when they played with neutral toys as opposed to aggressive toys. However, children from middle-class families displayed higher aggression and lower prosocial behaviors when they played with aggressive toys than when they played with neutral toys. Sanson and Di Muccio concluded that "aggressive toys seemed to be inhibiting prosocial behaviors, while neutral toys promoted it" (p. 97).

In summary, researchers in the 1990's corrected for past methodological problems, but the findings are still inconclusive. Although Watson and Peng (1992) and Goff (1995) found that children displayed more real aggression and pretend aggression when they played with violent toys than when they played with nonviolent toys, Connor (1991) did not observe real aggression when children played with macro war toys consisting of child size accessories used to act out war themes. Furthermore, Sanson and Di Muccio (1993) found that the effect of toys on aggression was not as consistent as the effect of toys on prosocial behaviors.

In addition, differences were found in the frequency of aggression based on the social economic status of the children in the play groups.

*Does War Play Without War Toys Contribute to Aggression?*

Only two observational studies have discriminated between real aggression and the aggression children act out during play activities without war toys (Frey & Hoppe-Graff, 1994; Wegener-Spöhring, 1989). First, Frey and Hoppe-Graff investigated the real aggression and playful aggression of 28 Brazilian children, ages 2–4 years. Frey and Hoppe-Graff included rough-and-tumble play, play fighting, role playing, and sociodramatic play in their definition of playful aggression. Real aggression was identified when there was evidence that a child's actions were to intentionally harm, threaten, or offend a peer. In addition, three types of real aggression were examined: bullying, reactive aggression, and instrumental aggression. The sample consisted of 14 girls and 14 boys from two nursery schools. One nursery school was located on a university campus catering to middle-class parents. The second school was located in a favela (slum district) providing services for the poor. The children were divided into four groups (seven children in each group) based on sex and setting (girls/favela, girls/university, boys/favela, and boys/university). Each child was observed 12 times, 15 minutes per observation. The observer took notes on children's physical and verbal behaviors including facial expressions and gestures. These notes were transcribed and used to identify and categorize acts of real and playful aggression.

Real aggression was more common among boys than girls in the middle-class setting, but not in the favela setting. Two boys, in the middle-class setting, exhibited aggressive behaviors more frequently than the other children did. The authors suggested that in middle-class nursery schools only some boys, not all boys, are more aggressive than girls. Middle-class girls were as likely as the boys to be victims of aggression. However, in both settings, girls were rarely victims of reactive aggression. Boys in the middle-class setting engaged in more acts of playful aggression than boys in the favela setting. Playful aggression was rare among girls in the university setting. In both settings, girls were rarely the victims in playful aggression. When children participated in playful aggression, both girls and boys preferred boy playmates. However, acts of playful aggression were not always, or even often, targeted towards a person. All children, except middle-class boys, were more likely to exhibit reactive aggression, followed by bullying and instrumental aggression. In contrast, bullying was the most common form of aggression among middle-class boys. The authors concluded that, for middle-class boys, acts of playful aggression coincide with acts of bullying.

Although girls' rates of aggression were low, girls who exhibited frequent acts of bullying were more likely to react aggressively to attacks by others. Furthermore, children who exhibited more acts of playful aggression were also more likely to exhibit real aggression and vice versa than children who did not display acts of playful aggression (Frey & Hoppe-Graff, 1994, p. 266). Although Frey and Hoppe-Graff distinguished between real aggression and playful aggression, their definition of playful aggression included play fighting and rough-and-tumble play. Therefore, the findings may not be consistent with an analysis that excludes play, such as rough-and-tumble play and play fighting, where no overt pretense is observed.

Wegener-Spöhring (1989) also discriminated between real aggression and the aggression that occurs during the children's aggressive games. In their study, aggression was classified as either external (i.e. outside the children's play theme) or internal (i.e. within the children's play theme). Wegener-Spöhring observed free play in 10 West Germany kindergarten classrooms that banned war toys. Verbatim written records were recorded of the children's play. Themes of destruction and violence were observed and onomatopocia vocalizations were common. Boys played the strong and aggressive roles. Only two times did the researcher observe girls taking on these roles.

Through their written records, Wegener-Spöhring (1989) determined that the boys maintained a balance in their aggressive games by regulating the aggressive and frightening play theme so it did not become over powering and the participants were able to remain in the play. When aggressive acts remained in the "let's pretend" mode, the children continued their friendly interactions. Wegener-Spöhring suggested that this reveals that "war can be played in a peaceful, cooperative, and imaginative way" (p. 44). However, real aggression can occur in the proximity of the game. This often happened when children's play became stagnate, was interrupted, or the teacher intervened. The children's bad moods were one sign of real aggression (Wegener-Spöhring, 1989). Unlike Frey and Hoppe-Graff (1994), Wegener-Spöhring excluded play fighting and rough-and-tumble play from their definition of aggressive games, but they did not limit their observations to war play.

*Addressing War Play in the Classroom*

In the book "The War Play Dilemma," Carlsson-Paige and Levin (1987) described four options available to early childhood educators for addressing the issue of war play. First, war play can be banned. However, banning war play may encourage children to become deceptive and participate in war play behind teachers' backs.

Furthermore, the children's desires to participate in war play activities may produce unwarranted feelings of guilt and anxiety. Finally, it is uncertain whether the developmental needs met by participation in war play can be satisfied when such play is banned (Carlsson-Paige & Levin, 1987, 1988).

Second, teachers can allow unrestricted war play. Although this approach does not lead to feelings of guilt or deceptive behaviors, children's play is in danger of becoming merely imitations of what they have seen, rather than constructions of their new understandings. Finally, neither banning war play nor allowing unrestricted war play allows teachers to address the political socialization of children in regard to war and global conflict (Carlsson-Paige & Levin, 1988).

Third, teachers can allow war play, but set limits on space, time, materials and/or social interactions (e.g. no physical contact). This option allows the children to use war play as a tool for meeting their developmental needs and sets limits to help children feel safe. However, without the teacher's active facilitation of their play, children are left to meet their own developmental needs and develop unguided political and social concepts. "There is no meaningful connection between the ideas children are working to understand through play and the teachers' values and goals" (Carlsson-Paige & Levin, 1987, p. 48).

An alternative approach is for teachers to become active facilitators of children's war play. Through this approach, teachers allow war play into the classroom when the children initiate it. They observe what the children are working on and actively intervene by expanding on what the children are doing and saying (Carlsson-Paige & Levin, 1988). This allows teachers to help children become more constructive rather than imitative in their play, as well as influences their political ideas (Carlsson-Paige & Levin, 1987).

A few studies have explored the effects of classroom rules and teacher interventions on children's war play (Fortis-Diaz, 1997; Gronlund, 1992; Jordan & Cowan, 1995). Jordan and Cowan used an ethnographic approach in a kindergarten classroom that prohibited war play. Data were collected by a non-participant observer who recorded field notes of the children's behaviors during a free play period once a week. Jordan and Cowan found that rules including no running, no shouting, use equipment properly, no car crashes, and no guns put constraints on children's warrior narratives. Although no action figures or war toys were in the classroom, the children used their imagination to transform the available materials to suit the purpose of their play (e.g. a baby carriage was turned into a car).

At the beginning of the Jordan and Cowan (1995) study, boys initiated warrior narratives that involved destruction, fighting, good guys, and bad guys in the doll corner. Story lines included heroes protecting the weak and attacking the bad guys. The boys transformed knives and tongs into weapons and a doll bed was used as a boat. Jordan and Cowan suggested that the boys were "establishing an accommodation between their needs and the classroom environment" (p. 733). However, the teacher attempted to control the children's behavior by enforcing a rule of no warrior narratives in the doll corner and discouraging the transformation of doll corner materials into warrior weapons. The rule was successful at eliminating warrior narratives including transformations of materials from the doll corner.

However, the boys moved the warrior narratives from the doll corner to the construction area and the car mat (Jordan & Cowan, 1995). The boys invented ways to continue playing without violating rules about running and shouting. Eventually, as time went on, there was less acting out of warrior narratives and more talking through warrior narratives with toy cars and construction materials. Jordan and Cowan suggested that the "warrior narratives went underground and became part of a deviant masculine subculture with the characteristic secret identity and hidden meanings" (p. 736). The boys protested to both teachers and peers that they were not making weapons, guns were transformed into water pistols, cars were crashed quietly, and swords were concealed under overalls and only used behind the teacher's back (Jordan & Cowan, 1995). Rather than resorting to violence, children learned to use the classroom rules to gain power over their peers (Jordan et al., 1995). Jordan and Cowan's findings support Carlsson-Paige and Levin's (1987) hypothesis that banning war play encourages children to become deceptive and participate in war play behind teachers' backs. Jordan and Cowan's study, is the only observational study that has examined the effect of banning war play on children's play behaviors.

In their informal observations of children in a preschool laboratory program, Ritchie and Johnson (1982) noticed children's superhero play was more aggressive than their other play. Although they did not ban superhero play, they reduced the children's interest in superhero play by structuring rich play environments and elaborating on concepts such as transportation with field trips, props, and play materials. The children who continued to participate in superhero play were children who felt powerless, lacked social skills, used avoidance techniques (e.g. avoid eye contact), and denied their feelings. These children also found it difficult to move from dramatic play to sociodramatic play. The teachers used positive redirection to help the children leave the superhero play and join a new activity.

It may be even more important for teachers to help children with behavioral disorders reduce the frequency of their aggressive play. Sherburne et al. (1988) conducted a study to examine whether a contingency statement strategy followed by a time-out for overt acts of aggression or a verbal prompting strategy would be more successful at reducing aggressive play in the classroom. The participants were six children with behavioral disorders and five typically developing children between the ages of three and five years old. Data was collected during two, 20 minute, free play sessions. No violent toys were available in the classroom. Prior to the experimental conditions, a baseline of the children's aggressive theme play was established. Following the baseline condition, either the contingency statement strategy that included a time-out for overt acts of aggression or the verbal prompting strategy was used during the first 20 minute play period. The other strategy was used during the second 20 minute play period. The contingency statement strategy consisted of bringing a rug into the classroom on which children were allowed to play aggressive themes. If children were observed participating in guns or other aggressive play themes they were asked to play on the rug. The children were placed in time-out when they displayed overt acts of aggression. In the verbal prompting strategy, the rug was not available and children were verbally redirected to play something else. The contingency statement strategy, followed by a time-out for overt aggressive acts, was found to be more effective at reducing violent or aggressive play than the verbal prompting strategy. Aggressive theme play was more frequent and more variable in the verbal prompts condition than in the contingency statement condition (Sherburne et al., 1988). By limiting war play to a specific area in the classroom or redirecting children's play, the teachers helped children reduce their participation in war play (Ritchie & Johnson, 1982; Sherburne et al., 1988), but they failed to address the sociopolitical ideas in the children's play (Carlsson-Paige & Levin, 1987).

Although no systematic studies have been conducted on the active facilitation of children's war play, two kindergarten teachers have provided anecdotal reports (Fortis-Diaz, 1997; Gronlund, 1992). Influenced by Carlsson-Paige and Levin's (1987) suggestion to actively facilitate children's war play, Gronlund chose to investigate the effects of adopting new rules in an effort to help the children in her kindergarten class understand violence and aggression. The superhero play in the classroom was based on the cartoon Ninja Turtles and involved karate kicking that needed constant adult supervision. She observed that the "children seemed obsessed with repeating the same actions over and over again" (p. 22). She began her endeavor by watching the cartoons and discussing them with the children. Initially, she interviewed the 30 children individually, but the children provided teacher appropriate answers (e.g. "No weapons allowed," "Children should never hurt each other," p. 23), rather than using their own words. She concluded that the children were too young to analyze their own play. However, it is possible that the children's answers were based on the fact that it was their teacher, rather than an unbiased observer, asking the questions. To overcome this obstacle, Gronlund chose to have the children act out stories that she encouraged them to write in journals. Other researchers (Dyson, 1994; Paley, 1984) have also used writing and drama (acting out stories they have written) as a means to explore children's fascination with war play, particularly superhero play. These researchers found that boys were more likely than girls to write about superheroes.

After Gronlund (1992) expressed her interest in the children's superhero play, the children openly chased each other on the playground using the cartoon lingo, rather than secretly expressing this behavior and language. The teacher concluded that she perceived less real aggression, but that the children's fake fighting did result in injury due to their limited motor skills. Gronlund incorporated "the idea of stunt men and stunt women who practice very carefully and plan fake fights" to counter this draw back (p. 23).

Fortis-Diaz (1997), also a kindergarten teacher, observed the aggressive play of the 24 children in her classroom. She observed that a particular group of boys displayed the most frequent aggressive acts. The boys frequently made guns out of Legos and cube-a-link blocks. When allowed to bring toys from home, they brought in war toys that included battleships, action figures, and war planes that contributed to their aggressive behavior.

Based on Gronlund's (1992) approach to war play, Fortis-Diaz (1997) decided to become active in the children's play. She had daily discussions with the children about their play. She observed that the children's ideas for war play often came from television programs. One group of boys used the television show "COPS" as a resource for their play. Through these discussions, she learned that the children had a very limited understanding of what police officers do. Based on the show "COPS," the children believed that to be a police officer you had to chase and shoot bad guys. Fortis-Diaz tried to expand the children's knowledge by discussing other duties of police officers and also invited a police officer to speak to the class. She tried to redirect the children's aggressive play by suggesting different scenarios and play settings. By placing bad guys in real places with real people familiar to the children, the children were able to make changes in the characters and the characters' actions. The teacher also compared the children's play to story books where the heroes and villains did not use guns. This helped to make the play less imitative and more creative. Fortis-Diaz found that intervening in the children's play, decreased the children's episodes of shooting and chasing. The boys no longer made guns out of the cube-a-link and the shooting noises and scenes of death decreased.

The findings of these studies demonstrate that the teacher's approach to war play can affect the type and amount of real aggression or pretend aggression that is exhibited by children in the early childhood classroom. Although Wegener-Spöhring (1989) observed that children displayed real aggression when teachers interrupted children's aggressive games, others have observed a decrease in aggression when teachers and parents intervene in play (Costabile et al., 1992;

Gronlund, 1992; Jordan & Cowan, 1995). Banning or limiting war play changes where and how children express war play in the classroom (Jordan & Cowan, 1995), but these methods of reducing children's war play do not ensure children's developmental needs are met or sociopolitical ideas are addressed (Carlsson-Paige & Levin, 1987). Helping to facilitate war play may decrease aggression, influence children's values, and foster children's ability to think of alternatives for solving conflicts both in play and in the world (Carlsson-Paige & Levin, 1987, 1988, 1990; Fortis-Diaz, 1997; Gronlund, 1992). However, more research is needed to determine whether it is more beneficial to ban children's war play, limit the war play, or facilitate children's war play. In addition, researchers may choose to examine how teachers shape children's war play including how they expand on what children are doing or saying during play, what sensitive questioning techniques they use, and what strategies are selected to assist children in finding alternative solutions to the imaginary problems in their play.

## METHODOLOGICAL ISSUES IN WAR PLAY

Although there have been reports of increased aggression in children's war play (Carlsson-Paige & Levin, 1987, 1990; Levin & Carlsson-Paige, 1995), the only available evidence is based on teacher surveys and the anecdotal reports of parents and early childhood professionals (Carlsson-Paige & Levin, 1987; Levin & Carlsson-Paige, 1995). Furthermore, parent questionnaires and preliminary observational data indicate that the incidence of war play in children's play is low (Boyd, 1997; Costabile et al., 1992).

Methodological problems have also prevented researchers from discovering a clear relationship between war toys (i.e. the manufactured toys specifically designed to be used in war play), and aggression (Jenvey, 1988; Sutton-Smith, 1988). Researchers often fail to distinguish between real aggression and playful aggression or measure pre-existing levels of aggression (Sutton-Smith, 1988). In 1995, Goldstein noted that war play research is often conducted in short periods of time. Longitudinal studies are needed to determine what the long-term effects are on children who participate in war play. As children develop into adults, their war play experiences in childhood remain with them as part of their history and may have an effect on their adult behaviors.

Goldstein (1995) also argued that war play research is rarely conducted in the natural environment where children play. When researchers have observed children in their natural settings, these observations of real aggression and pretend aggression were often limited to indoor free play (Goff, 1995; Watson & Peng, 1992; Wegener-Spöhring, 1989). Furthermore, several researchers manipulated the type of toys available for the children during play (Connor, 1991; Goff, 1995; Watson & Peng, 1992). When researchers have examined real and pretend aggression, without introducing war toys into the natural classroom setting, they did not limit their observations to acting out warrior themes in dramatic play (Frey & Hoppe-Graff, 1994; Wegener-Spöhring, 1989). Although Frey and Hoppe-Graff found that children who exhibit more acts of playful aggression are also more likely to exhibit real aggression and vice versa, their definition of playful aggression included rough-and-tumble play and play fighting, as well as pretend aggression.

According to Corsaro (1997), as children participate in the world of adults, they act on the information with their limited experience and knowledge and create new meanings. Children share these meanings with their peers as they participate together in play (Corsaro, 1985, 1997). Interpretive methods can be used to understand the meanings children create as they participate in the war play that naturally occurs within the peer culture. Interpretive methods are useful for investigating the meanings children create, because these methods allow researchers to explore children's understandings within the context of their daily lives. Researchers can uncover the meanings children create by observing and participating with them in their natural environments. Through the use of interpretive methods, researchers can learn about beliefs, rituals, and routines of children's peer culture (Corsaro & Miller, 1992).

Ethnography is an interpretive method that can be used to uncover meanings in children's cultures (Corsaro & Miller, 1992). The main goal of researchers who conduct ethnographic studies is to describe what happens in a particular setting, the perceptions of people's behaviors, and the context in which those behaviors occur. The social world is not understood in terms of simple causal relationships or universal laws; rather it is assumed that human actions are based upon social meanings that include rules, beliefs, values, intentions, and motives (Hammersley & Atkinson, 1995). Because human behavior is studied within the context of the culture, it is important for researchers to learn the social meaning of the culture they study (Hammersley & Atkinson, 1983). To understand behavior, an approach must be used that allows researchers to access the meaning that guides behavior. The goal of the ethnographer is to acquire the knowledge of the culture in the process of learning how to participate in it. Learning to understand behavior by learning the culture and interpreting the world in the same way as the people in the culture (Bogdan & Biklen, 1992). Ethnographers achieve this goal by observing and participating with children in their natural setting (Corsaro & Miller, 1992). Jordan and Cowan (1995) used an ethnographic approach in the design of their study, but these researchers used a non-participant observer, so it is unknown if they were able to capture children's real meanings.

# FUTURE APPROACHES TO THE STUDY OF AGGRESSIVE PLAY

Many studies have been conducted on children's real aggression (e.g. Coie et al., 1991; Crick & Grotpeter, 1995; Farver, 1996; Graham & Hoehn, 1995; Huesmann et al., 1984; Kupersmidt et al., 1995), but the research on children's "pretend" aggression in war play is scarce (Boyd, 1997). Even less is known about the real and pretend aggression that children exhibit when they act out war themes in dramatic play without aggressive toys. Although war play includes imaginary play, current research is not based on the theories of Piaget or Vygotsky. Goldstein (1995) suggests that piagetian or social-cognitive developmental theories are not the base for war play research because, researchers have been concerned with "the effects that aggressive play has on aggressive behavior and not on other possible effects, such as cognitive and social skills, self-presentation and social identity" (pp. 132–133). Children who frequently participate in real aggression may not be interested in pretend aggression or have the social skills to participate in the play. Children must maintain control of their physical movements and impulses to prevent actual harm to peers in imaginary play. Further research is needed to determine what cognitive, social, and self-regulating skills are needed for a child to be a successful participant in pretend aggression.

Previous researchers noted war play is within the culture of boys, but not all boys participate in war play. Future research using interpretive methods can examine peer groups of boys who participate in war play, the meanings they give to pretend aggression, and the roles they play in aggressive episodes. According to Corsaro (1997), children act on information from the adult world and try to make sense of it with their limited understanding. Children bring this limited understanding into their peer culture and collectively invent and create new meanings to address the concerns of the peer culture. Together children negotiate, share, and create cultures with adults and peers. However, "children's interactions and communications with adults raise problems, confusion, and uncertainties which are later reproduced in the activities and routines that make up peer culture" (Corsaro, 1985, p. 73). Children try to resolve issues from the adult world that they do not understand or that they find disturbing as they participate in imaginary play with their peers. As children participate in the world, adults warn children of dangers through conversation, television, movies, and fairy tales (Corsaro, 1997). These warnings of danger in the world may motivate children to participate in pretend aggression as a way to gain a sense of control and to overcome fears. In war play, children can become more powerful than the dangers and conquer their fears and anxieties (Corsaro, 1985).

Future researchers may also choose to use interpretive methods to examine the process of children's interactions in pretend aggression (Frey & Hoppe-Graff, 1994). Goldstein (1995) suggests that researchers examine where and how pretend aggression develops including who initiates it, where, with whom, what behaviors are used, and the duration of the play scripts. Goldstein also suggests examining the children's social relationships and the social consequences of their play. Finally, future research should consider variables that influence children's play including the characteristics of the children, the social environment, and the physical setting (Jenvey, 1988).

Research is also needed to discover the attitudes, beliefs, and behaviors of children from various cultures and levels of social economic status (SES). Researchers have found that children from low SES families tend to display more aggressive behaviors than children from middle-class families (Dodge et al., 1994; Kupersmidt et al., 1995; Ramsey, 1988; Spivack & Shure, 1974). However, Frey and Hoppe-Graff (1994) found that boys from middle-class families participate in more pretend aggression than do boys from low SES families. It is possible that displaying aggressive behaviors is more acceptable for boys from low-income families than boys whose families have higher incomes. The boys from higher income families may use pretend aggression to exhibit aggressive behaviors in ways that are more socially accepted by the adults in their families. Several of the war play studies reviewed in this paper were conducted outside of the U.S. (Costabile et al., 1992; Frey & Hoppe-Graff, 1994; Jordan & Cowan, 1995; Wegener-Spöhring, 1989). Cultural differences may also exist in children's and parent's attitudes, beliefs, and behaviors toward real aggression and pretend aggression. An interesting study could be conducted to examine the real aggression and pretend aggression in a culture with limited access to war cartoons and war toys.

Differences in attitudes, beliefs, and behaviors may also be found among children's peer cultures. Although children typically do not like to play with children who are aggressive (Cairns et al., 1988; Crick & Grotpeter, 1995; Dumas et al., 1994; Graham & Hoehn, 1995), researchers have found that aggressive children are not rejected by all social circles (Cairns et al., 1988; Farver, 1996; Parkhurst & Asher, 1992). Children who participate in real aggression may not be well liked by the majority of their peers, but they are able to make friends with other aggressive children (Cairns et al., 1988; Farver, 1996). Similarly, children who participate in pretend aggression are likely to play with other children who enjoy this activity (Fortis-Diaz, 1997). Children who participate in real and/or pretend aggression may create a subculture within the early childhood classroom. Researchers have reported only small groups of boys frequently participating in both real and pretend aggression (Frey & Hoppe-Graff, 1994; Goff, 1995). It is possible that a child, who frequently displays real aggression, is drawn to pretend aggression and by participating in this activity contributes to the aggression of the peer group. Future investigators could examine the type of play and the roles children take when they move from a peer group who participates in war play to a peer group who typically does not participate in this type of play. Corsaro (1997) reported that "few studies have followed children as they make transitions from family to peer group and from one peer group to another" (p. 118).

Qualitative studies are also needed to explore children's perceptions and parental beliefs regarding pretend and real aggression. Costabile et al. (1992) suggests that future studies are needed to clarify the relationship between parental attitudes and children's behaviors using observations rather than parental reports of children's behavior. Observational research in the home will also help to determine when and how pretend aggression develops. Corsaro (1997) suggests that researchers examine the negotiation processes between parents and children to discover how children negotiate with parents for access to children's television and toys. Investigators may want to explore how children communicate with parents and peers about the war cartoons they watch and the war toys they use to recreate and reinvent the television dramas in their imaginary play.

Preschool teachers are partners in children's production of peer culture and their reproduction of the adult world (Corsaro & Schwarz, 1991). In early childhood classrooms, peers work together to establish communal activities, but teachers provide the structure for these activities and are powerful influences on the children's behaviors. The teacher's personal characteristics, behaviors, classroom rules, and expectations can have an impact on children's tendencies to exhibit aggressive behavior in the classroom (Frude, 1988; Ramsey, 1986; Van Acker et al., 1996). Researchers have demonstrated that if a teacher reacts passively to children's aggression in the classroom, the aggressive behaviors increase (Berkowitz, 1958; Levin, 1955; Sherburne et al., 1988). Wegener-Spöhring (1989) observed that children displayed real aggression when teachers interrupted children's aggressive games, but others have observed a decrease in aggression when teachers and parents intervene in play (Costabile et al., 1992; Gronlund, 1992; Jordan & Cowan, 1995).

Future research is needed to investigate how children perceive teacher interventions in episodes of pretend aggression and in episodes of real aggression. Do children perceive the interventions as helpful or intrusive? Corsaro & Schwarz (1991) suggest that "an important aspect of children's peer culture is the partial break down of teacher control" (p. 236). In play, children collectively oppose adult control by devising strategies to overcome the burden of classroom rules (Corsaro, 1997).

Jordan and Cowan (1995) and Corsaro (1985) reported on children's attempts to overcome the limits set by classroom teachers. Jordan and Cowan found that when war play was banned in the early childhood classroom, the play went underground and became part of a subculture. Boys protested that they were not making weapons, guns were transformed into water pistols, cars were crashed quietly, and swords were concealed under overalls and only used behind teacher's back.

Corsaro (1985) described similar behaviors when he observed the imaginary play of two boys pretending to hunt with guns in a classroom where guns were banned. The boys overcame the rules by using the available resources in the classroom to achieve their personal goals. In an effort to evade the no guns rule, the boys used broomsticks as rifles and shot at imaginary animals rather than real people. Corsaro (1997) suggests that when children work together to overcome the official school rules, it contributes to their group identity. Future investigators may also choose to explore how the children not involved in the war play perceive the children's and teachers' behaviors. Finally, future studies need to be conducted in classrooms that facilitate rather than ban children's war play.

## IMPLICATIONS FOR EARLY CHILDHOOD EDUCATORS

In their 1993 position statement on violence, the National Association for the Education of Young Children (NAEYC) suggested that early childhood educators should help children cope with violence by implementing violence prevention in their programs. Early childhood teachers may help to prevent the negative effects of children's participation in war play by how they intervene in children's play and the rules they establish in their classrooms.

Before teachers try to change the behaviors of children who participate in episodes of aggression, they need to think about the purpose for their intervention. Is the behavior real aggression or is it pretend aggression? Observation of the children's behaviors is the key to identifying the type of aggression that is displayed. By observing children and talking to them about their play, teachers can determine where ideas for pretend aggression originate and what it means to them.

Bandura (1973) suggests that aggressive behaviors can be eliminated if the social conditions and positive reinforcements that maintain behavior are removed. Teachers can encourage parents concerned about the amount of pretend and real aggression their children participate in to limit the violent television programs they allow their children to watch. Parents not only introduce children to television and toys, but they control children's access to these cultural materials. Parents may be encouraging children to participate in aggressive play based on the toys they buy their children and the television programs they allow their children to view (Corsaro, 1997).

Teachers may want to use interventions that focus on specific peer groups rather than individual children. Farver (1996) suggests teachers can intervene by helping to restructure young children's peer groups. Reorganizing peer groups may provide children with aggressive behaviors a chance to participate with peers who can model positive techniques for solving problems and appropriate ways of displaying emotions in conflict. Participating with a different group of children may also foster variety in the play of children who appear to be obsessed with acting out pretend aggression.

Teachers can also use social problem solving to reduce aggressive behaviors (Pepler & Slaby, 1994). Researchers have found that teaching conflict resolution strategies leads to more social competence and less aggression in the classroom (Benton-Murray, 1994; DeMasters & King, 1994). Teachers can improve children's problem solving skills by helping them to think of alternative possibilities and consider the consequences of their action (Spivack & Shure, 1974).

Boyd (1997) suggested that teachers intervene in pretend aggression out of concern for children's safety. However, banning does not eliminate the children's desire to participate in war play. According to Jordan and Cowan (1995), when war play is banned, it goes underground. Children continue to participate in war play, but they try to conceal their activities from the teacher through deception and lies. "Children sneak around the room or playground, trying to hide this kind of play from adults, and turn their snack crackers into pretend guns which they gobble up before they can be accused of violating the 'no guns in school' rule" (Levin, 2003, p. 83). Banning war play denies teachers the "opportunity to teach about values, respect, safety, and living in a democratic social group" (Boyd, 1997, p. 23). Without guidance from a caring teacher, children create their own meanings about the violence they witness. Often leaving "children feeling unsafe and seeing the world as a dangerous place where fighting, weapons, and superpowers are necessary to keep oneself safe" (Levin, 2003, p. 83).

Teachers can reduce aggressive behaviors by changing children's aggressive scripts and normative beliefs about aggression (Huesmann, 1988; Huesmann & Eron, 1984, 1989). Teachers can help to change children's scripts and beliefs about aggression by actively facilitating war play rather than banning it. Through this approach teachers allow war play into the classroom when the children initiate it. They observe what children are working on and actively intervene by expanding on what the children are doing and saying (Carlsson-Paige & Levin, 1988). This allows teachers to help children become more constructive rather than imitative in their play, as well as influences their political ideas (Carlsson-Paige & Levin, 1987).

The following discussion occurred when a teacher asked a group of kindergarten children to sit down and explain to her what they were doing. The children explained that they were recruiting children to play Beetleborgs, a superhero game based on a television cartoon. According to the children, Beetleborgs are superheroes who kill bad guys.

Scott said, "Teacher, I have an idea." The teacher said, "Okay Scott." Scott said, "Why do they have to shoot?" The teacher asked, "Who?" Scott said, "The Beetleborgs. Why?" Amy said, "To kill the bad people." Scott said, "Why? You don't have to kill them, you could just put them in jail. You don't have to kill a person to be the boss." Amy said, "They're really bad people." The teacher said, "I heard Scott say, you don't have to kill people that are bad, to stop them just put them in jail." Ted said, "They can break out of the bars." Scott said, "Ted, why are they bad and why do they want to be the boss?" Amy said, "They don't like us, they don't like the Beetleborgs." Scott said, "Why can't the monsters, you know like in the Pocahontas movie they fighted, but then the Pocahontas said you don't have to fight to be the boss. Why did you have to fight?" Amy said, "They can break out of jail." Scott said, "Can't you just put more people on the list and some people as the guards?" The teacher said, "You know what? I didn't think I was in kindergarten. I thought I was listening to adults talk about this, because you know what I heard Scott say? You don't have to kill people. If they're bad, just put them in jail and get lots of guards." Scott said, "Why don't you make a plan where there's a lot of Beetleborgs, but no killing other people, like them guys." He pointed to the children in the room. Amy said, "See we're not doing that. Only imaginary people that's what we always do." Ted said, "Yeah, but I know another one we can play without guns or without arrows, only with machines." Amy said, "Can we make like a big thing that every single people could fit in. It's like on Star Wars." The teacher said, "Oh, like a big spaceship?" Amy said, "Yeah" (adapted from Malloy, 2000).

Through this discussion, the children's play was transformed from a destructive game of fighting with guns to a creative and exciting plan to build a flying spaceship. Although the teacher in this scenario facilitated a discussion on war play by reflecting the children's words, other teachers may need to use direct questions. For example, "Can you think of a way to solve that problem where no one gets hurt and where everyone feels safe?" (Levin, 2003, p. 91).

Teachers also help to change war play scripts by providing alternative content for play through reading books about dinosaurs or planning field trips to the zoo. Likewise teachers can intervene in children's war play by addressing the needs of the victims. Teachers can introduce rescue vehicles and medical equipment to change the script from killing to helping the victims of aggression. Guest speakers from the community including police officers and firefighters may also provide accurate content for children's play (Levin, 2003). Helping to facilitate war play may decrease aggression, influence children's values, and foster children's ability to think of alternatives for solving conflicts both in play and in the world (Carlsson-Paige & Levin, 1987, 1988, 1990; Fortis-Diaz, 1997; Gronlund, 1992).

# REFERENCES

Bandura, A. (1973). *Aggression: A social learning analysis.* Englewood Cliffs, NJ: Prentice-Hall.

Bandura, A., Ross, D., & Ross, S. A. (1963). Imitation of film-mediated aggressive models. *Journal of Abnormal and Social Psychology, 66,* 3–11.

Bateson, G. (1972). *Steps to an ecology of mind.* New York: Chandler.

Benton-Murray, J. M. (1994). *Increasing the growth in prosocial, nonviolent, problem-solving skills of kindergarten students through conflict resolution skills.* Plantation, FL: Nova Southeastern University (ERIC Document Reproduction Service No. ED 374 907).

Berkowitz, L. (1958). The expression and reduction of hostility. *Psychological Bulletin, 55,* 257–283.

Berkowitz, L. (1964). Aggression cues in aggressive behavior and hostility catharsis. *Psychological Review, 71,* 104–122.

Berkowitz, L. (1984). Some effects of thoughts on anti- and prosocial influences of media events: A cognitive-neoassociation analysis. *Psychological Bulletin, 95,* 410–427.

Bogdan, R. C., & Biklen, S. K. (1992). *Qualitative research for education: An introduction to theory and methods* (2nd ed.). Boston: Allyn and Bacon.

Bonte, E. P., & Musgrove, M. (1943). Influences of war as evidenced in children's play. *Child Development, 14,* 179–200.

Boyatzis, C. J. (1997). Of Power Rangers and v-chips. *Young Children, 52*(7), 74–79.

Boyatzis, C. J., Matillo, G. M., & Nesbitt, K. M. (1995). Effects of "The Mighty Morphin Power Rangers" on children's aggression with peers. *Child Study Journal, 25,* 45–55.

Boyd, B. J. (1997). Teacher response to superhero play: To ban or not to ban? *Childhood Education, 74,* 23–28.

Brotman, S. N. (1987). *The telecommunications deregulation source book.* Boston: Artech House.

Bushman, B. J. (2002). Does venting anger feed or extinguish the flame? Catharsis, rumination, distraction, anger, and aggressive responding. *Personality and Social Psychology Bulletin, 28*(6), 724–731.

Bushman, B. J., Baumeister, R. F., & Phillips, C. M. (2001). Do people aggress to improve their mood? Catharsis beliefs, affect regulation opportunity, and aggressive responding. *Journal of Personality and Social Psychology, 81*(1), 17–32.

Cairns, R. B., Cairns, B. D., Neckerman, H. J., Gest, S. D., & Gariepy, J. L. (1988). Social networks and aggressive behavior: Peer support or peer rejection? *Developmental Psychology, 24,* 815–823.

Cameron, S. M., Abraham, L. K., & Chernlcoff, J. B. (1971, April). The effect of exposure to an aggressive cartoon on children's play. Paper presented at the annual meeting of Eastern Psychological Association, New York, NY (ERIC Document Reproduction Service No. ED 055 297).

Carlsson-Paige, N., & Levin, D. E. (1987). *The war play dilemma: Balancing needs and values in the early childhood classroom.* New York: Teachers College Press.

Carlsson-Paige, N., & Levin, D. E. (1988). Young children and war play. *Educational Leadership, 45,* 81–84.

Carlsson-Paige, N., & Levin, D. E. (1990). *Who's calling the shots?: How to respond effectively to children's fascination with war play and war toys.* Philadelphia, PA: New Society.

Caulfield, M. J. (2002). The influence of war play theme on cooperation and affective meaning in preschoolers' pretend play (Doctoral dissertation, Rutgers The State University of New Jersey – New Brunswick, 2002). *Dissertation Abstracts International, 62,* 11-A.

Coie, J. D., Dodge, K. A., Terry, R., & Wright, V. (1991). The role of aggression in peer relations: An analysis of aggression episodes in boys' play groups. *Child Development, 62,* 812–826.

Comstock, G. (1991). *Television in America*. Newbury Park, CA: Sage.

Connor, K. (1989). Aggression: Is it in the eye of the beholder? *Play and Culture*, 2, 213–217.

Connor, K. M. (1991). War toys, aggression and playfighting (Doctoral dissertation, University of Pennsylvania, 1991). *Dissertation Abstracts International*, 52, 1746B.

Corsaro, W. A. (1985). *Friendship and peer culture in the early years*. Norwood, NJ: Ablex.

Corsaro, W. A. (1997). *The sociology of childhood*. Thousand Oaks, CA: Pine Forge Press.

Corsaro, W. A., & Miller, P. J. (1992). *Interpretive approaches to children's socialization*. San Francisco: Jossey-Bass.

Corsaro, W. A., & Schwarz, K. (1991). Peer play and socialization in two cultures. In: B. Scales, M. Almy, A. Nicolopoulou & S. Ervin-Tripp (Eds), *Play and Social Context of Development in Early Care and Education* (pp. 234–254). New York: Teachers College.

Costabile, A., Genta, M. L., Zucchini, E., Smith, P. K., & Harker, R. (1992). Attitudes of parents toward war play in young children. *Early Education and Development*, 3, 356–369.

Cramer, P., & Hogan, K. A. (1975). Sex differences in verbal and play fantasy. *Developmental Psychology*, 11, 145–154.

Crick, N. R., & Grotpeter, J. K. (1995). Relational aggression, gender, and social-psychological adjustment. *Child Development*, 66, 710–722.

DeMasters, R. H., & King, E. S. (1994). *Conflict resolution: Teaching social skills in a kindergarten classroom*. Charlottesville, VA: University of Virginia (ERIC Document Reproduction Services ED 373 905).

Dodge, K. A., Pettit, G. S., & Bates, J. E. (1994). Socialization mediators of the relation between socioeconomic status and child conduct problems. *Child Development*, 65, 649–665.

Dollard, J., Miller, N. E., Doob, L. W., Mowrer, O. H., & Sears, R. R. (1939). *Frustration and aggression*. New Haven, CT: Yale University.

Dumas, J. E., Blechman, E. A., & Prinz, R. J. (1994). Aggressive children and effective communication. *Aggressive Behavior*, 20, 347–358.

Dyson, A. H. (1994). The Ninjas, the X-Men, and the Ladies: Playing with power and identity in an urban primary school. *Teachers College Record*, 96, 219–239.

Ellis, G. T., & Sekyra, F. (1972). The effect of aggressive cartoons on the behavior of first grade children. *The Journal of Psychology*, 81, 37–43.

Engel, B. S. (1984). Between feeling and fact: Listening to children. *Harvard Educational Review*, 54, 304–314.

Eron, L. D., Gentry, J. H., & Schlegel, P. (Eds) (1994). *Reason to hope: A psychosocial perspective on violence and youth*. Washington, D.C.: American Psychological Association.

Farver, J. M. (1996). Aggressive behavior in preschoolers' social networks: Do birds of a feather flock together? *Early Childhood Research Quarterly*, 11, 333–350.

Feshbach, S. (1956). The catharsis hypothesis and some consequences of interaction with aggressive and neutral play objects. *Journal of Personality*, 24, 449–462.

Fortis-Diaz, E. (1997, May). *Just who are these "bad guys," anyway?: An attempt at redirecting children's aggressive play* (ERIC Documentation Reproduction Service No. ED 409 092).

Frey, C., & Hoppe-Graff, S. (1994). Serious and playful aggression in Brazilian girls and boys. *Sex roles*, 30, 249–268.

Fromberg, D. P. (1992). A review of research on play. In: C. Seefeldt (Ed.), *The Early Childhood Curriculum: A Review of Current Research* (pp. 42–84). New York: Teachers College.

Frost, J. L., Wortham, S. C., & Reifel, S. (2001). *Play and child development*. Columbus, OH: Prentice-Hall.

Frude, N. (1988). Aggression in the classroom. In: J. G. Howells (Ed.), *Modern Perspectives in Psychosocial Pathology* (pp. 58–74). New York: Brunner/Mazel.

Goff, K. E. (1995). *The relation of violent and nonviolent toys to play behavior in preschoolers.* Unpublished doctoral dissertation, Iowa State University, Ames IA.

Goldstein, J. (1995). Aggressive toy play. In: A. D. Pellegrini (Ed.), *The Future Of Play Theory* (pp. 127–147). Albany, NY: State University of New York.

Graham, S., & Hoehn, S. (1995). Children's understanding of aggression and withdrawal as social stigmas: An attributional analysis. *Child Development, 66,* 1143–1161.

Gronlund, G. (1992). Coping with Ninja Turtle play in my kindergarten classroom. *Young Children, 48*(1), 21–25.

Hammersley, M., & Atkinson, P. (1983) *Ethnography principles in practice.* New York: Tavistock.

Hammersley, M., & Atkinson, P. (1995). *Ethnography principles in practice* (2nd ed.). New York: Routledge.

Hapkiewicz, W. G., & Stone, R. D. (1974). The effect of realistic vs. imaginary aggressive models on children's interpersonal play. *Child Study Journal, 4,* 47–58.

Huesmann, L. R. (1988). An information processing model for the development of aggression. *Aggressive Behavior, 14,* 13–24.

Huesmann, L. R., & Eron, L. D. (1984). Cognitive processes and the persistence of aggressive behavior. *Aggressive Behavior, 10,* 243–251.

Huesmann, L. R., & Eron, L. D. (1989). Individual differences and the trait of aggression. *European Journal of Personality, 3,* 95–106.

Huesmann, L. R., Eron, L. D., Lefkowitz, M. M., & Walder, L. O. (1984). Stability of aggression over time and generations. *Developmental Psychology, 20,* 1120–1134.

Huesmann, L. R., Podolski, C. L., & Moise-Titus, J. (2003). Longitudinal relations between children's exposure to television violence and their aggressive and violent behavior in young adulthood: 1977–1992. *Developmental Psychology, 39*(2), 201–221.

Huston, A. C., Donnerstein, E., Fairchild, H., Feshbach, N. D., Katz, P. A., Murray, J. P., Rubinstein, E. A., Wilcox, B. L., & Zuckerman, D. (1992). *Big world, small screen: The role of television in American society.* Lincoln, NE: University of Nebraska.

James, N. C., & McCain, T. A. (1982). Television games preschool children play: Patterns, themes, and uses. *Journal of Broadcasting, 26,* 783–800.

Jenvey, V. (1988, August). What do we really know about the effects of toys on children's behaviour and development? Paper presented at the Australian Development Conference, Sydney, Australia (ERIC Document Reproduction Service No. ED 302 324).

Jordan, E., & Cowan, A. (1995). Warrior narratives in the kindergarten classroom: Renegotiating the social contract? *Gender and Society, 9,* 727–743.

Jordan, E., Cowan, A., & Roberts, J. (1995). Knowing the rules: Discursive strategies in young children's power struggles. *Early Childhood Research Quarterly, 10,* 339–358.

Kostelnik, M. J., Whiren, A. P., & Stein, L. C. (1986). Living with He-Man: Managing superhero fantasy play. *Young Children, 41*(4), 3–9.

Kupersmidt, J. B., Griesler, P. C., DeRosier, M. E., Patterson, C. J., & Davis, P. W. (1995). Childhood aggression and peer relations in the context of family and neighborhood factors. *Child Development, 66,* 360–375.

LaVoie, J. C., & Adams, G. R. (1974, May). Understanding of guns, gun play, and aggressivity among 5–9 year old children. Paper presented at the annual meeting of the Midwestern Psychological Association, Chicago, IL (ERIC Document Reproduction Service No. 101 253).

Levin, D. E. (2003). *Teaching young children in violent times: Building a peaceable classroom* (2nd ed.). Cambridge, MA: Educators for Social Responsibility.

Levin, D. E., & Carlsson-Paige, N. (1995). The Mighty Morphin Power Rangers: Teachers voice concern. *Young Children, 50*(6), 67–72.

Levin, H. (1955). The influence of classroom control on kindergarten children's fantasy aggression. *The Elementary School Journal*, *55*, 462–466.

Liebert, R. M., & Baron, R. A. (1972). Some immediate effects of televised violence on children's behavior. *Developmental Psychology*, *6*, 469–475.

Liebert R. M., Sprafkin, J. N., & Davidson, E. S. (1982). *The early window: Effects of television on children and youth* (2nd ed.). New York: Pergamon.

Mallick, S. K., & McCandless, B. R. (1966). A study of catharsis of aggression. *Journal of Personality and Social Psychology*, *4*, 591–596.

Malloy, H. L. (2000). *The battleground in kindergarten: A contrast between pretend aggression and real aggression in a full-day kindergarten classroom*. Unpublished doctoral dissertation, Iowa State University, Ames.

Mendoza, A. (1972). The effects of exposure to toys conducive to violence (Doctoral dissertation, University of Miami, 1972). *Dissertation Abstracts International*, *33*, 2769A.

Mussen, P., & Rutherford, E. (1961). Effects of aggressive cartoons on children's aggressive play. *Journal of Abnormal and Social Psychology*, *62*, 461–464.

National Association for the Education of Young Children (1993). NAEYC position statement on violence in the lives of children. *Young Children*, *48*(6), 80–84.

Nielsen, M., & Dissanayake, C. (2001). A study of pretend play and false belief in preschool children: Is all pretense metarepresentational? In: S. Reifel (Ed.), *Theory in Context and Out: Play and Culture Studies* (pp. 199–215). Westport, CT: Albex.

Nilsson, N. (1989, July). Do children need to be introduced to violence? The use of toys of war and violence. Paper presented at the International Conference on Early Education and Development, Hong Kong (ERIC Document Reproduction Service No. ED 312 049).

Paley, V. G. (1984). *Boys and girls: Superheroes in the doll corner*. Chicago: University of Chicago Press.

Parkhurst, J. T., & Asher, S. R. (1992). Peer Rejection in middle school: Subgroup differences in behavior, loneliness, and interpersonal concerns. *Developmental Psychology*, *28*, 231–241.

Pepler, D. J., & Slaby, R. G., (1994). Theoretical and developmental perspectives on youth and violence. In: L. D. Eron, J. H. Gentry & P. Schlegel (Eds), *Reason to Hope: A Psychosocial Perspective on Violence and Youth* (pp. 27–58). Washington, DC: American Psychological Association.

Piaget, J. (1951). *Play, dreams, and imitation in childhood*. New York: W. W. Norton (Original French edition published 1945).

Potts, R., Huston, A. C., & Wright, J. C. (1986). The effects of television form and violent content on boys' attention and social behavior. *Journal of Experimental Child Psychology*, *41*, 1–17.

Ramsey, P. G. (1988). Social skills and peer status: A comparison of two socioeconomic groups. *Merrill-Palmer Quarterly*, *34*, 185–202.

Rautman, A. L. (1943). Children's play in war time. *Mental Hygiene: New York*, *27*, 549–553.

Ritchie, K. E., & Johnson, Z. M. (1982, November). Superman comes to preschool: Superhero TV play. Paper presented at the annual meeting of the National Association for the Education of Young Children, Washington, D.C. (ERIC Document Reproduction Service No. ED 248 003).

Sanson, A., & Di Muccio, C. (1993). The influence of aggressive and neutral cartoons and toys on the behavior of preschool children. *Australian Psychologist*, *28*, 93–99.

Scales, B., & Cook-Gumperz, J. (1993). Gender in narrative and play: A view from the frontier. *Advances in Early Education and Day Care*, *5*, 167–195.

Sherburne, S., Utley, B., McConnell, S., & Gannon, J. (1988). Decreasing violent or aggressive theme play among preschool children with behavior disorders. *Exceptional Children*, *55*, 166–172.

Smilansky, S. (1968). *The effects of sociodramatic play on disadvantaged preschool children.* New York: Wiley.

Spivack, G., & Shure, M. B. (1974). *Social adjustment of young children: A cognitive approach to solving real-life problems.* San Francisco: Jossey-Bass.

Sutton-Smith, B. (1988). War toys and childhood aggression. *Play and Culture, 1,* 57–69.

Sutton-Smith, B. & Kelly-Byrne, D. (1984). *The masks of play.* New York: Leisure Press.

Turner, C. W., & Goldsmith, D. (1976). Effects of toy guns and airplanes on children's antisocial free play behavior. *Journal of Experimental Child Psychology, 21,* 303–315.

Van Acker, R., Grant, S. H., & Henry, D. (1996). Teacher and student behavior as a function of risk for aggression. *Education and Treatment of Children, 19,* 316–334.

Vygotsky, L. S. (1978). *Mind in society: The development of higher psychological processes.* Cambridge, MA: Harvard University Press.

Watson, M. W., & Peng, Y. (1992). The relation between toy gun play and children's aggressive behavior. *Early Education and Development, 3,* 370–389.

Wegener-Spöhring, G. (1989). War toys and aggressive games. *Play and Culture, 2,* 35–47.

Williams, D. E., & Schaller, K. A. (1993). Peer persuasion: A study of children's dominance strategies. *Early Child Development and Care, 88,* 31–41.

Wolf, D. P. (1984). Superheroes: Yes or no?: An interview with Carolee Fueigna and Michelle Heist. *Beginnings, 1*(1), 29–32.

Wolff, C. M. (1976). The effects of aggressive toys on aggressive behaviors in children (Doctoral dissertation, University of Montana, 1976). *Dissertation Abstracts International, 37,* 2487B.

# *LOS PADRES Y LOS MAESTROS*: PERSPECTIVES OF PLAY AMONG BILINGUAL STAKEHOLDERS IN PUBLIC SCHOOLS

Mari Riojas-Cortez and Belinda Bustos Flores

## ABSTRACT

*This manuscript presents findings regarding teachers' and parents' beliefs about play in bilingual early childhood classrooms. The participants of this study included Mexican or Mexican American bilingual early childhood teachers from different parts of the state of Texas. Participants of the study also included Mexican or Mexican American parents who had children enrolled in bilingual early childhood classrooms in South Texas. Data were collected through a Likert-scale survey and interviews about play. Three functions of play that emerged from the interviews paralleled the three play constructs as derived by factor analysis.*

Children's opportunities within school are dependent on teachers' beliefs and practices. Knowing teachers' philosophies and practices allows us to get a better picture of how success may be provided for children within the classroom. Similarly, knowing parents' beliefs about education helps in the understanding of their children's development and learning. In the case of language minority children, teachers' views and practices become even more crucial due to the

Social Contexts of Early Education, and Reconceptualizing Play (II)
Advances in Early Education and Day Care, Volume 13, 267–288
Copyright © 2004 by Elsevier Ltd.
ISSN: 0270-4021/doi:10.1016/S0270-4021(04)13010-3

persistent lack of school success among minority populations, particularly for groups like Latinos (Valencia, 2000).

Some educators believe that the learning opportunities for minority children must be drills and memorization exercises (Escobedo, 1993). In the case of early childhood classrooms, many teachers, administrators, and parents see learning centers as disconnected from academics since young children often engage in different types of play. In her observations of bilingual early childhood classrooms Riojas (1998) noted teacher directed activities as the norm, rather than child initiated play activities. Thus, the lack of information or misconceptions on the part of the stakeholders keeps them from embedding play as a spontaneous activity in which children practice their cognitive, language, socio-emotional, and physical skills.

# THEORETICAL FRAMEWORK

*Significance of Play for Child Development*

The research on play shows its importance for learning and development. It is through play that children enhance communication skills with peers and adults as well as their ability to recreate the world and come to understand it. Through play, children acquire some of the first concepts and make use of the conceptual skills (Weininger, 1979). Therefore, many early childhood educators and organizations advocate the need for all children to play (Stone, 1995). There are many theorists who have greatly contributed to the theories of play. Most of the beliefs regarding play and child development have evolved from the theories of Piaget (1962), Vygotsky (1967), Eriksen (1950), and Bruner (1983), among others. Bruner, for example, states that play is an episode or imitation of life. Erikson explains play as a development progressive stage in which the child adds new ideas and knowledge about the world in every state. Piaget provides a cognitive explanation of play. Vygostky emphasizes the effect that the sociocultural environment has on children's play.

*Young Bilingual Children*

Although research indicates the importance of play for the development of all children, research regarding young bilingual children has mostly focused on policy, program implementation, first and second language development, biliteracy, and the inclusion of culture in the curriculum. Very limited research has been conducted on bilingual teachers' beliefs about how children learn (Flores, 2001) as well as teaching and learning strategies (such as play) in bilingual early childhood programs in public school settings (Riojas-Cortez, 1998; Sutterby, 2002). There are a few studies that have focused on the play of Mexican and/or Mexican American children (Christman, 1979; Farver & Howes, 1993; Genishi & Galvan, 1983; Riojas, 1998; Sutterby, 2002; Trueba & Delgado-Gaitán, 1985). Riojas found that there is a greater evidence of academic knowledge when Mexican American preschoolers are allowed and encouraged to engage in sociodramatic play which displays their funds of knowledge, thus refuting the deficit notion that young minority children must participate in repetition and drill exercises to assure academic success. In general these studies describe how Mexican and Mexican American children play, but do not focus on the teachers' beliefs of play. The research also lacks for Mexican American parents' perspectives of play.

### Bilingual Parents

Of recent interest to early childhood educators are cross-cultural views of play held by different communities. The functionality of play for different communities becomes very important in terms of the educational benefits of play. The literature, however, only provides a glimpse of the parents' perspectives of play particularly minority parents in the U.S. (Bartkowiak & Goupil, 1992; Segal & Adcock, 1982). Other studies have examined parents' beliefs about their child's abilities and learning experiences, but have not specifically addressed the issues of play (Galper et al., 1997). Often the literature includes advice to parents on how to play with their children (Bronsil, 2001; Cohen, 2002; Kalata, 1998; Siegel, 2001; Tyce, 2002), but do not discuss what the parents think about play in a school setting (Malone & Landers, 2001).

Only one reference was found in which parents along with faculty's notions of play were explored during an evening meeting at a school located in a diverse community (Kieff & Casbergue, 2000). During this "Get-Acquainted Night," the group was asked to define play and to describe the role of play in the classroom. Kieff and Casbergue noted that the responses given were indicative of the multiple perspectives individuals hold about play. They suggest that, "the meaning and value of play are embedded in one's knowledge about play, past experiences with play, and cultural values regarding play" (p. 2). However, the authors do not provide detail as to how each group responded; therefore, it was difficult to ascertain if these multiple perspectives were mostly provided by parents or faculty.

The purpose of this study is to explore the beliefs about play of bilingual early childhood teachers in public schools and parents who have children enrolled in bilingual early childhood classrooms. The two research questions that drive this study are:

(1)  What are parents' and teachers' beliefs about play?
(2)  Are there differences between parents' and teachers' beliefs about play?

This study is significant because it begins a discussion about how bilingual early childhood teachers and parents view play as a tool for teaching and learning in bilingual early childhood classrooms.

# METHOD

## *Design*

A mixed-method was used to explore the research questions. During the preliminary phase of the study, parents ($n = 12$) and teachers ($n = 6$) were interviewed using open-ended questions regarding play. During the secondary phase, parents and teachers were surveyed using the Survey of Teachers' and Parents' Play Beliefs. A total of 136 completed surveys were used for the data analysis. All individuals were assured that confidentiality would be maintained. Interview data, field notes, and factor analysis constructs were triangulated to assure trustworthiness.

## *Phase One*

*Preliminary Procedures: Interviews*
*Parents' sample description.* Twelve parents were individually interviewed, but not surveyed, regarding their cultural practices including play. The parents interviewed reside in a rural school district in South Texas. The parents' occupations ranged from entry white-collar to blue-collar occupations. The lowest level of education appeared to be a homemaker who dropped-out of high school in the 9th grade, but wanted to obtain her GED (General Education Degree). The highest level of education was a parent who had a Master's Degree in Accounting.

*Teachers' sample description.* Six Mexican American bilingual early childhood teachers were also interviewed regarding their notions of play. All interviewed bilingual early childhood teachers were from the same inner-city school district in South Texas, but from different schools. The teachers held the same Texas credentials – bilingual education and early childhood certification. Three of the teachers had masters' degree in different areas such as bilingual education, educational administration, and early childhood education. Of the other three teachers, one is currently enrolled in an early childhood masters' degree program; the other two plan to start graduate studies in the future. One of the teachers was a "*normalista*," a teacher who was trained at a "normal" school in Mexico and through "Project Alianza,"[1] obtained her Texas teacher credentials.

These bilingual early childhood teachers had an average of 15 years of classroom experience. The interviews revealed that they knew the importance of acknowledging the children's language and culture for school success since the education system often negates these differences. One of the teachers indicated how she was inspired to teach in a school that reflected her culture and the importance of demonstrating proficiency in the children's home language:

> I looked at all the school[s], but I wanted a school that resembled my childhood. I wanted to make sure that the school that I interviewed at was 97% Hispanic. But the classroom was a bilingual PK-4; I knew the language, but not sufficiently as I should. I'm still learning it-the way it should be. It took me two years to get it. I'm so excited that I went back, because the Spanish is inside you; it just doesn't come out naturally.

All of them talked about the importance of the development of the children's home language for academic learning:

> I try to have a lot of print rich environment, colorful and if you notice I have a sign ¡*Se Habla Español*! [We Speak Spanish!] . . . if the kids are going to be taught in two languages and one of the books that I read . . . was "Pepita Talks Twice" and kids love when we read it. And you know, they identify themselves and that way they know it's important to know two languages.

In addition, the teachers mentioned the importance of maintaining the children's culture. The teachers understood that it is imperative that the children's culture be reflected in their classrooms so that children can feel a sense of belonging. Teachers' view of culture goes beyond holidays and celebrations. Values, beliefs, feelings, and traditions form part of these teachers' classrooms:

> *Bueno nosotros tenemos mucha música en español, tenemos mucho de las canciones de Crí Crí y las de Orozco. Al principio [de clase] también yo les pido fotografías de cada uno de los niños y ellos presentan a su familia. En épocas conmemorativas, por ejemplo, en Diciembre hacemos tamales y ellos mismos platican como lo hacen, porque la mayoría de los papás de los niños hacen tamales y los venden.*

> [Well, we have a lot Spanish music. We have all the songs by Crí Crí and the ones from Orozco. At the beginning of the school year, I also ask them [the children] for family photographs, and then they present their families. During holidays, like Christmas, we make tamales and they [the children] talk about how they make them because most of the parents make tamales and they sell them.]

In addition to language and culture, another important aspect of culture included parental involvement. The teachers agreed that if parents are not part of the culture of the classroom, learning is unlikely to occur.

*Qualitative Data Analysis*
The qualitative data were analyzed by finding patterns through the parents' and teachers' interviews and comments. Patterns revealed three functions regarding parents' and teachers' perspectives of play. Function 1 includes *"diversión"* meaning that children engage in play for enjoyment only after finishing their work in the learning centers. Function 2 includes *"diversión con aprendizaje"* or learning with enjoyment as Isabel (one of the teachers) stated, "[play] has lots of choices for fun learning." Function 3 involves *"aprendizaje"* which signifies learning.

Phase Two

*Secondary Procedures: Survey*
*Parent sample descriptions.* The Survey of Teachers' and Parents' Play Beliefs was administered to Mexican and/or Mexican American parents of children enrolled in bilingual programs at different schools in South Texas. A total of 64 parents were given the play survey. Most of the parents chose to complete the Spanish version of the survey. Graduate students assisted in administering the survey to parents who needed assistance. Surveyed parents were also encouraged to provide any comments. Additional comments to open-ended questions were collected from parents (16 of the 64) prior to the first session of a five-day parent institute regarding children's play and literacy at one of the schools. The level of education of all parents ranged from elementary to college level (see Table 1).

*Teacher sample descriptions.* The survey was also administered at a national bilingual conference and in different school districts in South Texas. The volunteer participants of the study included Mexican American bilingual early childhood teachers ($n = 72$). Teachers were encouraged to write any comments on the survey regarding the items. These comments were also used in the analysis. The level of education of all teachers' ranged from bachelor's to master's degree.

*Measure*
The Survey of Teachers' and Parents' Play Beliefs conceptual framework evolved from assumptions made about play by a diverse group in attendance during a "Get-Acquainted Night" at a school (Kieff & Casbergue, 2000). As noted by Kieff and Casbergue, individuals' perspectives of play are reflective of experience,

***Table 1.*** Groups Educational Level Crosstabulation.

| | Educational Level | | | Total |
|---|---|---|---|---|
| | Elementary | Secondary | College | |
| Membership group | | | | |
| Parents | | | | |
| Count | 14 | 31 | 18 | 63[a] |
| Total (%) | 10.4 | 23.0 | 13.3 | 46.7 |
| ECE teachers | | | | |
| Count | | | 72 | 72 |
| Total (%) | | | 53.3 | 53.3 |
| Total | | | | |
| Count | 14 | 31 | 90 | 135 |
| Total (%) | 10.4 | 23.0 | 66.7 | 100.0 |

[a] One parent did not respond.

knowledge, and cultural values. Therefore, to explore teachers and parents' beliefs of play in this present study, the first author created Likert-items indicative of the responses reported by Kieff and Casbergue. A total of fourteen items are included and are measured using a 5-point Likert scale ranging from 5 = Strongly Agree to 1 = Strongly Disagree. Participants' demographic data such as membership group (parent or teacher), occupational status, and educational level is also collected. The survey was developed in both English and Spanish. Bilingual colleagues familiar with the notion of play examined both versions for consistency across languages and the concept. To determine the overall reliability of the survey, the five negatively oriented items (nos. 7, 8, 11,13, 14) were reversed coded to depict the same positive orientation as the other nine, $1 = 5$, $5 = 1$. Overall reliability analysis of the survey demonstrated a significant high alpha reliability, $\alpha = 0.79$ $(F(13) = 62.91, p < 0.000)$.

Then to identify the underlying constructs of play captured by the items in the scale, we conducted an exploratory factor analysis. Although there were only 14 items, principal component factor analysis was used to discover underlying patterns among the variables (Darlington, 2002; Dunteman, 1989; Grimm & Yarnold, 2000). Principal component factor analysis is appropriate when there are at least three or more variables being measured and is ideal when researching between 10 and 100 variables. A principal components factor analysis using varimax rotation was run to determine the number of uncorrelated constructs measured by the survey, to determine internal consistency, and to achieve parsimony. The Kaiser-Meyer-Olkin Measure of Sampling Adequacy was very high $= 0.827$, indicating that

***Table 2.*** Principal Components Factor Analysis Rotated Component Matrix.

|  | Component | | |
| --- | --- | --- | --- |
|  | Developmental Aspects of Play | Social Playtime | Role of Play |
| 10. Play supports academic learning by giving children a chance to practice what they have learned. | 0.762 | −0.116 | 0.086 |
| 3. Play is fun. | 0.698 | −0.309 | −0.093 |
| 6. Play is how children learn to get along. | 0.651 | −0.292 | 0.161 |
| 9. Play is painting and building with blocks. | 0.633 | 0.231 | 0.040 |
| 2. Play is the way children express themselves. | 0.631 | −0.276 | 0.407 |
| 5. Play is the way children develop physically. | 0.569 | −0.167 | 0.285 |
| 4. Play is the way children learn about their world. | 0.526 | −0.054 | 0.452 |
| 11. Play is a socialization activity best left to recess or physical education. | −0.274 | 0.735 | 0.023 |
| 13. When children play at school, they are wasting learning time. | −0.308 | 0.716 | −0.273 |
| 14. Play should be a reward for work well done. | −0.021 | 0.712 | −0.265 |
| 8. After school and on weekends, that's when children can play. | −0.250 | 0.665 | −0.077 |
| 7. Play is running off all that energy. | 0.097 | 0.538 | 0.108 |
| 12. Play is the basis for the curriculum in the classroom. | 0.020 | −0.022 | 0.883 |
| 1. Play is a child's work. | 0.396 | −0.190 | 0.494 |

the sample size was more than adequate. The Bartlett's Test of Sphericity was significant and confirmed ($p < 0.001$) that the items were correlated, and thus it was appropriate to run the analysis. The principal component factor analysis resulted in three constructs: (a) developmental aspects of play; (b) social playtime; and (c) role of play. Factor loading coefficients ranged from moderate (0.494) to strong (0.762). These three constructs accounted for 55% of the variance in the survey items (see Table 2).

Alpha reliability was used to determine internal consistency for each of the three constructs; the $F$-test was used to test the significance for each of the three constructs. Alpha reliability ranged from a significant strong $\alpha = 0.76$ ($p < 0.0001$) to a significant moderate $\alpha = 0.46$ ($p < 0.0001$) coefficient (see Table 3).

*Survey Data Analysis*

A multivariate analysis of variance (MANOVA) was used to determine if there were group differences among the surveyed participants. Groups were compared based on level of education and group membership. Two levels of education were

***Table 3.*** Reliability of Play Constructs.

| Factor/Construct | Alpha Reliability | df | $F$-test |
|---|---|---|---|
| Developmental aspects of play | 0.76 | 6 | 23.49[****] |
| Social playtime | 0.73 | 4 | 60.19[****] |
| Role of play | 0.46 | 1 | 52.90[****] |

[****]$p < 0.0000$.

determined for the participants: (1) elementary thru secondary; and (2) college level. Two levels of membership group were determined: parents and bilingual early childhood teachers. Scale scores were computed for each of the constructs as determined by the factor analysis. Educational level and membership group were used as fixed factors to examine group differences on the developmental aspects of play, social playtime, and role of play scale scores as dependent variables. Post-hoc univariate tests were run to determine differences among the individual items for the groups. The Bonferroni adjustment was employed to reduce the probability of Type I error (Stevens, 1996).

# RESULTS

The three play constructs as determined through factor analysis included developmental aspects of play, social playtime, and role of play in the classroom. These three play constructs were also evident in the teachers' interviews. The MANOVA results indicated that membership group and educational level did have a main significant effect on the three play constructs as indicated by the multivariate tests ($p < 0.001$). The observed power for membership group was high (0.999) and the $\eta^2 = 0.21$ was also high. For educational level, the power was high (0.991) as was the $\eta^2 = 0.16$.

The between subjects test revealed that membership group did significantly modulate each of the three constructs: (a) developmental aspects of play ($F(1) = 25.224, p < 0.001$); (b) social playtime ($F(1) = 12.52, p < 0.001$); and (c) role of play ($F(1) = 3.966, p < 0.001$). The observed power ranged for the developmental aspects of play was high (0.999) as was social playtime (0.94). The observed power was moderate (0.50) for role of play. Further, the results showed that educational level also appeared to significantly influence social playtime ($F(1) = 24.56, p < 0.001$). The between subjects descriptive findings demonstrated the group differences on the three play constructs (see Table 4).

In general, the surveyed teachers' and parents' comments described their understanding of play and why children play. The findings were supported by

***Table 4.***  Between Subjects Descriptive Statistics.

| | Membership Group | Educational Level | Mean | Std. Dev. |
|---|---|---|---|---|
| Developmental aspects of play | Parents | Primary-secondary | 29.27 | 4.26 |
| | | College | 28.89 | 2.82 |
| | | Total | 29.16*** | 3.89 |
| | ECE teachers | College | 33.22 | 2.60 |
| | | Total | 33.22*** | 2.60 |
| | Total | Primary-secondary | 29.27 | 4.26 |
| | | College | 32.36 | 3.15 |
| | | Total | 31.33 | 3.83 |
| Social playtime | Parents | Primary-secondary | 17.20 | 3.91 |
| | | College | 12.44 | 2.93 |
| | | Total | 15.84** | 4.23 |
| | ECE teachers | College | 9.23 | 3.23 |
| | | Total | 9.23** | 3.23 |
| | Total | Primary-secondary | 17.20 | 3.2 |
| | | College | 9.87 | 3.4 |
| | | Total | 12.35*** | 4.98 |
| Role of play | Parents | Primary-secondary | 6.178 | 2.04 |
| | | College | 6.45 | 2.28 |
| | | Total | 6.25* | 2.09 |
| | ECE teachers | College | 7.6250 | 2.36 |
| | | Total | 7.62* | 2.36 |
| | Total | Primary-secondary | 6.18 | 2.04 |
| | | College | 7.39 | 2.38 |
| | | Total | 6.99 | 2.34 |

*Membership group means significant differ for role of play, $p < 0.05$.
**Membership group means significant differ for social playtime, $p < 0.01$.
***Membership group means significant differ for developmental aspects of play, $p < 0.001$. Educational level means significant differ for social playtime, $p < 0.001$.

the interviews and comments from the parents and teachers. When asked, "*¿Qué es el juego* [What is play]?," the parents responded in Spanish and English that it was "*diversión* [enjoyment], *manera de aprender en sus primeros años* [a way to learn in their early years], having fun, learning." The responses of this particular group of parents revealed the three functions of play. This finding in itself is very significant, since some bilingual early childhood teachers argue that the reason that they do not offer a play-based curriculum in their classroom is because of the parents' expectations. Five out of the six interviewed teachers defined play as a way for children to develop problem solving, language, and socialization skills. They also mentioned that play was hands-on learning and exploration.

The three functions of play that emerged from the interviews paralleled the three play constructs as derived by factor analysis and will be discussed below:

| Factor Analysis: Play Constructs | Emerging Themes: Functions of Play |
| --- | --- |
| Developmental Aspects of Play | Diversión con Aprendizaje |
| Social playtime | Diversión |
| Role of Play | Aprendizaje |

### *Developmental Aspects of Play: Diversión con Aprendizaje*

Essentially, the developmental aspects of play constructs reflected the teachers' and parents' beliefs about play allowing children to learn with enjoyment. When examining the individual items that comprise the developmental aspects of play construct, we noted the slight differences between parents and teachers, with a greater variance noted mostly for parents than teachers. These differences were significant as determined by the post-hoc tests (see Table 5). The greater variance in most of the parents' mean scores suggested that not all parents view the developmental aspects of play the same way as teachers.

***Table 5.*** Developmental Aspects of Play Item Descriptive Statistics and *F*-Tests.

| | Group | | | | $F$ |
| --- | --- | --- | --- | --- | --- |
| | Parents | | ECE Teachers | | |
| | Mean | Std. Dev. | Mean | Std. Dev. | |
| Play supports academic learning by giving children a chance to practice what they have learned. | 4.17 | 0.87 | 4.83 | 0.4468 | 48.20[*] |
| Play is fun. | 4.50 | 0.62 | 4.90 | 0.30 | 23.80[*] |
| Play is how children learn to get along. | 4.40 | 0.68 | 4.92 | 0.278 | 34.92[*] |
| Play is painting and building with blocks. | 3.56 | 1.26 | 4.21 | 1.36 | 7.96 |
| Play is the way children express themselves. | 4.22 | 0.92 | 4.88 | 0.33 | 31.34[*] |
| Play is the way children develop physically. | 4.43 | 0.78 | 4.89 | 7.36 | 20.35[*] |
| Play is the way children learn about their world. | 4.13 | 0.95 | 4.73 | 0.84 | 15.44[*] |

[*]$p < 0.003$ (Bonferroni adjustment).

Both parents and teachers agreed that play supports academic learning by giving children a chance to practice what they have learned. Isabel sheds light about parents' concerns regarding play in the classroom, particularly as it relates to academic issues:

> Some parents get upset if the child is talking too much or draws a messy picture. They express concern that their children have a voice in what they play with . . . It takes having the parents come into the classroom and just observe what is going on in the classroom. Once the child begins to discuss some of the concepts they have learned in play, then the parents' buy into what play is all about and encourage their child to do better. A few parents will come into the classroom and play with their children, but I have only seen this in about seven parents. It appears to be harder for parents to see the value of play if they only have one or two children.

The parents, as she indicated, usually changed their minds about play in the classroom once they saw what their children were able to do through play.

Furthermore, most teachers and parents agreed that play is the way children learn how to get along. For example, Minerva, a prekindergarten teacher mentioned how through the negotiation of roles children practice acceptance of others:

> *Ellos juegan con todo en drama. Por ejemplo, este, se visten ellos juegan al restaurante, hacen con plastilina tacos, hacen comida, la venden y juegan al papá y a la mamá. Aprenden a tomar turnos cuando ellos están jugando. A veces al principio es difícil para ellos porque los dos quieren ser mamá o los dos quieren ser los papás, pero ellos aprenden a que tienen que esperar su turno y que tienen que darle la oportunidad al otro primero.*

> [They play with everything in the drama center. For example, they dress up and play restaurant; they make tacos or food with clay, and role-play the father and the mother. They learn to take turns when they are playing and sometimes at the beginning it's difficult for them because both want to be the mother or both want to be the father, but they learn that they have to take turns and let the other one go first.]

Nora, another teacher, appeared to agree with Minerva's comment because she has noticed that play allows children to form "clicks" who go from center to center engaging in different types of play, but at the same time building friendships. She likes to see children develop friendships because the exchange of ideas allows for their creativity and their imagination to flourish.

In contrast, the parents interviewed often mentioned that a way to discipline their children when they do not get along with others was to take toys away or the play privileges. This is an example of "*diversión con aprendizaje*" [learning with enjoyment] in terms of social skills. Parents felt that the removal of toys and play teaches children social responsibility.

Another developmental aspect of play was painting and building with blocks. Minerva provided an example of developmental aspects of play and described how her children played with blocks in her classroom:

> *Los niños juegan con los bloques, si, unos al principio comenzaron a ponerlos nada más como en línea unos al ladito del otro como si estuvieran en línea y ahorita los niños están edificando como aviones, bicicletas – se están subiendo y están subiendo . . .*

> [The children play with the blocks. At the beginning some would start putting them like in a line one next to the other as if they were in a line. Now the children are building airplanes, bicycles – they are going higher and higher [conceptually] . . .]

A parent described how her son, Enrique, enjoyed playing with blocks, particularly constructing with Legos that were given to him by his grandfather:

> He plays mostly with blocks so he builds things and he's running back and forth showing us what he builds or, if not like last night he made what he called a Falcon's Ord; it's from the Power Rangers; it's some bird and he'll make like this little shooting sounds, you know and stuff. He's very loud when he plays; he makes a lot of noise.

Play allows children to develop cognitively and physically through building with blocks which also encourages interaction. Teachers and parents tended to agree that play is the way children express themselves. Only one teacher noted the importance of play for language development:

> The role [of play] is that children learn to communicate better with other peers and learn from others new vocabulary, speak English, interact with no barriers. It is important to keep an eye on the students because we can tell from their play how they think, speak, and what kind of imagination they have.

Although most parents may not have the theoretical background regarding play, once they observe it for a period of time, they begin to understand how their children develop through play. For example, one parent who had only a primary education expressed the importance of play, "*El juego es muy importante para el desarrollo de los niños.*" [Play is very important for children's development.]

The teachers also indicated how much their children have developed conceptually through play. Minerva reflected that she wanted to have more time to observe her children, but she felt like she was limited in many aspects such as the time she spent observing and interacting with children during play. She cited two major reasons. She felt that her children could not make too much noise in her classroom because of the teachers around her and since she could not close the classroom door, she felt like she still needed to have children work quietly so as not to disturb the other classrooms. Another reason included her own ability to "abdicate" power; she still felt that she could not let children freely engage in play. Minerva did not know why she felt this way because deep down inside she knew that by allowing children to freely choose activities they would learn more than if she controlled their learning. She was determined to share with parents how children develop through play:

*Bueno aquí vamos a hacerlo de acuerdo a como yo vea al niño. Si yo veo que está interesado pues vamos a enseñarle eso, pero si yo veo que no, no puedo enseñarle porque es como un bebé, le digo, mire, verdad los bebés pasan por cierto proceso primero gatean y cuando un bebé gatea, ¿usted lo va ha apresurar a que corra? Pues no, se va a caer, ¿verdad? Entonces tenemos que respetar el proceso. Allí les empiezo a decir a los papás verdad, no esperemos que al forzarlos ha aprender lo que ellos no quieren o pueden. Ahorita tengo niños de 3, 4, y 5 [años] hay unos niños ya interesados en los números y las letras . . .*

[Well, here we're going to do it depending on how I see the child. If I see that he's interested in something then we're going to teach him that, but if I see that he is not then I cannot teach him that because it's like a baby, babies go through a certain process. First they crawl and when a baby crawls, do you pressure him to run? Of course not, because he can fall, right? Then we have to respect that process and I start telling them not to force children to learn what they don't want or can. Now I have 3- 4- and 5-year olds that are interested in numbers and letters . . .]

Other teachers' reflections supported Minerva's views. A comment that resembled Minerva's thinking but added a different perspective was given by Lupita, a kindergarten teacher:

*Porque como maestras nos enseñan la teoría sobre el juego, pero como padres cuando vemos a un niño jugar pensamos, "no estes jugando, ponte a trabajar," aunque sepamos que el juego es bueno para el desarrollo del niño.* [We learn play theory as teachers, but as parents, when we see a child playing we think, "don't play, get to work," even though we know that play is good for a child's development.]

Lupita's own personal beliefs regarding play conflict with her theoretical and pedagogical knowledge and practices. Lupita and Minerva both serve as examples that even though teachers may know the benefits of play for child development, their own biases become obstacles for the implementation of play in their classrooms.

### Social Playtime-Diversión

The survey items that loaded on the social playtime construct reflected traditional views of play being only *diversión* or for enjoyment. Play was classified as a social activity restricted to recess, after school or weekend, and a means to minimize children's energy (see Table 6). When examining the post-hoc univariate analysis for the individual items that comprise the social playtime construct, we noted the differences between parents and teachers. Parents agreed to a greater degree than teachers that play was a social playtime. A teacher clarified this notion, when she writes, "It is a combination of both – learning and play."

Some parents felt that the purpose of school was for learning and not playing, as a parent describes, "*No, no, los niños tienen que trabajar . . . el juego es para después.*" [Children must work; play comes later.] Nevertheless, other parents

***Table 6.*** Social Playtime Item Descriptive Statistics & $F$-Tests.

| | Group | | | | $F$ |
|---|---|---|---|---|---|
| | Parents | | ECE Teachers | | |
| | Mean | Std. Dev. | Mean | Std. Dev. | |
| Play is a socialization activity left to recess or physical education. | 2.98 | 1.40 | 1.21 | 0.63 | 94.67[*] |
| When children play at school, they are wasting learning time. | 2.70 | 1.38 | 1.10 | 0.344 | 89.80[*] |
| Play should be a reward for work well done. | 3.63 | 1.30 | 2.23 | 1.64 | 29.88[*] |
| After school and on weekends, that's when children can play. | 2.90 | 1.30 | 1.48 | 1.05 | 48.20[*] |
| Play is running off all that energy. | 4.10 | 0.94 | 3.49 | 1.71 | 6.13 |

[*]$p < 0.003$ (Bonferroni adjustment).

disagreed and suggested that, "children should play at school." Teachers generally disagreed that play was a waste of time.

As compared to teachers, parents were more likely to agree that play should be a reward for work well done. Parents did reveal that they denied play privileges when children misbehaved. In essence for parents, children's playtime is an earned privilege. Teachers generally disagreed that play was a reward. However, a couple of surveyed teachers' comments suggested that play could be reward at times such as "in special centers" and in the upper grades.

### Role of Play – Aprendizaje

The two items that comprised this construct defined the role of play (see Table 7). Parents and teachers saw play as a child's work. In other words, play is what children do. Not all teachers believed that play was essential in an early childhood

***Table 7.*** Role of Play Item Descriptive Statistics & $F$-Tests.

| | Group | | | | $F$ |
|---|---|---|---|---|---|
| | Parents | | ECE Teachers | | |
| | Mean | Std. Dev. | Mean | Std. Dev. | |
| Play is the basis for the curriculum in the classroom. | 2.78 | 1.25 | 3.26 | 1.75 | 3.263 |
| Play is a child's work. | 3.67 | 1.33 | 4.50 | 1.15 | 14.87[*] |

[*]$p < 0.003$ (Bonferroni adjustment).

curriculum. Within the role of play construct these two items appeared to have conflicting perspectives. Although, there is a propensity to believe that the role of play is children's work, both teachers and parents were not as decisive as to its role in the bilingual early childhood curriculum. When we examine the univariate post-hoc results, we noted the parent and teacher differences (see Table 7).

Although some teachers felt play was the basis of the curriculum, they clarified that it depended on the grade level of the children, "Prek-3 or -4," from kindergarten children. One kinder teacher wrote: "Depends, because nowadays kinder is much more demanding as to what children have to know." Interesting, another pre-kinder teacher wrote, "[Play] is part of the curriculum, not the basis." Another wrote, "I wouldn't say it is the basis, but a means." Surveyed teachers' comments suggested that "hidden behind play" or the "purpose of play" is "the way a child learns."

Noteworthy is that parents had a distinct cultural view of play and when it should occur. Although some parents' value play, the primary purpose of school is for learning academics in order to help their children succeed in life. Mexican-American parents highly value education (Sosa, 1993) because they believe that education is a way to succeed in life and perhaps that is the reason that they see play as "*diversión con aprendizaje*" [learning with enjoyment] rather than as a primary means to acquire concepts or knowledge or "*aprendizaje*" [learning].

Five of the teachers interviewed revealed that their parents never questioned why their children engaged in play activities during class time. For example, Minerva shared how at first she had to gain the parents' trust:

> *A los papás les gusta. He tenido padres de familia que han estado aquí observando y han estado jugando con los niños y se quedan sorprendidos, "hay maestra, mire como está jugando y mira allá que están haciendo" y les gusta mucho inclusive tengo muchas personas que me ayudan . . .*
>
> [Parents like it. I have had parents that come to observe and they play with their children and they are surprised, "Oh teacher, look how he's playing and look over there what they're doing" and they like it a lot, as a matter of fact I have many people [parents] that help me . . .]

Once she was able to gain the trust, the parents, especially the mothers were no longer "*desconfiadas*" [distrustful] of what she did in her classroom. The trust that she gained helped her in the implementation of play in her classroom.

### *Mexican American Views of Play – Los Juegos Infantiles*

The survey did not include a question about culture, but during the interviews, the teachers were asked what they thought about how Mexican Americans viewed play. All of the teachers mentioned how family gatherings allowed children and adults to engage in different aspects of play. Terri, one of the teachers, remembered her *abuela* [grandmother] prompting her to play "*a las comadritas*"[2] with the kitchen items available at her home [the grandmother's]. She also indicated how family gatherings were also seen as a type of play.

Four of the teachers mentioned "*juegos infantiles*" [children's games]. *Juegos infantiles* are traditional games played by children throughout Latin America. These types of games include children organizing themselves for different physical movements and lots of language play. The games have rules that must be followed in order for them to be played. Isabel shared that her students like to play "*A la Rueda de San Miguel.*" *A La Rueda de San Miguel* [Saint Michael's Circle] originated in the 16th century as *Las Ollas de Churumbel* in Spain. To play *A La Rueda de San Miguel*, a child stands in the middle of a circle of children who walk around holding hands while singing the following song:

A la rueda, rueda
De San Miguel, San Miguel
Todos traen su caja de miel
A lo maduro, a lo maduro
Que se voltee _____ de burro.

As they sing the last line, the child in the middle points to another child while calling out the name and that child *se voltea de burro* [turns around facing outside the circle]. The game continues until all children are facing outside the circle. The nonsense lyrics are attractive to children because of their rhythmic sounds, which are difficult to translate because the rhythmic and rhyming patterns are lost. Other favorite *juegos infantiles* included *Los Elefantes* [The Elephants] and *A la Víbora de la Mar* [The Sea Snake]. Throughout centuries, these *juegos infantiles* have been adapted to fit the sociocultural context in which children live. For example, Mendez-Negrete (2002) recalled that as a migrant child while working in the fields, she played *las escondidas* [hide and go seek] with other children and pretended to hide from *la migra* [the immigration officers].

Many parents, particularly those from Mexico and other Latin American countries, recalled how they used to play these games when they were in school and realized that they had not passed these traditions on to their children. Mexican American parents, particularly those who were second and third generations, were not familiar with the games and wondered why they did not play these games during their childhood. This is an example how the acculturation process often results in cultural loss.

One of the teachers interviewed, Nora, also sheds light on the loss of cultural traditions such as *juegos infantiles* among bilingual early childhood teachers. She described the loss of ethnic identity and cultural traditions as a result of the acculturation process:

The Americanized bilingual teachers do not teach children the traditional games. The ones that we remember when we were little, when we sang those songs. But we really didn't revisited going back to college or like I have an assistant who's from Mexico and she's excellent; she was a teacher there. Now she's studying here to do that [become a teacher] and then I notice that she brings a lot of the culture . . . that we were aware of at one time and we kind of lost and we're trying to regain and we're trying to get into it where they [the district] bring in teachers over the summer [from Mexico] to train us on the games, because we tend to forget. But it's painful 'cause it's play – what we can do with children especially the Mexican-American children or the recent immigrants.

Nora, together with the rest of the bilingual early childhood teachers from her school, refuse to loose their cultural traditions and so they are going to be working with a Mexican Consulate representative to teach them how to play the traditional *juegos infantiles*. For Nora and her colleagues, this regained cultural knowledge will help them to assist children in connecting with their cultural background.

Minerva only referred to *juegos infantiles* when she reminisced about how she used to play growing up in Mexico. When asked about how she thought Mexicans or Mexican-Americans viewed play, she automatically thought about how the parents need to learn about the benefits of play:

Si lo ven muy bien creo yo que lo ven bien pero sobretodo como maestra debe uno enseñarle a los padres porque si, hay unos que dicen, "hay maestra no va a aprender las letras, los números" entonces tiene uno que como decirles lo de la importancia del juego. Hay unos que todavía no aceptan que porque vienen a la escuela que tienen que aprender los números que tienen que aprender las letras.

[I think they look at it [play] okay, but above all as a teacher we need to teach parents because there are some that think, 'oh teacher, he's not going to learn the letters or the numbers,' so we need to tell them about the importance of play. Although there are some who still do not accept because they feel that if their children come to school, they need to learn numbers and letters.]

Play was defined within the teachers' and parents' culture. This view of play reflects *diversión con aprendizaje* [learning with enjoyment]. These findings show us that one way of incorporating the child's culture in their learning is by playing *juegos infantiles*. Although Mexican American children should also be exposed to traditional American children's games, *juegos infantiles* reflect the other aspect of their culture. This will assist in avoiding cultural loss and promoting pride in the children's cultural traditions.

## DISCUSSION

This study provides a glimpse of bilingual Mexican American parents' and teachers' views of play. The analysis of the data provides evidence that bilingual early childhood teachers as well as parents seem to understand functions of play. The survey was limited in that it did not ask about cultural and language issues regarding play, but the interviews displayed the teachers' perspectives of play in terms of their cultural background. This is an important finding particularly when dealing with bilingual early childhood classrooms. The fact that this issue emerged from the qualitative data also indicates a strong significance. The survey needs to be redesigned to better reflect Mexican American linguistic and cultural aspects of play.

Of interest is the finding in which play serves different functions including enjoyment, learning with enjoyment, and learning. These bilingual early childhood teachers seem to understand the concept of play, but are still somewhat reluctant to implement it and are more likely to have the children engage in *"diversión con aprendizaje"* [learning with enjoyment]. This is also closely aligned with the parents' views. This play function appears to be a comfort zone for teachers since most of them revealed that they understand the value of play and know how to implement it, but are not ready to do so. This finding is not necessarily negative; it just means that teachers also go through a period of transformation as they reflect on their practices.

Surprisingly, only one of the teachers interviewed about the role of play mentioned its connection to first and second language development. Since a goal of bilingual early childhood classrooms is first and second language acquisition, teachers need to make the crucial connection that through play children learn and develop language skills. This is an important finding because often teachers working with minority children focus on the repetition of language skills as a basis for language development. However, teachers who provide a free play environment allow children to use language in different contexts for different purposes thus, allowing them to increase their language knowledge in English or Spanish (Riojas, 1998).

The last important finding includes the views regarding play of Mexican Americans. These teachers seemed to agree that children engage in play that reflects their culture and this allows the teachers to discover information about the children that otherwise they may never know. Riojas-Cortez (2001) supports this belief by stating that play creates a context in which children can practice and share their culture – their funds of knowledge.

# CONCLUSION

As we have seen in this study, play serves many functions in the Mexican American community, *diversión con aprendizaje*, *diversión*, and *aprendizaje*. In the case of teachers, we have noted cognitive dissonance between theory and practice. Thus, personal beliefs influence how play is perceived and implemented in the early childhood classroom. It is important for teachers to continuously engage in critical reflection to determine whether their beliefs about minority children and play are impeding the implementation of a play-based curriculum in which children can flourish.

Although this mixed-methods study sheds light on Mexican American parents' and teachers' beliefs about play and how these beliefs are culturally bound, this initial exploration is limited. Future studies should also examine how teachers' beliefs about play are actualized in their classroom, especially when there are minority children present. Furthermore, other studies exploring preservice teachers' preconceived notions of play in relation to teaching minority children. This may help researchers and other educators understand what needs to be accomplished in teacher preparation programs to prepare preservice teachers in challenging any deficit views they may hold or encounter.

In addition, more studies are needed that explore different minority groups' notions of play in the public schools. Play studies need to use an anthropological perspective in which minority children are observed during play in naturalistic environments and which use natural settings to engage minority parents in conversations about their beliefs about play in the schools. Such studies would help teachers and researchers understand that play is universal and serves different functions. Moreover, in revealing rich cultural traditions that often occur on a daily basis, such as *juegos infantiles*, these studies would serve to further raise all teachers' cultural awareness of the importance of these games. Even when teachers are not bilingual, these cultural traditions can be incorporated into the early childhood curriculum through the assistance of parent volunteers and other community members. If we are truly attempting to erase the gap between home and school, all teachers must see these cultural traditions as a means of promoting minority children's development. This type of validation assures minority children's academic success.

# NOTES

1. Project Alianza is funded by the W. R. Kellogg Foundation and a collaboration of Intercultural and Developmental Research Association and the Mexican and American Solidarity Foundation. The views presented here are those of the authors and not of these organizations.
2. Term of endearment for very close friends.

# REFERENCES

Bartkowiak, E. T., & Goupil, M. A. (1992). Parents' beliefs regarding early childhood education (*ERIC Document* No. 367 & 478).

Bronsil, E. (2001). Games children play. *Montessori Life, 12*(2), 7.

Bruner, J. (1983). Play, thought, and language. *Peabody Journal of Education, 60*(3), 60–69.

Christman, M. L. (1979). A Look at sociodramatic play among Mexican American children. *Childhood Education, 56*(2), 106.

Cohen, L. (2002). Promoting play at school and home. *Independent School, 61*(4), 94–98.

Darlington, R. B. (2002). *Factor Analysis*. Retrieved on September 17, 2002 from http://comp9.psych.cornell.edu/Darlington/factor.htm.

Dunteman, G. H. (1989). *Principal components analysis*. Sage University paper series on quantitative application in the social sciences (Series No. 07-069). Beverly Hills: Sage.

Eriksen, E. (1950). *Childhood and society*. New York: W. W. Norton.

Escobedo, T. H. (1993). Curricular issues in early education for culturally and linguistically diverse populations. In: S. Riefel (Ed.), *Advances in Early Childhood Education and Day Care*. JAI Press.

Farver, J., & Howes, C. (1993). Cultural differences in American and Mexican mother-child pretend play. *Merrill-Palmer Quarterly, 39*, 344–358.

Flores, B. B. (2001). Bilingual education teachers' beliefs and their relation to self-reported practices. *Bilingual Research Journal, 25*(3), 275–299.

Galper, A., Wigfield, A., & Seefeldt, C. (1997). Head start parents' beliefs about their children's abilities, task values, and performances on different activities. *Child Development, 68*(5), 897–907.

Genishi, C., & Galvan, J. (1983). Getting started: Mexican American preschoolers initiating dramatic play. In: J. Frost & S. Sunderlin (Eds), *When Children Play: Proceeding of the International Conference on Play and Play Environments*. Wheaton, MD: Association for Childhood Education International.

Grimm, L. G., & Yarnold, P. R. (2000). *Reading and understanding multivariate statistics*. Washington, DC: American Psychological Association.

Kalata, D. E. T. (1998). Parents! Let's play. *Young Children, 53*(5), 40–41.

Kieff, J. E., & Casbergue, R. M. (2000). *Playful learning and teaching: Integrating play into preschool and primary programs*. Boston: Allyn and Bacon.

Malone, M. D., & Landers, M. A. (2001). Mothers' perceptions of the toy play of preschoolers with intellectual disabilities. *International Journal of Disability, Development, and Education, 48*(1), 91–102.

Mendez-Negrete, J. (2002). Las Hijas de Juan: Daughters betrayed. San Jose, CA: Chusma House Publishing.

Piaget, J. (1962). *Play, dreams, and imitation in childhood*. New York: W. W. Norton.

Riojas, M. (1998). *A microethnography of Mexican American children during sociodramatic play in a preschool classroom*. Unpublished Dissertation, The University of Texas at Austin.

Riojas-Cortez, M. (2001). Preschoolers' funds of knowledge displayed through sociodramatic play episodes in a bilingual classroom. *Early Childhood Education Journal, 29*(1), 35–40.

Segal, M., & Adcock, D. (1982). The value of pretending (*ERIC Document* No. 215 & 780).

Siegel, D. (2001). Some bright ideas for play with your child. *The Exceptional Parent, 31*(10), 52–53.

Sosa, A. S. (1993). *Thorough and fair: Creating routes to success for Mexican-American students*. Charleston, WV: Clearinghouse on Rural Education and Small Schools.

Stevens, J. (1996). *Applied multivariate statistics for the social sciences* (3rd ed.). Mahwah, NJ: Lawrence Erlbaum.

Stone, S. J. (1995). Wanted: Advocates for play in the primary grades. *Young Children, 50*(6), 45–54.

Sutterby, J. (2002). *Todos somos amigos: Cross-cultural and cross-linguistic play interactions in two-way immersion prekindergarten classroom.* Unpublished dissertation, The University of Texas at Austin.

Trueba, H., & Delgado-Gaitán, C. (1985). Socialization of Mexican children for cooperation and competition: Sharing and copying. *Journal of Educational Equity and Leadership, 5*(3), 189–204.

Tyce, C. (2002). Mathematical adventures in role play. *Mathematics Teaching, 179*, 19–23.

Valencia, R. R. (2000). Inequalities and the schooling of minority students in Texas: Historical and contemporary conditions. *Hispanic Journal of Behavioral Sciences, 22*(4), 445–459.

Vygotsky, L. S. (1967). Play and its role in the mental development of the child. *Soviet Psychology, 5*(30), 6–18.

Weininger, O. (1979). *Play and education: The basic tool for early childhood learning.* Springfield, IL: Charles C. Thomas.

# SUBJECT INDEX

Imaginary play, 235, 237, 238, 239, 255, 257, 258
Inference(s), 211
Instrumental competencies, 143, 144, 156
Interdisciplinary perspectives, 55, 56
Interpretivist, 166, 167, 169, 172
Interviews, 10, 106, 108, 110, 114, 121, 241, 267, 270, 272, 275, 277, 282, 285

La Milpa metaphor, 158

Male hegemony, 266, 299
Male privilege, 72, 75
Mathematical thinking, 43
Meaning making, 165, 166, 179, 180, 186, 190, 196, 209, 210, 216
Mexican American, 137, 141, 143, 144, 153, 155, 267, 270, 272, 282, 284, 285

Narrative, 109, 110, 111, 178, 207, 209, 211, 215, 216
Nombres de carino, 147–154, 156–159

Parents, 12, 19, 86, 87, 98, 142, 146, 147, 151, 156, 225, 231, 233, 237, 241, 246, 247, 252, 257, 268, 270, 272, 278, 281, 284
Peer culture, 235, 236, 239, 241, 243, 254, 255, 257
Peer group, 63, 257
Perspective(s), 27, 41, 55, 58, 61, 64, 70, 78, 81, 84, 106, 119, 138, 143, 167, 174, 196, 202, 213, 232, 239, 286
Phenomenology, 105
Play, 10, 39, 40, 42, 57, 74, 93, 112, 125, 146, 165, 167, 170, 174, 178, 189, 197, 200, 209, 212, 216, 223, 236, 249, 254, 257, 268, 274, 284, 286
Play fighting, 213, 220, 222, 226, 232, 247, 248, 254
Playground rules, 226
Playgrounds, 141, 145, 225, 226
Policy supports, 93, 105
Poststructuralism, 72, 74, 78, 169
Poverty, 4, 7, 8, 10, 12, 13, 15, 17, 18, 20, 24, 26, 31, 33, 59, 98

Pretend aggression, 235, 237, 239, 242, 244, 254, 256, 259
Problem solving, 40, 41, 60, 211, 259, 277
Professional development of teachers, 100, 102, 106, 116, 126, 135, 232

Quality in early care and education, 93, 95, 96, 97, 100, 111, 116, 119, 127

Reader response, 8
Real aggression, 237, 238, 243, 244, 245, 246, 247, 252, 255, 257
Reconceptualizing, 165, 166, 167, 168, 173, 184, 200, 201, 232
Resilience, 59, 60, 63, 64
Rhetorics, 173, 174, 175, 176, 178, 181, 184, 194, 198
Rough and tumble (R&T) play, 219, 220, 221, 222, 224, 227, 229, 230, 232, 247, 254
Rough housing, 230, 231
Rules about play, 183

Social and economic inequality, 4, 6, 8, 29
Social class, 5, 6
Social cognition, 4, 6
Social Interaction, 39, 40, 41, 42, 49, 50, 51, 153, 154, 179
Social justice, 8, 56, 62, 64, 72, 79, 82, 84, 87
Spatial tasks, 42
Specialized coursework, 101, 126
Superhero, 238, 242, 243, 250, 251, 252, 260

Task structure, 40, 41, 42, 47, 48, 49, 51
Teacher reflection, 65, 216
Teachers, 19, 31, 34, 40, 41, 49, 50, 57, 64, 68, 69, 73, 75, 80, 85, 93, 96, 99, 100, 102, 105, 107, 110, 114, 118, 124, 139, 151, 199, 210, 214, 225, 237, 249, 257, 268, 275, 279, 281, 284, 286
Text, 8, 12, 13, 22, 28, 74, 110, 169, 183, 184, 188, 191, 196, 208, 216
Theory-practice, 201